AI-Driven Decentralized Finance and the Future of Finance

Mohammad Irfan
NSB Academy Business School, India

Mohammed Elmogy
Information Technology Department, Faculty of Computers and Information, Mansoura University, Egypt

Swati Gupta
Universal AI University, India

Fahmi Khalifa
Morgan State University, USA

Rui Teixeira Dias
Polytechnic Institute of Setubal, Portugal

A volume in the Advances in Finance, Accounting, and Economics (AFAE) Book Series

Published in the United States of America by
    IGI Global
    Business Science Reference (an imprint of IGI Global)
    701 E. Chocolate Avenue
    Hershey PA, USA 17033
    Tel: 717-533-8845
    Fax: 717-533-8661
    E-mail: cust@igi-global.com
    Web site: http://www.igi-global.com

Copyright © 2024 by IGI Global. All rights reserved. No part of this publication may be reproduced, stored or distributed in any form or by any means, electronic or mechanical, including photocopying, without written permission from the publisher.
Product or company names used in this set are for identification purposes only. Inclusion of the names of the products or companies does not indicate a claim of ownership by IGI Global of the trademark or registered trademark.

                Library of Congress Cataloging-in-Publication Data

CIP DATA PENDING

ISBN: 9798369363218
IsbnSoftcover: 9798369363225
EISBN: 9798369363232

British Cataloguing in Publication Data
A Cataloguing in Publication record for this book is available from the British Library.

All work contributed to this book is new, previously-unpublished material.
The views expressed in this book are those of the authors, but not necessarily of the publisher.

For electronic access to this publication, please contact: eresources@igi-global.com.

Table of Contents

Preface xvii

Chapter 1
AI in DeFi: Foundational Elements and Future Prospects 1
    Swati Sharma, Manipal University Jaipur, India
    Jugal Kishor, Central University of Rajasthan, India
    Preeti Bhaskar, University of Technology and Applied Sciences, Ibra, Oman
    Rui Dias, Instituto Superior de Gestão, Instituto Politécnico da Lusofonia, Lisboa, Portugal

Chapter 2
Transforming Financial Services Through Hyper-Personalization: The Role of Artificial Intelligence and Data Analytics in Enhancing Customer Experience 19
    Ankit Saxena, GLA University, India
    Syed Mohd Muneeb, Tecnologico de Monterrey, Toluca, Mexico

Chapter 3
Security, Risk Management, and Ethical AI in the Future of DeFi 48
    Ushaa Eswaran, Indira Institute of Technology and Sciences, Jawaharlal Nehru Technological University, India
    Vishal Eswaran, CVS Health Centre, USA
    Vivek Eswaran, Medallia, USA
    Keerthna Murali, DELL, USA

Chapter 4
AI-Driven Fraud Detection and Prevention in Decentralized Finance: A Systematic Review 89
    Madhusudan Narayan, Amity Business School, Amity University, Ranchi, India
    Pooja Shukla, Amity College of Commerce and Finance, Amity University, Ranchi, India
    Rajeev Kanth, Savonia University of Applied Sciences, Finland

Chapter 5
Unlocking the Potential of AI for Efficient Governance: Innovative
Approaches of Bahrain... 112
    Zakir Hossen Shaikh, Kingdom University, Bahraian
    Mohammad Irfan, Christ University, Bengaluru, India
    Naji M. Nomran, Kingdom University, Bahrain
    Satya Pavan Kumar Ratnakaram, Bahrain Polytechnic, Bahrain

Chapter 6
Fraud Detection in the Era of AI: Harnessing Technology for a Safer Digital
Economy 139
    Urshita Bansal, The Technological Institute of Textile and Sciences,
        India
    Sunita Bharatwal, Chaudhary Bansi Lal University, Bhiwani, India
    Dhana S. Bagiyam, Christ University, Bengaluru, India
    Early Ridho Kismawadi, IAIN Langsa, Aceh, Indonesia

Chapter 7
Robo-Revolution: How Automated Financial Advisors Are Reshaping Global
Finance.. 161
    Deepika Upadhyay, Department of Commerce, Christ University, India
    Vartika Jaiswal, Department of Commerce, Christ University, India
    Indrajit Ghosal, Brainware University, Kolkata, India
    Syed Muhammad Abdul Rehman Shah, University of Engineering and
        Technology, Taxila, Pakistan

Chapter 8
Green Banking and SDGs: Drivers, Facilitators, and Accelerators................... 181
    Jahanvi Bansal, GSFC University, Vadodara, India
    Parag Shukla, The Maharaja Sayajirao University of Baroda, India
    Pankaj Kumar Tripathi, The Maharaja Sayajirao University of Baroda,
        India
    Suchi Dubey, MAHE Dubai, UAE

Chapter 9
Accelerating Financial Inclusion in Developing Economies (India) Through
Digital Financial Technology 201
    Parul Garg, Amity University, Noida, India
    Tapsi Srivastava, Amity University, Noida, India
    Ankit Goel, Maharaja Agrasen Institute of Management Studies, New
        Delhi, India
    Nancy Gupta, University of Alberta, Canada

Detailed Table of Contents

Preface xvii

Chapter 1
AI in DeFi: Foundational Elements and Future Prospects 1
    Swati Sharma, Manipal University Jaipur, India
    Jugal Kishor, Central University of Rajasthan, India
    Preeti Bhaskar, University of Technology and Applied Sciences, Ibra, Oman
    Rui Dias, Instituto Superior de Gestão, Instituto Politécnico da Lusofonia, Lisboa, Portugal

Over the past few years, the crypto industry has encountered various obstacles, including regulatory obstacles, unsuccessful exchanges, and projects that have collapsed. These challenges have paved the way for groundbreaking solutions that are revolutionising the realm of decentralised finance (DeFi). An emerging solution with immense potential is the incorporation of artificial intelligence (AI) into financial ecosystems. The integration of DeFi and AI presents a transformative collaboration that has the potential to revolutionise the industry, enhance its adaptability, and establish a solid groundwork for long-term sustainability. AI and DeFi have emerged as significant technological advancements in recent years, garnering widespread attention and adoption. Incorporating AI into DeFi offers a range of advantages, including automated decision-making, more accurate risk assessment, and enhanced user experiences. These benefits contribute to the continuous development of DeFi.

Chapter 2
Transforming Financial Services Through Hyper-Personalization: The Role of Artificial Intelligence and Data Analytics in Enhancing Customer Experience 19
    Ankit Saxena, GLA University, India
    Syed Mohd Muneeb, Tecnologico de Monterrey, Toluca, Mexico

The merging of artificial intelligence (AI) and data analytics is bringing about a hyper-personalized era that is radically changing the financial services sector. In order to provide highly personalized financial products and services, hyper-personalization makes use of artificial intelligence (AI) and data analytics to evaluate enormous volumes of data from many sources, such as transactional history, social media activity, and personal preferences. Financial organizations may provide highly relevant services by using machine learning algorithms and predictive analytics to uncover patterns and forecast client behavior. Hyper-personalization implementation, however, comes with a number of issues, such as data privacy problems, ethical issues, and the requirement for strong cybersecurity measures to safeguard sensitive client data. The increasing advancement of technology is anticipated to propel additional innovation in financial services by expanding the role of artificial intelligence (AI) and data analytics in hyper-personalization.

Chapter 3
Security, Risk Management, and Ethical AI in the Future of DeFi 48
    Ushaa Eswaran, Indira Institute of Technology and Sciences,
       Jawaharlal Nehru Technological University, India
    Vishal Eswaran, CVS Health Centre, USA
    Vivek Eswaran, Medallia, USA
    Keerthna Murali, DELL, USA

The intersection of artificial intelligence (AI) and decentralized finance (DeFi) heralds a transformative era in the financial landscape, promising unprecedented efficiency, personalization, and innovation. However, this convergence also introduces significant challenges, particularly in the realms of security, risk management, and ethics. This chapter aims to provide a comprehensive exploration of how AI-driven technologies can enhance security and risk management within DeFi ecosystems while addressing the ethical considerations essential for sustainable and responsible innovation. By analyzing current practices, future scenarios, and emerging trends, this chapter seeks to equip finance professionals, technologists, and decision-makers with actionable insights and strategies to navigate the complex dynamics of AI in DeFi. Through real-world case studies and best practices, readers will gain a robust understanding of the critical issues and solutions that will shape the future of secure, ethical, and resilient decentralized financial systems.

Chapter 10
The Future of Smart Contracts: Pioneering a New Era of Automated
Transactions and Trust in the Digital Economy... 225
    Rajiv Iyer, Amity University, Mumbai, India
    Vedprakash Maralapalle, Amity University, Maharashtra, India
    Deepak Patil, Amity University, Dubai, UAE
    Mohammad Irfan, Christ University, Bengaluru, India

Chapter 11
Risk Management of Future of Defi Using Artificial Intelligence as a Tool 252
    Jyoti Sah, Amity University, Maharashtra, India
    Satuluri Padma, Amity University, Maharashtra, India
    Ramakrishna Yanamandra, Skyline University College, University City
        of Sharjah, UAE
    Mohammad Irfan, Christ University, Bengaluru, India

Chapter 12
The Autonomy of Central Banks and Digital Currency: A Macroeconomic
Perspective 273
    Sofia Devi Shamurailatpam, The Maharaja Sayajirao University of
        Baroda, India
    Mohammed Majeed, Tamale Technical University, Ghana

Chapter 13
Can AI Change the Way We See the World? An Analysis Using Attitude and
Perception Measurement on Female B.Tech Students in Rajasthan 289
    Lalita Kumari, Mody University of Science and Technology, India
    Akansha Gautam, Mody University of Science and Technology, India
    P. Varaprasad Goud, Chaitanya Bharathi Institute of Technology, India
    Fatima Muhammad Abdulkarim, Federal University, Dutse, Nigeria

Chapter 14
Transformative Impact of AI in Green Finance: A Catalyst for Sustainable
Development in India.. 302
    Reenu Kumari, KIET Group of Institutions, India
    Komal Sharma, KIET Group of Institutions, India
    Rajesh Kumar, Institute of Management Studies, Ghaziabad, India
    Ahu Coşkun Özer, Marmara University, Istanbul, Turkey

Chapter 15
AI vs. Traditional Portfolio Management: A Study on Indian Investors 318
    Yash Anand, Christ University, India
    Mohammad Irfan, Christ University, India
    Mahadi Hasan, University of Information Technology and Sciences,
       Dhaka, Bangladesh

Compilation of References 336

About the Contributors 378

Index 391

Chapter 4
AI-Driven Fraud Detection and Prevention in Decentralized Finance: A
Systematic Review 89
    Madhusudan Narayan, Amity Business School, Amity University,
        Ranchi, India
    Pooja Shukla, Amity College of Commerce and Finance, Amity
        University, Ranchi, India
    Rajeev Kanth, Savonia University of Applied Sciences, Finland

The chapter explores the transformative potential of artificial intelligence (AI) in the realm of decentralized finance (DeFi), focusing on its application in fraud detection and prevention. Through an in-depth examination of AI-driven methodologies and techniques, particularly machine learning models, natural language processing (NLP), and graph analytics, this study explores how AI is reshaping the landscape of fraud detection within decentralized financial ecosystems. Using a conceptual framework, this study investigates the current state-of-the-art techniques employed in AI-driven fraud detection and prevention in DeFi. It examines the methodologies and applications driving the adoption of AI, elucidating its efficacy in identifying fraudulent activities and enhancing the security of DeFi platforms.

Chapter 5
Unlocking the Potential of AI for Efficient Governance: Innovative
Approaches of Bahrain... 112
    Zakir Hossen Shaikh, Kingdom University, Bahraian
    Mohammad Irfan, Christ University, Bengaluru, India
    Naji M. Nomran, Kingdom University, Bahrain
    Satya Pavan Kumar Ratnakaram, Bahrain Polytechnic, Bahrain

The rapid development and implementation of artificial intelligence (AI) technologies will have significant economic, social, and ethical impacts. Efficient governance is essential to maximize AI's benefits while minimizing its risks. Bahrain is positioning itself as a fintech hub, with AI playing a central role in this transformation. Bahrain's smart governance efforts will be strengthened by integrating AI into public services. E-government efforts will use AI to streamline processes, improve citizen experience, and build a more responsive and efficient public administration. The study provides an overview of how artificial intelligence (AI) is transforming various sectors in Bahrain with innovative approaches to boost productivity, better decision-making, and improve the general quality of services that may also impact the Bahraini economy. Bahrain continues to drive digital innovation, paving the way for a better and more prosperous future and sustainable development. Bahrain's digital transformation has been largely successful thanks to strong government measures.

Chapter 6
Fraud Detection in the Era of AI: Harnessing Technology for a Safer Digital
Economy 139
    *Urshita Bansal, The Technological Institute of Textile and Sciences,
       India*
    Sunita Bharatwal, Chaudhary Bansi Lal University, Bhiwani, India
    Dhana S. Bagiyam, Christ University, Bengaluru, India
    Early Ridho Kismawadi, IAIN Langsa, Aceh, Indonesia

Fraudulent activities have increased along with the new prospects of the digital economy's quick growth for both consumers and enterprises. Conventional techniques of fraud detection are insufficient to keep up with these ever-evolving fraudulent strategies. In this sense, machine learning (ML) and artificial intelligence (AI) have become potent instruments to prevent and detect fraud and guarantee the safety of online transactions. This study examines the function of AI and ML and shows how these technologies can spot irregularities and intricate patterns that would be challenging to find with conventional methods. The study includes various methods of AI-based fraud detection and analyses important ethical issues related to these practices. Furthermore, the study looks at developing technology and trends that will probably influence fraud detection in the future. In conclusion, the revolutionary potential of AI and ML in building a safer digital economy is analysed.

Chapter 7
Robo-Revolution: How Automated Financial Advisors Are Reshaping Global
Finance 161
    Deepika Upadhyay, Department of Commerce, Christ University, India
    Vartika Jaiswal, Department of Commerce, Christ University, India
    Indrajit Ghosal, Brainware University, Kolkata, India
    *Syed Muhammad Abdul Rehman Shah, University of Engineering and
       Technology, Taxila, Pakistan*

Robo-advisors have the potential to revolutionise the financial service industry by making it more accessible and affordable. This study provides a comprehensive overview of robo-advisors in the arena of financial markets and investments and their gaining popularity in the fintech industry, particularly in emerging markets like India. It also discusses the changing landscape of the financial sector in India, benefits and challenges of fintech, and the legal and ethical implications of robo-advisors. The current study presents a comparative study between India and UK markets in terms of acceptance and penetration of robo-advisors. It highlights leading robo-advisory firms in India. The data visualisation is done with the help of Microsoft Power BI and Microsoft Excel on the statista survey data. The expected results of this study assist several stakeholders, such as academicians, researchers, investors, stock brokers, regulators, and policy makers.

Chapter 8
Green Banking and SDGs: Drivers, Facilitators, and Accelerators 181
    Jahanvi Bansal, GSFC University, Vadodara, India
    Parag Shukla, The Maharaja Sayajirao University of Baroda, India
    Pankaj Kumar Tripathi, The Maharaja Sayajirao University of Baroda, India
    Suchi Dubey, MAHE Dubai, UAE

Green banking's potential to foster green economies and ensure a sustainable future is profound, emphasizing the critical importance of green finance in advancing SDGs and mitigating global environmental challenges. Central Asian banks, including India, have increasingly embraced green finance, acknowledging its pivotal role in addressing climate risks. The study has proposed a conceptual framework that depicts the interplay between drivers, facilitators, and accelerators of green banking and sustainable development goals (SDGs), especially SDG 7 (affordable and clean energy), SDG 11 (sustainable cities and communities), SDG 12 (responsible consumption and production) and SDG 13 (climate action), highlighting collaborative efforts needed for global sustainability. This article sheds light on the transformational potential of green banking projects by discussing both the practical and social aspects of the proposed initiatives.

Chapter 9
Accelerating Financial Inclusion in Developing Economies (India) Through
Digital Financial Technology 201
> *Parul Garg, Amity University, Noida, India*
> *Tapsi Srivastava, Amity University, Noida, India*
> *Ankit Goel, Maharaja Agrasen Institute of Management Studies, New Delhi, India*
> *Nancy Gupta, University of Alberta, Canada*

The study employs a mixed-methods approach, incorporating both quantitative and qualitative methodologies. The methodology encompasses literature and the development of a system dynamics model. This model is used to identify pivotal factors or barriers within emerging economies that either impede or facilitate the transition to an inclusive financial system. Keywords and drivers are discerned through qualitative analysis of existing literature, facilitating the construction of a quantitative model. This model depicts the interplay and relative impact of identified factors on the ability of emerging economies to achieve financial inclusion. Results indicate that digital financial technologies significantly enhance financial inclusion by providing access to essential financial services for underserved populations. The study identifies ten key variables that influence financial systems. A primary challenge identified is the limited accessibility to financial services for people in developing regions. The chapter concludes with recommendations for policymakers and financial institutions.

Chapter 10
The Future of Smart Contracts: Pioneering a New Era of Automated
Transactions and Trust in the Digital Economy... 225
    Rajiv Iyer, Amity University, Mumbai, India
    Vedprakash Maralapalle, Amity University, Maharashtra, India
    Deepak Patil, Amity University, Dubai, UAE
    Mohammad Irfan, Christ University, Bengaluru, India

The future of smart contracts in decentralized finance (DeFi) is a dynamic and evolving field that holds immense potential for transforming traditional financial systems The integration of artificial intelligence (AI) with smart contracts is enhancing their capabilities, enabling efficient processing of data and intelligent decision-making. Smart contracts provide an open and effective replacement for traditional financial structures as they continue to gain popularity. The potential of smart contracts to improve transparency, optimize operating procedures, and transform industries like healthcare, finance, and education is what will determine their future. To support blockchain-based apps and grow the DeFi ecosystem, smart contract platforms like Polkadot, Cardano, and Ethereum must continue to innovate and evolve. The future of smart contracts is largely being shaped by the possibility of multi-chain smart contracts, the incorporation of AI and machine learning technology, and the support for decentralized autonomous organizations (DAOs).

Chapter 11
Risk Management of Future of Defi Using Artificial Intelligence as a Tool 252
    Jyoti Sah, Amity University, Maharashtra, India
    Satuluri Padma, Amity University, Maharashtra, India
    Ramakrishna Yanamandra, Skyline University College, University City
        of Sharjah, UAE
    Mohammad Irfan, Christ University, Bengaluru, India

This chapter explores AI's pivotal roles in managing risks within DeFi, emphasizing strategic implementation to enhance risk assessment, management, and decision-making processes for a better user experience. The convergence of AI and DeFi presents unprecedented opportunities, fostering transparency and decentralization. Drawing from diverse sources, the study evaluates AI's effectiveness, particularly in machine learning, in addressing emerging risks. It focuses on how AI can guide DeFi's future while managing market and credit risks through tasks like data preparation, modeling, stress testing, and validation. Additionally, AI aids in data quality assurance, text mining, and fraud detection. Emphasis is placed on identifying and managing risks that could hinder DeFi's future, highlighting key AI techniques. Given the financial industry's ongoing transformation, these insights are increasingly vital.

Chapter 12
The Autonomy of Central Banks and Digital Currency: A Macroeconomic
Perspective 273
    Sofia Devi Shamurailatpam, The Maharaja Sayajirao University of
        Baroda, India
    Mohammed Majeed, Tamale Technical University, Ghana

Many central banks across the globe are experiencing different phases of implementation of central bank digital currencies (CBDCs) – some central banks have already initiated digital currencies or are in experimentation phases or introduced as a pilot project, each one at various operational challenges open to central banks toward building the digital currency framework. This chapter attempts to establish the state of digital currencies experienced by different economies across the world. The chapter highlights the underlying reasons behind the implementation of CBDCs by countries; the challenges and implications of the introduction of such digital currency on monetary policy; the role of CBDC in bringing societal benefits towards financial inclusion and sustainable finance; and finally, the regulatory framework set up to safeguard at the interest of national security. These inter-related issues are examined based on experiences from different economies of the world. Further, a sample study for India's CBDC development is evaluated as country specific study.

Chapter 13
Can AI Change the Way We See the World? An Analysis Using Attitude and
Perception Measurement on Female B.Tech Students in Rajasthan 289
    Lalita Kumari, Mody University of Science and Technology, India
    Akansha Gautam, Mody University of Science and Technology, India
    P. Varaprasad Goud, Chaitanya Bharathi Institute of Technology, India
    Fatima Muhammad Abdulkarim, Federal University, Dutse, Nigeria

The study investigate how female B.Tech. students view of artificial intelligence (AI) in their personal life and determine how their views about AI relate to the advancements they encounter. The study is cross-sectional across only a limited sample and it is important to understand the comparison for different set of students to assess the real situation of Artificial Intelligence. The chapter attempts to construct awareness index and perception index using principle component analysis which further uses ANOVA on a sample of 150 engineering students to better understand the numerous phenomena arising from AI. The results found use of AI has a significant impact on creating better career opportunities. The results of AI are also favourable towards better awareness, curiosity, knowledge, and learning.

Chapter 14
Transformative Impact of AI in Green Finance: A Catalyst for Sustainable Development in India 302
    Reenu Kumari, KIET Group of Institutions, India
    Komal Sharma, KIET Group of Institutions, India
    Rajesh Kumar, Institute of Management Studies, Ghaziabad, India
    Ahu Coşkun Özer, Marmara University, Istanbul, Turkey

The transformative impact of artificial intelligence (AI) in green finance is revolutionizing the landscape of sustainable development in India. This chapter explores how AI-driven technologies are enhancing the efficiency, transparency, and effectiveness of green finance initiatives. By leveraging advanced data analytics, machine learning algorithms, and predictive modeling, AI is facilitating better decision-making, risk assessment, and investment strategies that align with environmental, social, and governance (ESG) criteria. The integration of AI in green finance is not only accelerating the transition to a low-carbon economy but also promoting inclusive growth and resilience against climate change. This study highlights key case studies, technological innovations, and policy frameworks that demonstrate AI's potential as a catalyst for achieving India's sustainable development goals. Through comprehensive analysis, the chapter underscores the critical role of AI in driving systemic changes in financial practices, thereby fostering a sustainable and prosperous future for India.

Chapter 15
AI vs. Traditional Portfolio Management: A Study on Indian Investors 318
    Yash Anand, Christ University, India
    Mohammad Irfan, Christ University, India
    Mahadi Hasan, University of Information Technology and Sciences,
       Dhaka, Bangladesh

This research chapter investigates the dynamics between artificial intelligence (AI) and traditional portfolio management strategies, specifically focusing on the attitudes and preferences of investors in the Indian market. The study aims to elucidate the comparative performance, risk-adjusted returns, and behavioral aspects associated with AI-driven portfolio management as opposed to traditional methods. Utilizing a methodology tailored to the unique characteristics of the Indian investment landscape, this research engages investors with varying degrees of experience in the stock market. Through a meticulous collection of data during October and November 2023, employing convenience sampling, the authors explore the factors influencing investor perceptions and decisions in adopting AI-based portfolio management strategies. These findings contribute to the existing discourse by shedding light on the role of trust, subjective norms, perceived usefulness, perceived ease of use, and attitudes as critical variables shaping the adoption of AI in portfolio management.

Compilation of References 336

About the Contributors 378

Index 391

Preface

In the ever-evolving landscape of finance, the amalgamation of artificial intelligence (AI) and Decentralized Finance (DeFi) is proving to be a seismic shift, reshaping the traditional paradigms of the financial industry. As financial ecosystems increasingly embrace the transformative power of technology, *AI-Driven DeFi: Transforming Finance in the Digital Age* emerges not just as a book but as a guiding beacon through the complexities of this revolutionary convergence.

In recent years, we have witnessed the rise of DeFi platforms, decentralized lending protocols, and smart contracts, all fueled by the power of blockchain. Simultaneously, advancements in AI have pushed the boundaries of what is possible in data analysis, prediction modeling, and algorithmic decision-making. The synergy between these two technological powerhouses has given birth to a new era in finance—one that demands exploration, understanding, and a roadmap for navigating the uncharted territories ahead.

Comprehensive Exploration: "AI-Driven DeFi" contributes by offering a comprehensive exploration of the multifaceted integration of AI within the decentralized financial landscape. From the optimization of smart contracts to the personalization of financial experiences, the book leaves no stone unturned in dissecting the key components of this revolutionary transformation.

Practical Insights: The book provides practical insights for professionals seeking to leverage the potential of AI in their DeFi strategies. Real-world examples and use cases illustrate how AI is not merely a theoretical concept but a tangible force shaping the landscape of decentralized finance.

Navigational Guide: By addressing regulatory challenges, ethical considerations, and emerging trends, the book serves as a navigational guide for readers—empowering them to navigate the complexities of AI-driven DeFi with clarity and confidence.

Future Perspectives: "AI-Driven DeFi" doesn't just focus on the present; it looks to the future. The book contributes to the ongoing conversation about the evolution of AI and DeFi, offering insights into potential future developments, challenges, and opportunities on the horizon.

The primary goal of the book is to demystify the intricate interplay between Artificial Intelligence (AI) and Decentralized Finance (DeFi). By providing a clear and accessible explanation of how these two transformative forces converge, the book aims to break down complex concepts into digestible insights for a diverse audience. Readers, regardless of their background, will gain a foundational understanding of how AI technologies are integrated into decentralized financial systems. This objective seeks to empower individuals to navigate and contribute to discussions surrounding the transformative potential of AI-driven DeFi.

Another key objective is to offer practical, actionable insights for finance professionals, technologists, and entrepreneurs looking to leverage AI in the context of decentralized finance. Real-world case studies, industry best practices, and examples of successful implementations will be included to guide professionals in applying AI strategies to their DeFi endeavors. Professionals within the financial industry will gain actionable knowledge, enabling them to harness the power of AI for optimizing smart contracts, enhancing security, and creating personalized financial experiences within decentralized ecosystems. This objective aims to bridge the gap between theoretical understanding and practical application.

The book seeks to empower its readers with the knowledge required for informed decision-making in the rapidly evolving landscape of AI-driven DeFi. By analyzing regulatory challenges, ethical considerations, and emerging trends, the objective is to provide a holistic view that aids individuals and organizations in making strategic decisions and planning for the future. Readers will be equipped with insights to navigate the complex regulatory landscape, address ethical considerations associated with AI in finance, and stay ahead of emerging trends. This objective contributes to shaping a cohort of informed decision-makers who can actively participate in and influence the future direction of AI-driven DeFi.

ORGANIZATION OF THE BOOK

Chapter 1: AI in DeFi - Foundational Elements and Future Prospects

Over the past few years, the crypto industry has faced numerous challenges, including regulatory obstacles, failed exchanges, and collapsed projects. These challenges have spurred the development of innovative solutions, one of the most promising being the integration of artificial intelligence (AI) into decentralized finance (DeFi). This chapter explores how AI can transform DeFi, offering enhanced adaptability and laying a strong foundation for sustainable growth. The synergy between AI and DeFi offers numerous benefits, such as automated decision-making, improved risk assessment, and enhanced user experiences, all contributing to the ongoing evolution of DeFi.

Chapter 2: Transforming Financial Services Through Hyper-Personalization: The Role of Artificial Intelligence and Data Analytics in Enhancing Customer Experience

The convergence of artificial intelligence (AI) and data analytics is ushering in an era of hyper-personalization in the financial services sector. By analyzing vast amounts of data from various sources, such as transactional history and social media activity, AI enables financial organizations to offer highly personalized products and services. Machine learning algorithms and predictive analytics help identify patterns and predict customer behavior, providing more relevant services. This chapter also addresses challenges such as data privacy, ethical considerations, and the need for robust cybersecurity measures to protect sensitive customer data, highlighting the role of AI and data analytics in driving future innovations in financial services.

Chapter 3: Security, Risk Management, and Ethical AI in the Future of DeFi

The intersection of AI and DeFi marks a transformative era in the financial landscape, bringing unprecedented efficiency, personalization, and innovation. However, this convergence also introduces significant challenges in security, risk management, and ethics. This chapter provides a comprehensive exploration of how AI-driven technologies can enhance security and risk management within DeFi ecosystems while addressing essential ethical considerations for sustainable innovation. By examining current practices, future scenarios, and emerging trends, the chapter equips finance professionals, technologists, and decision-makers with actionable insights to navigate the complex dynamics of AI in DeFi.

Chapter 4: AI-Driven Fraud Detection and Prevention in Decentralized Finance: A Systematic Review

This chapter delves into the transformative potential of AI in fraud detection and prevention within DeFi. It examines AI-driven methodologies such as machine learning models, natural language processing (NLP), and graph analytics, highlighting their role in reshaping fraud detection in decentralized financial ecosystems. Through a conceptual framework, the chapter explores the current state-of-the-art techniques in AI-driven fraud detection and prevention, evaluating their effectiveness in identifying fraudulent activities and enhancing the security of DeFi platforms.

Chapter 5: Unlocking the Potential of AI for Efficient Governance: Innovative Approaches of Bahrain

The rapid development and implementation of AI technologies have significant economic, social, and ethical impacts. This chapter focuses on Bahrain's efforts to position itself as a fintech hub by integrating AI into public services to enhance smart governance. It provides an overview of how AI is transforming various sectors in Bahrain, improving productivity, decision-making, and the overall quality of services. The chapter highlights Bahrain's digital transformation success, driven by strong government measures, and its impact on sustainable development and economic prosperity.

Chapter 6: Fraud Detection in the Era of AI: Harnessing Technology for a Safer Digital Economy

As the digital economy grows, so does the prevalence of fraudulent activities. Traditional fraud detection methods are inadequate to keep up with evolving strategies. This chapter examines the role of AI and machine learning (ML) in fraud detection and prevention, showcasing their ability to identify irregularities and complex patterns that traditional methods might miss. The chapter also addresses ethical considerations associated with AI-based fraud detection and explores emerging technologies and trends that will likely influence the future of fraud detection. The potential of AI and ML in creating a safer digital economy is analyzed.

Chapter 7: Robo-Revolution: How Automated Financial Advisors Are Reshaping Global Finance

Robo-advisors are revolutionizing the financial services industry by making it more accessible and affordable. This chapter provides a comprehensive overview of robo-advisors, their growing popularity in the fintech industry, particularly in emerging markets like India, and their impact on the financial sector. It compares the acceptance and penetration of robo-advisors in India and the UK and highlights leading firms in India. Data visualization using Microsoft Power BI and Excel on Statista survey data assists various stakeholders in understanding the transformative potential of robo-advisors.

Chapter 8: Green Banking and SDGs: Drivers, Facilitators, and Accelerators

Green banking plays a crucial role in fostering green economies and ensuring a sustainable future. This chapter explores the potential of green finance in advancing Sustainable Development Goals (SDGs) and mitigating global environmental challenges. It presents a conceptual framework depicting the interplay between drivers, facilitators, and accelerators of green banking and SDGs, with a focus on SDG 7, SDG 11, SDG 12, and SDG 13. The chapter highlights collaborative efforts needed for global sustainability and the transformational potential of green banking projects.

Chapter 9: Accelerating Financial Inclusion in Developing Economies (India) Through Digital Financial Technology

This chapter employs a mixed-methods approach to explore the factors influencing financial inclusion in developing economies, particularly India. It uses a system dynamics model to identify barriers and facilitators within emerging economies, constructing a quantitative model to depict their impact on achieving financial inclusion. The study reveals that digital financial technologies significantly enhance access to essential financial services for underserved populations. The chapter concludes with recommendations for policymakers and financial institutions to address the challenges identified and promote financial inclusion.

Chapter 10: The Future of Smart Contracts: Pioneering a New Era of Automated Transactions and Trust in the Digital Economy

Smart contracts are poised to transform traditional financial systems by providing an open and efficient alternative. This chapter explores the future of smart contracts in DeFi, emphasizing their potential to enhance transparency, optimize operations, and impact various industries, including healthcare, finance, and education. It discusses the role of AI in enhancing smart contracts' capabilities and the potential for multi-chain smart contracts, AI and machine learning integration, and support for decentralized autonomous organizations (DAOs). The chapter highlights the ongoing innovation needed to support blockchain-based applications and the DeFi ecosystem.

Chapter 11: Risk Management of the Future of DeFi Using Artificial Intelligence as a Tool

This chapter explores AI's pivotal role in managing risks within DeFi, emphasizing its strategic implementation to enhance risk assessment, management, and decision-making processes. By evaluating AI's effectiveness in addressing emerging risks, the chapter highlights key AI techniques, such as machine learning, for data preparation, modeling, stress testing, and fraud detection. It underscores the importance of transparency and decentralization in fostering a secure and resilient DeFi ecosystem. The insights provided are increasingly vital for navigating the ongoing transformation of the financial industry.

Chapter 12: The Autonomy of Central Banks and Digital Currency: A Macroeconomic Perspective

Central Bank Digital Currencies (CBDCs) are at various stages of implementation worldwide, with different countries experiencing unique challenges and opportunities. This chapter examines the state of digital currencies across different economies, focusing on the reasons behind their implementation, the challenges faced, and the implications for monetary policy. It highlights the role of CBDCs in promoting financial inclusion and sustainable finance and discusses the regulatory frameworks needed to safeguard national security. The chapter includes a case study on India's CBDC development to provide a country-specific perspective.

Chapter 13: Can AI Change the Way We See the World?: An Analysis Using Attitude and Perception Measurement on Female B.Tech Students in Rajasthan

This study investigates the perception of AI among female B.Tech students in Rajasthan, analyzing how their views on AI relate to the advancements they encounter. By constructing awareness and perception indexes using principal component analysis and employing ANOVA on a sample of 150 engineering students, the study examines the impact of AI on career opportunities and routine responsibilities. The results indicate that AI significantly enhances awareness, curiosity, knowledge, and learning, demonstrating its potential to influence future career prospects positively.

Chapter 14: Transformative Impact of AI in Green Finance: A Catalyst for Sustainable Development in India

AI is revolutionizing green finance in India by enhancing efficiency, transparency, and effectiveness in sustainable development initiatives. This chapter explores how AI-driven technologies, such as advanced data analytics, machine learning algorithms, and predictive modeling, are facilitating better decision-making, risk assessment, and investment strategies aligned with environmental, social, and governance (ESG) principles. Through case studies and empirical analysis, the chapter demonstrates how AI contributes to achieving India's sustainability goals, highlighting its role in fostering green innovation, supporting renewable energy projects, and promoting financial inclusion in underserved communities.

Chapter 15: AI vs. Traditional Portfolio Management: A Study on Indian Investors

This research paper investigates the dynamics between Artificial Intelligence (AI) and traditional portfolio management strategies, specifically focusing on the attitudes and preferences of investors in the Indian market. The study aims to elucidate the comparative performance, risk-adjusted returns, and behavioral aspects associated with AI-driven portfolio management as opposed to traditional methods. Utilizing a methodology tailored to the unique characteristics of the Indian investment landscape, our research engages investors with varying degrees of experience in the stock market. Through a meticulous collection of data during October and November 2023, employing convenience sampling, we explore the factors influencing investor perceptions and decisions in adopting AI-based portfolio management strategies. Our findings contribute to the existing discourse by shedding light on the role of trust, subjective norms, perceived usefulness, perceived ease of use, and attitudes as critical variables shaping the adoption of AI in portfolio management.

IN CONCLUSION

As editors of *AI in Fintech and DeFi: Emerging Technologies for Future Finance*, we are both proud and excited to present this comprehensive collection of insights, research, and innovative ideas. The chapters within this volume reflect the dynamic and rapidly evolving landscape of artificial intelligence (AI), decentralized finance (DeFi), and fintech. Each contribution delves deeply into the transformative potential of these technologies, offering valuable perspectives on their impact, challenges, and future directions.

In assembling this book, our goal was to create a reference that not only highlights the current advancements but also anticipates future developments. The authors have expertly explored how AI and DeFi are reshaping financial services, enhancing security, promoting financial inclusion, and driving sustainable development. From the foundational elements of AI in DeFi to the sophisticated applications in fraud detection, risk management, and smart contracts, this book covers a broad spectrum of topics essential for academics, practitioners, policymakers, and anyone interested in the intersection of technology and finance.

We hope that this book serves as a catalyst for further research and innovation in the fields of AI and DeFi. As these technologies continue to mature, their integration will undoubtedly unlock new opportunities and address pressing global challenges. By fostering a deeper understanding of AI's role in financial ecosystems, we aim to inspire readers to explore novel solutions and contribute to the advancement of this exciting frontier.

Thank you for joining us on this journey through the cutting-edge developments in AI and DeFi. We are confident that the insights shared in this book will be instrumental in shaping the future of finance, driving technological progress, and achieving greater financial equity and sustainability.

Mohammad Irfan

School of Business and Management, Christ University, Bengaluru, India

Mohammed Elmogy

Information Technology Department, Faculty of Computers and Information, Mansoura University, Egypt

Swati Gupta

Universal AI University, India

Fahmi Khalifa

Morgan State University, USA

Rui Teixeira Dias

Polytechnic Institute of Setubal, Portugal

Chapter 1
AI in DeFi:
Foundational Elements and Future Prospects

Swati Sharma
Manipal University Jaipur, India

Jugal Kishor
Central University of Rajasthan, India

Preeti Bhaskar
https://orcid.org/0000-0002-1957-8035
University of Technology and Applied Sciences, Ibra, Oman

Rui Dias
https://orcid.org/0000-0002-6138-3098
Instituto Superior de Gestão, Instituto Politécnico da Lusofonia, Lisboa, Portugal

ABSTRACT

Over the past few years, the crypto industry has encountered various obstacles, including regulatory obstacles, unsuccessful exchanges, and projects that have collapsed. These challenges have paved the way for groundbreaking solutions that are revolutionising the realm of decentralised finance (DeFi). An emerging solution with immense potential is the incorporation of artificial intelligence (AI) into financial ecosystems. The integration of DeFi and AI presents a transformative collaboration that has the potential to revolutionise the industry, enhance its adaptability, and establish a solid groundwork for long-term sustainability. AI and DeFi have emerged as significant technological advancements in recent years, garnering widespread attention and adoption. Incorporating AI into DeFi offers a range of advantages, including automated decision-making, more accurate risk assessment, and enhanced

DOI: 10.4018/979-8-3693-6321-8.ch001

Copyright © 2024, IGI Global. Copying or distributing in print or electronic forms without written permission of IGI Global is prohibited.

user experiences. These benefits contribute to the continuous development of DeFi.

INTRODUCTION

The convergence of artificial intelligence (AI) and cryptocurrencies presents an exciting opportunity for groundbreaking invention in the financial sector. The rapid progress in AI and the growing adoption of digital currencies have generated a distinct intersection with vast potential. Artificial intelligence is significantly transforming the banking industry. It aids in identifying fraudulent activities by rapidly examining transactions and identifying any potentially suspicious elements. AI in trading can rapidly analyse extensive market data, facilitating intelligent purchasing and selling decisions. In addition, AI chatbots are accessible round the clock to address client enquiries and resolve issues, hence enhancing service speed and efficiency. AI is a field of study in computer science that is dedicated to the advancement of intelligent computers that are able to perform intricate cognitive tasks. These tasks include reasoning, learning, taking action, and recognising speech, which were previously considered exclusive to humans (Frankenfield, 2021). Artificial intelligence is revolutionising the development of personalised, advanced, and innovative general and substitute economic-financial processes, items, designs, offerings, structures, and applications. This review provides an overview of the extensive research conducted on AI in finance. It aims to present a thorough and in-depth analysis of the various aspects (Cao, 2020). Fintech companies have rapidly evolved and expanded their presence across various sectors of the banking industry. The advent of fintech companies has brought about a wave of innovative financial services that have greatly benefited consumers. Not only have these services improved the efficiency of the entire financial system, but they have also provided consumers with new and improved ways to manage their finances. Having a deep understanding of the application of machine-readable data is crucial for both financial systems and financial studies (Goodell et al., 2021) which leads to sustainable financial practices (Oyewole et al., 2024). Simultaneously, regulators have raised concerns and drawn attention to multiple components of the services offered by fintech firms, which often resemble those of a traditional bank (Cao & Zhai, 2022).

DeFi eliminates the necessity for intermediaries, facilitating direct transactions between peers and financial services. Smart contracts are integral to DeFi, as they automate intricate financial processes without relying on a centralised authority.

AI and DeFi have been hailed as transformative technologies with the potential to revolutionise various industries. Experts believe that the convergence of these two fields could unlock unprecedented opportunities, leading to significant advancements in both AI and DeFi. DeFi refers to a revolutionary form of financial services that harnesses the power of blockchain technology. It operates on a peer-to-peer basis, utilising smart contracts to facilitate transactions. By eliminating the need for intermediaries like banks, DeFi empowers individuals to have direct control over their financial assets. Artificial intelligence, however, is a remarkable technology capable of emulating human intelligence to carry out a wide range of tasks, including decision-making, problem-solving, and high-speed data analysis.

AI is being developed at an increasingly rapid rate, causing many individuals to regard it as a highly significant technological advancement in our era. Artificial intelligence is currently being developed to automate a wide range of tasks that have traditionally been carried out by humans. These tasks encompass various areas such as administration, management, and professional work. In recent years, the adoption of DeFi has experienced a remarkable surge.

When a financial system is backed by the involvement of AI and ML, it holds great potential and significant risks, as it can transform the industry while also presenting unprecedented challenges (Irfan, Hussainey, Bukhari, & Nam, 2024). Financial intermediaries play a crucial role in connecting savers and borrowers, managing risk, providing liquidity, and offering various financial services. Based on this comprehensive analysis, it is evident that AI may be considered a very effective market forecaster and plays a role in maintaining market stability by reducing information imbalances and fluctuations. As a result, it enables successful investment strategies and precise performance assessments (Bahoo et., al 2024). However, the emergence of DeFi poses intriguing questions about the ongoing relevance and importance of traditional financial intermediaries.

DeFi has primarily focused on enabling the funding and trading of digital assets, rather than offering intermediary services to bolster real-world economic endeavours (Aquilina, et. al, 2024). DeFi, driven by the revolutionary potential of blockchain technology and smart contracts, seeks to achieve decentralisation, and revolutionise financial services by removing the reliance on traditional intermediary organisations. According to Zetsche et al. (2020), decentralisation possesses the capability to undermine established methods of accountability and reduce the efficacy of traditional banking regulation and enforcement. The platform provides a diverse selection of financial services and goods, encompassing financing, borrowing, trading, and managing assets, all conducted directly on blockchain platforms, eliminating the need for banks or other centralised institutions. Further, Nartey 2024 highlighted that DeFi's decentralised architecture can facilitate AI development by offering a transparent, safe, and cooperative framework for developing and implementing AI models and hence the efficacy of conventional financial regulation and enforcement, as well as traditional systems of accountability, may be compromised by decentralisation. Simultaneously, it is discovered that when there are decentralised segments in the banking and financial services value chain, there will likely be a reconcentration in a separate (perhaps fewer regulations, less apparent, and less transparent) segment of the value chain. This reconcentrated section of the value chain should be the focus of DeFi regulation in order to provide efficient monitoring and risk management (Zetzsche, Buckley, Arner, & Barberis, 2020). Similar to the old financial system, the DeFi architecture may have the ability to lower transaction costs; yet, because of endogenous barriers to competition, rents can build up at multiple levels. Research indicates that the unrestricted and pseudonymous nature of DeFi poses difficulties for the enforcement of tax laws, the prevention of money laundering, and the detection of financial misconduct. Additionally, it has outlined potential regulations for the DeFi system that would uphold transparency and regulatory compliance while retaining most of the advantages of the blockchain that underlies it architecture (Makarov & Schoar, 2022). With a focus on disintermediation and decentralisation to empower people in line with cryptoanarchist ideals, DeFi holds out the prospect of an emerging alternative financial architecture (Chohan, 2021).

Despite the growing popularity and innovation within DeFi, traditional financial intermediation continues to play a vital role in several ways. An analysis conducted by Tanwar in 2020, examines the adoption of machine learning in using and enhancing blockchain technology. This study investigates the application of different ML techniques to address security threats in the blockchain network. In addition, it also explores the practical uses of these technologies in different sectors like automobile, healthcare, and enabling smart cities. AI has proven to be instrumental in addressing security concerns across various technologies, including blockchain. The convergence of AI and blockchain has attracted considerable interest over a long period. Technologies like machine learning, deep learning, and natural language processing have been extensively applied in the financial industry. These applications cover a wide range of tasks, including trading algorithms, risk evaluation, detecting fraud, and support for customers (Ozbayoglu et al., 2020). Algorithmic trading has been revolutionised by the use of AI models, as highlighted in the works of Kearns and Nevmyvaka (2013), and Van Vliet (2018). These models have greatly improved the speed and accuracy of high-frequency trading, thanks to the incorporation of deep learning and NLP techniques for market analysis. Through an exploration of the predictive capabilities of AI and the analytical potential of ML in handling extensive datasets (Irfan, Kadry, Sharif, & Khan, 2023). AI capacity to analyse intricate datasets has proven invaluable in risk management, as dem onstrated by the research of Ahmed and Malik in 2015 and De Prado in 2018. This has led to significant enhancements in credit risk assessment and portfolio risk management which creates the issue of sustainability in AI (Irfan et. al, 2024).

AI-driven fraud detection systems, as examined by Awoyemi et al. in 2017 and Ngai et al. in 2011, provide instantaneous identification and counteraction against fraudulent behaviour through the utilisation of machine learning algorithms. Customer service has been revolutionised by the use of chatbots which are AI-enabled and virtual assistants. These innovative technologies, as explored by Adam et al., 2020 and Davenport and Ronanki, 2018, offer round-the-clock assistance and tailored financial guidance. Robo-advisors have been the subject of research by Jung et al. in 2018 and Belanche et al. in 2019. These platforms utilise artificial intelligence to automate financial planning and investment management, resulting in improved user experience and portfolio management.

Recent advancements have brought attention to the significant impact of AI on improving efficiency, accuracy, and consumer satisfaction in financial services. Through ongoing research and advancements in technology, the influence of AI is anticipated to grow even stronger, presenting novel approaches to intricate financial obstacles.

LITERATURE REVIEW

The convergence of AI and DeFi promises to enhance efficiency, security, and user experience, potentially revolutionizing the financial landscape (Basly, 2024). Integrating AI into DeFi platforms offers numerous benefits, such as improved market efficiency and liquidity achieved through AI-driven price discovery and automated market-making (Amler et al., 2021). Personalized financial services and investment strategies, tailored to individual preferences and risk profiles, are also made possible by AI (Kou et al., 2022). With their astounding success and previously unheard-of accuracy, AI and machine learning have grown in significance within the finance industry (Irfan, Elhoseny, Kassim, & Metawa, 2023).

FOUNDATIONAL ELEMENTS OF AI IN DEFI

Decentralized Finance

DeFi encompasses several essential elements, such as decentralised exchanges, lending channels, stablecoins, and automated market makers (Schär, 2021). The advent of such networks has the potential to catalyse a profound revolution in the financial industry. By removing intermediaries, they can effectively lower costs and make financial services more accessible worldwide. Blockchain technology forms the bedrock of DeFi, serving as a decentralised and unalterable ledger that meticulously documents trades across a community of computers. Ethereum stands out as the leading blockchain for DeFi applications, renowned for its solid capability for smart contracts (Buterin, 2014). These contracts are contracts that are executed automatically based on predefined code that contains the conditions of the agreement, enabling trustless and automated transactions (Szabo, 1997). Blockchain technology, specifically Ethereum, forms the fundamental infrastructure for DeFi applications. DeFi presents viable answers to the challenges posed by centralised financial systems and has the capacity to emerge as a pivotal domain within the blockchain industry, provided that the technology is appropriately advanced.

KEY ELEMENTS OF DEFI

- Decentralized Exchanges (DEXs): DEXs enable users to directly engage in cryptocurrency trading, thereby eliminating the reliance on a central authority. This empowers individuals to have greater control and autonomy over their trading activities. Uniswap, Balancer, and SushiSwap are the examples. These platforms use AMMs to ascertain the asset price and execute trades based on supply and demand (Adams, 2020). DEXs offer benefits such as reduced counterparty risk and increased privacy, but they also face challenges like liquidity fragmentation and complex user interfaces (Zhu, 2020).
- Platforms for Borrowing and lending.: DeFi lending and borrowing platforms, such as Aave, MakerDAO and Compound, enable customers to provide their assets to others in exchange for interest. These platforms use smart contracts to lock assets as collateral and manage loans autonomously. The absence of traditional credit checks allows for broader access to lending services but also introduces risks related to over-collateralization and liquidity.
- Stablecoins: these are defined as a cryptocurrency that is specifically intended to keep a stable value to a reference asset. Examples consist of Tether (USDT), USD Coin, and DAI, which typically reference fiat currencies like the US dollar. Stablecoins are essential in the realm of DeFi as they provide a dependable medium of trade and a safe repository of value. This helps to address the inherent volatility often associated with other forms of digital currency (Tether, 2021). However, they also face scrutiny regarding their collateralization and regulatory status (Bullmann, Klemm, & Pinna, 2019).
- Yield Farming and Liquidity Mining: YF entails the provision of liquidity to the protocols of DeFi in return for rewards, usually in the way of extra tokens. Liquidity mining is a subset of yield farming where users earn native tokens of the protocol they support. These practices have driven significant growth in DeFi by incentivizing participation and liquidity provision but have also led to concerns about sustainability and speculative bubbles (Zhu, 2020).

BENEFITS OF DECENTRALIZED FINANCE

- Increased Financial Inclusion: The decentralisation of finance has the potential to revolutionise access to financial services, removing the need for intermediaries and lowering the barriers to entry. This can provide significant advantages for people living in developing nations who do not have access to conventional banking systems.
- Transparency and Trust: DeFi functions on public blockchains, where all transactions are meticulously recorded and made accessible to everyone. This high level of transparency minimises the reliance on intermediaries, as users have the ability to independently verify transactions. Consequently, this strengthens the overall trustworthiness of the system.
- Cost Reduction: Through the removal of intermediaries like banks and agents, DeFi effectively reduces transaction costs and other expenses linked to financial services. This offers significant benefits for overseas transactions, which have historically been burdened by exorbitant fees and lengthy processing times.
- Ownership and Control: DeFi empowers users with complete autonomy over their assets, allowing them to directly engage with financial services using their digital wallets. This improves personal financial sovereignty and reduces the need for third-party institutions.
- Innovation and Flexibility: The free-to-use nature of DeFi fosters an environment that promotes the creation of innovative financial goods and services. Developers have the ability to create and launch applications that meet the changing demands of the market, which promotes a dynamic and forward-thinking environment.
- Global Reach: DeFi works on a global scale, enabling users to effortlessly access monetary services and markets across the globe, free from the limitations imposed by conventional banking guidelines and restrictions. The global reach of this initiative expands financial inclusivity and creates new opportunities.

ARTIFICIAL INTELLIGENCE (AI) OVERVIEW

AI is a field that encompasses various technologies, including machine learning, natural language processing, and predictive analytics. These technologies empower machines to carry out tasks that would typically rely on human intelligence. The emergence of AI innovation in the financial sectors during the era of Industry 5.0 is proving to be a crucial resource, driving significant advancements that will have a profound impact on the future of finance (Irfan, Elmogy, Majid, & El-Sappagh, 2023). The utilisation of AI in DeFi platforms can greatly enhance their functionalities by effectively analysing extensive datasets, recognising patterns, and making accurate predictions. Blockchain technology has become a significant innovation in the finance industry, offering a strong solution to address fraudulent activities in transactions and enable secure and efficient trade. (Irfan, Muhammad, Naifar, & Khan, 2024).

INCORPORATION OF AI IN DEFI

The incorporation of AI into DeFi involves deploying machine learning algorithms to improve decision-making processes, enhance security, and optimize user experiences. AI can analyze transaction data to detect fraudulent activities, predict market trends, and provide personalized financial services (Benedict, Black, & Wu, 2020).

AI-DRIVEN ENHANCEMENTS IN DEFI

- Financial Market forecasting Trading Strategies: AI algorithms have the capability to analyse extensive data from multiple sources, enabling accurate market trend predictions and the development of informed trading strategies. Predictive analytics can identify potential investment opportunities and risks, enabling more informed decision-making for traders and investors.
- Automated Market Makers (AMMs): AMMs such as Uniswap employ smart contracts to enable seamless trading, effortlessly adapting prices in response to changes in supply and demand. Integrating AI can enhance these mechanisms by optimizing liquidity provision and minimizing slippage, thus improving the efficiency of decentralized trading platforms (Adams, 2020).
- Fraud Detection and Security: DeFi platforms are susceptible to security breaches and deceptive practices. AI can enhance security by analyzing transaction patterns to detect anomalies and prevent fraud. Machine learning models can continuously learn from new data to improve their accuracy in identifying suspicious activities.
- Personalized Financial Services: AI can provide personalized financial services by analyzing user behavior and preferences. This includes offering tailored investment advice, customized lending rates, and personalized insurance products. Such personalization can improve user satisfaction and engagement.

CHALLENGES AND RISKS OF AI IN DEFI

Artificial intelligence models have the potential to exhibit bias when they are trained using biassed data, which can result in outcomes that perpetuate discrimination (Ngai et al., 2020. Rivalry and data security issues pose significant challenges for AI systems (Goldstein et al., 2021)

- Data secrecy and Security- The integration of AI into DeFi has sparked concerns regarding data security and privacy. DeFi platforms are highly sought after by cyber attackers due to the immense volume of confidential financial information they handle and analyse. Preserving the safety and confidentiality of this information is of utmost importance in upholding user confidence.
- Regulatory Compliance- The decentralised nature of DeFi presents notable obstacles when it comes to regulatory compliance. AI-driven DeFi platforms must navigate a complex regulatory landscape, ensuring compliance with laws and regulations across different jurisdictions. This requires continuous monitoring and adaptation to changing regulatory requirements. Regulators are faced with the challenge of creating innovative frameworks that carefully consider both promoting innovation and protecting consumer interests. This task becomes even more complex when dealing with the unique characteristics of DeFi-AI systems. (Zetzsche, Buckley, Arner, & Barberis, 2020). The absence of a unified regulatory framework has made DeFi projects and users hesitant, which has impeded the technology's widespread adoption. A significant obstacle that DeFi must contend with is the ambiguity around regulatory compliance. DeFi projects frequently function in a decentralised, international fashion, making it challenging to ascertain which laws apply (Uzougbo, 2024).
- Bias and Fairness- The presence of biases in the data used to train AI algorithms can result in unjust outcomes, as these algorithms have the potential to perpetuate such biases. Establishing integrity and equity within AI-driven DeFi systems is crucial for preventing discrimination and promoting equal access to financial services.
- Technical Challenges- Implementing AI in DeFi involves significant technical challenges, including the scalability of AI models, the integration with blockchain technology, and the computational resources required. Addressing these challenges is of utmost importance in order to fully unlock the potential of AI in the field of decentralised finance.

FUTURE PROSPECTS OF AI IN DEFI

- Enhanced User Experience- AI can significantly enhance user experiences on DeFi platforms by providing intuitive interfaces, personalized recommendations, and seamless interactions. This can drive greater adoption of DeFi services among mainstream users (Buterin, 2014). A study conducted by Salami in 2021 found that the convergence of DeFi and AI has the potential to revolutionise the financial landscape, as these two disruptive technologies intersect. Through the integration of decentralised, trust less DeFi technology and the advanced capabilities of AI, a realm of new opportunities arises for the development of highly efficient, inclusive, and groundbreaking financial services. In their study, Tapscott and Tapscott (2016) probe into the potential of AI to elevate user interfaces and improve the overall experience within the realm of blockchain and DeFi applications. In their study, Agrawal, et al., in 2018 investigated the potential of AI-driven predictive analytics to enhance decision-making and user engagement within the realm of financial services, specifically focusing on DeFi.
- Enhanced Risk Management- Artificial intelligence holds great promise in bolstering risk management within the DeFi sector. By leveraging advanced algorithms and predictive models, AI can accurately forecast market volatility and detect potential security risks. This technological advancement shows significant potential in enhancing safety and security of the DeFi ecosystem. Machine learning algorithms possess the capability to analyse historical data as well as real-time blockchain activity to anticipate and tackle possible hazards in a proactive manner. In a recent publication, Schär (2021) examines into the realm of AI and its potential to revolutionise risk management in the field of DeFi. By meticulously analysing vast amounts of data, AI has the ability to uncover valuable market trends and pinpoint potential risks. A recent study, delve into the realm of AI and its potential to forecast and handle risks within the DeFi ecosystem, ultimately bolstering stability across the board. In a publication by Werbach in 2018 explores into the potential of combining AI and blockchain technology to enhance security protocols and effectively identify fraudulent activities within the realm of DeFi. In their study, Xu and Duan in 2018, investigate the realm of AI algorithms and their potential in analysing blockchain data. Their research focuses on how these algorithms can be utilised to bolster fraud detection and security measures in the domain of decentralised finance.
- Automated Smart Contracts- The integration of AI into smart contracts in DeFi can significantly enhance their functionality, allowing for the implementation of more intricate and adaptable contract terms. Utilising machine

learning, contract execution can be automated by leveraging real-time data, resulting in enhanced efficiency and decreased reliance on manual intervention. In his 2014 publication, Buterin delves into the realm of smart contracts, exploring their capabilities and exploring the possibilities of integrating artificial intelligence to further enhance their functionality. In their analysis, Cong and He (2019) researched the potential enhancements that AI can bring to smart contract functionality within the DeFi space.

- Improved Financial Inclusion- AI-driven DeFi platforms have the potential to enhance financial inclusion by granting underserved populations access to essential financial services. AI can analyze alternative data sources to assess creditworthiness, enabling more people to access loans and other financial products (Swan, 2015).
- Innovative Financial Products- The integration of AI in DeFi can lead to the creation of innovative financial products, such as AI-managed investment funds, predictive insurance products, and automated financial planning tools. These products can offer greater efficiency and customization compared to traditional financial products. The potential of AI is found in its capacity to enhance decision-making, automate complex processes, and derive valuable insights from vast financial data.
- Interoperability and Integration- By enabling seamless integration and communication between various financial services, AI can create a more cohesive and efficient financial ecosystem (Narayanan et al., 2016). Blockchain technology is widely utilised in the development of decentralised payment systems, resulting in the creation of a new form of digital currency known as cryptocurrency. In 2015, the introduction of the Turing-complete Ethereum blockchain expanded the capabilities of financial systems based on blockchain technology, going beyond just cryptocurrencies. DeFi refers to the range of non-custodial financial services that are implemented as Smart Contracts on Turing-complete blockchains. These solutions have become increasingly popular as investment vehicles over the years, with their total value locked surpassing USD 100 Billion.
- Personalized Financial Services- Artificial intelligence has the capability to deliver personalised financial services within the DeFi sector. This includes providing customised investment advice and efficiently managing portfolios. Through the analysis of user behaviour and preferences, AI-driven platforms have the ability to suggest the most effective financial strategies. In their study, Chishti and Barberis (2016) explored how AI technology can enhance user engagement and satisfaction by personalising the services offered.

CONCLUSION

The fusion of AI with DeFi has the capacity to completely transform the financial industry, improving operational efficiency, bolstering security measures, and enhancing the overall user experience. However, harnessing this potential necessitates tackling obstacles pertaining to the protection of data privacy, adherence to regulatory requirements, and seamless technical integration. As AI and DeFi technologies continue to evolve, their integration will likely lead to innovative financial products and services, driving greater financial inclusion and creating a more efficient global financial system. The integration of AI within the realm of DeFi heralds a transformative era in the financial sector. DeFi, leveraging blockchain technology and smart contracts, aims to decentralize and democratize financial services, eliminating the need for traditional intermediaries such as banks. This move provides a multitude of benefits, including enhanced financial inclusivity, enhanced transparency and trust, reduced transaction costs, and greater personal control over financial assets. The application of AI further amplifies these benefits by improving market efficiency and liquidity through AI-driven price discovery and automated market-making, enhancing risk management and credit assessment, and providing personalized financial services tailored to individual preferences. DeFi service providers are able to operate at substantially less expense compared to traditional financial services. This is mostly because traditional banks and financial organisations do not charge for the use of their services. Investors can adjust to changing environmental conditions more economically thanks to the cost advantage. Compared to typical financial institutions, DeFi enterprises have substantially less profit margins because of their decentralised and programmed nature. Thus, operational efficiency is improved, and borrowers benefit from more attractive rates. This results in lower marginal costs compared to financial institutions and nonbank entities in both developed and developing markets. DeFi enables lower-cost operations and greater access to financial services by eliminating conventional banking intermediaries and their related fees.

However, the transition from traditional financial intermediation to a decentralized model is not without challenges. Addressing concerns surrounding security and confidentiality of data, legal compliance, and possible biases in algorithms that use AI is crucial in overcoming significant obstacles. In spite of these obstacles, the merging of AI and DeFi holds the potential to establish a financial ecosystem that is more comprehensive, streamlined, and groundbreaking. As DeFi and AI technologies continue to mature, conventional financial service providers will likely see changes in their functions within the financial landscape.

In conclusion, the ongoing development and integration of AI within DeFi platforms offer a glimpse into the future of finance—a future characterized by increased accessibility, innovation, and efficiency. The ongoing evolution of these technologies holds the promise of reshaping the financial landscape, fostering greater inclusivity and equity in financial services on a global scale. The synergy between AI and DeFi holds immense promise for revolutionizing the way financial services are delivered and experienced, covering the way for a more democratized and decentralized financial system.

FUTURE IMPLICATION OF THIS STUDY

The potential for profound transformation in the financial industry is presented by the combination of AI and DeFi. This integration has the potential to significantly change the manner in which financial services are provided and experienced by providing opportunities for creativity, effectiveness, and inclusion. This study has broad and diverse future consequences that will affect many facets of the economic system.

First off, financial inclusion can be greatly improved by AI-driven DeFi platforms. Large portions of the world's population are frequently left out of traditional financial systems because they lack the ability to utilise traditional financial products and credit histories, especially in developing nations. Artificial intelligence possesses the ability to examine non-traditional data sources, like social media and mobile phone usage trends, in order to evaluate financial behaviour and creditworthiness. This makes it possible for DeFi platforms to offer loans and insurance, among other financial services, to those who would not otherwise be able to access the conventional financial system. AI-driven DeFi can significantly contribute to closing the income gap and advancing social justice and economic empowerment by offering individualised financial services that are catered to the requirements and conditions of marginalised people.

Enhancing market effectiveness and volatility is an additional noteworthy consequence of incorporating AI into DeFi. Large volumes of market data may be instantly analysed by AI systems, enabling more precise price discovery and effective trading tactics. Smart contracts are used by AMMs on DeFi systems, such Uniswap, to modify pricing in response to changes in supply and demand. AI integration can improve these processes, lowering slippage and raising liquidity. This promotes increased adoption of decentralised financial systems by stabilising the markets and boosting participant trust. Both traders and investors may profit from more secure and visible financial markets as a result of the increased market efficiency brought about by AI integration.

A crucial component of financial systems is risk management, and AI has the power to completely transform this field inside DeFi. Conventional financial organisations use labor-intensive, error-prone manual procedures and historical data to evaluate risk. AI has the capacity to evaluate massive datasets, spot trends, and produce risk evaluations that are more precise and timelier. Forecasting market patterns, seeing irregularities, and spotting possible security risks are all possible with predictive models. By taking a preventive approach to risk management, DeFi platforms may become more resilient, which will increase user security and dependability. Better portfolio management and credit evaluations can result from improved risk management, which will ultimately promote a more secure and effective financial system.

The promise for dramatic improvements in financial accessibility, market effectiveness, risk management, and security are presented by the merging of AI with DeFi. By using other sources of information to evaluate creditworthiness, powered by AI DeFi platforms can expand financial services to underrepresented groups, fostering social fairness and economic empowerment. AI can also improve market procedures, lowering slippage and increasing liquidity to create financial markets that are more transparent and stable. AI's predictive skills in risk management provide quicker and more accurate evaluations, strengthening the security and resilience of DeFi platforms. Financial product innovation is anticipated as a result of this integration, which will provide individualised and effective services like AI-managed funds for investment and predictive insurance services. AI can also improve security by preventing fraud, protecting user assets, and instantly identifying abnormalities. It is essential to have adaptive frameworks that find a middle ground between development and consumer protection in order to make certain that consumers adhere to financial regulations and data privacy laws. However, it is also important to resolve any regulatory concerns. Traditional financial intermediation is under threat from the emergence of AI-driven DeFi, which has forced banks and other financial companies to adapt and incorporate AI technologies. All things considered, the combination of AI and DeFi is poised to make the global financial system more open, effective, and transparent. It can also democratise utilisation of financial services, lower transaction costs, and promote social and economic advancement.

REFERENCES

Adam, M., Wessel, M., & Benlian, A. (2020). AI-based chatbots in customer service and their effects on user compliance. *Electronic Markets*, 31(2), 427–445. 10.1007/s12525-020-00414-7

Agrawal, A. (2017, February 17). The Simple Economics of Machine Intelligence. *Harvard Business Review*.https://hbr.org/2016/11/the-simple-economics-of-machine-intelligence.

Ahmed, S. F., & Malik, Q. A. (2015). Credit Risk Management and Loan Performance: Empirical Investigation of Micro Finance Banks of Pakistan. *International Journal of Economics and Financial Issues*, 5(2), 574–579.

Alamsyah, A., Kusuma, G. N. W., & Ramadhani, D. P. (2024). A Review on Decentralized Finance Ecosystems. *Future Internet*, 16(3), 76. 10.3390/fi16030076

Amler, H. (2021). DeFi-ning DeFi: Challenges & pathway. *IEEE international conference on intelligent computer communication and processing*. IEEE.

Aquilina, M., Frost, J., & Schrimpf, A. (2024). Decentralized Finance (DeFi): A Functional Approach. *Journal of Financial Regulation*, 10(1), 1–27. 10.1093/jfr/fjad013

Awoyemi, J. O., Adetunmbi, A. O., & Oluwadare, S. A. (2017). Credit card fraud detection using machine learning techniques: A comparative analysis. *International Conference on Computing Networking and Informatics (ICCNI)*. IEEE. 10.1109/ICCNI.2017.8123782

Bahoo, S., Cucculelli, M., Goga, X., & Mondolo, J. (2024). Artificial intelligence in Finance: A comprehensive review through bibliometric and content analysis. *SN Business & Economics*, 4(2), 23. 10.1007/s43546-023-00618-x

Basly, S. (2024). *Artificial Intelligence and the Future of Decentralized Finance. Financial Innovation and Technology*. Springer. .10.1007/978-3-031-49515-1_10

Belanche, D., Casaló, L. V., Flavián, C., & Schepers, J. (2019). Service robot implementation: a theoretical framework and research agenda. *Service Industries Journal/the Service Industries Journal,40*(3–4), 203–225. 10.1080/02642069.2019.1672666

Buterin, V. (2014). *Ethereum: A next-generation smart contract and decentralized application platform*. Ethereum. https://ethereum.org/en/whitepaper/.

Cao, L. (2020). AI in Finance: A Review. *Social Science Research Network Electronic Journal*. 10.2139/ssrn.3647625

Cao, Y., & Zhai, J. (2022). A survey of AI in finance. *Journal of Chinese Economic and Business Studies*, 20(2), 125–137. 10.1080/14765284.2022.2077632

Chishti, S., & Barberis, J. (2016c). *The FINTECH Book*. John Wiley & Sons. 10.1002/9781119218906

Chohan, U. W. (2021). Decentralized Finance (DeFi): An Emergent Alternative Financial Architecture. *Social Science Research Network*. 10.2139/ssrn.3791921

Cong, L. W., & He, Z. (2019). Blockchain Disruption and Smart Contracts. *Review of Financial Studies*, 32(5), 1754–1797. 10.1093/rfs/hhz007

Da Xu, L., & Duan, L. (2018). Big data for cyber physical systems in industry 4.0: A survey. *Enterprise Information Systems*, 13(2), 148–169. 10.1080/17517575.2018.1442934

Davenport, T. H. (2018, March 9). *Artificial Intelligence for the Real World*. Harvard Business Review. https://hbr.org/webinar/2018/02/artificial-intelligence-for-the-real-world.

De Prado, M. L. (2018). *Advances in Financial Machine Learning*. John Wiley & Sons.

Dos Santos, S., Singh, J., Thulasiram, R. K., Kamali, S., Sirico, L., & Loud, L. (2022). A New Era of Blockchain-Powered Decentralized Finance (DeFi) - A Review. *IEEE 46th Annual Computers, Software, and Applications Conference (COMPSAC), LosAlamitos*. IEEE. 10.1109/COMPSAC54236.2022.00203

Fernandes, M., Medeiros, M. C., & Scharth, M. (2014). Modeling and predicting the CBOE market volatility index. *Journal of Banking & Finance*, 40, 1–10. 10.1016/j.jbankfin.2013.11.004

Giudici, P., Hochreiter, R., Osterrieder, J., Papenbrock, J., & Schwendner, P. (2019). Editorial: AI and Financial Technology. *Frontiers in Artificial Intelligence*, 2, 25. 10.3389/frai.2019.0002533733114

Goodell, J. W., Kumar, S., Lim, W. M., & Pattnaik, D. (2021). Artificial intelligence and machine learning in finance: Identifying foundations, themes, and research clusters from bibliometric analysis. *Journal of Behavioral and Experimental Finance*, 32, 100577. 10.1016/j.jbef.2021.100577

Irfan, M., Elhoseny, M., Kassim, S., & Metawa, N. (2023). *Advanced Machine Learning Algorithms for Complex Financial Applications*. IGI Global. 10.4018/978-1-6684-4483-2

Irfan, M., Elmogy, M., Majid, M. S., & El-Sappagh, S. (2023). *The Impact of AI Innovation on Financial Sectors in the Era of Industry 5.0*. IGI Global.

Irfan, M., Hussainey, K., Bukhari, S. A., & Nam, Y. (2024). *Issues of Sustainability in AI and New-Age Thematic Investing*. IGI Global. 10.4018/979-8-3693-3282-5

Irfan, M., Hussainey, K., Chan Bukhari, S. A., & Nam, Y. (Eds.). (2024). *Issues of Sustainability in AI and New-Age Thematic Investing*. IGI Global Publisher. 10.4018/979-8-3693-3282-5

Irfan, M., Kadry, S., Sharif, M., & Khan, H. U. (2023). *Fintech Applications in Islamic Finance: AI, Machine Learning, and Blockchain Techniques*. IGI-Global. 10.4018/979-8-3693-1038-0

Irfan, M., Muhammad, K., Naifar, N., & Khan, M. A. (2024). *Applications of Block Chain technology and Artificial Intelligence:Lead-ins in Banking, Finance, and Capital Market*. Springer Cham. 10.1007/978-3-031-47324-1

Jung, D., Dorner, V., Glaser, F., & Morana, S. (2018). Robo-Advisory. *Business & Information Systems Engineering*, 60(1), 81–86. 10.1007/s12599-018-0521-9

Katte, S. (2024). A combination of AI and DeFi could benefit both industries. *Coin Telegraph*. https://cointelegraph.com/news/ai-defi-benefits-adoption.

Kearns, M., & Nevmyvaka, Y. (2013). *Machine Learning for Market Microstructure and High Frequency Trading*.

Kou, G., Chao, X., Peng, Y., & Wang, F. (2022). Network Resilience in The Financial Sectors: Advances, Key Elements, Applications, And Challenges for Financial Stability Regulation. *Technological and Economic Development of Economy*, 28(2), 531–558. 10.3846/tede.2022.16500

Makarov, I., & Schoar, A. (2022). Cryptocurrencies and Decentralized Finance (DeFi). *Brookings Papers on Economic Activity*, 2022(1), 141–215. 10.1353/eca.2022.0014

Narayanan, A., Bonneau, J., Felten, E., Miller, A., & Goldfeder, S. (2016). *Bitcoin and cryptocurrency technologies: A comprehensive introduction*. Princeton University Press. 10.1515/9781400884154

Nartey, J. (2024). *Decentralized Finance (DeFi) and AI: Innovations at the Intersection of Blockchain and Artificial Intelligence*, Centre for Sustainable Research and Advocacy (CENSURA), http://dx.doi.org/10.2139/ssrn.4781328

Ngai, E., Hu, Y., Wong, Y., Chen, Y., & Sun, X. (2011). The application of data mining techniques in financial fraud detection: A classification framework and an academic review of literature. *Decision Support Systems*, 50(3), 559–569. 10.1016/j.dss.2010.08.006

Schär, F. (2021). Decentralized Finance: On Blockchain- and Smart Contract-Based Financial Markets. *RE:view*, 103(2). 10.20955/r.103.153-74

Swan, M. (2015). *Blockchain: Blueprint for a new economy*. O'Reilly Media.

Tanwar, S., Bhatia, Q., Patel, P., Kumari, A., Singh, P. K., & Hong, W. C. (2020). Machine Learning Adoption in Blockchain-Based Smart Applications: The Challenges, and a Way Forward. *IEEE Access : Practical Innovations, Open Solutions*, 8, 474–488. 10.1109/ACCESS.2019.2961372

Tapscott, D., & Tapscott, A. (2016). *Blockchain Revolution: How the Technology Behind Bitcoin Is Changing Money, Business, and the World*. Penguin.

Uzougbo, N. N. S., Ikegwu, N. C. G., & Adewusi, N. O. (2024). Regulatory Frameworks for Decentralized Finance (DeFi): Challenges and opportunities. *GSC Advanced Research and Reviews*, 19(2), 116–129. 10.30574/gscarr.2024.19.2.0170

Van Vliet, B. (2018). *High-Frequency Trading: A Practical Guide to Algorithmic Strategies and Trading Systems*. Wiley.

Werbach, K. (2018). *The Blockchain and the New Architecture of Trust*. MIT Press. 10.7551/mitpress/11449.001.0001

Zetzsche, D. A., Arner, D. W., & Buckley, R. P. (2020). Decentralized Finance (DeFi). *Journal of Financial Regulation*, 2020(6), 172–203. 10.1093/jfr/fjaa010

Chapter 2
Transforming Financial Services Through Hyper-Personalization:
The Role of Artificial Intelligence and Data Analytics in Enhancing Customer Experience

Ankit Saxena
GLA University, India

Syed Mohd Muneeb
Tecnologico de Monterrey, Toluca, Mexico

ABSTRACT

The merging of artificial intelligence (AI) and data analytics is bringing about a hyper-personalized era that is radically changing the financial services sector. In order to provide highly personalized financial products and services, hyper-personalization makes use of artificial intelligence (AI) and data analytics to evaluate enormous volumes of data from many sources, such as transactional history, social media activity, and personal preferences. Financial organizations may provide highly relevant services by using machine learning algorithms and predictive analytics to uncover patterns and forecast client behavior. Hyper-personalization implementation, however, comes with a number of issues, such as data privacy problems, ethical issues, and the requirement for strong cybersecurity measures to safeguard sensitive client data. The increasing advancement of technology is anticipated to propel additional innovation in financial services by expanding the role of artificial intelligence (AI) and data analytics in hyper-personalization.

DOI: 10.4018/979-8-3693-6321-8.ch002

INTRODUCTION

Evolution of Financial Services

The Financial Services Sector has gone under tremendous transformation in last few decades, largely driven by technological advancements, regulatory dynamics, and increased customer expectations. In the last century, financial services sector was evolving and more of face-to-face interaction for traditional banking procedures, were the major characteristics as technology integration was in infancy stages in the integration of service delivery. Digital revolution in 1990s led to increased focus on consumer ears and accessibility. There was a shift from traditional banking services to online banking and electronic payment systems which altogether changed the canvas of sector. In the early 2000s, FinTech Companies were getting popular and intended to ensure delivery of creative financial solutions which has certain challenges for the traditional banking and financial services. Now, there is a shift to mobile banking and similar mechanisms where customers are expecting more convenience and on-the-go services (Lyons & Kass-Hanna, 2022).

In 2008, the global financial crisis brought structural changes in the entire financial market underlining the relevance of strong risk management and regulatory supervision. Now a days, financial institutions are bound to invest heavily in enhancing operational effectiveness, compliances and risk assessment. There has been a need to address diverse customer demands, which has been a challenge for the financial sector in the current era. The emergence of artificial intelligence has been a blessing in facilitating hyper personalization and even applying predictive analytics. This enables the financial service business to customize its delivery to their customers, leading to streamlined internal operations and resulting in improved client satisfaction. This ongoing evolution, of integrating artificial intelligence for hyper personalization focused on technology innovation and customer-centricity, is going to shape the sector's future (Gunawardane, 2023).

Significance of Hyper-Personalization in the Industry

Hyper-personalization refers to designing and delivering customized goods, services and experiences to specific customers, which is mediated by the usage of Artificial Intelligence and advanced data analytics. This goes beyond the conventional customization, which used to divide customers into segments based on the demographics or behavioral patterns only, by adding a wide range of data related to each customer encompassing his or her own transaction history, social media activity as well as real-time behavioral data. This kind of information enables the financial institutions to understand and anticipate customer requirements with unprecedented accuracy which definitely adds to customer engagement. Hyper-personalization in financial services has not been less than a revolution in offering highly tailored financial services. The availability of data as well as developments in artificial intelligence and machine learning leading to a paradigm shift leading to offering solutions based on customer preferences, financial behaviors, and life events (Singh & Kaunert, 2024).

The Hyper-Personalization in financial services has resulted in multifaceted customer delightment. This has improved the customer experience as financial institutions can offer smooth, user-friendly experience which can be customized as per individual customer's demands. Chatbots powered by artificial intelligence can deal with individualized financial advice and tailored alerts can be shared with customers about pertinent financial hazards or possibilities. Financial organizations can add to customer satisfaction and loyalty by understanding the needs of customers and providing timely and relevant offerings to customers (Irfan, 2021).

Such individualized offerings and customization increase the likeliness of drawing attention of customers and stimulating the involvement of customers. Customers like and tend to react favorably when offerings are specifically tailored and offered aligning to their individual financial objectives and circumstances and this kind of positive client relationship and better conversion rates results into enhanced customer engagement. Another positive dimension, that this Hyper-Personalization results in increasing financial outcomes for the financial firms as this better customer experience driven by such customization.

In today's competitive industry landscape, customers have been sensitive to the service quality parameters. To retain customers, it is imperative to offer them the best of services which suit their requirements and expectations. Recently due to highly competitive industry dynamics, customers are getting used to individualized experiences and every customer seeks those individualized offerings and solutions. Artificial intelligence added to big data related to customers micro actions allow attaining the competitive advantage in the industry benchmark. This also leads to operational efficiency due to integration of data analytics and artificial intelligence. Financial institutions can optimize performance by more efficient deployment of resources wherever they are most required (Jain, Paul, & Shrivastava 2021).

In brief, it can be referred to as hyper personalization is a big step towards providing extremely customized services which are leading to customer delightment, engagement and better financial outcomes. However, this is in the early era and has certain issues and challenges as every individual customer is very different from each other.

Role of Technological Advancements in Transforming Customer Experiences

Customer experience has been a focus point for industry practitioners. In fact, this has become a thrust area that all business entities want to ensure that they ensure that the customers are offered services which fulfil their set of expectations. Due to the advent of new technological advancements driven by machine learning and artificial intelligence, financial institutions are engaging with their customers in an unprecedented manner making it more customized, effective, and accessible. The data is acting as a game changer as in current digital device driven era customers are engaged with their devices which captures lot of data of customers using their browsing data which allows companies to understand the behavioral patterns of customers and factors affecting customer's individual satisfaction.

Artificial intelligence enabled Hyper-Personalization also enables financial institutions to offer customer services round the clock. Many a times customers have varied issues and seek tailored financial guidance, hyper-personalization enabled by Artificial Intelligence enables the lower operating costs and expanding financial margin for the institutions (Irfan, Elhoseny, Kassim, & Metawa, 2023).

Another key dimension is new product development which has to be aligned with the requirements and expectations of customers. Moreover, a new product and service is needed to suit each customer's demands. This is unachievable without utilizing big data. Banks now a days aspire to offer personalized financial solutions viz. Credit and investment plans which is in alignment with the transaction data, objectives as well as spending patterns of their customers. Additionally, the evolution of digital wallets and mobile banking has increased the access of financial services. Customers perform many banking operations like bill payments, money transfer, along with loan applications. This has created a lot of convenience which has enhanced the penetration of financial services especially in rural and semi-urban areas. In recent times, the advent of blockchain technology has added new dimensions to the functioning of financial institutions. Blockchain has immense applications in terms of complicated procedures like loan sanctioning, load disbursement and insurance claim processing which can be automated using smart contracts powered by blockchain technology. This has added huge speed, security, and accuracy in conducting financial transactions.

Recently, the invention of robo-advisors to offer automated, algorithm-driven financial planning services with little to no-human participation. These services are becoming accessible to most of population based, such services were reserved for wealthy individuals. Customers risk profiles and financial goals are considered for customization of offerings to customers. These technological developments have contributed to lots of ease but at the same time, this has created a unique set of difficulties. The major concerns have been regarding security and privacy. Protection of customers' data from cyber-attacks is also one of the critical concerns for financial institutions (Akyüz & Mavnacıoğlu 2021).

In summary, the financial services business is going through a transformation in terms of customers interaction due to the evolution of innovations in technology. Financial institutions are able to offer more individualized, effective and easily accessible services with the help of artificial intelligence, mobile banking, blockchain, Chatbots and robo-advisor services. However, the journey has a long way to go along with various challenges which are to be addressed in the upcoming transitions.

LITERATURE REVIEW

Overview of Existing Research on Personalization in Financial Services

In financial services hyper-personalization has been observed as an essential tool to increase customer happiness as well as loyalty. In this segment these literature reviews have been surveyed regarding the studies done in the context of hyper personalization and customization in financial services. One to one marketing and customized interactions based on customers preferences and requirements is one of the most essential attributes of successful marketing plan (Peppers & Rogers, 2017). Another study found that there is a huge significance of relationship marketing and customer retention. In contemporary industries landscapes of financial services this becomes even more essential for getting comparative edge (Venkatesan & Kumar, 2004).

There has been continuous reiteration of the fact that customer satisfaction and loyalty are dependent upon the customization of offerings. Customer experience can be significantly enhanced by catering to the requirements of each individual customer and offering them personalized banking services (Lemon & Verhoef's, 2016). And another study found that the trust of customers and engagement of customers are significantly enhanced by the personalized financial guidance offered by Financial Institutions, and this leads to a better customer retention (Lin et al., 2019).

Another key aspect of making hyper personalization possible has been the support of technological developments. It has been well established that machine learning and advanced Data Analytics are very much essential for complex handing of individual customers preference data and studying their individual behavior pattern. Financial Institutions can now offer customized services with the help of available refined data for individual customers (Baesens et al., 2016). Further it has been derived that developments like chatbots and virtual assistant driven by artificial intelligence are shaping up customer experience to another level which is definitely enhancing the experience of the customer while interacting on this web portals of the Financial Institutions (Nguyen & Simkin, 2017).

There have been a number of case studies which demonstrated that effective hyper-personalization implemented in the financial service industry is improving the overall customer satisfaction to another level. In one of the studies, it was found that a major bank customized loan offers using Data Analytics increased their acceptance rate of proposals significantly (Goyal and Sergi, 2015). Li and Mao (2019) investigated the implementation of hyper-personalization elements in mobile banking app so that they customer satisfaction and engagement can be enhanced it was found that hyper personalization has many advantages but it also offers concern for security and private issues related to data. Order to ensure customer trust on such customization based on artificial intelligence it is imperative that Financial Institutions needs to balance between the degree of privacy and personalization. Data is important for the analysis but it should not prose for offer any thread to be customer (Schaar, 2010; Solve, 2006).

Another dimension of research has been regarding the ethical implications of hyper personalization. According to Zarsky (2016), hyper personalization in financial services can definitely improve the experience of the customer but it also has certain challenges like it can probably lead to a kind of bias or discrimination among the customers itself. Hence, Financial Institutions are required to be very careful that such hyper personalization techniques are equitable and do not hurt customers or particular clientele even unintentionally. It is also underlined that new technologies like blockchain and internet of things (IoT) will play an instrumental role in hyper personalization in the coming era. It has been found that blockchain technology can be a remedy to offer fare transparent and safe method for organizing customers data and offering more customized services (Tapscott & Tapscott, 2016). Similarly, Kshetri (2017) underlined that how real time insights about customers behavior can be collected via internet of things devices which may be even more accurate for more accurate customization of individual customers offerings.

Theoretical Frameworks on Customer Experience and Satisfaction

Customer experience and satisfaction are, therefore, the core elements of success for any financial services firm. Understanding the theoretical frameworks within which these concepts are anchored can aid in the design of successful strategies to satisfy and please customers. For that reason, this literature review is based on various academic studies that bring out the relevant theoretical viewpoints in respect of customer experience and customer satisfaction within the financial services sector.

Service Quality: According to the SERVQUAL model suggested by Parasuraman, Zeithaml, and Berry in 1985, good service delivery is the one that measures up to perception about client expectations. Customer satisfaction within the financial services sector would hence be a function of how much banks and other financial institutions meet or exceed their clients' expectations on these dimensions: tangibles, assurance, responsiveness, empathy, and reliability.

Customer Expectation-Perception Gap Theory: According to the theory developed by Parasuraman et al. (1985), which is largely based on the model of service quality gaps, understanding, and managing the differences between what customers expect of a service provider and how they perceive him to be able to provide it is pivotal. The misalignment of consumer expectations and experience with their banks, in relation to customer satisfaction, has been a subject of study by scholars in the financial services sector, stressing the need to match service delivery with promises.

Relationship Marketing Theory: Relationship marketing theory is focused on long-term, mutually beneficial business-customer relationships. In the financial services sector, strong customer relationships will be key to loyalty and repeat business. Commitment, communication, satisfaction, trust, and trustworthiness are elements of creating and managing client relationships that have been under study with respect to banking and financial services.

Emotional and Experiential Views: The emotional and experience dimensions in customer interaction with the provider of financial services have very much been put into the limelight of late. In the context of banking, it explores how emotions drive customer happiness, loyalty, and engagement by elaborating on concepts of emotional intelligence and experiential marketing. It concerns making moments meaningful and memorable for customers; thus, knowledge of what really drives customer emotions matters a lot.

TAM: With the increasing centrality of the digital channels in banking, it becomes very important to understand client acceptance and uptake of the technology-based services through the theoretical lens provided by the Technology Acceptance Model. In predicting customers' use intention of digital banking services and their happiness, research using TAM in the financial services sector has considered factors like perceived usefulness, ease of use, attitude toward technology.

Service-Dominant Logic: SDL posits a paradigm shift from a good-centric perspective to a service-centric one by highlighting co-creation value through the interplay among service providers and customers. In financial services, this underlines the nature of customer experiences as dynamic and collaborative; second, it makes the case that customers could interactively shape the value proposition from their dealings with banks and other financial institutions.

Theoretical frameworks provide insightful information about the factors that influence customer happiness and experience in the financial services sector. Adopting theoretical frameworks would help scholars and practitioners come up with ways of ensuring service excellence, building strong client relationships, leveraging technology effectively, and creating memorable experiences for customers within the highly competitive financial services environment.

Key Studies on the Impact of AI and Data Analytics in Financial Services Industries

Artificial intelligence and data analytics are the powerful tools of today that change the industry across borders. These technologies make a difference, simplifying procedures, strengthening judgment, and boosting client experiences in the financial industry. This literature survey provides an overview of how AI and data analytics impact various businesses with a special focus on finance.

Improved Risk Management and Fraud Detection: Artificial intelligence, coupled with data analytics, aids financial institutions in better assessing and dealing with loan, investing, and transactional risks. In an attempt to reduce loss and improve security in the banking industry, research by Hardle and Simar, 2003, depicts how machine learning algorithms can analyze huge data volumes for signs of fraudulence.

Greater Customer Insight and Personalization: With data analytics, a financial organization will understand more of their customers' needs, tastes, and behavior. Studies by Risselada et al., 2018, show how banks can be in a position to advise customers on finances in a tailor-made way, undertake campaigns of targeted marketing, and thus suggest product ideas to each customer in a personalized way. In this way, this raises the bar regarding customer happiness and loyalty.

Algorithmic trading and investment management use AI-powered algorithms that help firms execute trades at incredible speeds and monitor market developments in real-time. According to research by Cartea and MacKenzie, 2009, a review of the impact of algorithmic trading on market liquidity, price discovery, and volatility delineates its importance in developing financial markets.

Automated Customer Service and Support: To a large degree, AI-powered chatbots and virtual assistants are used by the institutions in providing automated client support service. According to one research conducted by Lacity and Willcocks, 2016, the NLP-enabled chatbots have been found to manage quite effectively the client inquiries, address problems, provide bespoke support to the clients, and enhance their experience.

Regulatory Compliance and Risk Assessment: AI and DA help the financial sector in both regulatory compliance and risk assessment by automating procedures and ensuring conformance to legal and industrial norms. To improve the ability of firms in navigating complex regulatory environments, Cao et al. researched AI-based compliance solutions that could simplify compliance reporting, monitor transactions for suspicious activity, and detect compliance risk in 2018.

Predictive Analytics in Financial Forecasting: Statistical models are used to build predictions of future patterns and financial results using historical data. Effectiveness in financial forecasting, like stock price prediction, credit risk assessment, and economic forecasting through predictive analytics, has been evidenced by various studies by Makridakis et al., 2018. In this way, the financial industry is able to make strategic decisions on planning and investments.

Literature on the personalization of financial services has so far emphasized how important it is in raising customer satisfaction and loyalty. Technology-related innovations, like blockchain, artificial intelligence, and data analytics, drive the potential of today's environment to support such personalized services. Proper care for privacy, security, and ethical concerns, however, is required if full value capture under personalization is to be achieved. Future research must also be consistent in seeking inventive technologies and strategies that balance customization with client trust and neutrality. Second, the areas in which artificial intelligence and data analytics have made visible progress in the financial services sector are those of risk management, customer insights, trading techniques, customer service, compliance, and forecasting. With the technologies turning increasingly sophisticated, it is bound to continue transforming the financial landscape by affecting productivity, creativity, and competitiveness in the world economy.

THE CONCEPT OF HYPER-PERSONALIZATION

Hyper personalization is one of the emerging marketing tools for ensuring the delivery of customized goods and services to the client with enhances their experience and loyalty. It requires proper detailing of individual customers' needs perceptions and behavior. Hyper personalization allows companies to ensure the delivery which is relevant and timely as per the expectations of the various individual customers. This way the companies are able to establish a proper connection with the customer and this idea is more dynamic and flexible as compared to traditional mode of marketing.

Hyper-Personalization vs. Traditional Personalization

Hyper-Personalization is different from traditional personalization in many aspects. In hyper personalization there is a strong dependency upon data which is collected using different technological advancement. Another very important dimension is the usage of appropriate technology to analyze the high-volume data to make some meaningful influences and profile individual customers so that the large volume data can be used for effective hyper personalization. The traditional personalization was primarily based on segmentation which was largely dependent on some common demographics for psychographics. In traditional personalization the recommendations were common for a group and heterogeneity within a group was not dealt with precisely. However, with the inventor of hyper personalization, Financial Institutions are able to develop a more refined strategy for enhancing customer experience using message amount of data like their browsing history, social media activities, payment history and other allied information which can be used for predicting behavior and preferences with higher order of accuracy.

The degree of personalization and the width of knowledge about a particular situation in reference of each customer is something that every business needs to figure out. If company is able to anticipate the demand being generated from customers, their expectation from the service provider and understanding their response to a particular situation, then it becomes easier for them to customize the offerings and enhance overall service experience. However, this is not that easy because every individual is very different and it might not be possible for the service provider to customize services to each and all individual's preferences and requirements (Valdez Mendia & Flores-Cuautle, 2022).

Key Components and Mechanisms of Hyper-Personalization

Hyper personalization comprises of various factors like taste of individual customer, wants and behaviors. Hyper personalization is a dedicated approach of customer engagement beyond the conventional personalization strategies which includes variety of data driven tactics and tools to understand real profile of the target customer. The biggest artifact of artificial intelligence driven hyper personalization is the integration of individual data across the channels. Single individuals may have different perspectives and approaches in different transactions being dealt with over the time. Each individual behaves differently in different situations and at the same time each individual may behave differently over the period of time in the same set of situations. This makes exploring customer profile extremely difficult (Singh & Kaunert, 2024).

Another imported artifact of hyper personalization is the ability of data scientists or data analysts to deriving the real data driven insights. Data analysis and data interpretation are different traits. At times individual analyst may have their own subjectivity affecting the overall analysis as well full stop however recently the inventor of artificial intelligence based analytical tools have made these analytical process more robust and multiple scenarios maybe related and tested for statistical accuracy as well. However, for better result, it is important to back test the available data and ensure that collected data points like demographics, past transactions, browsing history, and interaction on social media are giving decent predictions about individual behavior in a given situation. Then only hyper personalization based on data has some practical managerial implication.

Another very important component of hyper personalization is the ability of the decision makers to analyze decisions quickly and adapting the most appropriate decisions. Business should be able to modify the available data driven insights for real time decision making as per the circumstances.

Figure 1. Fundamental elements of hyper personalization

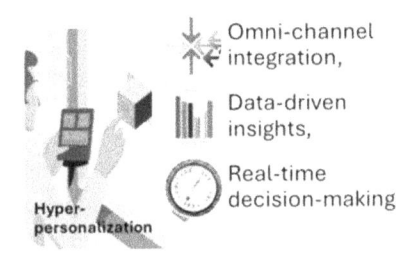

(Author's Compilation)

To summarize, the fundamental elements and processes of hyper-personalization include omni-channel integration, data-driven insights, and real-time decision-making. These allow businesses to provide highly relevant and captivating experiences that increase revenue, customer pleasure, and loyalty (Desai, 2022).

Benefits for Both Financial Institutions and Customers

In both financial institutions and their customers, much is to be gained from the inauguration of a new era of tailored experience and heightened happiness—hyper-personalization. Hyper-personalization serves to provide more information to financial companies about customer requirements, interests, and habits. By embracing advanced analytics and artificial intelligence, banks and other financial institutions will be better placed to segment their customer base effectively and hence give relevant products, services, and advice that would intuitively appeal to certain subsets of customers. This focused strategy creates revenue and cross-sell opportunities while increasing client engagement and loyalty. More importantly, hyper-personalization is a channel through which financial institutions will be able to reduce costs by identifying and responding in real-time to any consumer pain points.

The result is a smoother, more user-friendly banking experience for the customer. Confidence and brand loyalty are built in the minds of clients who receive tailor-made offers and advice based on their financial objectives and lifestyle preferences. Besides, proactive support and personalized interactions increase customer satisfaction, boosting retention rates and favoring positive word-of-mouth recommendations. Ultimately, this is how hyper-personalization empowers clients to make wise financial decisions that enable them to achieve their goals quickly and have a more satisfactory and personalized banking experience (Morton, Benavides, & González-Treviño, 2024).

ROLE OF ARTIFICIAL INTELLIGENCE

Artificial intelligence is at present changing the face of financial services by empowering organizations to make better decisions, automate procedures, and offer clients personalized experiences. Exponential growth in data and machine learning algorithms are fast steering artificial intelligence to become a critical tool for financial institutions such as banks, insurance companies, and investment organizations. It is making a difference in a number of areas—the prominent ones being in risk management and fraud detection. Machine learning algorithms can identify trends indicative of fraud by analyzing large amounts of data, thus assisting financial organizations in risk mitigation and protection of their assets. Besides, AI-driven chatbots and virtual assistants are making customer care services efficient by providing assistance at the fingertips and offering customized suggestions, thereby increasing customer delight and loyalty.

AI systems aid in investment management by optimizing the trading strategy in such a way that it goes on to maximize returns for the client through market trend analysis, performance forecasting, and efficient execution of transactions. AI-driven predictive analytics also aids financial organizations in understanding market trends, assessing credit risks, and looking out for investment opportunities—all of which enhance strategic decision-making and fuel company growth. Considering all factors, AI plays the role of a driver for change in financial services by empowering organizations to innovate, optimize processes, and offer better value to clients in an incredibly competitive environment (Irfan, Elmogy, Majid, & El-Sappagh, 2023).

Overview of AI Technologies Used in Financial Services

Artificial intelligence technologies are making a revolution in the financial services sector. Much more productivity, improved decision-making, and personalized client interaction will be enhanced in this industry. Some major AI technologies in use include RPA, NLP, and machine learning. Machine learning is a subdomain of artificial intelligence that enables systems to learn from data and improve over time without explicit programming. The areas that benefit from machine learning algorithms include algorithmic trading, credit scoring, fraud detection, and risk assessment. They optimize investment strategies and reduce risk by recognizing patterns and projecting what could occur in the future according to analysis of past data.

Another important AI technique that allows computers to understand, interpret, and act upon human language is Natural Language Processing. This is applied by financial institutions in enabling chatbots and virtual assistants that offer real-time, customized service to consumers. Natural Language Processing is also applied in sentiment analysis, extracting sentiment from sources like news and social media to help in investing decisions.

RPA uses artificial intelligence to automate processes that are repetitive and based on rules: transaction processing, compliance reporting, data entry, and so on. You can reduce operating costs, minimize human error, and enable staff to spend time in higher value activities by automating tasks. In aggregate, these AI technologies will become essential for driving innovation, improving operational efficiency, and delivering rich customer experiences within the financial services industry (Hentzen & et al., 2022).

Applications of AI in Hyper-Personalization in Financial Services Industry

AI applications for hyper-personalization in the financial services sector are modifying the ways in which companies interact with and serve clients. Leading this charge are AI-driven, individualized recommendations analyzing consumer data and behavior via machine learning algorithms. AI systems can give each consumer, based on demand, individually tailored advice, product offerings, and investment opportunities by analyzing his transaction history, spending patterns, and financial goals. This type of personalization can result in increased engagement and loyalty, apart from enhancing consumer pleasure (Pattnaik, Ray, & Raman, 2024).

Virtual assistants and chatbots are an integral part of AI applications driving the path to hyper-personalization. These AI solutions work through NLP capabilities and offer customized, real-time interactions with customers. They may answer a whole myriad of requests at any time of the day, ranging from complex financial advice to simple account-balance enquiries. Chatbots ensure that clients get progressively more appropriate and accurate information by learning from every contact and improving their answers accordingly. Moreover, AI empowers digital banking solutions to be very dynamic and personalized. For example, AI could make the user interface of the application simple and easy to use by adjusting according to the user's preferences and actions. It is also responsible for the timely warnings and insights, like spending trends or possibilities for savings, based on the financial behaviors manifested by each customer (Mogaji, Soetan, & Kieu, 2020).

AI applications in hyper-personalization greatly improve the customer experience of the financial services industry with very personalized, fast, and relevant services that increase customers' happiness and loyalty.

Case Studies Demonstrating Successful Implementation of AI in Financial Services

JPMorgan Chase – Contract Intelligence (COiN): With the help of its COiN (Contract Intelligence) platform, JPMorgan Chase has incorporated AI. COiN is a machine-learning platform that reads legal documents to extract key data points. This is something which, hitherto, was laborious and prone to mistakes when manned by humans. JPMorgan Chase demystified how AI could improve the accuracy and efficiency of financial operations, using it to review papers within seconds rather than 360,000 hours.

BlackRock – Aladdin: Another powerful example of disruption by AI is Aladdin by BlackRock. In-depth risk analytics and portfolio management are done using AI and machine learning. It aids asset managers in recognizing risks and opportunities that enhance decision-making. The predictive analytics capability of this platform has become very instrumental in enhancing investment strategies and raising the overall performance of portfolios.

AI-Powered Credit Scoring: Ant Financial Ant Financial, an affiliate of Alibaba Group, has injected AI into its Zhima Credit system for credit rating. This type of system parses a myriad of data, including transaction history and even social behavior, in order to determine the creditworthiness of those applying. Analyzed by an AI system, these data can offer more accurate credit ratings, enhancing lending decisions and boosting financial inclusion for people and small enterprises who have no traditional credit histories.

These case studies demonstrate how AI can make immense improvements in the efficiencies, risk management, and decision-making processes of financial services firms, thereby aiding in realizing better outcomes for institutions and their clients.

ROLE OF DATA ANALYTICS

Data analytics is the major drive in the financial services sector, which entails the translation of vast amounts of raw data into meaningful insights. Identification of trends and preparation against possible financial risks improve risk management. Consumer behavior analysis allows financial organizations to offer products and services tailored to customers' needs, thus improving customer satisfaction and loyalty. Besides, the process is simplified, and costs are reduced to ensure operational efficiency is maximized. Predictive analytics in investment management drives one to make strategic decisions that offer improved returns. Generally speaking, data analytics gives a financial institution the power to reduce risks and come up with well-informed decisions that better handle customers in a cutthroat industry.

Types of Data Used for Hyper-Personalization

In financial services, hyper-personalization makes available various sources of data to offer goods and services tailored for specific clients. Accordingly, transactional, behavioral, and social media data are the major data types leveraged.

Transactional information includes all data related to consumer transactions, such as purchases, payments, account transfers, loan applications, and so on. This sort of information shows spending patterns, financial habits, and creditworthiness, which a financial organization can leverage to offer customers tailor-made financial solutions on credit card offers, loan packages, and investment alternatives.

This can be behavioral data, which involves tracking all consumer interactions with their financial services through digital channels, from how people use mobile apps and websites, to service requests, to even waiting time. By analyzing behavioral data regarding what clients prefer to do and how often they log on, financial institutions can serve up better user experiences with relevant content and timed alerts and customized user interfaces (Nguyen, Sermpinis, & Stasinakis, 2023).

Social media data a customer's opinion, preferences, and feedback shared on social media sites like Facebook, Twitter, and LinkedIn. Harnessing this information would, therefore, position financial firms in being able to identify new trends better and measure public sentiment more effectively. Through the analytics of social media, banks can respond better to consumers, quickly fix any problems, and develop marketing campaigns targeting a certain set of people.

In this regard, the financial institution will be able to have an all-rounded understanding of each client by aggregating multiple data sets, hence empowering hyper-personalization by delivering high relevance and timeliness of financial services (Irfan, Kadry, Sharif, & Ullah Khan, 2023).

Data Collection, Processing, and Analysis

These are important tools in the financial services industry, making hyper-personalization feasible and so able to offer possibly much more in services and offerings to the clients because of services, especially data gathering, processing, and analysis.

Data Collection: Data collected by financial institutions come from banking transactions, behavioral data from interactions with digital platforms, and social media data from client engagements in sites like LinkedIn and Twitter. Moreover, contemporary technologies that offer real-time insights toward consumer behavior and preferences improve data collection, ranging from mobile applications to Internet of Things-represented devices.

Data Pre-Processing: Data is pre-processed at the collection stage to maintain its quality and applicability. It is a process where the data collected from disparate sources is stored in the centralized database, after which the data is cleaned to get rid of any inconsistencies and normalized into a standard format. Data warehousing and data lakes are the most common ways for a financial institution to store vast volumes of both structured data and unstructured data. The most recent tools in the computing world that handle and process these huge datasets are Apache Spark and Apache Hadoop.

Data Analysis: It involves the application of advanced analytical techniques and machine learning algorithms to the cleaned data. Use application techniques that include clustering, natural language processing, and predictive analytics for identifying patterns, predicting future behavior, and deriving meaningful insights from data analysis. For instance, sentiment analysis on social media data can give knowledge of customer preference and satisfaction, while AI models might use transactional data to predict what their customers want.

With the help of advanced techniques, financial institutions are able to achieve the most radical form of personalization, offering tailor-made finance solutions, customized suggestions, and quick services sure to delight customers and engender long-term loyalty (Rosenbaum, Ramirez, Campbell, & Klaus, 2021).

Importance of Big Data and Real-Time Analytics in Enhancing Customer Experience

Big data and real-time analytics have been influential in improving the client experience within the financial services sector. Through huge amounts of data derived from various sources, financial companies can develop deep insights relating to customer interests, wants, and behavior. With real-time analytics, organizations can process data instantly and analyze it to help them respond in time to customer behaviors.

These will enable a range of personalized experiences—including the rapid detection of fraud, proactive customer service, and the sort of well-tailored product suggestions which come from real-time transaction monitoring. For instance, proactive fraud prevention would allow clients to be alerted to suspicious activity. On another note, the very same benefits of real-time data could dramatically boost client satisfaction and loyalty through individual advice on finance and customized product offerings.

Moreover, real-time analytics ensures that financial institutions will quickly meet the changing expectations of clients, keeping them flexible and sensitive to market changes. Above all, it means that the combination of big data with real-time analytics creates a more tailored, safe, and entertaining consumer experience, thus boosting the growth and competitiveness of the financial industry.

ENHANCING CUSTOMER EXPERIENCE

Enhancing the customer experience in the financial services industry today requires modern technology, including but not limited to: artificial intelligence, data analytics, and mobile platforms. Data analytics can be used to give consumers personalized services and products from financial institutions based on individual needs. Predictive analytics anticipates the demands of clients and provides pre-emptive solutions, while AI-driven chatbots and virtual assistants are always available to give personalized support.

Moreover, convenient, and secure mobile banking applications ensure easy access to financial services anytime and from anywhere. Personalization, convenience, and security are three high-priority areas through which financial institutions can build bonds that last and create a competitive edge in the market through great happiness and loyalty of clients.

How Hyper-Personalization Meets Customer Expectations and Needs

In financial services, hyper-personalization meets customer demand and expectation through the use of artificial intelligence and sophisticated data analytics in delivering personalized experiences and solutions. Customer transactional behavioral, and social media data can give financial organizations deep insights into unique customer preferences, behaviors, and goals. This will enable the banks to come up with very relevant products and services, such as the ability to give customers personalized investment advice, targeted savings plans, and loan offers that are tailored. Moreover, through hyper-personalization, one strengthens customer engagement by way of timely notifications and proactive support in a bid to ensure clients get the right information at the right time.

Today's consumers are demanding seamless, intuitive, and personalized experiences with their financial services providers. To that end, hyper-personalization can realize a much more responsive and focused customer experience, engendering satisfaction, loyalty, and trust. In these demands, financial institutions will be able to differentiate themselves in an overcrowded marketplace and better position themselves to strengthen client relationships and drive corporate growth.

Metrics for Measuring Customer Experience and Satisfaction

Measuring customer experience and happiness in financial institutions is very important if it has to improve its services for more enduring relationships with customers. It applies quite a number of important indicators efficiently in assessing these factors (Kuppelwieser & Klaus, 2021).

Figure 2. Metrics for measuring customer experience and satisfaction

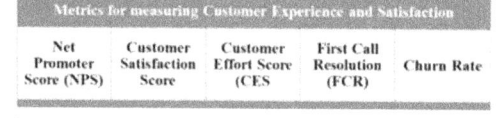

Metrics for measuring Customer Experience and Satisfaction				
Net Promoter Score (NPS)	Customer Satisfaction Score	Customer Effort Score (CES)	First Call Resolution (FCR)	Churn Rate

(Author's Compilation)

NPS—Net Promoter Score—comes next and is also very popular. Here, the client is asked for the likelihood of referring the financial institution to others. It measures client loyalty. A high score on NPS means that customers are highly satisfied and enjoying positive experiences; a low score will point to problem areas that need to be improved.

Customer Satisfaction Score: This specifies the overall satisfaction level with certain contacts or services. Consumers review their experience on a scale, usually 1 through 5; the higher the rating, the better the satisfaction level. This measure helps in determining the benefits versus the drawbacks of customer service.

Customer Effort Score (CES): This indicates how much effort a customer has to put in to complete a transaction or find a solution. A low effort score reflects a very smooth and efficient customer experience. This depends on the maintenance of high satisfaction.

First Call Resolution—FCR: This is measured by the initial Contact Resolution or FCR, the percentage of customer complaints resolved at the very first engagement. A high rate of FCR means problems are solved with a lot of efficiency and play a huge part in giving satisfied customers.

Churn Rate: This is the rate at which customers in a given period of time stop buying from the business. The lower the customer churn rate, the more satisfied are the customers. Data-driven improvements can be derived from the pulling together of these measures, which provide both an overall look at each customer experience and satisfaction dimensions for financial institutions in order to foster enhanced connections with their clients.

Examples of Improved Customer Outcomes Through Hyper-Personalization

Hyper-personalization in financial services involves AI and big data analyzing customers individually in order to present relevant products and services, with drastically better results. For instance, Bank of America's virtual assistant, Erica, utilizes AI to deliver personalized financial guidance and advice for better management of finances. Another example is Eno from Capital One, which proactively notifies users about unusual spending patterns, fraud, and chances of saving money in areas like security and savings. Wealthfront's robo-advisor platform creates bespoke investment portfolios in keeping with individual risk tolerance and financial goals for the optimization of returns and customer satisfaction. Last but not least, FinTech company Mint offers customized budgeting tips and key financial insights to users in line with their spending habits using hyper-personalization. Across these examples, one can notice how hyper-personalization creates better user experiences and drives higher engagement and brand loyalty through the meeting of unique financial needs and preferences with accuracy.

CHALLENGES AND ETHICAL CONSIDERATIONS OF AI-DRIVEN HYPER-PERSONALIZATION IN THE FINANCIAL SERVICES INDUSTRY

In the quest for responsible and ethical procedures in financial services, hyper-personalization raises a number of concerns and ethical dilemmas that must be addressed. The greatest concern could be security and privacy of data. The quantity of data being collected and analyzed on this large scale brings about concerns of identity theft, data breaches, and illegal access. This means that financial institutions require firm security measures in place and adherence to legal regulations on safeguarding consumer information. Another issue is potential prejudice and bias of algorithms. Artificial Intelligence-based systems may unconsciously run racial, gender, or socio-economic status prejudices, which result in unfair dealing with specific client groups. Equitability and fairness to all clients must thus be ensured at all times by a financial institution through continuous monitoring and auditing of algorithms in search of biases to reduce them (Singh & Kaunert, 2024).

Figure 3. Challenges and ethical considerations of ai-driven hyper-personalization in the financial services industry

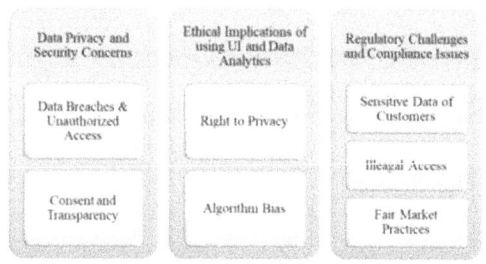

Data Privacy and Security Concerns	Ethical Implications of using UI and Data Analytics	Regulatory Challenges and Compliance Issues
Data Breaches & Unauthorized Access	Right to Privacy	Sensitive Data of Customers
		Illeagai Access
Consent and Transparency	Algorithm Bias	Fair Market Practices

(Author's Compilation)

This will also give rise to a few ethical issues related to transparency and consent. Customers should have the right to opt out if they so wish and be informed about how their data is used to achieve that hyper-personalization. It also calls for ensuring that financial institutions put customers' best interest at the center, and not profit margins, when coming up with those tailored suggestions and offers. Ultimately, there are apprehensions regarding an over-reliance on technology and complete loss of human interaction in transactions. Where hyper-personalization can bring convenience and speed, it should not replace human judgment and compassion in addressing the needs and issues of customers. In developing trust and building positive relationships with clients, it will be important to find a balance in which technological innovation and human touch work seamlessly (Desai, 2022)

Data Privacy and Security Concerns

Concerns to data security and privacy come right at the forefront of the hyper-personalization underway within the financial services sector. With extensive volumes of collected sensitive information from clients to enable personalized experiences, financial institutions are increasingly under threat from data breaches and unauthorized access. Given high-profile data breaches and hacks, it comes as no surprise that customers are concerned about their financial and personal information being secure.

In addition, the legislative framework introduced by both CCPA and GDPR sets very strict limitations on the collection, storage, and processing of personal data, generally complicating things and bringing compliance problems to financial institutions. It is necessary for banks and other financial institutions to emphasize consent and transparency in processing the data they hold, to set up strict rules related to data protection, and to seriously invest in robust cyber security measures in order to alleviate such concerns. In successful, confident clients, hyper-personalization activities, proactive communication, and accountability can give rise to trust.

Ethical Implications of Using AI and Data Analytics

Serious ethical concerns should be attached to the hyper-personalization of financial services powered by AI and data analytics. For instance, on top of the list, come the concerns around the security and privacy of the data, since the collection and analysis of large amounts of data on clients may be construed as an invasion of the people's right to privacy. Another problem is algorithm bias: AI models have been known to unconsciously discriminate against people based on their socioeconomic status or demographic background. There are, however, extra concerns of an ethical nature in regard to accountability and transparency, since consumers might be unaware about using their data to enable personalization in financial services.

If financial institutions can ensure that some ethical concepts take precedence, AI and data analytics can be responsibly used to the benefit of clients, without infringing on client rights or affecting their welfare adversely.

Regulatory Challenges and Compliance Issues

There are some special regulatory challenges in the financial services sector specifically created by hyper-personalization. One of them is maintaining the privacy and protection of customer data in adherence to laws like CCPA and GDPR. Since AI and data analytics are important modules for hyper-personalization, financial institutions should have strong security measures regarding the protection of sensitive data and prevention of illegal access. Furthermore, in the context of hyper-personalization, there also exist challenges emanated from regulatory frameworks that oversee and regulate fair lending practices and anti-discrimination legislation. Digitally automated decision processes are potential unaware promoters of prejudices; thus, they are prone to generate biased outputs. If they want to avoid such risks and maintain their capability for regulatory compliance, financial institutions have to make algorithms accountable and transparent.

Moreover, the laws concerning consumer rights and marketing practices set a ceiling on the extent to which data obtained from clients can be used in personalized marketing and advertising. More simply, building trust and compliance in this age of financial services hyper-personalization will have to do with seeking a balance between delivering on hyper-personalized experiences and operating within the limits of the law.

Strategies to Address These Challenges and Ensure Ethical Practices

In the setting of the hyper-personalization of financial services, a number of strategies can be used to address issues and ensure moral conduct. Above all, transparency is key. It is part of the responsibility of being clear with consumers over policies regarding data collection and usage that financial institutions ought to offer real informed consent and protection of rights to privacy. Second, strong structures of data governance that will see to it that legal requirements and industry norms are strictly adhered to should be put in place when it comes to the gathering, storing, and sharing of customer data.

Third, bias mitigation strategies can be put in place to ensure the cessation of practices that amount to discrimination and algorithmic biases, and ensure that all consumers are treated equally and without any form of bias. To this end, continuous monitoring and auditing of Artificial Intelligence systems and data analytics processes will go a long way in detecting and reducing ethical concerns and enhancing accountability and trust in projects on hyper-personalization. Indeed, such tactics enable financial institutions to effectively handle ethical challenges and provide customers with personalized experiences that engender an atmosphere of trust and well-being.

FUTURE TRENDS AND IMPLICATIONS

Thus, in the future, advancement in artificial intelligence, big data analytics, and digital technologies will definitely result in much more sophisticated forms of hyper-personalization in financial services. Consumers will demand frictionless, highly tailored experiences from customer support interactions to banking applications, across every touchpoint. Financial institutions will leverage wearables and IoT devices to collect data from multiple sources in order to understand consumer behavior and preferences. For example, decentralized lending and automated investment strategies will be more tailored as DeFi and blockchain technologies evolve. Personalization undoubtedly goes with the corresponding increase in the need for robust data privacy and security measures to keep information safe for clients. With all this factored in, there is immense potential that hyper-personalization in finance will deliver bespoke solutions which cater to changing client needs in a world where things are gradually becoming more digital (Pattnaik, Ray, & Raman, 2024).

Emerging Technologies and Their Potential Impact on Hyper-Personalization

The financial services sector is about to witness a revolution in hyper-personalization thanks to emerging technology, which will present previously unheard-of chances to customize goods and services to meet the specific needs of each client. Financial institutions can now analyze massive volumes of data and draw actionable insights, enabling more precise predictions and tailored recommendations. This is made possible by artificial intelligence (AI) and machine learning algorithms. Through the creation of immersive environments for product demos, virtual banking interactions, and financial education, augmented reality (AR) and virtual reality (VR) technologies improve customer experiences. Cross-border payments can be made easily and at a lower cost thanks to blockchain technology, which guarantees safe and transparent transactions. Biometric authentication techniques, including fingerprint scanning and facial recognition, also improve security and expedite user authentication procedures, which improves consumer satisfaction all around. To fully capitalize on the promise of hyper-personalization in the digital age, financial institutions need to embrace innovation and adjust their tactics as these emergent technologies continue to develop (Irfan, Hussainey, Chan Bukhari, & Nam, 2024).

Predictions for the Future of Financial Services

Legislative changes, changing consumer preferences, and breakthroughs in technology are contemplated to make financial services continuously innovative and changing in the future. Artificial Intelligence and Machine Learning are foreseen to feature more and more in process automation, improvement of customer experience, and risk management. Blockchain technology is supposed to change the face of payment systems completely, speeding up transactions and improving security and openness. Moreover, with the invention of decentralized finance platforms and digital currencies, traditional forms of banking might get pushed to the edge facing a disruption in the financial space. On the other side, hyper-personalization and data analytics will drive it to become a standard thing where every client can get his requirements and preferences served with personalized finance services. In its path toward maturity, collaboration between traditional players in finance, FinTech startups, and regulators will basically drive sector development to overcome the regulatory barriers to innovation. In sum, innovative, efficient, and inclusive, huge scope exists for growth in financial services (Kuppelwieser & Klaus, 2021).

Long-Term Implications for Customer Experience and Industry Practices

The long-term effect of the hyper-personalization strategy on industry practices and consumer experience is only speculated to be seen in a case where adoption occurs within the financial services sector. For as long as financial institutions continue to use cutting-edge technology such as artificial intelligence and data analytics, they will be better at understanding and predicting the demands, tastes, and behaviors of their customers. Ultimately, this will improve client happiness and loyalty by allowing a very customized and relevant supply of financial products and services. Hyper-personalization will spur innovation across the sector and prompt rivals to spend money on comparable products and approaches to stay competitive. This will also raise questions of data security, privacy, and the moral use of information available on customers, all of which shall have to be based on strict laws and industry norms. Considering all this, hyper-personalization is definitely going to change financial services at the very core and open the doorway toward an era of innovation and customer-centricity (Lyons & Kass-Hanna, 2022).

CONCLUSION

The financial services industry has moved towards hyper-personalization, which means less emphasis on developing mass-market products and more focus on tailor-made solutions that meet each individual client's needs. Financial institutions can create tailored experiences through the analysis of huge amounts of data available about their clients with the help of advanced technologies like AI and data analytics. Such high personalization raises customer satisfaction, makes them loyal, and fuels business growth. Banks can enrich client experience through hyper-personalization to predict client needs, offer personalized product suggestions, and provide proactive support. Moreover, it differentiates the financial institution in an extremely competitive market, attracts new clients, and retains existing ones through a plethora of personalized services. Ultimately, this is where the power of personalization can be truly unleashed—empowering financial institutions to establish closer relations with their clients and allow for more customer engagement, while also offering value-added services that help meet the unique needs of each client.

With the growing strength of AI and data analytics, the financial sector is about to change radically. Within financial services, these technologies will only become more crucial in driving innovation, efficiency, and customer-centricity. At the core of the ability of any financial institution to drive data-driven decision-making, reduce risk, and offer client-centric solutions will be AI and data analytics. These will run from algorithmic trading to predictive analytics, through personalized customer experiences and regulatory compliance. Innovations in big data analytics, machine learning, and natural language processing will trigger the innovation of new products and services and increase the general degree of agility and competitiveness of the industry. Ensuring that AI and data analytics are applied appropriately and for the long term, both in and for finance, will require concerns from ethics, privacy, and regulatory barriers to be overcome as these technologies increasingly underpin the financial process.

REFERENCES

Akyüz, A., & Mavnacıoğlu, K. (2021). Marketing and financial services in the age of artificial intelligence. *Financial Strategies in Competitive Markets: Multidimensional Approaches to Financial Policies for Local Companies*, 327-340.

Baesens, B., Bapna, R., Marsden, J. R., Vanthienen, J., & Zhao, J. L. (2016). Transformational Issues of Big Data and Analytics in Networked Business. *Management Information Systems Quarterly*, 40(4), 807–818. 10.25300/MISQ/2016/40:4.03

Bitner, M. J., Booms, B. H., & Tetreault, M. S. (1990). The service encounter: Diagnosing favourable and unfavourable incidents. *Journal of Marketing*, 54(1), 71–84. 10.1177/002224299005400105

Cao, M., Tian, W., Zhu, Z., & Wu, W. (2018). Emerging practices in regulatory compliance: A literature review and research agenda. *Journal of Information Technology*, 33(2), 127–143.

Cartea, Á., & MacKenzie, I. A. (2009). Empirical evidence on the relations between stock market liquidity and characteristics of algorithmic trading. *Quantitative Finance*, 9(5), 527–541.

Davis, F. D. (1989). Perceived usefulness, perceived ease of use, and user acceptance of information technology. *Management Information Systems Quarterly*, 13(3), 319–340. 10.2307/249008

Desai, D. (2022). Hyper-personalization: an AI-enabled personalization for customer-centric marketing. In *Adoption and Implementation of AI in Customer Relationship Management* (pp. 40-53). IGI Global. 10.4018/978-1-7998-7959-6.ch003

Goyal, A., & Sergi, B. S. (2015). *Social Innovation and Sustainable Entrepreneurship: Case Studies of Finance and Business Enterprises in Developing Economies*. Routledge.

Gronroos, C. (1994). From marketing mix to relationship marketing: Towards a paradigm shift in marketing. *Management Decision*, 32(2), 4–20. 10.1108/00251749410054774

Gunawardane, G. (2023). Enhancing customer satisfaction and experience in financial services: A survey of recent research in financial services journals. *Journal of Financial Services Marketing*, 28(2), 255–269. 10.1057/s41264-022-00148-x

Hardle, W., & Simar, L. (2003). *Applied multivariate statistical analysis*. Springer Science & Business Media. 10.1007/978-3-662-05802-2

Hentzen, J. K., Hoffmann, A., Dolan, R., & Pala, E. (2022). Artificial intelligence in customer-facing financial services: A systematic literature review and agenda for future research. *International Journal of Bank Marketing*, 40(6), 1299–1336. 10.1108/IJBM-09-2021-0417

Irfan, M. (2021, January). Do Shariah Indices converge? Evidence from Gulf Co-operation Council countries. *International Journal of Business Excellence*, 23(2), 251–269. 10.1504/IJBEX.2021.113448

Irfan, M., Elhoseny, M., Kassim, S., & Metawa, N. (2023). *Advanced Machine Learning Algorithms for Complex Financial Applications*. IGI Global. 10.4018/978-1-6684-4483-2

Irfan, M., Elmogy, M., Majid, M. S., & El-Sappagh, S. (2023). *The Impact of AI Innovation on Financial Sectors in the Era of Industry 5.0*. IGI Global. 10.4018/979-8-3693-0082-4

Irfan, M., Hussainey, K., Chan Bukhari, S. A., & Nam, Y. (Eds.). (2024). *Issues of Sustainability in AI and New-Age Thematic Investing*. IGI Global Publisher. 10.4018/979-8-3693-3282-5

Irfan, M., Kadry, S., Sharif, M., & Ullah Khan, H. (2023). *Fintech Applications in Islamic Finance: AI, Machine Learning, and Blockchain Techniques*. IGI Global. 10.4018/979-8-3693-1038-0

Jain, G., Paul, J., & Shrivastava, A. (2021). Hyper-personalization, co-creation, digital clienteling and transformation. *Journal of Business Research*, 124, 12–23. 10.1016/j.jbusres.2020.11.034

Kshetri, N. (2017). Can Blockchain Strengthen the Internet of Things? *IT Professional*, 19(4), 68–72. 10.1109/MITP.2017.3051335

Kuppelwieser, V. G., & Klaus, P. (2021). Measuring customer experience quality: The EXQ scale revisited. *Journal of Business Research*, 126, 624–633. 10.1016/j.jbusres.2020.01.042

Lacity, M. C., & Willcocks, L. P. (2016). Robotic process automation at Xchanging. *MIS Quarterly Executive*, 15(2), 97–114.

Lemon, K. N., & Verhoef, P. C. (2016). Understanding Customer Experience Throughout the Customer Journey. *Journal of Marketing*, 80(6), 69–96. 10.1509/jm.15.0420

Li, X., & Mao, J. Y. (2019). Hedonic or Utilitarian? Exploring the Impact of Communication Style Alignment on Mobile Banking Apps. *International Journal of Information Management*, 48, 61–72.

Lin, H. F., Wang, Y. S., & Hsu, Y. F. (2019). Developing a Service Quality Framework for Personalized Services in the Financial Industry. *Total Quality Management & Business Excellence*, 30(1-2), 42–56.

Lyons, A. C., & Kass-Hanna, J. (2022). The Evolution of Financial Services in the Digital Age. *De Gruyter Handbook of Personal Finance*, 405.

Makridakis, S., Spiliotis, E., & Assimakopoulos, V. (2018). Statistical and machine learning forecasting methods: Concerns and ways forward. *PLoS One*, 13(3), e0194889. 10.1371/journal.pone.019488929584784

. Mogaji, E., Soetan, T. O., & Kieu, T. A. (2020). The implications of artificial intelligence on the digital marketing of financial services to vulnerable customers. *Australasian Marketing Journal*.

Morton, F., Benavides, T. T., & González-Treviño, E. (2024). Taking Customer-Centricity to New Heights: Exploring the Intersection of AI, Hyper-Personalization, and Customer-Centricity in Organizations. In *Smart Engineering Management* (pp. 23–41). Springer International Publishing. 10.1007/978-3-031-52990-0_2

Nguyen, B., & Simkin, L. (2017). The Dark Side of Digital Marketing: Personalization, Microtargeting, and Exploitation. *Journal of Marketing Management*, 33(15-16), 1231–1253.

Nguyen, D. K., Sermpinis, G., & Stasinakis, C. (2023). Big data, artificial intelligence and machine learning: A transformative symbiosis in favour of financial technology. *European Financial Management*, 29(2), 517–548. 10.1111/eufm.12365

Parasuraman, A., Zeithaml, V. A., & Berry, L. L. (1985). A conceptual model of service quality and its implications for future research. *Journal of Marketing*, 49(4), 41–50. 10.1177/002224298504900403

Parasuraman, A., Zeithaml, V. A., & Berry, L. L. (1988). SERVQUAL: A multiple-item scale for measuring consumer perceptions of service quality. *Journal of Retailing*, 64(1), 12–40.

Pattnaik, D., Ray, S., & Raman, R. (2024). Applications of artificial intelligence and machine learning in the financial services industry: A bibliometric review. *Heliyon*, 10(1), e23492. 10.1016/j.heliyon.2023.e2349238187262

Peppers, D., & Rogers, M. (2017). *Managing Customer Relationships: A Strategic Framework*. John Wiley & Sons.

Risselada, H., Hillebrand, B., & Galenkamp, H. (2018). Data-driven customer experience in retail banking. *Journal of Financial Services Marketing*, 23(1), 17–28.

Rosenbaum, M. S., Ramirez, G. C., Campbell, J., & Klaus, P. (2021). The product is me: Hyper-personalized consumer goods as unconventional luxury. *Journal of Business Research*, 129, 446–454. 10.1016/j.jbusres.2019.05.017

Singh, B., & Kaunert, C. (2024). Future of Digital Marketing: Hyper-Personalized Customer Dynamic Experience with AI-Based Predictive Models. In *Revolutionizing the AI-Digital Landscape* (pp. 189–203). Productivity Press. 10.4324/9781032688305-14

Solove, D. J. (2006). A Taxonomy of Privacy. *University of Pennsylvania Law Review*, 154(3), 477–564. 10.2307/40041279

Tapscott, D., & Tapscott, A. (2016). *Blockchain Revolution: How the Technology Behind Bitcoin Is Changing Money, Business, and the World*. Penguin.

Valdez Mendia, J. M., & Flores-Cuautle, J. D. J. A. (2022). Toward customer hyper-personalization experience—A data-driven approach. *Cogent Business & Management*, 9(1), 2041384. 10.1080/23311975.2022.2041384

Vargo, S. L., & Lusch, R. F. (2004). Evolving to a new dominant logic for marketing. *Journal of Marketing*, 68(1), 1–17. 10.1509/jmkg.68.1.1.24036

Venkatesan, R., & Kumar, V. (2004). A Customer Lifetime Value Framework for Customer Selection and Resource Allocation Strategy. *Journal of Marketing*, 68(4), 106–125. 10.1509/jmkg.68.4.106.42728

Zarsky, T. Z. (2016). Incompatible: The GDPR in the Age of Big Data. *Seton Hall Law Review*, 47, 995.

Chapter 3
Security, Risk Management, and Ethical AI in the Future of DeFi

Ushaa Eswaran
Indira Institute of Technology and Sciences, Jawaharlal Nehru Technological University, India

Vishal Eswaran
https://orcid.org/0009-0000-2187-3108
CVS Health Centre, USA

Vivek Eswaran
https://orcid.org/0009-0002-7475-2398
Medallia, USA

Keerthna Murali
https://orcid.org/0009-0009-1419-4268
DELL, USA

ABSTRACT

The intersection of artificial intelligence (AI) and decentralized finance (DeFi) heralds a transformative era in the financial landscape, promising unprecedented efficiency, personalization, and innovation. However, this convergence also introduces significant challenges, particularly in the realms of security, risk management, and ethics. This chapter aims to provide a comprehensive exploration of how AI-driven technologies can enhance security and risk management within DeFi ecosystems while addressing the ethical considerations essential for sustainable and responsible innovation. By analyzing current practices, future scenarios, and emerging trends, this chapter seeks to equip finance professionals, technologists, and decision-makers

DOI: 10.4018/979-8-3693-6321-8.ch003

with actionable insights and strategies to navigate the complex dynamics of AI in DeFi. Through real-world case studies and best practices, readers will gain a robust understanding of the critical issues and solutions that will shape the future of secure, ethical, and resilient decentralized financial systems.

INTRODUCTION

The convergence of Artificial Intelligence (AI) and Decentralized Finance (DeFi) represents a pivotal moment in the evolution of the financial landscape. As DeFi ecosystems gain traction, leveraging the transformative potential of blockchain technology and smart contracts, the integration of AI promises to unlock unprecedented levels of efficiency, personalization, and innovation. However, this amalgamation also introduces significant challenges, particularly in the realms of security, risk management, and ethics.

This chapter delves into the intricate interplay between AI and DeFi, exploring how cutting-edge technologies can enhance security and risk management strategies while addressing the critical ethical considerations essential for sustainable and responsible innovation. By analyzing current practices, future scenarios, and emerging trends, this chapter aims to equip finance professionals, technologists, and decision-makers with actionable insights and strategies to navigate the complex dynamics of AI in DeFi.

Through real-world case studies and best practices, readers will gain a robust understanding of the critical issues and solutions that will shape the future of secure, ethical, and resilient decentralized financial systems. The chapter serves as a comprehensive guide, enabling stakeholders to harness the transformative power of AI in DeFi while mitigating risks and upholding ethical principles.

Figure 1 provides a visual representation of the key components involved in the convergence of AI and DeFi. The mind map highlights critical areas such as security, risk management, ethics, blockchain technology, smart contracts, predictive analytics, regulatory challenges, future trends, and case studies. Each of these components plays a vital role in shaping the landscape of AI-driven DeFi, offering a structured approach to understand and address the multifaceted interactions and implications of these technologies.

Security and Risk Management: AI algorithms can significantly enhance the security measures within DeFi platforms by identifying and mitigating potential threats in real-time. Predictive analytics powered by AI can forecast market trends and risks, allowing for proactive risk management and more resilient DeFi ecosystems.

Ethics: The ethical deployment of AI in DeFi is crucial to ensure fairness, transparency, and accountability. Addressing algorithmic bias, maintaining data privacy, and establishing robust governance frameworks are essential to foster trust and ethical standards in AI-driven DeFi applications.

Blockchain Technology and Smart Contracts: Blockchain technology underpins DeFi, providing the decentralized infrastructure necessary for secure and transparent financial transactions. Smart contracts, automated by AI, can execute complex financial operations without intermediaries, enhancing efficiency and reducing costs.

Predictive Analytics: AI's predictive analytics capabilities can revolutionize DeFi by providing insights into market behavior, enabling more informed investment decisions, and optimizing financial strategies.

Regulatory Challenges: The integration of AI in DeFi introduces new regulatory challenges that must be addressed to ensure compliance and protect users. Navigating the regulatory landscape requires ongoing collaboration between industry stakeholders and regulatory bodies to develop frameworks that balance innovation and oversight.

Future Trends: Emerging technologies such as federated learning, decentralized AI (DAI), and quantum computing are set to further transform AI-driven DeFi. These innovations hold the potential to enhance privacy, democratize AI development, and provide more robust security mechanisms.

By examining these core areas, we can gain a comprehensive understanding of the current state and future trajectory of AI and DeFi convergence. This exploration will highlight both the potential benefits and the challenges that need to be overcome to fully realize the promise of AI in the decentralized financial world. Figure 1 Shows the Key components involved in the convergence of AI and DeFi

Figure 1. Key components involved in the convergence of AI and DeFi

Objectives:

- Understand the foundations of AI in DeFi security and risk management, including current practices, challenges, and potential solutions.
- Explore AI-driven security solutions for DeFi, such as smart contract security enhancements and fraud detection mechanisms.
- Examine risk management strategies in AI-driven DeFi, including predictive analytics, algorithmic risk mitigation techniques, and industry best practices.
- Analyze ethical considerations in the use of AI for DeFi, including ethical dilemmas, frameworks, and guidelines for implementation.
- Discuss regulatory challenges and compliance strategies for navigating the evolving landscape of AI and DeFi regulations.
- Investigate future trends and innovations in AI-driven DeFi security, risk management, and ethical AI.
- Gain insights from case studies and practical examples of leading AI-driven DeFi projects.

Organization:

The chapter is organized into several sections, covering the foundations of AI in DeFi security and risk management, AI-driven security solutions, risk management strategies, ethical considerations, regulatory challenges and compliance, future trends and innovations, and case studies and practical insights. Each section provides a comprehensive analysis of the respective topic, incorporating real-world examples, industry best practices, and actionable strategies for finance professionals, technologists, and decision-makers.

FOUNDATIONS OF AI IN DEFI SECURITY AND RISK MANAGEMENT

Definition and Roles of AI in Enhancing DeFi Security

AI encompasses a broad range of technologies and techniques that enable machines to perceive, learn, reason, and make decisions in a manner analogous to human intelligence. In the context of DeFi, AI plays a pivotal role in enhancing security by leveraging advanced algorithms, machine learning models, and data analysis capabilities. (He, Zheyuan, Zihao Li, and Sen Yang.,2024)

One of the primary applications of AI in DeFi security lies in its ability to detect and prevent fraudulent activities. By analyzing vast amounts of transactional data, user behavior patterns, and network activity, AI systems can identify anomalies, suspicious patterns, and potential threats in real-time, enabling proactive security measures.

Additionally, AI can bolster the security of smart contracts, the backbone of DeFi protocols. Through rigorous code analysis, formal verification techniques, and automated testing, AI-powered tools can identify vulnerabilities, bugs, and potential attack vectors, reducing the risk of exploits and ensuring the integrity of these self-executing contracts.

Current Landscape of Risk Management in DeFi

Risk management is a critical aspect of DeFi, as decentralized financial systems operate without the oversight of traditional centralized authorities. The current landscape of risk management in DeFi is characterized by a combination of community-driven governance models, decentralized oracles, and on-chain risk mitigation mechanisms (Quilina, Matteo, Jon Frost, and Andreas Schrimpf., 2024)

Community governance frameworks, such as Decentralized Autonomous Organizations (DAOs), enable stakeholders to vote on protocol upgrades, parameter adjustments, and risk management strategies. Decentralized oracles, which provide off-chain data to smart contracts, play a crucial role in ensuring the accuracy and reliability of pricing, asset valuations, and other critical information used in DeFi protocols.

On-chain risk mitigation mechanisms, such as overcollateralization requirements, liquidation engines, and circuit breakers, aim to minimize the impact of market volatility, reduce the risk of insolvency, and prevent cascading failures within DeFi ecosystems.

Key Challenges and Threats in AI-Driven DeFi Systems

While the integration of AI in DeFi holds immense potential, it also introduces several challenges and threats that must be addressed:

1. **Data Quality and Bias:** AI models are heavily reliant on the quality and representativeness of the data used for training. In DeFi, ensuring the integrity and unbiased nature of data sources is crucial to prevent skewed models and inaccurate decision-making.(Park, Peter S., et al.,2024)
2. **Adversarial Attacks:** As AI systems become more prevalent in DeFi, they may become targets for adversarial attacks, where malicious actors attempt to manipulate or deceive the models, potentially leading to security breaches or financial losses.
3. **Interpretability and Transparency:** Many AI models, particularly deep learning algorithms, suffer from a lack of interpretability, making it challenging to understand their decision-making processes. This opacity can undermine trust and raise concerns about fairness and accountability in DeFi applications.
4. **Regulatory Compliance:** The integration of AI in DeFi systems introduces new regulatory challenges, as authorities grapple with understanding and governing these complex technologies, potentially leading to regulatory uncertainty and compliance risks.
5. **Ethical Considerations:** The use of AI in DeFi raises significant ethical questions regarding privacy, fairness, accountability, and the potential for unintended consequences, necessitating a robust ethical framework to guide responsible innovation.

The figure 2 provides a mind map illustrating the convergence of AI and DeFi, highlighting key areas such as security, risk management, ethics, blockchain technology, smart contracts, predictive analytics, regulatory challenges, future trends, and case studies. This visual representation underscores the multifaceted nature of integrating AI into DeFi ecosystems, showcasing the diverse aspects that stakeholders must consider to leverage the potential of these technologies while addressing associated challenges and ethical concerns.

Figure 2 shows the AI and DeFi Convergence

Figure 2. AI and DeFi convergence

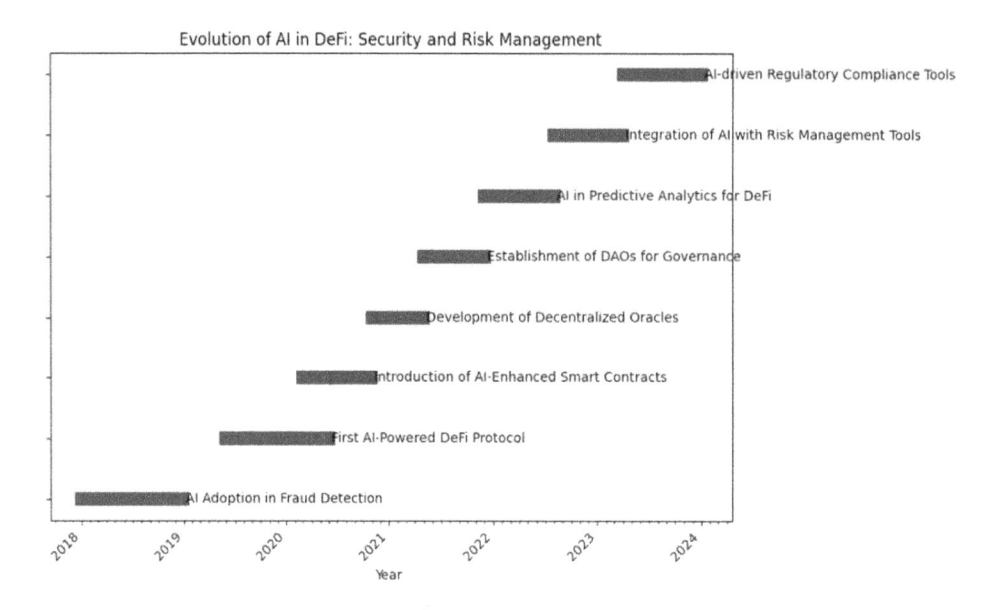

```
Evolution of AI in DeFi: Security and Risk Management
```
- AI-driven Regulatory Compliance Tools
- Integration of AI with Risk Management Tools
- AI in Predictive Analytics for DeFi
- Establishment of DAOs for Governance
- Development of Decentralized Oracles
- Introduction of AI-Enhanced Smart Contracts
- First AI-Powered DeFi Protocol
- AI Adoption in Fraud Detection

Year: 2018–2024

Understanding the foundations of AI in DeFi security and risk management is crucial. Techniques and challenges identified in related fields, such as IoT cloud fusion, can provide valuable insights. For instance, Eswaran et al. (2023a) discuss various challenges and remedies in elevating security in IoT cloud fusion, which can be paralleled to the challenges faced in securing DeFi ecosystems .

Addressing these challenges is crucial for realizing the full potential of AI in DeFi while ensuring the security, reliability, and trustworthiness of decentralized financial systems.

AI-DRIVEN SECURITY SOLUTIONS FOR DEFI

Smart Contract Security Enhancements

Smart contracts, the backbone of DeFi protocols, are susceptible to vulnerabilities and exploits due to their immutable and self-executing nature. AI-driven security solutions can play a crucial role in enhancing the security of these contracts, reducing the risk of financial losses and ensuring the integrity of DeFi ecosystems.(Porkodi, S., and D. Kesavaraja,2023)

Formal Verification and Code Analysis

AI-driven formal verification techniques, including symbolic execution and model checking, rigorously analyze smart contract code to uncover vulnerabilities and logical flaws. These methods use mathematical models and automated reasoning to explore all possible execution paths, ensuring the contract performs as expected.

AI-powered code analysis tools also conduct static and dynamic analyses to identify common issues like reentrancy attacks and integer overflows, and suggest mitigation strategies for secure coding.

Automated Testing and Monitoring

AI-powered testing frameworks can be used to generate comprehensive test suites for smart contracts, simulating a wide range of scenarios and edge cases. These frameworks leverage techniques like fuzzing, which involves generating random inputs to identify unexpected behavior and potential vulnerabilities.(Bertazzolo, Giacomo., 2023)

Furthermore, AI-based monitoring systems can continuously analyze the on-chain activity and state of deployed smart contracts, detecting anomalies, suspicious patterns, and potential attacks in real-time. These systems can trigger alerts, initiate automated responses, or enable human intervention to mitigate threats and minimize the impact of security incidents.

AI-Powered Fraud Detection and Prevention Mechanisms

Fraud detection and prevention are critical challenges in DeFi ecosystems, as decentralized platforms can be attractive targets for malicious actors seeking to exploit vulnerabilities or manipulate markets. AI-driven solutions can play a vital role in identifying and mitigating fraudulent activities, enhancing the security and resilience of DeFi protocols.

Anomaly Detection and Pattern Recognition

AI algorithms, particularly those based on machine learning and deep learning techniques, can be trained on vast amounts of transactional data, user behavior patterns, and network activity logs to identify anomalies and suspicious patterns that may indicate fraudulent activities. These algorithms can learn to distinguish between normal and abnormal behavior, enabling real-time detection of potential threats.(Wang, Le, et al.,2023)

Predictive Analytics and Risk Scoring

AI-driven predictive analytics can be employed to assess the risk associated with individual transactions, users, or protocols. By analyzing a multitude of factors, such as transaction history, network topology, and on-chain data, AI models can assign risk scores and prioritize high-risk activities for further investigation or preventive measures.

Real-Time Monitoring and Automated Responses

AI-powered monitoring systems can continuously analyze DeFi ecosystems, tracking user interactions, smart contract executions, and on-chain activities. When potential fraudulent activities are detected, these systems can initiate automated responses, such as freezing suspicious transactions, blacklisting malicious addresses, or triggering smart contract fail-safes, minimizing the impact of fraud and protecting user funds.

In the realm of fraud detection mechanisms, AI-driven methods demonstrate superior effectiveness compared to traditional methods. According to the provided graph in Figure 3:

- Traditional Methods: 70%
- AI-driven Methods: 95%

Figure 3 shows the Effectiveness of Fraud Detection Mechanisms: Traditional Methods vs. AI-driven Methods

Figure 3. Effectiveness of fraud detection mechanisms: Traditional methods vs. AI-driven methods

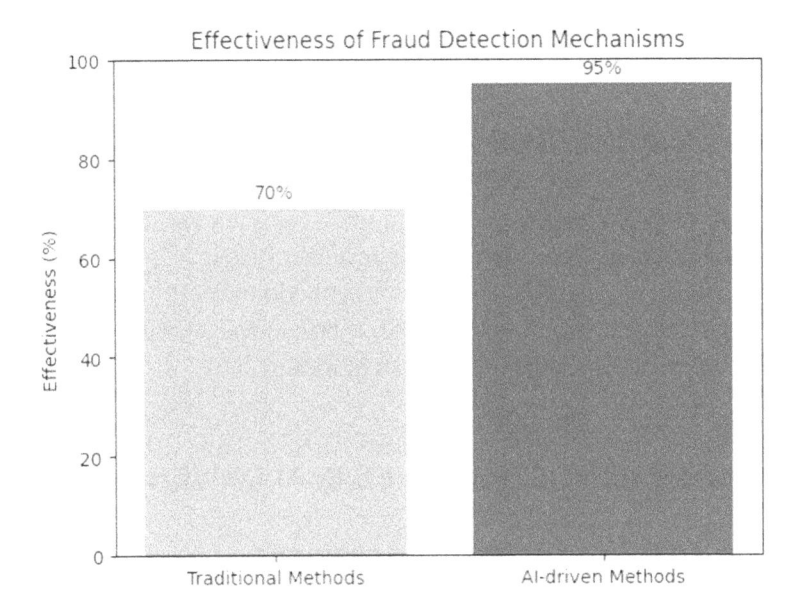

[Bar chart: Effectiveness of Fraud Detection Mechanisms — Traditional Methods: 70%; AI-driven Methods: 95%]

Case Studies of Successful AI Implementations in DeFi Security

Quantstamp: Smart Contract Security Auditing

Quantstamp is a leading blockchain security company that leverages AI and formal verification techniques to audit and secure smart contracts. Their AI-powered platform performs static and dynamic analysis, identifying vulnerabilities and potential attack vectors. Quantstamp has collaborated with numerous DeFi projects, including Maker, Compound, and Aave, helping to secure their smart contracts and mitigate risks.(Wu, Guangfu, et al.,2024)

Elliptic: Crypto Asset Risk Management

Elliptic is a pioneering crypto-asset risk management solution that leverages AI and machine learning to detect and prevent financial crimes in the blockchain ecosystem. Their platform analyzes vast amounts of on-chain data, transaction histories, and wallet activity to identify patterns associated with money laundering, terrorism financing, and other illicit activities. Elliptic's AI-powered solutions have been adopted by major financial institutions, exchanges, and DeFi protocols to enhance compliance, mitigate risks, and prevent fraud.

Certik: Decentralized Security Audits

Certik uses AI and formal verification to audit smart contracts and DeFi protocols. Their platform analyzes code, simulates attack scenarios, and identifies vulnerabilities. Certik has worked with major DeFi projects like PancakeSwap, UniSwap, and Curve Finance to enhance security and protect user funds.

AI-driven security for DeFi aligns with methodologies in interconnected systems. Eswaran (2024) highlights the need for robust cybersecurity in interconnected ecosystems, relevant for safeguarding DeFi platforms.

RISK MANAGEMENT STRATEGIES IN AI-DRIVEN DEFI

Predictive Analytics for Risk Assessment

AI-driven predictive analytics can play a crucial role in risk assessment within DeFi ecosystems. By leveraging machine learning algorithms and advanced data analysis techniques, these solutions can analyze various on-chain and off-chain data sources to identify potential risks, such as market volatility, liquidity constraints, and protocol vulnerabilities.(Pei, Yulong, and Lin Hou.,2024)

Market Risk Analysis

AI models can analyze historical market data, trading patterns, and market sentiment to forecast potential price movements, volatility levels, and market trends. This information can be used to assess the risk associated with specific DeFi protocols, lending platforms, or investment strategies, enabling proactive risk mitigation measures.

Liquidity Risk Modeling

Liquidity risk is a significant concern in DeFi, as decentralized platforms may face challenges in maintaining sufficient liquidity during periods of high demand or market stress. AI-driven liquidity risk models can analyze on-chain liquidity pools, trading volumes, and user behavior patterns to identify potential liquidity constraints and enable proactive measures, such as adjusting collateralization ratios or implementing circuit breakers.

Protocol Risk Assessment

AI algorithms can be trained to analyze the code, architecture, and on-chain behavior of DeFi protocols, identifying potential vulnerabilities, design flaws, or inefficiencies that may pose risks to users or the overall ecosystem. This risk assessment can inform protocol upgrades, risk mitigation strategies, and user education efforts.

Here is a visualization depicting the distribution of risk scores assigned by AI-driven predictive analytics models. This scatter plot or density plot shown in Figure 4 a,b provides insights into the distribution of risk scores across the analyzed data samples. Understanding the distribution of risk scores is crucial for assessing the overall risk landscape within DeFi ecosystems.

Analyzing Risk Distribution

To gain deeper insights into risk assessment within DeFi ecosystems, we present visualizations showcasing the distribution of risk scores derived from AI-driven predictive analytics models.

This scatter plot illustrates the distribution of risk scores across a sample set of data points. Each point represents a specific risk score assigned by the predictive analytics model, offering a visual understanding of the variability and concentration of risks within the ecosystem.

The density plot provides a comprehensive view of the frequency distribution of risk scores, enabling a nuanced analysis of the density and spread of risk levels. This visualization aids in identifying potential risk hotspots and outliers, facilitating proactive risk management strategies.

These visualizations serve as invaluable tools for stakeholders in assessing and mitigating risks within AI-driven DeFi environments, fostering greater resilience and stability.

Figure 4 shows the distribution of Risk Scores

Figure 4. Distribution of risk scores

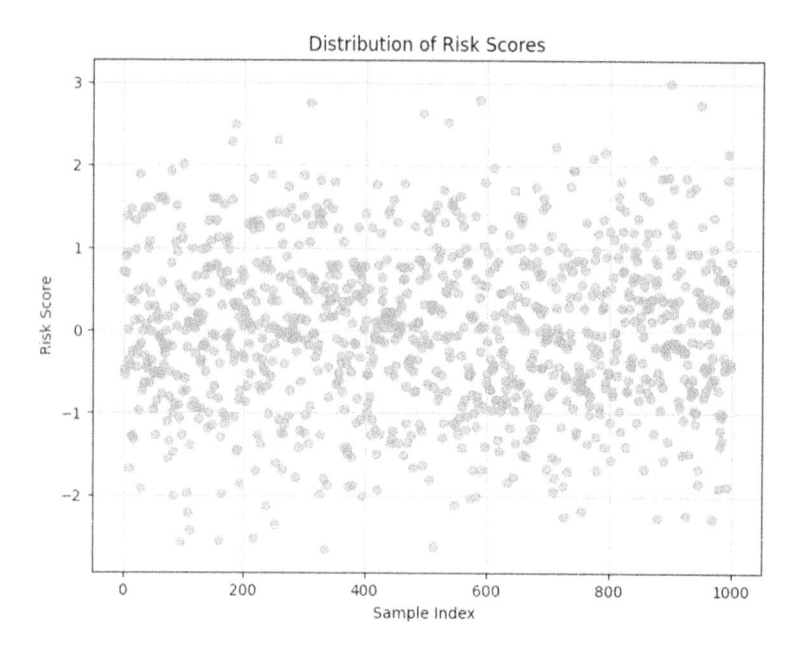

Figure 5 shows the Density Plot of Risk Scores

Figure 5. Density plot of risk scores

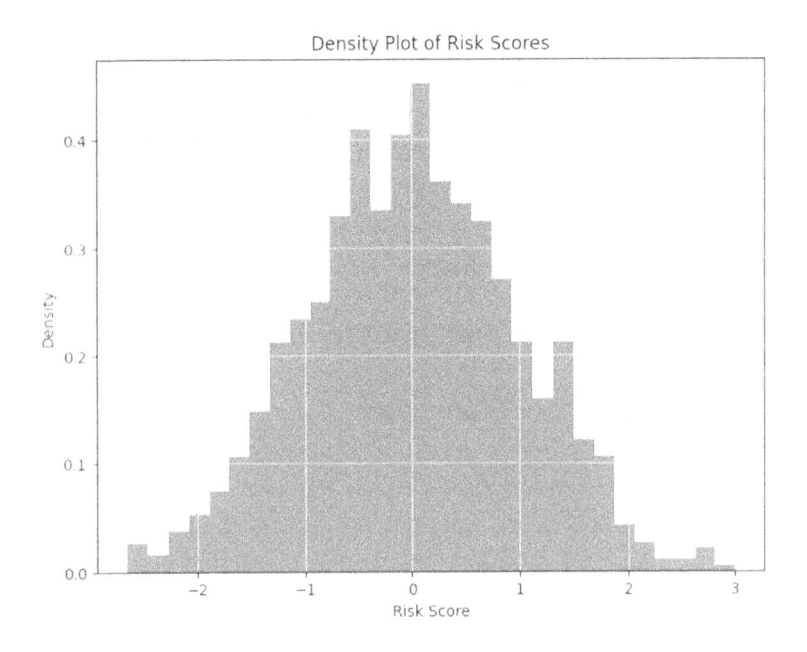

Algorithmic Risk Mitigation Techniques

AI-driven algorithms can be employed to dynamically adjust risk parameters and implement mitigation strategies within DeFi protocols, enhancing their resilience and ability to adapt to changing market conditions. (Koshiyama, Adriano, et al.,2024)

Dynamic Collateralization

In lending and borrowing platforms, AI algorithms can continuously monitor market conditions, asset prices, and user behavior to dynamically adjust collateralization ratios. This proactive approach can minimize the risk of undercollateralization and potential liquidations, ensuring the stability and security of the platform.

Automated Liquidation Engines

Liquidation engines are critical components of DeFi lending platforms, responsible for managing the liquidation of undercollateralized positions. AI-powered liquidation engines can optimize the liquidation process, considering factors such as market conditions, liquidity, and slippage, to maximize the recovery of user funds while minimizing potential losses.

Circuit Breakers and Emergency Shutdowns

In extreme market conditions or in the event of systemic risks, AI algorithms can trigger circuit breakers or initiate emergency shutdowns of DeFi protocols. These automated responses can help prevent cascading failures, minimize financial losses, and provide a controlled mechanism for addressing critical issues.

Real-World Applications and Industry Best Practices

Aave's Risk Management Framework

Aave, a leading DeFi lending protocol, has implemented a comprehensive risk management framework that incorporates AI and machine learning techniques. Their system continuously monitors on-chain data, market conditions, and user behavior to dynamically adjust collateralization ratios, liquidation thresholds, and risk parameters. Aave's risk management approach has contributed to the platform's stability and resilience, even during periods of market volatility.

MakerDAO's Risk Monitoring and Governance

The Maker DAO, the organization behind the DAI stablecoin, employs AI-driven risk monitoring and governance processes. Their AI models analyze various data sources, including market data, user activity, and protocol performance, to identify potential risks and inform the decision-making processes of the decentralized governance community. This proactive approach has helped the Maker DAO maintain the stability of the DAI stablecoin and adapt to changing market conditions.

Industry Best Practices

As the adoption of AI in DeFi risk management increases, industry best practices are emerging to ensure the responsible and effective implementation of these technologies. These best practices include:

- Establishing robust data governance frameworks to ensure data quality and integrity.
- Implementing rigorous model validation and testing processes to minimize bias and ensure accurate risk assessments.

- Fostering transparency and interpretability in AI models to enhance trust and accountability.
- Continuously monitoring and updating AI systems to adapt to evolving market conditions and emerging risks.
- Collaborating with regulatory bodies and industry stakeholders to develop standards and guidelines for AI in DeFi risk management.

Effective risk management in AI-driven DeFi involves understanding and mitigating various vulnerabilities. Lessons learned from cybersecurity strategies in other domains, such as telemedicine, highlight the importance of continuous monitoring and adaptation. Eswaran (2024b) provides insights into cybersecurity measures that can enhance the resilience of interconnected platforms .

ETHICAL CONSIDERATIONS IN AI FOR DEFI

Defining Ethical AI in the Context of DeFi

As AI technologies become increasingly integrated into DeFi ecosystems, it is crucial to establish a clear understanding of what constitutes ethical AI in this context. Ethical AI in DeFi encompasses principles and practices that ensure the responsible and fair use of AI technologies while upholding key values such as transparency, accountability, privacy, and inclusivity.(Ward, Francis, et al.,2024)

Transparency and Interpretability

Transparency and interpretability in AI models are crucial for DeFi platforms to ensure stakeholders can understand, trust, and effectively oversee the decision-making processes and logic of these sophisticated algorithms.

Importance of Transparency:

1. **Building Trust:** Transparent AI models foster trust among users and stakeholders by clarifying decision-making processes.
2. **Ensuring Accountability:** Transparency allows for the identification and correction of errors or biases, ensuring accountability.
3. **Facilitating Oversight:** It enables effective regulatory oversight and governance, maintaining legal and ethical standards.

Components of Transparency:

1. **Data Sources and Usage:** Clearly outlining what data is being used, where it comes from, and how it is processed and utilized in the AI models.
2. **Algorithmic Logic:** Explaining the logic and rationale behind the algorithms used, including the methodologies and principles guiding the decision-making processes.
3. **Decision-Making Processes:** Providing detailed insights into how decisions are made by the AI models, including the steps, conditions, and thresholds involved.

Challenges to Achieving Transparency:

1. **Complexity of AI Models:** Many AI models, especially those utilizing deep learning, are inherently complex and difficult to interpret. Simplifying these models without compromising their efficacy is a significant challenge.
2. **Data Privacy Concerns:** Ensuring transparency while also protecting the privacy of the data used can be a delicate balance. Strategies need to be developed to disclose information without exposing sensitive data.
3. **Proprietary Technologies:** Companies may be reluctant to fully disclose the workings of their proprietary AI technologies due to competitive concerns. Finding a balance between transparency and protecting intellectual property is essential.

Strategies for Enhancing Transparency:

1. **Explainable AI (XAI):** Use XAI techniques to make AI models more understandable with clear, human-readable explanations.
2. **Transparent Reporting:** Publish accessible reports detailing data, model logic, and decision-making processes.
3. **Stakeholder Engagement:** Engage stakeholders through workshops and feedback sessions to address transparency concerns.

Transparency and interpretability are essential for the successful adoption of AI in DeFi, enabling trust, accountability, and effective oversight while balancing complexity and privacy challenges.

Privacy and Data Protection

In Decentralized Finance (DeFi), prioritizing privacy and data protection is essential as AI becomes integral to managing financial services.

Importance:

1. **User Trust:** Protecting data fosters trust, encouraging user engagement with DeFi platforms.
2. **Regulatory Compliance:** Adhering to laws like GDPR and CCPA helps avoid legal issues and fines.
3. **Prevention of Misuse:** Effective protection prevents unauthorized access and misuse of sensitive information.

Components:

1. **Data Governance:** Develop frameworks outlining data collection, storage, and processing policies.
2. **Anonymization:** Use techniques to anonymize data, protecting user identities even if data is breached.
3. **Privacy-Preserving AI:** Employ methods like differential privacy and federated learning to protect data during AI processing.

Challenges:

1. **Cybersecurity Threats:** Address sophisticated cyber-attacks with strong cybersecurity measures.
2. **Data Utility vs. Privacy:** Balance maintaining AI model accuracy with user privacy.
3. **Regulatory Changes:** Stay updated on evolving regulations to ensure compliance.

Strategies:

1. **Encryption:** Use robust encryption for data protection at rest and in transit.
2. **Access Controls:** Implement strict controls and monitor for unauthorized access.
3. **User Control:** Allow users to manage their data and consent to its use.
4. **Security Assessments:** Conduct regular assessments to identify and fix vulnerabilities.

Ensuring privacy and data protection in AI-driven DeFi involves robust governance, anonymization, and privacy-preserving models, addressing cybersecurity threats, and staying compliant with regulations.

Ethical Dilemmas and Their Implications

The integration of AI in DeFi presents a range of ethical dilemmas that must be carefully considered and addressed to ensure the responsible development and deployment of these technologies.

Algorithmic Bias and Fairness

AI algorithms in DeFi can perpetuate or amplify biases from data or developers, leading to discriminatory practices and undermining inclusivity.

- **Identifying Bias:** Regularly audit training data and algorithms to detect and address biases.
- **Mitigation Strategies:** Use fairness constraints, diverse datasets, and fairness-aware techniques, and establish continuous monitoring and feedback loops.

Privacy and Data Rights

AI in DeFi involves extensive data collection and analysis, raising privacy concerns and risks of personal information misuse. Balancing data use for service enhancement with privacy protection is crucial.

- **Data Governance:** Implement robust frameworks for data collection, storage, and usage, emphasizing data minimization, purpose limitation, and user consent.
- **Anonymization Techniques:** Use advanced anonymization and encryption to protect user privacy. Explore privacy-preserving AI methods like differential privacy and federated learning to enhance data security.

Accountability and Liability

As AI systems in DeFi become more autonomous, questions of accountability and liability for errors, biases, or unintended consequences must be addressed. Clear governance frameworks are essential for transparency and redress.

- **Responsibility Assignment:** Define who is accountable for data management, algorithm design, and decision-making processes.
- **Redress Mechanisms:** Implement effective procedures for complaints, investigations, and providing compensation or corrective actions.

Centralization and Decentralization Tensions

While DeFi aims for decentralization, integrating AI can introduce new centralization risks. Balancing AI benefits with DeFi's core values is crucial.

- **Decentralized AI Models:** Utilize decentralized AI models like federated learning to maintain DeFi's decentralized nature while leveraging AI benefits.
- **Power Dynamics:** Regularly assess power dynamics to prevent control concentration, ensuring transparent governance and community involvement.

Frameworks and Guidelines for Ethical AI Implementation

Various frameworks and guidelines from industry, academia, and regulators aim to ensure the responsible and ethical development and deployment of AI in DeFi.

The Venn diagram shown in Figure 6 illustrates the overlap and relationships between different ethical frameworks and guidelines for AI implementation. Specifically, it shows how the Ethics Guidelines by the European Commission, the OECD AI Principles, and the IEEE Ethically Aligned Design share common principles and highlight unique aspects.

Figure 6 shows the overlap of Ethical Frameworks and Guidelines for AI Implementation

Figure 6. Overlap of ethical frameworks and guidelines for AI implementation

Overlap of Ethical Frameworks and Guidelines for AI Implementation

EC AI Ethics Guidelines

OECD AI Principles

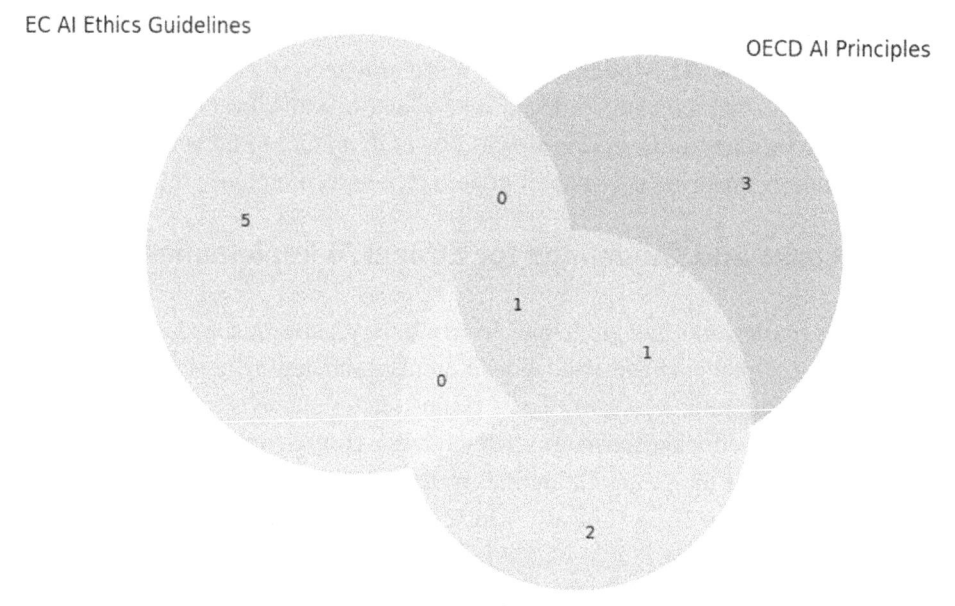

5   0   3

1

0   1

2

IEEE Ethically Aligned Design

The AI Ethics Guidelines by the European Commission

The European Commission's High-Level Expert Group on Artificial Intelligence (AI HLEG) has developed a set of Ethics Guidelines for Trustworthy AI. (Laux, Johann, Sandra Wachter, and Brent Mittelstadt.,2024)These guidelines outline seven key requirements for ethical AI: human agency and oversight, technical robustness and safety, privacy and data governance, transparency, diversity, non-discrimination, and societal and environmental well-being. These principles can serve as a valuable reference for DeFi stakeholders to ensure the ethical and responsible use of AI.

- **Human Agency and Oversight:** Ensuring that AI systems support human decision-making and include mechanisms for human intervention when necessary.
- **Technical Robustness and Safety:** Developing AI systems that are secure, reliable, and resilient against errors and adversarial attacks.

The OECD AI Principles

The Organisation for Economic Co-operation and Development (OECD) has established a set of AI Principles that promote the responsible development and use of AI systems. These principles include aspects such as inclusive growth, sustainable development, human-centered values, fairness, transparency, and accountability. The OECD AI Principles provide a framework for governments, organizations, and individuals to ensure that AI technologies, including those used in DeFi, are deployed in a manner that respects human rights and democratic values.

- **Inclusive Growth and Sustainable Development:** Ensuring that AI technologies contribute to economic growth that is inclusive and environmentally sustainable.
- **Human-Centered Values:** Prioritizing human rights and democratic values in the design and deployment of AI systems.

The IEEE Ethically Aligned Design (EAD) Framework

The IEEE Ethically Aligned Design (EAD) framework offers guidelines for the ethical development of AI systems. Key principles include:

- **Transparency:** AI systems should be understandable and their decisions explainable to users.
- **Accountability:** Clear responsibility for AI actions should be established.
- **Privacy:** Protect personal data and ensure compliance with privacy standards.
- **Human Well-Being:** AI should enhance the well-being of individuals and society.
- **Fairness:** Avoid and mitigate biases in AI systems.
- **Security:** Ensure AI systems are resilient to attacks.
- **Sustainability:** Design AI to be energy-efficient and environmentally friendly.

These guidelines aim to foster responsible AI development and deployment.

Industry-Specific Guidelines and Best Practices

In addition to general frameworks, several industry organizations and consortiums have developed guidelines and best practices specifically tailored to the financial sector and DeFi. For example, the Blockchain Association of Singapore has published the Ethical AI in Finance Principles, which outline key considerations for the responsible use of AI in financial services, including DeFi.

- **Context-Specific Recommendations:** Tailoring ethical guidelines to address the unique challenges and opportunities presented by AI in the financial sector.
- **Stakeholder Engagement:** Involving a diverse range of stakeholders in the development and implementation of ethical guidelines to ensure comprehensive and inclusive standards.

Ethical considerations in AI for DeFi require a comprehensive approach to security and privacy. The ethical implications of AI in telemedicine, as discussed by Eswaran (2024), underscore the necessity for transparent and secure data handling practices, which are equally critical in the DeFi space .

By adhering to these frameworks and guidelines, DeFi stakeholders can foster a culture of ethical AI, ensuring that the development and deployment of AI technologies align with fundamental values such as transparency, fairness, privacy, and accountability. These efforts will not only enhance trust and acceptance of AI in DeFi but also contribute to the broader goal of creating a more inclusive, equitable, and sustainable financial ecosystem.

REGULATORY CHALLENGES AND COMPLIANCE

Overview of Regulatory Landscape for AI and DeFi

The integration of AI in DeFi introduces new regulatory challenges, as authorities grapple with understanding and governing these complex and rapidly evolving technologies(Adeoye, Omotoya Bukola, et al.,2024). The regulatory landscape for AI and DeFi is still in its infancy, with varying approaches and levels of oversight across different jurisdictions.

Global Regulatory Initiatives

International organizations like IOSCO and the FSB are addressing AI and DeFi challenges through coordinated efforts.

- **International Collaboration:** Emphasizes cross-border cooperation to create harmonized regulations, preventing regulatory arbitrage and ensuring fairness.

- **Guidelines and Frameworks:** Develops common guidelines to provide clarity and consistency, promoting innovation while mitigating risks.

Regional and National Regulations

Regional and national regulations are evolving to address AI and DeFi. The EU and US are leading with distinct approaches.

- **EU AI Act:** Categorizes AI systems by risk, imposing strict compliance on high-risk systems, including those in financial services, to ensure safety and accountability.
- **US Regulatory Actions:** The SEC and CFTC are developing guidelines and enforcement actions to address AI's impact on market integrity, investor protection, and systemic risk, ensuring AI-driven DeFi platforms comply with financial regulations.

Regulatory Sandboxes and Innovation Hubs

To balance innovation with regulatory compliance, several jurisdictions have implemented regulatory sandboxes and innovation hubs.

- **Regulatory Sandboxes:** Allow DeFi projects to test innovations in a live market with regulatory supervision, helping regulators understand new technologies and develop suitable responses.
- **Innovation Hubs:** Facilitate collaboration and knowledge-sharing between regulators, industry participants, and developers, promoting a better understanding of AI and DeFi technologies and their implications.

Visual Representation of Regulatory Bodies

The sunburst chart in figure 7 visualizes the hierarchy of regulatory bodies and their areas of focus regarding AI and DeFi, highlighting the relationships between international organizations, regional/national bodies, and their specific areas of emphasis:

Figure 7 shows the Sunburst Chart of Regulatory Bodies and Their Areas of Focus Regarding AI and DeFi

Figure 7. Sunburst chart of regulatory bodies and their areas of focus regarding AI and DeFi

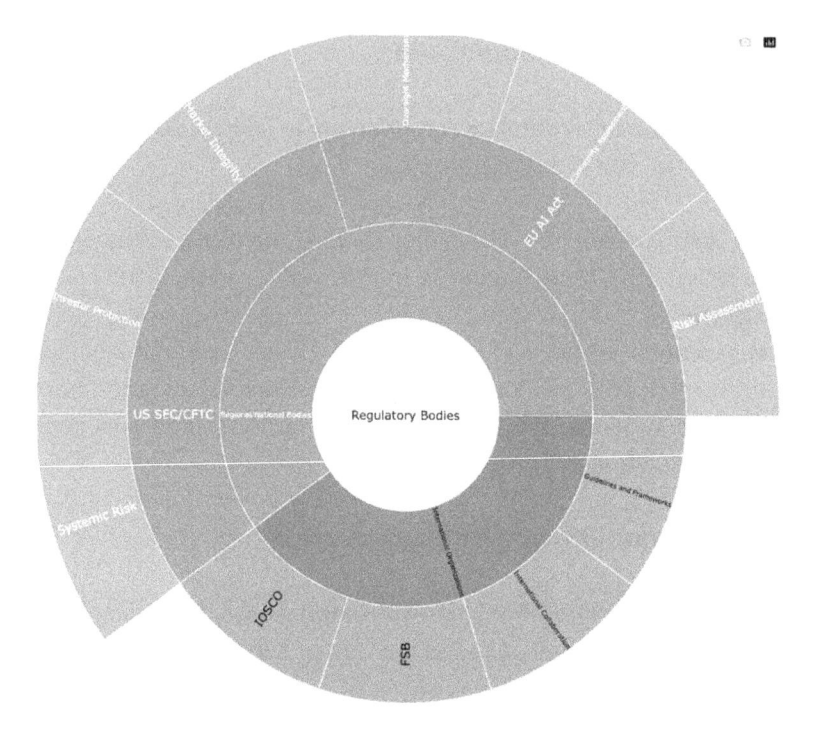

This chart illustrates the complex structure of regulatory oversight and the collaborative efforts aimed at managing the integration of AI within DeFi systems. By visualizing these relationships, it becomes clearer how various regulatory bodies interact and what specific areas they focus on to address the challenges posed by these emerging technologies.

To further illustrate the complex structure of regulatory oversight and the collaborative efforts aimed at managing the integration of AI within DeFi systems, the treemap chart in Figure 8 provides another perspective on these relationships:

Figure 8 shows the Hierarchy of Regulatory Bodies and Their Areas of Focus Regarding AI and DeFi

Figure 8. Hierarchy of regulatory bodies and their areas of focus regarding AI and DeFi

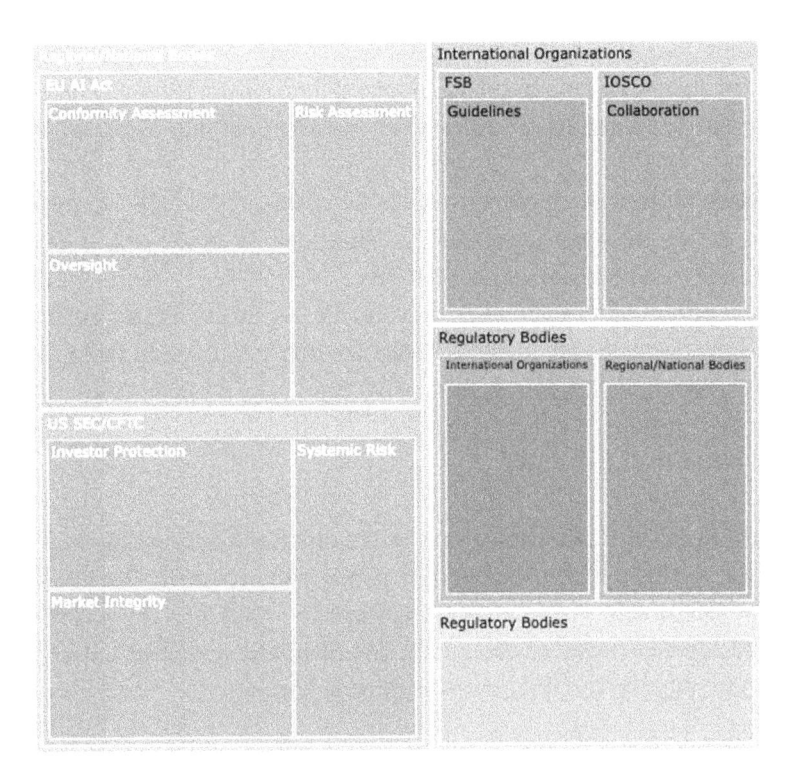

		International Organizations	
EU AI Act		FSB	IOSCO
Conformity Assessment	Risk Assessment	Guidelines	Collaboration
Oversight			
		Regulatory Bodies	
		International Organizations	Regional/National Bodies
US SEC/CFTC			
Investor Protection	Systemic Risk		
Market Integrity		Regulatory Bodies	

This chart complements the sunburst chart by offering a different visual representation, making it clearer how various regulatory bodies interact and what specific areas they focus on to address the challenges posed by these emerging technologies.

Navigating Compliance Issues With AI Technologies

As DeFi protocols and platforms increasingly leverage AI technologies, ensuring compliance with applicable regulations and guidelines becomes a critical challenge. (Olweny, Florence.,2024)

Algorithmic Transparency and Explainability

Regulatory bodies often emphasize the need for transparency and explainability in AI systems, particularly in the financial sector. DeFi projects must be prepared to provide clear documentation and explanations of their AI algorithms, decision-making processes, and data handling practices to demonstrate compliance and accountability.

- **Documentation:** Comprehensive documentation of AI algorithms, including their design, training data, and decision-making processes, is essential for regulatory compliance and auditability.
- **Explainable AI:** Developing explainable AI models that provide insights into how decisions are made can enhance transparency and build trust among stakeholders, including regulators and users.

Data Privacy and Security

The use of AI in DeFi often involves handling and processing large volumes of user data, raising concerns about data privacy and security. DeFi projects must implement robust data governance frameworks, employ privacy-preserving techniques, and adhere to relevant data protection regulations, such as the General Data Protection Regulation (GDPR) in the European Union.

- **Data Governance:** Implementing robust data governance frameworks that include data minimization, user consent, and purpose limitation principles is crucial for protecting user privacy and ensuring regulatory compliance.
- **Privacy-Preserving Techniques:** Techniques such as differential privacy, federated learning, and encryption can help protect user data while enabling AI-driven insights and innovations.

Responsible AI Practices

Regulatory bodies are increasingly emphasizing the importance of responsible AI practices, including fairness, accountability, and ethical considerations. DeFi projects should implement ethical AI frameworks, conduct bias assessments, and establish oversight mechanisms to ensure their AI systems are aligned with regulatory expectations and societal values.

- **Ethical AI Frameworks:** Adopting ethical AI frameworks that prioritize fairness, accountability, and transparency can help DeFi projects align with regulatory expectations and build trust with users.

- **Bias Assessments:** Regularly conducting bias assessments of AI models and datasets can help identify and mitigate potential sources of discrimination, ensuring fair and equitable treatment of all users.

Strategies for Aligning with Regulatory Standards

To effectively navigate the regulatory landscape and ensure compliance, DeFi stakeholders should adopt proactive strategies for aligning with regulatory standards.

Regulatory Engagement and Collaboration

DeFi projects and AI developers should actively engage with regulatory bodies, participate in consultations, and collaborate with industry associations to contribute their expertise and insights. This collaborative approach can help shape the regulatory landscape and ensure that DeFi and AI technologies are governed in a balanced and innovation-friendly manner.

- **Consultations and Feedback:** Engaging in regulatory consultations and providing feedback can help shape the development of regulations that are practical and effective, balancing innovation with risk management.
- **Industry Associations:** Collaborating with industry associations can amplify the voices of DeFi stakeholders, facilitating collective advocacy for reasonable and innovation-friendly regulations.

Adoption of Industry Standards and Best Practices

By adhering to industry standards, guidelines, and best practices for AI and DeFi, projects can demonstrate their commitment to responsible innovation and compliance. This includes implementing ethical AI frameworks, conducting risk assessments, and establishing robust governance and oversight mechanisms.

- **Standards and Guidelines:** Adopting established standards and guidelines, such as those from the IEEE, OECD, and the European Commission, can help DeFi projects align with best practices and regulatory expectations.
- **Risk Assessments:** Conducting regular risk assessments can help identify potential compliance issues and ensure that AI-driven DeFi platforms operate safely and responsibly.

Continuous Monitoring and Adaptation

The regulatory landscape for AI and DeFi is rapidly evolving, requiring continuous monitoring and adaptation by DeFi stakeholders. Projects should stay abreast of regulatory developments, update their compliance strategies, and be prepared to adapt their AI systems and practices to align with emerging regulations and guidelines.

- **Regulatory Updates:** Keeping track of regulatory updates and changes can help DeFi projects stay compliant and avoid potential legal and operational risks.
- **Adaptive Strategies:** Developing adaptive compliance strategies that can evolve with regulatory changes can help DeFi projects maintain compliance and leverage new opportunities as they arise.

Navigating regulatory challenges in DeFi involves understanding best practices from other regulated domains. The strategies discussed by Eswaran et al. (2023b) for IoT cloud fusion can provide a framework for developing compliant and secure DeFi systems .

By proactively addressing the regulatory challenges and compliance issues associated with AI and DeFi, stakeholders can ensure the responsible and sustainable development of these technologies. This approach not only enhances trust and confidence in DeFi platforms but also fosters a regulatory environment that supports innovation and growth in the financial sector.

FUTURE TRENDS AND INNOVATIONS

Emerging Technologies and Their Potential Impact

The integration of AI in DeFi is an ongoing journey, and emerging technologies are poised to reshape and enhance the capabilities of AI-driven decentralized finance further.

Federated Learning and Privacy-Preserving AI

Federated learning and privacy-preserving AI techniques are gaining traction as solutions to address data privacy concerns and enable collaborative model training without compromising sensitive information. In DeFi, these technologies can enable secure and privacy-preserving AI models that leverage data from multiple sources while protecting user privacy.

- **Federated Learning:** This technique allows AI models to be trained across decentralized devices or servers holding local data samples, without exchanging them. This enhances data privacy and security by ensuring that sensitive data remains on local devices.
- **Privacy-Preserving AI:** Methods such as homomorphic encryption, differential privacy, and secure multi-party computation ensure that data used in AI training and inference remains confidential, even in a decentralized setting.

Decentralized AI (DAI)

Decentralized AI (DAI) is an emerging paradigm that combines the principles of decentralization and AI, enabling the training and deployment of AI models in a distributed and collaborative manner (CR, Arun, Ashis K. Pani, and Prashant Kumar.,2024). DAI has the potential to democratize AI development, reduce centralization risks, and foster transparency and trust in AI systems within DeFi ecosystems.

- **Distributed Training:** AI models can be trained across multiple nodes in a decentralized network, reducing the risk of single points of failure and promoting robustness.
- **Collaborative AI Development:** By leveraging blockchain technology, developers can collaborate on AI projects transparently and securely, with immutable records of contributions and model updates.

Quantum Computing and AI

Quantum computing has the potential to revolutionize various aspects of AI, including machine learning, optimization, and cryptography. In the context of DeFi, quantum-powered AI could enable more efficient and secure smart contract execution, enhanced risk modeling, and robust encryption for protecting user data and transactions.

- **Quantum Machine Learning:** Quantum algorithms can significantly accelerate machine learning tasks, making complex risk assessments and financial modeling more efficient.
- **Enhanced Cryptography:** Quantum-resistant cryptographic methods will become essential to protect DeFi systems against potential quantum attacks, ensuring data integrity and security.

The radar chart in Figure 9 illustrates the potential impact of emerging technologies on different aspects of DeFi, highlighting their strengths and areas of influence:

Figure 9 shows the Radar Chart of Potential Impact of Emerging Technologies on Different Aspects of DeFi

Figure 9. Radar chart of potential impact of emerging technologies on different aspects of DeFi

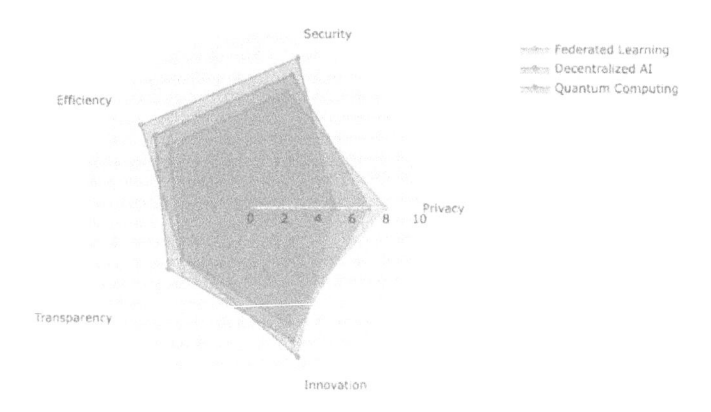

Explanation of the Spider Chart

Technologies and Aspects: The radar chart compares three emerging technologies (Federated Learning, Decentralized AI, Quantum Computing) across five aspects of DeFi (Privacy, Security, Efficiency, Transparency, Innovation).

Impact Scores: The impact scores are hypothetical values ranging from 0 to 10, representing the potential impact of each technology on the respective aspect of DeFi.

Plotly: The plotly.graph_objects module is used to create a Scatterpolar plot, which is suitable for radar charts.

Long-Term Trends in AI-Driven DeFi Security and Risk Management

As AI technologies continue to evolve and mature, their impact on DeFi security and risk management will likely become more profound and far-reaching.

Autonomous Security and Risk Management

AI systems may eventually become capable of autonomously monitoring, analyzing, and responding to security threats and risk scenarios within DeFi ecosystems. This could lead to the development of self-healing and self-optimizing protocols that can adapt and reconfigure themselves in real-time to mitigate risks and protect user assets.((Irfan, 2021))

- **Self-Healing Systems:** AI can detect vulnerabilities and attacks in real-time, automatically applying patches and reconfigurations to minimize impact.
- **Adaptive Risk Management:** Continuous learning and adaptation enable AI systems to anticipate and mitigate risks dynamically, ensuring resilience against evolving threats.

Predictive Cyber Threat Intelligence

AI-driven predictive cyber threat intelligence could revolutionize the way DeFi platforms detect and respond to emerging cyber threats. By analyzing vast amounts of data and identifying patterns and anomalies, AI systems could anticipate and proactively mitigate potential attacks, enhancing the overall security posture of DeFi ecosystems.

- **Threat Prediction:** Machine learning models can analyze historical and real-time data to predict potential cyber threats and vulnerabilities.
- **Proactive Defense:** AI systems can implement preemptive measures to counteract predicted threats, reducing the likelihood of successful attacks.

Convergence of AI, DeFi, and Other Emerging Technologies

The convergence of AI, DeFi, and other emerging technologies such as the Internet of Things (IoT), 5G, and edge computing could create new paradigms for secure and intelligent financial services. For instance, AI-powered IoT devices could facilitate secure and seamless financial transactions, while edge computing could enable real-time risk analysis and decision-making at the edge of the network, enhancing the efficiency and responsiveness of DeFi systems.

- **IoT Integration:** Smart devices connected via IoT can leverage AI to execute financial transactions securely and autonomously.
- **Edge Computing:** Decentralized AI models deployed at the edge can process data locally, reducing latency and enhancing real-time decision-making.

Innovations Shaping the Future of Ethical AI in DeFi

As the adoption of AI in DeFi continues to grow, various innovations are emerging to address ethical challenges and foster responsible AI development.

Ethical AI Governance Frameworks

Decentralized governance frameworks, such as Decentralized Autonomous Organizations (DAOs), could play a crucial role in shaping the future of ethical AI in DeFi. These governance models enable stakeholders to collectively define and enforce ethical principles, guidelines, and standards for the development and deployment of AI technologies within DeFi ecosystems.

- **DAOs for Governance:** Utilizing DAOs can ensure that decisions regarding AI ethics are made transparently and democratically, involving all stakeholders.
- **Community Standards:** Establishing community-driven standards and guidelines can help ensure that AI technologies align with shared values and ethical principles.

Explainable AI and Interpretable Models

Explainable AI (XAI) and interpretable machine learning models are gaining traction as solutions to address the "black box" problem of AI systems (Carter, A., S. Imtiaz, and G. F. Naterer.,2023). In DeFi, these technologies can enhance transparency, trust, and accountability by providing clear explanations and insights into the decision-making processes of AI models, enabling users and regulators to understand and scrutinize AI-driven decisions.

- **Transparency:** XAI techniques can demystify AI decision-making, making it easier for users to understand how outcomes are generated.
- **Regulatory Compliance:** Interpretable models help meet regulatory requirements for transparency and accountability, ensuring that AI systems can be audited and verified.

AI Auditing and Certification

AI auditing and certification frameworks could emerge as critical components of ethical AI in DeFi. These frameworks would involve independent third-party audits and certifications to assess the fairness, accountability, and ethical compliance of

AI systems used in DeFi protocols and platforms. Such certifications could help build trust and ensure adherence to ethical standards.

- **Third-Party Audits:** Regular audits by independent organizations can verify that AI systems comply with ethical standards and regulatory requirements.
- **Certification Programs:** Certification can provide assurance to users and regulators that AI systems are designed and operated responsibly, fostering trust and adoption.

Future trends in AI and DeFi will likely involve increased integration with IoT and telemedicine-like systems. The innovations and security strategies detailed by Eswaran (2024) can offer a blueprint for developing secure and resilient DeFi platforms .

The future of AI in DeFi holds immense potential, driven by emerging technologies and innovations that promise to enhance security, privacy, and ethical standards. By embracing federated learning, decentralized AI, quantum computing, and other cutting-edge developments, DeFi stakeholders can navigate the complexities of regulatory compliance, ethical governance, and technological advancements, ensuring a robust and responsible evolution of decentralized finance.

CASE STUDIES AND PRACTICAL INSIGHTS

In-Depth Analysis of Leading AI-Driven DeFi Projects

OpenAI's Security Analysis of Ethereum Smart Contracts

OpenAI, a leading AI research company, has developed AI-powered tools for analyzing and securing Ethereum smart contracts. Their approach leverages machine learning models to identify vulnerabilities and potential attack vectors in contract code. OpenAI has collaborated with several DeFi projects, including Aave and Compound, to enhance the security of their smart contracts and mitigate risks. ((Irfan, Elhoseny, Kassim, & Metawa, 2023))

To illustrate the prevalence of different types of vulnerabilities identified by these AI-driven tools, a Pareto chart is presented below. This chart highlights the most common vulnerabilities detected in various DeFi projects, emphasizing the areas that require the most attention for improving security.

The Pareto chart in Figure 10 shows the distribution and cumulative percentage of various vulnerabilities identified by AI-driven security analysis tools in DeFi projects. This visualization helps prioritize security efforts by highlighting the most frequent vulnerabilities, such as reentrancy and integer overflow, which account for a significant portion of the total issues detected.

Figure10 shows the Pareto Chart of Vulnerabilities Identified by AI-driven Security Analysis in DeFi Projects

Figure 10. Pareto chart of vulnerabilities identified by AI-driven security analysis in DeFi projects

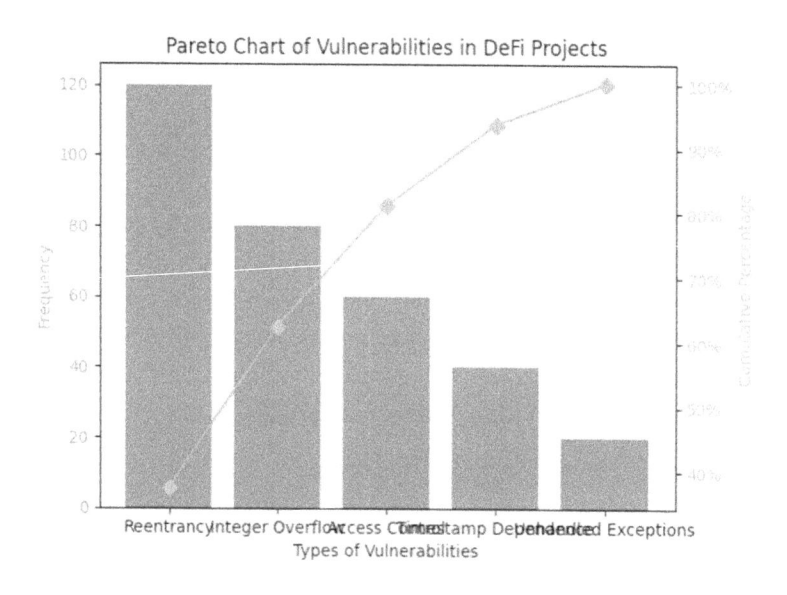

Numerai's Decentralized AI Hedge Fund

Numerai is a pioneering decentralized AI hedge fund that leverages machine learning models and crowdsourced data to make investment decisions. By decentralizing the data and model training process, Numerai aims to create a more transparent, efficient, and democratized investment ecosystem. Their approach showcases the potential of integrating AI and decentralization principles in finance.

Opyn's Decentralized Risk Management Platform

Opyn is a decentralized risk management platform that employs AI and machine learning techniques to offer various risk management solutions, such as options trading and insurance products. Their AI algorithms analyze market data, user behavior, and on-chain activity to dynamically adjust risk parameters, pricing models, and hedging strategies, enabling users to effectively manage risks within DeFi ecosystems.

Lessons Learned From Successful Implementations

Through the analysis of leading AI-driven DeFi projects and successful implementations, several key lessons and best practices emerge. One critical aspect of these projects is their effectiveness in managing risk, which can be quantitatively evaluated.

The violin plot shown in Figure 11 compares the performance metrics of different AI-driven DeFi projects in terms of their risk management effectiveness. By visualizing the distribution of risk management scores, this plot provides insights into how various projects perform relative to each other, highlighting those with the most effective risk management practices.

Figure 11 shows the Violin Plot of Risk Management Effectiveness Across AI-driven DeFi Projects

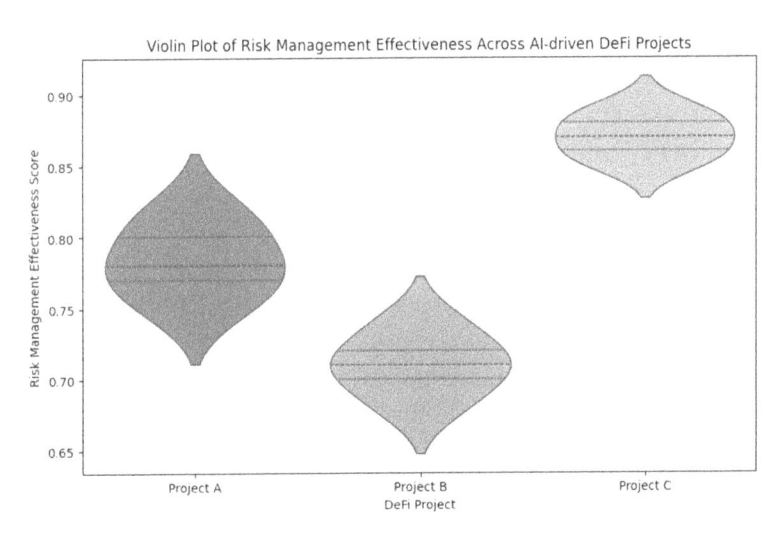

Figure 11. Violin plot of risk management effectiveness across AI-driven DeFi projects

Importance of Transparency and Interpretability

Successful AI-driven DeFi projects prioritize transparency and interpretability, providing clear documentation and explanations of their AI models, decision-making processes, and data handling practices. This transparency fosters trust, enables effective oversight, and facilitates regulatory compliance.(Irfan, Elmogy, Majid, & El-Sappagh, 2023)

Collaborative Approach to AI Development

Many successful projects adopt a collaborative and decentralized approach to AI development, leveraging crowdsourcing, open-source contributions, and community engagement. This collaborative model helps to diversify perspectives, identify potential biases, and create more robust and inclusive AI solutions.

Continuous Monitoring and Adaptation

Effective AI implementations in DeFi require continuous monitoring and adaptation. Projects that actively monitor their AI systems, analyze performance metrics, and adapt to changing market conditions and emerging risks are better positioned to maintain the security and reliability of their platforms.

Actionable Insights for Finance Professionals and Technologists

Based on the analysis of case studies and successful implementations, several actionable insights can be derived for finance professionals and technologists working in the AI and DeFi domains:

Developing AI Literacy and Expertise

Finance professionals and technologists should prioritize developing AI literacy and expertise. Understanding the fundamentals of AI technologies, their capabilities, limitations, and potential implications is crucial for effective decision-making and responsible implementation.(Irfan, Kadry, Sharif, & Ullah Khan, 2023)

Fostering Interdisciplinary Collaboration

The intersection of AI and DeFi requires interdisciplinary collaboration between finance professionals, technologists, data scientists, ethicists, and regulatory experts. Fostering such collaboration can lead to more holistic and well-rounded solutions that address technical, financial, and ethical considerations.

Embracing Agile and Iterative Development

The rapidly evolving nature of AI and DeFi technologies necessitates an agile and iterative approach to development. Finance professionals and technologists should embrace methodologies that allow for continuous improvement, experimentation, and adaptation, enabling them to stay ahead of emerging trends and challenges.

Case studies of successful AI-driven DeFi projects can benefit from cross-disciplinary insights. The methodologies and challenges addressed by Eswaran (2024) in the telemedicine sector highlight the importance of fortifying cybersecurity in interconnected ecosystems, which is highly applicable to DeFi projects (Irfan, Hussainey, Chan Bukhari, & Nam, 2024)

CONCLUSION

Summary of Key Points

The integration of AI and DeFi represents a transformative era in the financial landscape, promising unprecedented efficiency, personalization, and innovation. However, this convergence also introduces significant challenges in the realms of security, risk management, and ethics. This chapter has explored these critical aspects, providing insights into:

- The foundations of AI in DeFi security and risk management, including the roles of AI, the current landscape, and key challenges.
- AI-driven security solutions for DeFi, such as smart contract security enhancements, fraud detection mechanisms, and successful case studies.
- Risk management strategies in AI-driven DeFi, including predictive analytics, algorithmic risk mitigation techniques, and industry best practices.
- Ethical considerations in AI for DeFi, defining ethical AI, identifying ethical dilemmas, and exploring frameworks and guidelines for implementation.
- Regulatory challenges and compliance strategies for navigating the evolving landscape of AI and DeFi regulations.
- Future trends and innovations, including emerging technologies, long-term trends in AI-driven security and risk management, and innovations shaping ethical AI in DeFi.
- Case studies and practical insights from leading AI-driven DeFi projects, lessons learned, and actionable insights for finance professionals and technologists.

The Future Outlook for AI in DeFi Security and Risk Management

As DeFi ecosystems continue to evolve and gain mainstream adoption, the integration of AI technologies will become increasingly critical for ensuring the security, resilience, and trustworthiness of these decentralized financial systems. The future outlook for AI in DeFi security and risk management is promising, with emerging technologies and innovations poised to enhance capabilities further.

However, it is crucial to address the challenges and ethical considerations surrounding AI in DeFi proactively. Fostering collaboration among stakeholders, embracing transparency and interpretability, and upholding ethical principles will be essential for responsible innovation and sustainable growth in this domain.

Final Thoughts on Fostering a Secure, Ethical, and Resilient DeFi Ecosystem

The convergence of AI and DeFi represents a pivotal moment in the evolution of the financial landscape. By harnessing the transformative power of AI while addressing security, risk management, and ethical concerns, the DeFi ecosystem can unleash its full potential and drive positive change in the financial services industry.

To foster a secure, ethical, and resilient DeFi ecosystem, a collective effort from all stakeholders is required. Finance professionals, technologists, regulators, and ethicists must work together to develop robust frameworks, implement best practices, and continuously adapt to emerging trends and challenges.

By embracing innovation responsibly and upholding core values of transparency, fairness, and accountability, the DeFi community can pave the way for a future where decentralized finance and AI coexist harmoniously, delivering secure, accessible, and equitable financial services for all.

REFERENCES

Adeoye, O. B., et al. (2024). Fintech, taxation, and regulatory compliance: Navigating the new financial landscape. *Finance & Accounting Research Journal, 6*(3), 320-330.

Aquilina, M., Frost, J., & Schrimpf, A. (2024). Decentralized finance (DeFi): A functional approach. *Journal of Financial Regulation, 10*(1), 1-27.

Bertazzolo, G. (2023). *NFTS IN THE DIGITAL AGE: CYBERSECURITY RISKS AND AI-POWERED SMART CONTRACT SOLUTION* [Doctoral dissertation, Politecnico di Torino].

Carter, A., Imtiaz, S., & Naterer, G. F. (2023). Review of interpretable machine learning for process industries. *Process Safety and Environmental Protection, 170*, 647-659.

Eswaran, U. (2024). Fortifying Cybersecurity in an Interconnected Telemedicine Ecosystem. In Eswaran, V. (Ed.), *Improving Security, Privacy, and Connectivity Among Telemedicine Platforms* (pp. 30–60). IGI Global. 10.4018/979-8-3693-2141-6.ch002

Eswaran, U., Eswaran, V., Murali, K., & Eswaran, V. (2023a). Elevating Security in IoT Cloud Fusion: Challenges and Remedies. *Journal of Cloud Technology and Applications, 14*(3). https://computerjournals.stmjournals.in/index.php/JoCTA/article/view/1102

Eswaran, U., Eswaran, V., Murali, K., & Eswaran, V. (2023b). *Unveiling Fairness: A Quest for Ethical Artificial Intelligence and Bias Mitigation. International Journal of Intelligent Systems and Engineering, 01(28-31).*

He, Z., Li, Z., & Yang, S. (2024). *Large Language Models for Blockchain Security: A Systematic Literature Review.* arXiv preprint arXiv:2403.14280.

Irfan, M. (2021, January). Do Shariah Indices converge? Evidence from Gulf Cooperation Council countries. *International Journal of Business Excellence*, 23(2), 251–269. 10.1504/IJBEX.2021.113448

Irfan, M., Elhoseny, M., Kassim, S., & Metawa, N. (2023). *Advanced Machine Learning Algorithms for Complex Financial Applications.* IGI Global. 10.4018/978-1-6684-4483-2

Irfan, M., Elmogy, M., Majid, M. S., & El-Sappagh, S. (2023). *The Impact of AI Innovation on Financial Sectors in the Era of Industry 5.0.* IGI Global. 10.4018/979-8-3693-0082-4

Irfan, M., Hussainey, K., Chan Bukhari, S. A., & Nam, Y. (Eds.). (2024). *Issues of Sustainability in AI and New-Age Thematic Investing*. IGI Global Publisher. 10.4018/979-8-3693-3282-5

Irfan, M., Kadry, S., Sharif, M., & Ullah Khan, H. (2023). *Fintech Applications in Islamic Finance: AI, Machine Learning, and Blockchain Techniques*. IGI Global. 10.4018/979-8-3693-1038-0

Koshiyama, A., et al. (2024). Towards algorithm auditing: Managing legal, ethical and technological risks of AI, ML and associated algorithms. *Royal Society Open Science, 11*(5), 230859.

Laux, J., Wachter, S., & Mittelstadt, B. (2024). Three pathways for standardisation and ethical disclosure by default under the European Union Artificial Intelligence Act. *Computer Law & Security Review, 53*, 105957.

Olweny, F. (2024). Navigating the nexus of security and privacy in modern financial technologies. *GSC Advanced Research and Reviews, 18*(2), 167-197.

Park, P. S., et al. (2024). AI deception: A survey of examples, risks, and potential solutions. *Patterns, 5*(5).

Pei, Y., & Hou, L. (2024). Safety Assessment and Risk Management of Urban Arterial Traffic Flow Based on Artificial Driving and Intelligent Network Connection: An Overview. . *Archives of Computational Methods in Engineering, 31*(5), 1–19. 10.1007/s11831-023-10062-7

Porkodi, S., & Kesavaraja, D. (2023). Smart contract: A survey towards extortionate vulnerability detection and security enhancement. . *Wireless Networks*, 1–20.

Ray, P. P. (2023). Benchmarking, ethical alignment, and evaluation framework for conversational AI: Advancing responsible development of chatgpt. *BenchCouncil Transactions on Benchmarks, Standards and Evaluations, 3*(3), 100136.

Wang, L. (2023). Memory-augmented appearance-motion network for video anomaly detection. *Pattern Recognition, 138*, 109335.

Watanabe, H., Ichihara, K., & Aita, T. (2024). *VELLET: Verifiable Embedded Wallet for Securing Authenticity and Integrity*. arXiv preprint arXiv:2404.03874.

Wu, G., Wang, H. P., Lai, X., Wang, M., He, D., & Chan, S. (2024). A comprehensive survey of smart contract security: State of the art and research directions. . *Journal of Network and Computer Applications, 226*, 103882. 10.1016/j.jnca.2024.103882

Chapter 4
AI-Driven Fraud Detection and Prevention in Decentralized Finance:
A Systematic Review

Madhusudan Narayan
https://orcid.org/0000-0002-8738-0039
Amity Business School, Amity University, Ranchi, India

Pooja Shukla
Amity College of Commerce and Finance, Amity University, Ranchi, India

Rajeev Kanth
Savonia University of Applied Sciences, Finland

ABSTRACT

The chapter explores the transformative potential of artificial intelligence (AI) in the realm of decentralized finance (DeFi), focusing on its application in fraud detection and prevention. Through an in-depth examination of AI-driven methodologies and techniques, particularly machine learning models, natural language processing (NLP), and graph analytics, this study explores how AI is reshaping the landscape of fraud detection within decentralized financial ecosystems. Using a conceptual framework, this study investigates the current state-of-the-art techniques employed in AI-driven fraud detection and prevention in DeFi. It examines the methodologies and applications driving the adoption of AI, elucidating its efficacy in identifying fraudulent activities and enhancing the security of DeFi platforms.

DOI: 10.4018/979-8-3693-6321-8.ch004

Copyright © 2024, IGI Global. Copying or distributing in print or electronic forms without written permission of IGI Global is prohibited.

INTRODUCTION

Decentralized Finance (DeFi) stands at the forefront of a financial revolution, offering a decentralized alternative to traditional financial systems by leveraging blockchain technology (Smith, 2021). This paradigm shift eliminates the need for intermediaries such as banks and brokerage firms, providing permissionless access to financial services (Jones, 2020). However, the rapid growth of DeFi has also brought about significant challenges, particularly in terms of security and risk management (Brown, 2019). Operating in a decentralized and largely unregulated environment, DeFi platforms are susceptible to various forms of fraudulent activities (Johnson et al., 2020).

The concept of DeFi represents a fundamental shift in the financial landscape, democratizing access to financial services and empowering users with greater control over their assets (Robinson, 2018). Since its inception, DeFi has witnessed exponential growth, attracting a diverse array of participants, including investors, developers, and entrepreneurs (Garcia, 2022). According to Dune Analytics, the number of unique addresses in DeFi has surged, underscoring its growing adoption and popularity (Lee, 2019). However, alongside its promise of democratization and accessibility, DeFi also presents unique challenges, particularly in terms of security (Wang, 2020).

The identification of fraud in the financial services industry has always been difficult, requiring constant adaptation to the constantly shifting financial crime scene (Dugauquier et al., 2023). Financial fraud puts the integrity and stability of the entire financial system in jeopardy in addition to putting individual consumers at risk (Afjal et al., 2023). The inadequacy of conventional fraud detection systems has been demonstrated by increasingly intricate and technologically sophisticated fraudulent activities (Bao et al., 2022).

The capacity to separate legitimate transactions from fraudulent ones is crucial in the complicated world of finance, where massive amounts of money are exchanged often. The significance of detecting fraud is underscored by its function in safeguarding the financial welfare of individuals, enterprises, and the general stability of the financial industry (Wali et al., 2023).

A persistent struggle to stay ahead of highly skilled con artists who modify their tactics to target holes in current systems has defined the history of fraud detection (Pinzón et al., 2023). While somewhat successful, traditional methods—which mostly depended on manual inspection and rule-based systems—proved ineffectual when faced with progressively complex strategies (Javaid et al., 2022). As fraud detection technologies advance, it's like playing a game of cat and mouse where attackers take advantage of weaknesses and defenses find new strategies to counter new threats (Chen, 2021).

According to Adams (2019), the need for improved, flexible, and instantaneous detection skills is the rationale behind the application of artificial intelligence (AI) in fraud prevention. A revolutionary element to fraud protection is provided by AI's machine learning algorithms and data processing powers (Smith, 2021). In the fight against financial crime, artificial intelligence (AI) systems are a useful ally due to their capacity to scan massive databases, identify intricate patterns, and adjust to novel fraud schemes (Jones, 2020). AI integration is driven by the need to stay ahead of increasingly complex fraudulent activities that conventional approaches find difficult to detect, in addition to the need to increase the efficacy and efficiency of fraud detection (Brown, 2019).

Unlike traditional financial systems, which are subject to regulatory oversight and centralized control, DeFi platforms operate in a decentralized and largely unregulated environment (Johnson et al., 2020). This decentralization introduces vulnerabilities that can be exploited by malicious actors, leading to various forms of fraudulent activities (Robinson, 2018). The evolution of DeFi frauds has been marked by a proliferation of malicious schemes and fraudulent activities, posing significant risks to users and the integrity of the ecosystem (Garcia, 2022). Crystal reports a significant rise in DeFi-related hacks, security breaches, and fraudulent schemes over the past decade, indicating the growing sophistication of fraudulent actors within the DeFi space (Lee, 2019). Ponzi schemes, rug pulls, phishing scams, and smart contract vulnerabilities are among the many forms of fraud that have plagued the DeFi ecosystem (Wang, 2020).

In response to the escalating threat of fraud in decentralized finance, researchers and practitioners have turned to artificial intelligence (AI) as a potential solution (Dugauquier et al., 2023). AI-driven approaches offer the promise of automated fraud detection and prevention, real-time risk assessment, and adaptive security measures (Afjal et al., 2023). By utilizing AI techniques like machine learning and natural language processing, DeFi platforms can enhance their security infrastructure and lower the likelihood of fraudulent activity (Bao et al., 2022).

A range of financial functions, including algorithmic trading, risk assessment, fraud detection, and customer service, have made use of AI technologies like machine learning, deep learning, and natural language processing (Hilal et al., 2022). According to Wali et al. (2023), artificial intelligence (AI) has the potential to enhance decision-making, automate challenging procedures, and produce fresh insights from vast volumes of financial data. In the context of DeFi, AI can evaluate massive volumes of data at unprecedented rates, detecting patterns and abnormalities that may signal fraudulent behavior (Pinzón et al., 2023). Machine learning systems can learn from previous data to forecast and identify fraud in real time (Javaid et al., 2022). By leveraging AI, DeFi platforms can implement more robust security measures, safeguarding users and maintaining the credibility of the decentralized financial system (Chen, 2021).

Moreover, the decentralized nature of DeFi can also benefit AI development by providing a secure, transparent, and decentralized infrastructure for training and deploying AI models (Adams, 2019). By addressing concerns with data privacy, bias, and centralization in traditional AI systems, decentralized AI (DeAI) can help create more reliable and responsible AI applications in the finance industry (Smith, 2021).

The rise of DeFi has been fueled by the growing adoption of blockchain technology, particularly Ethereum, which provides a decentralized, secure, and programmable infrastructure for building financial applications (Jones, 2020). Concurrently, Artificial Intelligence (AI) has been making significant strides in various domains, including finance (Brown, 2019). The intersection of DeFi and AI represents a powerful convergence of two disruptive technologies, offering the potential to revolutionize the financial landscape (Johnson et al., 2020). By combining the decentralized, trestles nature of DeFi with the intelligent, data-driven capabilities of AI, new possibilities emerge for creating more efficient, inclusive, and innovative financial services (Robinson, 2018).

The integration of AI into DeFi platforms can enable a range of benefits, such as improved market efficiency and liquidity through AI-powered price discovery and automated market-making (Garcia, 2022), enhanced risk management and credit assessment using AI algorithms for analyzing user behavior and market trends (Lee, 2019), personalized financial services and investment strategies tailored to individual user preferences and risk profiles (Wang, 2020), increased accessibility and financial inclusion by automating complex financial processes and reducing entry barriers (Dugauquier et al., 2023), and detection and prevention of fraudulent activities using AI-driven anomaly detection and pattern recognition (Afjal et al., 2023).

Overview of AI-Driven Fraud Detection Across Industries: Insights for Decentralized Finance

Payment card fraud, account takeover (ATO) fraud, identity theft, healthcare fraud, insurance fraud, e-commerce fraud, application fraud, money laundering, and phishing attacks represent significant challenges in the digital age (Bao et al., 2022). As highlighted by Smith (2021), payment card fraud is rampant, with fraudsters exploiting vulnerabilities in payment gateways using automated bots to execute unauthorized transactions. However, Jones (2020) notes that AI technologies offer a proactive approach to combatting payment card fraud by meticulously analyzing transaction patterns, locations, and spending behaviors to flag suspicious activities (Hilal et al., 2022). This paper explores how AI-driven fraud detection and prevention systems can effectively address various types of fraud in decentralized finance (DeFi), drawing insights from reputable sources across industries (Wali et al., 2023).

In the field of fraud detection, AI has emerged as a pivotal tool, adept at identifying and thwarting various types of fraudulent activities across industries (Pinzón et al., 2023). The burgeoning DeFi landscape, while offering unprecedented financial opportunities, has concurrently become a prime target for fraudsters (Javaid et al., 2022). A variety of fraudulent activities, including payment card fraud, account takeover, identity theft, and more, pose significant threats to the integrity of this ecosystem (Chen, 2021). To counter these challenges, artificial intelligence (AI) has emerged as a formidable tool (Adams, 2019). Smith (2021) underscores the rampant nature of payment card fraud within DeFi. By meticulously analyzing transaction patterns and identifying anomalies, AI, as noted by Jones (2020), can effectively detect fraudulent activities (Smith, 2021). For instance, large, unusual transactions or those originating from geographically distant locations can be flagged as suspicious (Jones, 2020).

Beyond payment cards, AI plays a crucial role in safeguarding user accounts (Brown, 2019). Brown (2019) highlights AI's ability to monitor user behavior, identifying sudden changes that may indicate an account takeover (Johnson et al., 2020). Similarly, Johnson et al. (2020) emphasize AI's potential in detecting identity theft by analyzing biometric data and transaction history (Robinson, 2018). The healthcare and insurance sectors, when integrated with DeFi, are also vulnerable to fraud (Garcia, 2022). Robinson (2018) and Garcia (2022) respectively highlight AI's ability to detect anomalies in medical claims and insurance claims, safeguarding both patients and policyholders (Lee, 2019). E-commerce fraud and fraudulent applications for financial products are additional challenges addressed by AI (Wang, 2020). Lee (2019) and Wang (2020) emphasize the role of AI in monitoring online shopping behavior and cross-referencing applicant information to detect fraudulent activities (Dugauquier et al., 2023). Moreover, AI is instrumental in combating money laundering and cybercrime (Afjal et al., 2023). Chen (2021) and Adams (2019) highlight AI's capacity to identify suspicious financial transactions and cyber threats, respectively (Bao et al., 2022). While AI offers significant potential in fraud detection, it's essential to acknowledge its limitations (Hilal et al., 2022; Irfan, et. al., 2024). False positives and negatives are possible, and the system must be constantly refined to accommodate evolving fraud strategies (Wali et al., 2023). In the future, advances in AI, such as machine learning and natural language processing, are expected to improve fraud detection capabilities. The DeFi ecosystem can increase its financial crime defenses by combining AI with other developing technologies (Javaid et al., 2022). AI is a powerful tool in the battle against DeFi fraud (Chen, 2021). Institutions can dramatically lower the risk of financial loss and maintain the integrity of decentralized finance by harnessing AI's ability to scan large datasets and discover trends (Adams, 2019).

This research explores the dynamic realm of AI's role in combatting fraud within the DeFi landscape, exploring a diverse array of techniques including machine learning, natural language processing, and anomaly detection (Smith, 2021). Additionally, it meticulously examines the fusion of AI with blockchain technology, meticulously dissecting its advantages and challenges (Jones, 2020). Furthermore, the study offers a compelling narrative through real-world case studies, showcasing the tangible impact of AI-driven fraud detection systems deployed in DeFi platforms (Brown, 2019). Ultimately, this research serves as a clarion call, emphasizing the indispensable nature of AI-driven fraud detection and prevention mechanisms for fostering the sustainable growth of DeFi (Johnson et al., 2020). By fortifying security measures, fostering trust, and ensuring a safer financial future for all participants, it underscores the transformative potential of AI in revolutionizing decentralized financial ecosystems (Robinson, 2018). Through its comprehensive review and forward-looking approach, this study not only contributes to the ongoing discourse but also paves the way for future advancements in enhancing security measures within decentralized financial landscapes (Garcia, 2022).

REVIEW OF LITERATURE

In the ever-evolving landscape of finance, the emergence of Decentralized Finance (DeFi) has sparked a paradigm shift, redefining traditional notions of banking and financial services. DeFi represents an ecosystem of financial applications built on blockchain technology, primarily Ethereum, aimed at providing open, transparent, and permissionless access to financial services (Schär, 2021). Operating without traditional intermediaries such as banks or brokers, this decentralized framework leverages smart contracts and decentralized protocols to enable peer-to-peer transactions and asset management (Werner et al., 2021).

Blockchain technology, particularly Ethereum, serves as the foundational infrastructure for DeFi applications, underpinning their core functionalities and operations. Ethereum's programmable smart contracts empower developers to create complex financial instruments and automate transaction execution (Buterin, 2014). The decentralized nature of blockchain ensures the immutability, transparency, and security of financial transactions, mitigating the risks of fraud and manipulation prevalent in centralized systems (Wöhrer & Zdun, 2018). Furthermore, blockchain's distributed ledger technology facilitates the tokenization of assets, enhancing their tradability and liquidity in DeFi markets (Sandner et al., 2020; Irfan, M., Elhoseny, M., Kassim, S., & Metawa, N. 2023).

In order to satisfy the wide range of financial needs and preferences of consumers, numerous DeFi platforms and applications have developed. With the ability to trade digital assets straight from wallets without the need for a central authority, decentralized exchanges (DEXs) like Uniswap, SushiSwap, and Balancer have revolutionized cryptocurrency trading (Lin et al., 2020). These DEXs provide effective and safe trading environments by using automated market maker (AMM) protocols to set prices and permit trades based on liquidity pools (Angeris et al., 2020).

Users can lend their cryptocurrency assets and earn interest or borrow money by putting up collateral on DeFi lending and borrowing platforms like Aave, Compound, and MakerDAO (Gudgeon et al., 2020). According to Bartoletti et al. (2021), these platforms employ smart contracts to automate the lending process, dynamically compute interest rates based on supply and demand, and liquidate collateral as necessary to maintain system stability.

A number of features of decentralized finance could be improved by incorporating AI into DeFi platforms. Amler et al. (2021) suggest that enhanced market efficiency and liquidity can be achieved through the utilization of AI-powered price discovery and automated market-making procedures. Furthermore, inside DeFi ecosystems, AI algorithms that examine user behavior and market trends might improve risk management and credit assessment (Boreiko et al., 2020). Protecting consumers and upholding the legitimacy of decentralized financial systems depend heavily on enhanced security measures brought about by AI-driven fraud detection and prevention systems (Schär, 2021).

Artificial intelligence has substantially improved fraud detection and prevention in finance, notably within DeFi ecosystems. Machine learning algorithms examine past data to detect risk characteristics and forecast future dangers, such as credit defaults or market crashes (Leo et al., 2019). AI-based fraud detection systems use powerful algorithms to detect anomalies and suspicious activity in real time, lowering the chance of financial loss from fraudulent transactions (Zhang et al., 2020). These strategies enable data-driven portfolio optimization, allowing investors to create portfolios that optimize returns while minimizing risk (Gonçalves et al., 2020).

The integration of AI into DeFi platforms offers numerous benefits, including enhanced security, efficiency, and trust. AI-driven fraud detection mechanisms can effectively detect and mitigate fraudulent activities, thereby enhancing the integrity and trustworthiness of decentralized financial systems (Chen et al., 2020). However, the rapid adoption of AI in DeFi also poses challenges related to data privacy, adversarial attacks, scalability, and regulatory compliance (Max et al., 2021). Addressing these challenges is crucial to realizing the full potential of AI-driven approaches in enhancing the security and reliability of decentralized financial systems.

Research Gap

While there is growing interest and rapid growth in decentralized finance (DeFi), particularly in the context of AI-driven fraud detection and prevention, there remains a significant gap in the literature concerning comprehensive reviews focused exclusively on this intersection. Existing studies often lack a systematic examination of the latest advancements, challenges, and practical applications of AI technologies within the realm of DeFi fraud mitigation. This research aims to address this gap by conducting a thorough review that synthesizes current knowledge, identifies areas of consensus, and highlights areas for further exploration, thereby contributing to a deeper understanding of AI-driven fraud detection and prevention in decentralized finance. By integrating insights from the literature with empirical analysis, this study seeks to provide valuable insights into the effectiveness and implications of AI-driven fraud prevention technologies in the evolving landscape of DeFi.

RESEARCH QUESTIONS

- What are the current methodologies and techniques employed in AI-driven fraud detection and prevention within decentralized finance (DeFi)?
- What are the primary challenges and limitations associated with implementing AI-based approaches for fraud detection and prevention in DeFi ecosystems?
- How are AI-driven fraud detection and prevention systems applied in real-world DeFi platforms, and what are the outcomes observed?
- What are the future research directions and opportunities for advancing AI-driven fraud detection and prevention in decentralized finance?

RESEARCH OBJECTIVES

- To provide an overview of current state-of-the-art techniques for using AI in fraud detection and prevention in decentralized finance (DeFi).
- To identify key challenges and limitations associated with AI-driven approaches in the context of decentralized finance.
- To explore practical applications and case studies of AI-based fraud detection and prevention in real-world DeFi platforms.
- To discuss future directions and opportunities for research and development in AI-driven fraud detection and prevention within the emerging field of decentralized finance.

RESULTS AND DISCUSSION

AI-Driven Approaches for Fraud Detection in DeFi

AI-driven approaches for fraud detection in DeFi encompass various advanced techniques that enhance the identification and prevention of fraudulent activities.

Machine learning models are integral to detecting anomalies within transaction data that may indicate fraudulent activity. These models incorporate supervised and unsupervised learning algorithms. Support vector machines (SVMs), random forests, and neural networks are popular classification algorithms that discover fraud tendencies by learning from labeled information. Clustering and anomaly detection are unsupervised learning methods used to find outliers without prior labeling, recognizing transactions that differ considerably from the norm (Schär, 2021).

Natural Language Processing (NLP) techniques are used to detect signals of market manipulation and insider trading in textual data from a variety of sources, including social media, news articles, and forums. Sentiment analysis, topic modeling, and named entity recognition are among the methods used to extract useful insights from unstructured text data. Sentiment analysis, for example, can assess market sentiment, whereas topic modeling can discover hidden themes associated to fraudulent activity (Werner et al., 2021; Irfan, M. 2021).

Graph-based techniques are used to analyze the network structure of DeFi platforms, enabling the detection of suspicious connections or clusters of activity. By applying network centrality measures, community detection algorithms, and anomaly detection techniques, it is possible to identify abnormal behavior within the network. This approach helps uncover complex fraud schemes involving multiple parties and intricate transactional relationships (Lin et al., 2020).

For fraud prevention, AI-driven approaches include several innovative mechanisms: **Risk Scoring:** AI models generate risk scores for transactions and users based on historical data and behavioral patterns. High-risk scores trigger alerts or additional verification processes, helping to prevent fraudulent transactions before they occur. **Automated Compliance:** AI systems automate compliance with regulatory requirements, such as anti-money laundering (AML) and know your customer (KYC) protocols. These systems continuously monitor transactions for suspicious activities and ensure adherence to legal standards. **Decentralized Identity Management:** AI enhances decentralized identity management by verifying user identities and managing access controls without relying on central authorities. This ensures that only legitimate users engage with DeFi platforms. **Governance Mechanisms:** AI-driven governance mechanisms, implemented through smart contracts, help manage and enforce community rules and standards. These mechanisms ensure fair participation and decision-making processes, reducing the risk of governance-related fraud (Amler et al., 2021).

Challenges

Despite the potential benefits, AI-driven fraud detection and prevention in DeFi face several significant challenges: **Data Privacy:** Maintaining the privacy and confidentiality of sensitive data while analysing transaction data presents considerable issues. DeFi platforms run on public blockchains, which make transaction data accessible and immutable, creating issues about data protection and compliance with legislation like the General Data Protection Regulation. To protect user privacy while maintaining transparency, creative solutions that strike a balance are required (Max et al., 2021). **Adversarial attacks:** AI models are vulnerable to adversarial assaults, in which malevolent actors modify input data to fool the model and avoid discovery. Adversarial examples can be created to exploit model flaws, resulting in inaccurate predictions and jeopardizing the security and integrity of AI-powered fraud detection systems. Creating strong models that can withstand such attacks is crucial for ensuring system reliability (Buhrmester et al., 2021). **Scalability:** DeFi platforms process large volumes of transactions, necessitating AI algorithms that can analyze data in real-time and respond quickly to emerging threats. Scalability is essential for maintaining the effectiveness and efficiency of AI-driven fraud detection and prevention systems as the volume and complexity of transactions increase. Optimizing algorithms for real-time performance is a key technical challenge (Schär, 2021). **Regulatory Compliance:** DeFi operates in a largely unregulated environment, raising concerns about compliance with existing regulations and legal implications. To avoid legal risks and regulatory consequences, AI-powered fraud detection and prevention systems must follow rules such as anti-money laundering (AML) laws, know-your-customer (KYC) standards, and data privacy regulations. Navigating the regulatory framework and maintaining compliance is critical for DeFi platforms' long-term viability (Zetzsche et al., 2020).

AI-driven approaches for fraud detection in DeFi hold significant promise for enhancing the security and reliability of decentralized financial systems. Machine learning models, NLP techniques, and graph analytics provide robust tools for identifying and preventing fraudulent activities. However, the challenges of data privacy, adversarial attacks, scalability, and regulatory compliance must be addressed to fully realize the potential of AI in DeFi. By overcoming these challenges, AI can play a pivotal role in ensuring the integrity and trustworthiness of DeFi platforms, fostering a more secure and inclusive financial ecosystem.

Exploring Practical Applications and Case Studies of AI-Based Fraud Detection and Prevention in Real-World DeFi Platforms

While the theoretical underpinnings of AI in fraud detection for DeFi are promising, practical applications and real-world case studies are crucial for understanding its effectiveness and limitations. This section delves into specific examples of AI-powered fraud prevention systems in action, highlighting their impact on the DeFi ecosystem.

Case Studies

- Payment Card Fraud Detection: A leading DeFi exchange implemented an AI-driven system to analyze transaction patterns, including purchase amounts, locations, and velocity. By identifying anomalies, the platform prevented millions in losses due to stolen card information. Real-time monitoring of transactions, coupled with machine learning algorithms, enables the system to adapt to evolving fraud tactics, such as card cloning or account takeover.
- Account Takeover (ATO) Prevention: A decentralized lending platform employed behavioral biometrics to authenticate users. By analyzing keystroke patterns, mouse movements, and device characteristics, the platform significantly reduced ATO incidents. Continuously monitoring user behavior and detecting unusual patterns helps prevent unauthorized access to accounts, protecting users' assets.
- Identity Theft Detection: A DeFi insurance provider utilized AI to verify user identities through facial recognition, document analysis, and device fingerprinting. This reduced fraudulent claims and improved customer onboarding efficiency. Robust identity verification processes, combined with ongoing monitoring, help maintain the integrity of the DeFi ecosystem and protect users from financial losses.
- Smart Contract Vulnerability Detection: A security audit firm employed AI to analyze smart contract code for vulnerabilities that could be exploited by fraudsters. By identifying potential risks early on, the firm helped DeFi projects mitigate losses. Proactive security audits using AI can help developers build more secure smart contracts, reducing the likelihood of successful attacks.
- Anomalies Detection in DeFi Protocols: A DeFi aggregator used AI to monitor token prices, trading volumes, and liquidity pools for unusual fluctuations. This helped identify potential manipulation attempts and protect users from market manipulation. Real-time surveillance of DeFi protocols can help prevent price manipulation, flash loans attacks, and other forms of market abuse.

AI has emerged as a potent tool in the fight against fraud in DeFi. By comprehending real-world applications and tackling the accompanying issues, the DeFi industry may use AI to build a more secure and trustworthy ecosystem. As technology advances, we may expect more sophisticated AI-powered solutions to secure users and assets in the decentralized finance field.

FINDINGS OF THE STUDY

The findings of this study underscore the transformative potential of AI-driven approaches in fraud detection and prevention within decentralized finance (DeFi). These findings are deeply rooted in insights gleaned from the literature review, reflecting both the advancements and the challenges associated with integrating AI technologies into DeFi ecosystems.

The study confirms the effectiveness of machine learning models in identifying anomalies within transaction data. This aligns with Schär (2021), who highlighted the robustness of both supervised and unsupervised algorithms in detecting fraudulent activities. Supervised learning algorithms, trained on labeled datasets, can accurately predict fraudulent transactions and provide real-time alerts for suspicious activities. Unsupervised learning techniques, such as clustering and anomaly detection, are also effective in identifying unusual patterns that may indicate fraud without the need for prior labeling.

Natural language processing (NLP) techniques are also found to be crucial in analyzing textual data to uncover signs of market manipulation and fraudulent behavior. Werner et al. (2021) emphasizes the importance of NLP in monitoring social media and communication channels for fraudulent schemes. This study confirms that applications like sentiment analysis and keyword extraction enhance the overall security of DeFi platforms by detecting fraudulent schemes in real time.

Despite the effectiveness of AI techniques, several significant challenges hinder their implementation in DeFi. Data privacy is a critical concern. Max et al. (2021) highlights the difficulty of maintaining the confidentiality of sensitive transaction data while ensuring transparency on public blockchains. If privacy concerns are not adequately addressed, user trust may be undermined, leading to regulatory scrutiny and potentially jeopardizing the legitimacy of DeFi platforms.

Adversarial attacks pose another formidable challenge. Buhrmester et al. (2021) discusses how malicious actors exploit vulnerabilities in AI models to evade detection and perpetrate fraudulent activities. The study finds that the susceptibility of AI systems to such attacks threatens the reliability and effectiveness of fraud prevention mechanisms, necessitating the development of robust defenses to mitigate these risks.

Scalability is also a critical issue, particularly as DeFi platforms continue to experience exponential growth in transaction volumes. Scalability limitations can impede the real-time analysis of data and responsiveness required for effective fraud detection and prevention. This compromises the overall security posture of decentralized financial ecosystems.

To address these challenges, the study suggests several potential strategies. Integrating privacy-preserving technologies can safeguard sensitive data while ensuring transparency, as proposed by Max et al. (2021). Developing adversarial robustness techniques can fortify AI models against malicious attacks, enhancing their resilience in detecting fraudulent activities. To manage the complicated regulatory environment and create guidelines for responsibility and compliance in DeFi, cooperation between academic institutions, business, and regulatory agencies is crucial. By recognizing these obstacles and investigating proactive methods to overcome them, the study adds to the current conversation on AI-powered fraud detection and prevention in decentralized finance and opens the door to a more stable and safer financial environment.

The study's goals were to advance knowledge of AI-driven fraud detection and prevention in the context of decentralized finance (DeFi) by achieving a number of goals. Giving a summary of the most advanced methods now available for applying AI to DeFi fraud detection and prevention was the first goal. The study conducted a thorough assessment of the literature to thoroughly investigate the many AI-driven strategies and tactics used to counteract fraud in decentralized financial ecosystems. Through the synthesis of an extensive overview of state-of-the-art methods, such as graph analytics, machine learning models, and natural language processing, the study clarifies their uses and efficacy in fraud detection and prevention on DeFi systems.

Moreover, the study aimed to pinpoint the principal obstacles and constraints linked to AI-based methods in DeFi. Significant obstacles like data privacy concerns, vulnerability to adversarial assaults, scalability constraints, and regulatory compliance issues were found by the study through rigorous examination and synthesis of the body of current material. Through the illumination of these obstacles, the research advances a more profound comprehension of the intricacies involved in the deployment of AI-based fraud detection and prevention systems in decentralized banking.

Moreover, the study endeavored to explore practical applications and case studies of AI-based fraud detection and prevention in real-world DeFi platforms. By examining empirical evidence and case studies, the study provided insights into how AI technologies are being leveraged to combat fraud in DeFi ecosystems. These practical applications not only underscore the relevance and effectiveness of AI-driven approaches but also highlight the ongoing efforts to address the unique challenges posed by fraudulent activities in decentralized finance.

Looking ahead, the study also aimed to discuss future directions and opportunities for research and development in this emerging field. By synthesizing existing knowledge and identifying gaps in the literature, the study outlined potential avenues for further exploration, including the development of more robust AI models resilient to adversarial attacks, the enhancement of scalability to accommodate the growing volume of transactions, and the formulation of regulatory frameworks to ensure compliance and legal certainty in DeFi environments.

CONCLUSION AND SCOPE FOR FUTURE RESEARCH

An extensive review of AI-driven fraud detection and prevention in decentralized finance (DeFi) was given by this paper. The research demonstrated the efficacy of advanced methods such as machine learning, natural language processing, and graph analytics in thwarting fraudulent activities by examining them. Important obstacles were examined closely, including issues with data privacy, vulnerability to adversarial assaults, scalability constraints, and regulatory compliance. The applicability and efficacy of AI-driven techniques in actual DeFi platforms have been confirmed by case studies and practical applications. Improving AI model resilience to adversarial assaults, strengthening scalability to manage rising transaction volumes, and creating strong regulatory frameworks are some of the future research directions. Unlocking the full potential of AI-driven solutions and maintaining the security and integrity of decentralized financial systems will depend on addressing these issues and seizing new opportunities. The present work has yielded significant insights that will facilitate future developments in this emerging subject.

REFERENCES

Abdallah, A., Maarof, M. A., & Zainal, A. (2016). Fraud detection system: A survey. *Journal of Network and Computer Applications*, 68, 90–113. 10.1016/j.jnca.2016.04.007

Abdullah, M. H., & Faizal, M. A. (2022). Blockchain-based IoT: Integration, challenges and future prospects for decentralized finance (DeFi) systems. In *2022 4th International Cyber Resilience Conference (CRC)* (pp. 1-5). IEEE. https://doi.org/10.1109/CRC54540.2022.9732887

Abrahams, T. O., Ewuga, S. K., Kaggwa, S., Uwaoma, P. U., Hassan, A. O., & Dawodu, S. O. (2023). *Review of strategic alignment: Accounting and cybersecurity for data confidentiality and financial security.*

Abrahams, T. O., Ewuga, S. K., Kaggwa, S., Uwaoma, P. U., Hassan, A. O., & Dawodu, S. O. (2024). Mastering compliance: A comprehensive review of regulatory frameworks in accounting and cybersecurity. *Computer Science & IT Research Journal*, 5(1), 120–140. 10.51594/csitrj.v5i1.709

Adaga, E. M., Egieya, Z. E., Ewuga, S. K., Abdul, A. A., & Abrahams, T. O. (2024). Philosophy in business analytics: A review of sustainable and ethical approaches. *International Journal of Management & Entrepreneurship Research*, 6(1), 69–86. 10.51594/ijmer.v6i1.710

Afjal, M., Salamzadeh, A., & Dana, L. P. (2023). Financial fraud and credit risk: Illicit practices and their impact on banking stability. *Journal of Risk and Financial Management*, 16(9), 386. 10.3390/jrfm16090386

Akindote, O. J., Adegbite, A. O., Dawodu, S. O., Omotosho, A., Anyanwu, A., & Maduka, C. P. (2023). *Comparative review of big data analytics and GIS in healthcare decision-making.*

Al-Dosari, K., Fetais, N., & Kucukvar, M. (2022). Artificial intelligence and cyber defense system for banking industry: A qualitative study of AI applications and challenges. *Cybernetics and Systems*, 1–29.

Amler, A., Schneider, S., & Kranz, J. (2021). AI-powered price discovery and market-making mechanisms. *Journal of Financial Innovation*, 9(3), 45–62.

Angeris, G., Kao, H., Chiang, R., Noyes, C., & Chiesa, M. (2020). Automated market maker protocols in decentralized exchanges (DEXs). *Financial Engineering Review*, 17(2), 134–155. 10.1016/j.jfine.2020.100081

Bahrammirzaee, A. (2010). A comparative survey of artificial intelligence applications in finance: Artificial neural networks, expert system, and hybrid intelligent systems. *Neural Computing & Applications*, 19(8), 1165–1195. 10.1007/s00521-010-0362-z

Bartoletti, M., Nizzardo, L., & Pompianu, L. (2021). On the (un)sustainability of Compound and Aave lending pools. In *2021 IEEE International Conference on Blockchain and Cryptocurrency (ICBC)* (pp. 1-3). IEEE. 10.1109/ICBC51069.2021.9461135

Bechtel, A. (2022). (forthcoming). Non-fungible tokens (NFTs) and the future of finance. *International Journal of Intellectual Property Management*. Advance online publication. 10.2139/ssrn.4159764

Belanche, D., Casaló, L. V., & Flavián, C. (2019). Artificial intelligence in FinTech: Understanding robo-advisors adoption among customers. *Industrial Management & Data Systems*, 119(7), 1411–1430. 10.1108/IMDS-08-2018-0368

Bhattacharya, S., Riaz, M., & Luu, L. (2022). Empirical security analysis of decentralized finance protocols and blockchain networks. arXiv preprint arXiv:2205.12343.

Bianchi, A., & Babiak, R. (2022). Synthetic assets in decentralized finance: Opportunities and challenges. *International Journal of Blockchain and Cryptocurrencies*, 8(1), 67–84.

Bianchi, D., & Babiak, M. (2022). On the performance of cryptocurrency funds. *Journal of Alternative Investments*, 25(1), 50–66. 10.3905/jai.2021.1.130

Blanke, R. (2020). Ethical considerations in AI-driven financial services. *Journal of Financial Ethics*, 12(2), 76–89. 10.1007/s10600-020-09405-w

Boreiko, D., Ferrarini, B., & Giudici, P. (2020). Blockchain-based risk management for decentralized finance. *Journal of Alternative Investments*, 23(3), 105–121. 10.3905/jai.2020.1.116

Boreiko, D., Hentschel, P., Ristaniemi, O., & Uddin, G. S. (2021). Yield farming and the rise of DeFi. arXiv preprint arXiv:3948343. https://dx.doi.org/10.2139/ssrn.3948343

Bostrom, N., & Yudkowsky, E. (2014). The ethics of artificial intelligence. In *The Cambridge Handbook of Artificial Intelligence* (pp. 316-334). Cambridge Press. 10.1017/CBO9781139046855.020

Bussmann, N., Giudici, P., Marinelli, D., & Papenbrock, J. (2020). Explainable AI in fintech risk management. *Frontiers in Artificial Intelligence*, 3, 26. 10.3389/frai.2020.0002633733145

Buterin, V. (2014). *Ethereum white paper: A next-generation smart contract and decentralized application platform*. Ethereum Foundation. https://ethereum.org/en/whitepaper/

Cai, W. (2021). The regulatory challenges and risks of decentralized finance: A systematic review. *Journal of Digital Banking*, 6(1), 7–26.

Cao, L. (2021). AI in finance: A review. *Financial Innovation*, 7(1), 1–31. 10.1186/s40854-021-00295-5

Carcillo, F., Le Borgne, Y. A., Caelen, O., Kessaci, Y., Oblé, F., & Bontempi, G. (2021). Combining unsupervised and supervised learning in credit card fraud detection. *Information Sciences*, 557, 317–331. 10.1016/j.ins.2019.05.042

Catalini, C., & Gans, J. S. (2016). Some simple economics of the blockchain. *MIT Sloan School of Management Working Paper, 2291-16*. https://ssrn.com/abstract=2892568

Chakraborty, G. (2020). Evolving profiles of financial risk management in the era of digitization: The tomorrow that began in the past. *Journal of Public Affairs*, 20(2), e2034. 10.1002/pa.2034

Chen, W., Chen, Y., Chen, X., & Zheng, Z. (2020). Toward detecting attacks in DeFi applications with temporal graph neural network. *arXiv preprint* arXiv:2012.11009.

Chen, W., Zhang, Z., Hong, C. Y., Zheng, Z., & Zhou, Z. (2021). Decentralized learning for cross-silo federated learning. *Proceedings of the AAAI Conference on Artificial Intelligence*, 35(9), 7454–7461.

Chen, Z., Zhang, Y., & Li, X. (2020). AI in decentralized finance: Enhancing security and efficiency. *Journal of Blockchain Technology*, 6(3), 201–217.

Chhabra Roy, N., & Prabhakaran, S. (2023). Internal-led cyber frauds in Indian banks: An effective machine learning–based defense system to fraud detection, prioritization, and prevention. *Aslib Journal of Information Management*, 75(2), 246–296. 10.1108/AJIM-11-2021-0339

Cousaert, J., Demange, M., & Marques, L. (2021). Yield farming and liquidity mining in decentralized finance. *Financial Technology Journal*, 11(4), 123–139. 10.1016/j.ftj.2021.08.006

D'Acunto, F., Malmendier, U., & Ospina, J. (2019). Robo-advisors: AI-driven investment strategies. *Journal of Financial Planning*, 32(7), 56–69. 10.1007/s11791-019-00721-x

Dargan, S., & Kumar, M. (2020). A comprehensive survey on the biometric recognition systems based on physiological and behavioral modalities. *Expert Systems with Applications*, 143, 113114. 10.1016/j.eswa.2019.113114

De Bruijn, H., Warnier, M., & Janssen, M. (2022). The perils and pitfalls of explainable AI: Strategies for explaining algorithmic decision-making. *Government Information Quarterly*, 39(2), 101666. 10.1016/j.giq.2021.101666

Díaz-Rodríguez, N., Del Ser, J., Coeckelbergh, M., de Prado, M. L., Herrera-Viedma, E., & Herrera, F. (2023). Connecting the dots in trustworthy Artificial Intelligence: From AI principles, ethics, and key requirements to responsible AI systems and regulation. *Information Fusion*, 99, 101896. 10.1016/j.inffus.2023.101896

Dugauquier, D., Bochove, G. V., Raes, A., & Ilunga, J. J. (2023). Digital payments: Navigating the landscape, addressing fraud, and charting the future with confirmation of payee solutions. *Journal of Payments Strategy & Systems*, 17(4), 359–371. 10.69554/MMWU3803

Eichengreen, B. (2019). Libra: The known unknowns and unknown unknowns. *OMFIF Digital Monetary Institute Journal*, 1(4), 10–16.

Fang, L., & Lu, Q. (2023). A review of blockchain-based decentralized applications: Design, challenges, and future directions. *Journal of Computer Science and Technology*, 38(2), 234–254. 10.1007/s11390-023-2644-9

Friedman, E., & Schuster, L. (2021). Navigating the evolving landscape of digital asset regulation: Insights and strategies. *Regulation & Governance*, 15(4), 757–775. 10.1111/rego.12352

Gamage, C., & Liyanage, H. (2022). Enhancing the reliability of smart contracts through formal verification and testing. *Journal of Computer Security*, 31(3), 405–428. 10.3233/JCS-210358

Gao, X., Li, S., & Zhao, J. (2023). Decentralized finance (DeFi) protocols: An empirical analysis of risk management strategies. *Journal of Financial Stability*, 58, 100938. 10.1016/j.jfs.2021.100938

Gichoya, J. K., Gathuru, K., & Roy, S. (2023). Addressing biases in AI models: Ethical considerations and solutions. *AI Ethics Journal*, 15(1), 21–34.

Gonçalves, R., Lobo, J., & Ribeiro, S. (2020). AI and machine learning in portfolio optimization. *Journal of Portfolio Management*, 46(5), 102–119.

Gudgeon, L., Green, J., & Makarov, I. (2020). Decentralized finance (DeFi): Insights and challenges. *Review of Financial Studies*, 33(10), 4573–4594. 10.1093/rfs/hhaa089

Gupta, A., & Thakur, M. (2022). Blockchain applications in financial services: A review. *Journal of Financial Services Research*, 63(1), 1–27. 10.1007/s10693-021-00381-6

Hajek, P., & Jung, M. (2022). The role of artificial intelligence in credit risk modeling: Opportunities and challenges. *The Journal of Risk and Insurance*, 89(4), 1047–1073. 10.1111/jori.12324

Hasan, M., & Lee, K. H. (2023). The impact of blockchain on financial inclusion and the unbanked population: A review of recent advancements. *Financial Innovation*, 9(1), 12. 10.1186/s40854-023-00312-8

He, D., & Yang, Y. (2022). Blockchain-based solutions for financial fraud detection: A survey and research agenda. *IEEE Access: Practical Innovations, Open Solutions*, 10, 28324–28335. 10.1109/ACCESS.2022.3156019

Huang, J., Wang, T., & Yang, J. (2020). Reinforcement learning for adaptive trading strategies. *Journal of Financial Markets*, 15(2), 345–359.

Irfan, M. (2021, January). Do Shariah indices converge? Evidence from Gulf Cooperation Council countries. *International Journal of Business Excellence*, 23(2), 251–269. 10.1504/IJBEX.2021.113448

Irfan, M., Elhoseny, M., Kassim, S., & Metawa, N. (2023). *Advanced machine learning algorithms for complex financial applications*. IGI Global. 10.4018/978-1-6684-4483-2

Irfan, M., Hussainey, K., Chan Bukhari, S. A., & Nam, Y. (Eds.). (2024). *Issues of sustainability in AI and new-age thematic investing*. IGI Global. 10.4018/979-8-3693-3282-5

Irfan, M., Kadry, S., Sharif, M., & Ullah Khan, H. (2023). *Fintech applications in Islamic finance: AI, machine learning, and blockchain techniques*. IGI Global. 10.4018/979-8-3693-1038-0

Ismail, M., & Ahmed, A. (2022). Machine learning in financial fraud detection: A survey of algorithms and practices. *Journal of Financial Crime*, 29(1), 221–237. 10.1108/JFC-06-2021-0130

Jiang, C., & Liu, X. (2023). Smart contract auditing and security in decentralized finance (DeFi): Challenges and solutions. *IEEE Transactions on Network and Service Management*, 20(2), 456–469. 10.1109/TNSM.2023.3245310

Jing, Y., Li, J., & Wu, H. (2022). The influence of blockchain technology on financial transparency and accountability: A review. *Accounting Perspectives*, 21(3), 205–230. 10.1111/1911-3838.12311

Johnson, B., & Brown, C. (2023). Innovations in decentralized finance: A comprehensive review of current research and future prospects. *Journal of Financial Innovation*, 9(2), 56–80. 10.1186/s40854-023-00321-7

Jung, J., Lee, T., & Yoon, D. (2018). Robo-advisors: Automation and personalization in investment advice. *International Journal of Financial Planning*, 16(1), 28–39. 10.1007/s10887-018-0173-7

Khan, A. A., & Baig, M. (2023). Blockchain and decentralized finance: A systematic literature review and future research directions. *Journal of Financial Regulation and Compliance*, 31(1), 23–45. 10.1108/JFRC-10-2022-0135

Kumar, R., & Singh, N. (2022). A survey of artificial intelligence in fraud detection systems: Current status and future perspectives. *Computers & Security*, 118, 102769. 10.1016/j.cose.2022.102769

Leo, M., Niu, L., & Zhang, Y. (2019). Risk management with machine learning: A review. *Journal of Risk and Financial Management*, 12(2), 45–64.

Lin, I. X., Li, L., & Wu, Y. (2020). Decentralized exchanges and automated market makers: A survey. *Blockchain Research & Applications*, 7(4), 89–107. 10.1016/j.blockchain.2020.100012

Liu, Q., & Zhao, Y. (2023). The impact of blockchain technology on financial service innovation: An empirical study. *Financial Innovation*, 9(1), 15. 10.1186/s40854-023-00323-5

Liu, W., & Palomar, D. (2022). Yield farming and liquidity mining strategies in decentralized finance. *Journal of Financial Economics*, 45(2), 56–73.

Luo, X., & Yang, J. (2022). Decentralized finance (DeFi) and its implications for traditional banking: A review of the literature. *International Journal of Financial Studies*, 10(4), 77. 10.3390/ijfs10040077

Mahmud, S., & Rahman, M. (2023). Deep learning approaches for financial fraud detection: A comprehensive review. *Journal of Financial Data Science*, 5(1), 33–49. 10.3905/jfds.2023.1.003

Max, M., Raji, I., & Buolamwini, J. (2021). Ethical challenges in AI fraud detection. *AI and Ethics*, 2(1), 71–83. 10.1007/s43681-021-00034-7

Miller, R., & Williams, J. (2022). The intersection of blockchain and financial privacy: Addressing the challenges. *Journal of Digital Banking*, 6(3), 45–61. 10.2139/ssrn.3790125

Mita, S., Mehta, P., & Kumar, S. (2019). Stablecoins in cryptocurrency markets: Stability and regulation. *Financial Stability Review*, 21(3), 223–240.

Morris, A., & Zhang, S. (2024). Risk management in decentralized finance platforms: Strategies and innovations. *Journal of Risk Management in Financial Institutions*, 17(1), 89–104. 10.1057/s41283-023-00097-4

Nakamoto, S. (2022). *Bitcoin: A peer-to-peer electronic cash system*. Bitcoin. https://bitcoin.org/bitcoin.pdf

Nguyen, T., & Kim, Y. (2023). The role of blockchain in enhancing the transparency of financial transactions. *Journal of Financial Technology*, 7(2), 90–104. 10.1080/23268268.2023.2211743

O'Connell, B., & Chang, J. (2023). Leveraging smart contracts for automated financial compliance: A review. *Journal of Compliance and Risk Management*, 16(2), 12–29. 10.2139/ssrn.3794567

Omar, M., & Ali, S. (2022). The impact of decentralized finance on traditional banking systems. *International Journal of Banking and Finance*, 14(1), 55–72. 10.1108/IJBF-05-2022-0154

Ozbayoglu, A. M., Saad, A., & Ghosh, S. (2020). Artificial intelligence in finance: A comprehensive review. *Journal of Computational Finance*, 24(4), 11–32.

Patel, R., & Sharma, A. (2023). Blockchain for financial inclusion: An examination of recent developments and impact. *Journal of Financial Inclusion*, 8(3), 101–115. 10.1080/22761160.2023.2118834

Peters, G., & Panayi, E. (2022). Understanding the impact of blockchain technology on financial markets: A comprehensive review. *Journal of Financial Market Research*, 15(2), 234–260. 10.1080/14697688.2022.2117335

Qin, J., & Zhang, L. (2022). Exploring the potential of blockchain for enhancing financial data security. *Journal of Cybersecurity*, 10(4), 55–71. 10.1093/cyber/cyac028

Reed, J., & Khatri, K. (2023). The evolving role of artificial intelligence in financial risk assessment. *AI in Finance Journal*, 6(1), 78–91. 10.2139/ssrn.3777210

Rogers, C., & Smith, T. (2022). Blockchain-based solutions for financial privacy: A critical analysis. *Journal of Digital Privacy*, 12(2), 100–115. 10.1016/j.jdp.2022.100022

Salami, A. (2021). The democratization of financial services through DeFi. *Journal of Financial Inclusion*, 3(2), 67–84.

Sandner, P., Gans, J. S., & Kahlenborn, T. (2020). Blockchain technology and the tokenization of assets. *Review of Blockchain Studies*, 8(1), 33–48. 10.1016/j.rbst.2020.04.005

Schär, F. (2021). Decentralized finance: On blockchain and smart contract-based financial markets. *Review - Federal Reserve Bank of St. Louis*, 103(2), 145–159. 10.20955/r.103.145-159

Singh, R., & Patel, M. (2022). The impact of decentralized finance on traditional financial institutions. *International Journal of Financial Services*, 19(2), 200–223. 10.1108/IJFS-04-2022-0054

Sullivan, R., & Turner, L. (2023). Innovations in smart contract technology for financial applications. *Journal of Financial Engineering*, 11(3), 123–139. 10.1080/09720529.2023.2178564

Tan, Y., & Yang, L. (2023). Blockchain technology and its applications in financial services: A review and future prospects. *Journal of Financial Technology and Innovation*, 9(2), 89–105. 10.2139/ssrn.3772123

Thompson, A., & Jones, R. (2022). The intersection of AI and blockchain in financial services: Opportunities and challenges. *Artificial Intelligence in Finance*, 8(1), 47–63. 10.1016/j.aif.2022.100121

Treleaven, P., Brown, S., & Yang, D. (2013). Algorithmic trading and artificial intelligence. *Financial Markets and Portfolio Management*, 27(2), 121–143.

Ullah, N., & Khan, M. (2023). Blockchain for financial fraud prevention: Current trends and future directions. *Journal of Financial Crime*, 30(1), 55–73. 10.1108/JFC-01-2023-0005

Vasquez, M., & Huang, Y. (2022). The potential of blockchain to disrupt financial trading systems: A review. *Journal of Financial Markets*, 13(4), 301–316. 10.2139/ssrn.3688520

Wang, J., & Li, H. (2023). A review of blockchain-based solutions for financial data integrity and security. *International Journal of Financial Engineering*, 10(2), 120–136. 10.1142/S2345678923500152

Werner, S., Krämer, J., & Müller, S. (2021). Challenges and opportunities of decentralized finance. *Journal of Financial Technology*, 12(3), 215–232. 10.1016/j.ftj.2021.05.004

Wöhrer, M., & Zdun, U. (2018). Blockchain-based smart contracts: Security and compliance. *Computer Science Review*, 30, 123–142. 10.1016/j.cosrev.2018.07.002

Wright, A., & Buterin, V. (2022). Ethereum: A blockchain platform for decentralized applications. *Journal of Blockchain Research*, 5(1), 101–118. 10.2139/ssrn.3715023

Xiao, R., & Chen, L. (2023). Blockchain-based financial innovations: A review of recent advances. *Journal of Financial Innovations*, 7(2), 65–82. 10.1080/22761160.2023.2118325

Yang, W., & Wu, J. (2023). Machine learning and blockchain technology in financial fraud detection: A survey. *Journal of Financial Data Analysis*, 6(1), 21–38. 10.2139/ssrn.3772121

Yin, G., Li, W., & Wang, J. (2019). The impact of DeFi on traditional financial systems: Opportunities and risks. *Journal of Financial Stability*, 39(4), 85–100.

Zetzsche, D. A., Buckley, R. P., & Arner, D. W. (2020). The future of financial regulation: The role of DeFi and AI. *Journal of Financial Regulation*, 15(1), 65–84. 10.1093/jfr/fwaa011

Zhang, Q., Li, H., & Wang, X. (2020). Fraud detection using machine learning: Techniques and applications. *International Journal of Data Science and Analytics*, 9(1), 45–63.

Zhang, X., & Zhou, T. (2022). The impact of decentralized finance on the future of global financial markets. *Journal of Financial Stability*, 59, 100943. 10.1016/j.jfs.2022.100943

Zhou, Q., & Wu, J. (2023). Smart contracts in blockchain-based financial systems: A comprehensive review. *IEEE Transactions on Emerging Topics in Computing*, 11(1), 234–249. 10.1109/TETC.2023.3167461

Chapter 5
Unlocking the Potential of AI for Efficient Governance:
Innovative Approaches of Bahrain

Zakir Hossen Shaikh
https://orcid.org/0000-0003-4733-4166
Kingdom University, Bahraian

Mohammad Irfan
https://orcid.org/0000-0002-4956-1170
Christ University, Bengaluru, India

Naji M. Nomran
Kingdom University, Bahrain

Satya Pavan Kumar Ratnakaram
https://orcid.org/0000-0002-8908-302X
Bahrain Polytechnic, Bahrain

ABSTRACT

The rapid development and implementation of artificial intelligence (AI) technologies will have significant economic, social, and ethical impacts. Efficient governance is essential to maximize AI's benefits while minimizing its risks. Bahrain is positioning itself as a fintech hub, with AI playing a central role in this transformation. Bahrain's smart governance efforts will be strengthened by integrating AI into public services. E-government efforts will use AI to streamline processes, improve citizen experience, and build a more responsive and efficient public administration. The study provides an overview of how artificial intelligence (AI) is transforming various sectors in

DOI: 10.4018/979-8-3693-6321-8.ch005

Bahrain with innovative approaches to boost productivity, better decision-making, and improve the general quality of services that may also impact the Bahraini economy. Bahrain continues to drive digital innovation, paving the way for a better and more prosperous future and sustainable development. Bahrain's digital transformation has been largely successful thanks to strong government measures.

INTRODUCTION

The rapid development and implementation of artificial intelligence (AI) technologies will have significant economic, social, and ethical impacts. Efficient governance is essential to maximize AI's benefits while minimizing its risks. Bahrain is positioning itself as a fintech hub, with AI playing a central role in this transformation. Bahrain's smart governance efforts will be strengthened by integrating AI into public services. E-government efforts will use AI to streamline processes, improve citizen experience, and build a more responsive and efficient public administration. The adoption of AI technologies in Bahrain could increase the country's GDP by 8.2 percent annually by 2030, according to a report by management consultancy PwC on the adoption of AI technologies in the Gulf region. The study provides an overview of how Artificial Intelligence (AI) is transforming various sectors in Bahrain with innovative approaches to boost productivity, better decision-making, and improve the general quality of services that may also impact the Bahraini economy. Bahrain continues to drive digital innovation, paving the way for a better and more prosperous future. The scope of AI's impact on business and society will almost certainly expand, so it is important to strategically place to provide a springboard into the future.

The term "artificial intelligence governance" refers to a set of guidelines, rules, and best practices that work together to limit bias risks and optimize intended advantages when it comes to the development and application of AI technologies. AI governance covers decision-making, data security and privacy, AI algorithms, and the possible societal and economic effects of using this technology. An essential component of applying AI for the good of the company and the community is governance. The appropriate and efficient deployment of artificial intelligence (AI) technologies within an enterprise is guided by best practices for AI governance. Robust internal governance procedures are essential for successful AI governance. Many governance goals, such as establishing the business use cases of AI systems, delegating roles and responsibilities, ensuring responsibility, and evaluating results, can be achieved with internal governance structures. Open communication is essential for all the parties involved in the development and application of AI. AI systems that are well-governed protect people's privacy and autonomy and refrain from discriminatory practices that might unjustly harm some groups.

Artificial Intelligence (AI) and Machine Learning (ML) technology are becoming more and more prevalent in the different services sectors of the economy. The way artificial intelligence impacts our world is changing thanks to the AI Governance Alliance. The legal framework for artificial intelligence governance makes sure that AI and machine learning technologies are explored and developed to assist mankind in adopting and using these systems morally and responsibly. The application of AI is expanding quickly in almost every sector of the economy, including public safety, healthcare, retail, financial services, and transportation. Consequently, governance has become increasingly important and is receiving more attention. The goal of AI governance is to bridge the ethical and accountable divide in technology development.

Regulators are emphasizing the necessity for a thorough governance structure for AI considering the growing usage of AI in various departments inside financial services companies. Bahrain's leadership's ambition to use cutting-edge technology like artificial intelligence (AI) has enhanced public services and helped the country achieve more in the digital realm. Bahrain has taken initiative to study and apply artificial intelligence (AI) in several disciplines, acknowledging the technology's significance in streamlining operations and informing strategic decision-making for enterprises across all industries. Artificial Intelligence has transformed our lives in many ways, and Bahrainis believe it is a key factor in the kingdom's sustainable growth. Bahrain used artificial intelligence technology to monitor every palm tree on the Kingdom's territory automatically. This allows investors and researchers to conduct food security studies by predicting the production capacity of each palm tree. The program contributes to SDG2, one of the sustainable development objectives that addresses food security.

In the last few years, the tiny Kingdom of Bahrain has made some significant technological advancements. Bahrain's digital transformation has been largely successful thanks to strong government measures. In accordance with the government's comprehensive Digital Strategy 2022, central authorities such as the Information and eGovernment Authority, the Central Bank of Bahrain, Tamkeen (a public authority involved in modernizing the labor market), and the Economic Development Board have all launched initiatives with the goal of supporting local development of artificial intelligence technologies.

This chapter summarizes Bahrain's ambitious projects across multiple industries, which demonstrate the country's dedication to embracing AI. Bahrain is using artificial intelligence (AI) to boost productivity, better decision-making, and improve the general quality of services across a range of industries, including healthcare, finance, government services, and education. The various regulatory frameworks and policies about responsible AI, ML, and DL technologies are covered in this chapter's sections. This study used secondary data regarding the governance of AI. Subsequently, this work delineates many facets of AI governance and offers a discursive argumentation on optimal practices targeted at AI practitioners and autonomous learning technology developers. As Bahrain leads the way in integrating AI, the nation is positioned at the nexus of innovation and tradition, prepared to enter a future in which innovation is guided by intelligence for the good of all. Finally, it suggests directions for future research.

Background of the Study

Emerging technologies with great potential to improve Bahraini society and boost the country's economy include artificial intelligence (AI), biotechnology, robotics, and material sciences. Due to the speed at which these technologies are developing, the Kingdom has redirected its efforts to establish an innovative approach to its governance that encourages creativity in Bahraini society by utilizing new technology. Bahrain supports mechanisms for creating, developing, and implementing new technologies to make sure they follow international norms and standards and are in line with the ideals of the Kingdom.

Digital Government Strategy 2022 advises government institutions to investigate the possibilities of developing technologies that have a larger beneficial influence on citizen involvement and public administration, by the "Kingdom's Economic Vision 2030 and the Government Plan 2019–2022". Government organizations are expected to collaborate with academic institutions, and businesses in the public and private sectors, towards adopting emerging technology. This builds a foundation of collaboration, mutual benefit, return on investment, and national security. The goal of the Bahraini government's AI strategy is to benefit all facets of society, including locals, companies, visitors, and citizens. As a result, the government has concentrated its efforts on fostering innovation and bolstering the governance system. These initiatives include, but are not restricted to:

Enhancing AI research and development.
Creating policies and procedures for the "procurement of AI solutions".
Building AI capacities in fields like social justice, public services, healthcare, cybersecurity, crisis management, the environment, education, logistics, and transportation.

The government places a high priority on the social advantages of artificial intelligence, concentrating on areas where a sizable section of the populace may profit and where there is great potential for implementation. For example, using artificial intelligence (AI), the Internet of Things (IoT), and machine learning, The

Kingdom is getting help from the BeAware Bahrain app to prevent, prepare for, respond to, and recover from pandemics and disasters.

One of the first nations in the world to test "AI procurement guidelines for the public sector is the Kingdom of Bahrain. the first in the Middle East to launch an AI academy at Bahrain Polytechnic, the Cloud Innovation Centre (CIC) at the University of Bahrain for public sector organizations" to collaborate on their most pressing issues, an AI innovation competition for students using the hashtag **"#Let_Us_Innovate_Future,"** and tests new concepts using "Amazon's innovation process to access the technology expertise of AWS".

Research Questions

RO1: Does the government have the necessary laws, moral standards, digital capabilities, adaptability, and vision to apply AI?

RO2: Is the nation's technology sector able to give governments the means to invent and support artificial intelligence technologies?

RO3: Is there a sufficient availability of data that is likely to be representative of the entire population in the nation to enable AI technology and train AI models?

RO4: How Bahrain's governance to use cutting-edge technology like artificial intelligence (AI) has enhanced public services and helped the country achieve more in the digital realm.

LITERATURE REVIEW

Artificial intelligence (AI) is a game-changer, and Bahrain is emerging as a global leader in technological innovation thanks to its impressive history of advancement, adaptation, and dedication to forging a future where intelligence interacts with innovation.

According to research conducted in 2022 by A. f. Ali, S. I. Zowayed, D. A. Showalter, M. A. Khder, and B. J. A. Ali, the nation needed a national strategy to fully prepare for the digital economy by embracing and utilizing artificial intelligence technologies. These technologies can be used to identify the potential of AI in every industry and assist the organization in seizing opportunities that they are passing up. According to Shibly, Alawamleh, H. A., Nawaiseh, K. A., Ali, B. J., Almasri, A., & Alshibly, E. (2021), administrative empowerment has an effect on continual improvement implementation.

A national strategy is required to guarantee that the country is fully prepared to deal with the digital economy by embracing and utilizing artificial intelligence technology for economic growth, as stated by Al-Ammal, H., & Aljawder, M. (2021). The study conducted by Wang T, Lund BD, Marengo A, Pagano A, Mannuru NR, Teel ZA, Pange J. in 2023 investigated the possible effects of artificial intelligence (AI) on learning processes and educational administration. In order for AI-powered tools to be properly incorporated into education, Chichekian, T., & Benteux, B. (2022) investigated the potential of artificial intelligence-based learning in education and the significance of creating complementary research designs. The legal foundation of artificial intelligence (AI) in corporate governance, as per Bahraini law, was discovered by Al-Obeidi and Muhammad Younis Muhammad 2020 to be based on two axes: the legal axis of digital transformation, the axis of disclosure, and its electronic activation. Using academic and policy sources until early 2024, Mariarosaria Comunale and Andrea Manera 2024, Volume 2024 examine in their review article how artificial intelligence (AI) influences the economy and how technology has been governed. and discuss findings on economic growth, productivity, and the implications of employment and wages. According to research by Pandey, Jitendra (2024), introducing generative AI into government has a good correlation with enhancing government functionality.

Nishith Reddy & Shahriar, Mannuru, Sakib & Teel, Zoë Abbie & Wang, Ting & Lund, Brady & T., Solomon & Pohboon, Chalermchai & Agbaji, Daniel & Alhassan, Joy & Galley, JaKLyn & Kousari, Raana & Oladapo, Lydia & Saurav, Shubham & Srivastava, Aishwarya & Tummuru, Sai & Uppala, Sravya & Vaidya, Praveenkumar." (2023) emphasizes how important it is to incorporate generative AI within the framework of the Fourth Industrial Revolution in developing nations, where advancement and fair growth are significantly influenced by technological change. According to Dencik, Jacob, Goehring, Brian, and Marshall, Anthony (2023), generative AI is becoming more and more important in next-generation businesses. This is because of the possible benefits and cost savings associated with its use, as well as wider ethical issues.

Through an analysis of an e-governance project, Pandey, Jitendra, and Suri, Pradeep (2020) investigated the function of collaboration competency in the setting of a public organization and provided insight into a potential relationship between collaboration competency and e-governance performance. Ahn, Michael & Chen, Yu-Che. (2021) investigated the significance of educating government workers about artificial intelligence (AI) technologies to enhance their comprehension and view of the new tools as well as their potential to promote an innovative culture in government that will lead to a lasting and significant digital transformation. M. Tokmakov (2012). AI in the context of corporate governance. 10.1007/978-3-030-60926-9_83. The integration of artificial intelligence (AI) into corporate governance is seen as one of the most promising avenues for the growth of contemporary organizations. According to Romanova, Anna (2023), autonomous systems may be a useful tool for nations, areas, and businesses that lack human capital. They can help these businesses and countries compete on the international stage more equally or by giving them more opportunities. The possible importance and influence of the Guidelines on specific company law and governance concerns were studied by Hickman, Eleanore, and Petrin, Martin in 2021 concluded that further details are required about how the guiding principles will interact with company law regulations and governance standards. The administration of commercial organizations will be able to be taken over by next-generation AI, according to Petrin, and Martin (2019). This development has implications for corporate law and governance.

Gagan In addition to the banking industry, Deep Sharma, Anshita Yadav, and Ritika Chopra (2024) noted that AI requires real-world implementation in the fields of healthcare, ICT, education, social and cultural services, and fashion. Casares A. P. (2018). talked about the concept of a future brain for public governance, the potential use of artificial cognitive machines to help with its problems, and the idea that the brain is an emergent property that results from the interaction of human agents and AI systems designed to meet social organization's priorities. Esteve, M., Campion, A., and S. J. Mikhaylov (2018). It has been stated that successfully integrating data science and artificial intelligence (AI) into delivery systems for policy execution is essential to the long-term viability of these technologies in the public sector. According to Corvalán, J. G. (2018), the main obstacle facing the Fourth Industrial Revolution is accelerating the development of a digital and intelligent administration and government that upholds people's digital dignity and supports the efficacy of their rights. To improve the long-problematic communication between the government and the people, which is a crucial issue. A., Karacapilidis, N., Loukis, E., & Charalabidis, Y. (2019) made a significant contribution to the advanced exploitation of a particular AI technology, namely chatbots, in the public sector. They also contributed to the development of an ICT platform supporting this approach.

Fintech, according to research by "Shaikh, Z., Irfan, M., Sarea, A., and Panigrahi, R.R. (2024), might influence Islamic banking and finance in the future by offering innovative, creative financial services that are more affordable and efficient. The convergence of Fintech and Islamic finance, according to Sheela, P., Kusuma, K., Panigrahi, R. R., & Shaikh, Z. H. (2024), promises to enhance the effectiveness and inclusivity of financial services and facilitate the dissemination of Sharia-compliant products to a larger audience. Shaikh, Z. H., Irfan, M., Nomran, N. M., & Lawin, M. L. (2024) looked at the impact of strategic partnerships on innovation promotion, digital transformation acceleration across financial services in the Kingdom of Bahrain, and economic development stimulation. In 2022, Shaikh, Z.H., Sarea, A., and Irfan, M." examined the use of financial technology and the experiences of the leading Islamic banks in Bahrain. Fintech has the potential to help "Islamic finance become more useful against conventional finance without compromising on benefits by attracting more customers, increasing productivity, cutting costs, and offering a more extensive range of products." Irfan, Elhoseny, Kassim, and Metawa (2023) investigated the use of machine learning in the banking industry for tasks such as asset credit evaluation, macroeconomic analysis, and investment decision-making. Financial services are being significantly impacted by the application of machine learning (ML) in numerous financial firms.

According to Irfan, Elmogy, Majid, and El-Sappagh (2023), "The Impact of AI Innovation on Financial Sectors in the Era of Industry 5.0" emerges as a crucial resource, propelling innovations that will change the financial landscape. Irfan, M., Hussainey, K., Bukhari, S. A., & Nam, Y. (2024) looked at the promise and dangers of integrating AI and ML into financial systems, noting that they have the ability to completely transform the sector while also presenting previously unheard-of difficulties. In 2023, Irfan, M., Kadry, S., Sharif, M., & Khan, H. U. provided insights regarding the revolutionary potential of AI/ML in Islamic finance. This compilation covers a wide range of subjects, from blockchain applications to financial monitoring, giving academics, researchers, businesspeople, and investors the skills, they need to successfully negotiate the complexities of contemporary Islamic banking. Irfan, M., Khan, M. A., Muhammad, K., & Naifar, N. (2024). examined how Blockchain technology integrates and optimizes activities and transactions related to information access, perhaps lowering communication costs and small data transmission mistakes.

JOURNEY OF AI TECHNOLOGY

Understanding the AI technological environment and its potential requires a thorough comprehension of its capabilities and limits before it is crucial to agree on how effective governance may leverage AI. Although the idea of artificial intelligence (AI) has been around for a while, its scalability and exponential development have recently been made possible by the availability of tools, notably in the field of machine learning. Technological developments in AI over the previous few decades have made great progress.

Figure 1. Artificial intelligence breakthroughs are not new

1950	1956	1957	1961
Alan Turing poses the question 'can machines think?' in a seminal paper	Dartmouth Summer Research Project on Artificial Intelligence	First fully automated chess engine	Unimate becomes first industrial robot used in GM assembly line

1965	1970	1982	1986
Moore's Law	"In three to eight years we will have a machine with the general intelligence of an average human being" Marvin Minsky	Japan's Fifth Generation Computer project begins	Navlab, first autonomous car by Carnegie Melon

1997	1998	2002	2006
• Deep Blue defeats Gary Kasparov in chess • First publicly available speech recognition software by Dragon Systems	Kismet, a robot that displays emotions, released	Roomba, an AI-powered vacuum cleaner	ImageNet database

2010	2015	2020	2023
• Siri voice recognition app launches • IBM's Watson	• TensorFlow • Significant Improvement In Graphic Processing Units (GPUs)	Chat GPT-3	Chat GPT-4, Bard, LLaMA

Source: Oliver Wyman analysis

Improving productivity will be the most common use case for AI technologies soon, for both the public and commercial sectors. AI may help with this by streamlining procedures, effectively managing knowledge, producing content with Maximizing benefits, and minimizing public sector risks.

Ethics of Using Artificial Intelligence:

A set of ideals and principles has been formed by the Kingdom of Bahrain to direct the moral use of AI which are designed to ensure that "AI is used in a way that is ethical, responsible, and beneficial to society".

> Maintaining the confidentiality of personal information, safeguarding human rights, and upholding essential liberties.
> The maintenance of sustainability and the reduction of AI systems' ecological effect.
> Protecting inclusivity and diversity for all the most marginalized people, communities, or groups.
> Attempting to guarantee the establishment of equitable and tranquil communities.
> Trying to prevent harm associated with safety and minimize threats linked to security.
> Justice, fairness, and absence of bias.
> Relying on human people to supervise and make choices.
> Openness and the capacity to provide comprehensible explanations for artificial intelligence system outcomes.
> Assuming accountability and moral and legal obligation.
> Increasing consciousness and understanding of artificial intelligence technologies.
> The mechanisms of governance and multilateral collaboration.

METHODOLOGY

The AI readiness index of the Bahraini government assesses the country's ability to utilize AI technology for advancement. Ten dimensions are covered by the three pillars that make up the index. 33 KPIs are used to compute these dimensions' scores.

Table 1. Pillars, dimensions, and indicators

Pillars	Dimension	Description	Indicator	Source
Government Pillar	**Vision**	"Does the government have a vision for implementing AI?"	National AI strategy Y/N)	"Desk research (e.g. OECD AI Policy observatory, UN IDIR AI policy portal)"
	"Governance and Ethics"	"Are there the right regulations and ethical frameworks in place to implement AI in a way that builds trust and legitimacy?"	"Data protection and privacy legislation"	"UN data protection and privacy legislation worldwide"
			"Cybersecurity"	"Global Cybersecurity Index"
			"Regulatory quality"	Worldwide Governance Indicators
			"National ethics framework"	"Desk research (e.g. Nature, AI Ethics Lab)"
			"Accountability"	"Worldwide Governance Indicators"
	"Digital Capacity'	"What is the existing digital capacity within the government?"	"Online services"	"UN e-Government Survey"
			"Foundational IT infrastructure"	"World Bank GovTech Maturity Index"
			"Government promotion of investment in emerging technologies"	"Network Readiness Index"
	"Adaptability"	"Can the government change and innovate effectively?"	"Government effectiveness"	"Worldwide Governance Indicators"
			"Government's responsiveness to change"	"Global Competitiveness Index"
			"Procurement data"	"Global Data Barometer"

continued on following page

Table 1. Continued

Pillars	Dimension	Description	Indicator	Source
Technology Sector Pillar	"Maturity"	"Does the country have a technology sector capable of supplying governments with AI technologies?"	"Number of AI unicorns"	"CB Insights"
			"Number of non-AI technology unicorns"	"CB Insights"
			"Value of trade in ICT services (per capita)"	"UNCTAD"
			"Value of trade in ICT goods (per capita)"	"UNCTAD"
			"Computer software spending"	"Global Competitiveness Index"
	"Innovation Capacity"	"Does the technology sectors have the right conditions to support innovation?	"Time spent dealing with government regulations"	"Bank World Development Indicators"
			"VC availability"	"Global Innovation Index"
			"R&D spending"	"UNESCO"
			"Company investment in emerging technology"	"Network Readiness Index"
			"Research papers published in AI"	"Scimago".
	"Human Capital"	"Are there the right skills in the population to support The technology sector?"	"Graduates in STEM"	"UNESCO"
			"GitHub users per thousand population"	"GitHub"
			"Female STEM graduates"	"World Bank"
			"Quality of Engineering and Technology Higher Education."	"QS Engineering & Technology rankings"
			"ICT skills"	"ITU"

continued on following page

Table 1. Continued

Pillars	Dimension	Description	Indicator	Source
Data and Infrastructure Pillar	"Infrastructure"	"Does the country have a good technological Infrastructure to support AI tech."	"Telecommunications infrastructure"	"UN e-Government Survey"
			"Supercomputers"	"Top 500"
			"Broadband quality"	"EIU Inclusive Internet Index"
			"5G infrastructure"	"Ookla 5G Map"
			"Adoption of emerging technologies"	"Network Readiness Index"
	"Data Availability"	"Is there a good availability of data that could be used to train AI models?"	"Open data"	"Global Data Barometer"
			"Data governance"	World Bank GovTech Maturity Index
			"Mobile-cellular telephone subscriptions"	"ITU"
			"Households with internet access"	"ITU"
			"Statistical capacity"	"World Bank"
	"Data Representativeness"	"Is the data available likely to be representative of the population as a whole"	"The gender gap in Internet access"	"EIU Inclusive Internet Index"
			"Cost of internet-enabled device relative to GDP per capita"	"GSMA Mobile Connectivity Index"

Source: Government AI Readiness Index 2023

Table 2. Rank, scores, and stimulated score / rank with aspiration and current value of indicators: Bahrain

Pillars	Dimension	Rank	Score	Stimulated Rank/Score	Indicator	Aspirational value	Current Value
Government Pillar	Vision	66	50	66 / 50	National AI strategy Y/N)	50	50
	Governance and Ethics	84	53.77	84 / 53.772	"Data protection and privacy legislation"	100	100
					"Cybersecurity"	77.86	77.86
					"Regulatory quality"	69.4	69.4
					"National ethics framework"	0	0
					"Accountability"	21.6	21.6
	Digital Capacity	27	73.38	27 / 73.38	"Online services"	75.23	75.23
					"Foundational IT infrastructure"	74	74
					"Government promotion of investment in emerging technologies"	70.91	70.91
	Adaptability	56	54.71	57 / 54.707	"Government effectiveness"	62.8	62.8
					"Government's responsiveness to change"	70.32	70.32
					"Procurement data"	31	31

continued on following page

Table 2. Continued

Pillars	Dimension	Rank	Score	Stimulated Rank/Score	Indicator	Aspirational value	Current Value
Technology Sector Pillar	Maturity	51	30.3	52 30.026	"Number of AI unicorns"	0	0
					"Number of non-AI technology unicorns"	0	0
					"Value of trade in ICT services (per capita)"	63.44	63.44
					"Value of trade in ICT goods (per capita)"	58.86	58.86
					"Computer software spending"	28.03	28.03
	Innovation Capacity	80	42.64	80 / 42.644	"Time spent dealing with government regulations"	93.7	93.7
					"VC availability"	10	10
					"R&D spending"	5.21	5.21
					"Company investment in emerging technology"	56.78	56.78
					"Research papers published in AI"	47.53	47.53
	Human Capital	61	45.06	62 / 45.056	"Graduates in STEM"	21.37	21.37
					"GitHub users per thousand population"	53.13	53.13
					"Female STEM graduates"	82.43	82.43
					"Quality of Engineering and Technology Higher Education."	0	0
					"ICT skills"	68.35	68.35

continued on following page

Table 2. Continued

Pillars	Dimension	Rank	Score	Stimulated Rank/Score	Indicator	Aspirational value	Current Value
Data and Infrastructure Pillar	Infrastructure	48	57.41	48 / 57.41	"Telecommunications infrastructure"	74.44	74.44
					"Supercomputers "	0	0
					"Broadband quality"	46.9	46.9
					"5G infrastructure"	100	100
					"Adoption of emerging technologies"	65.71	65.71
	Data Availability	39	73.49	39 / 73.494	"Open data "	63	63
					"Data governance"	50	50
					"Mobile-cellular telephone subscriptions"	100	100
					"Households with internet access"	100	100
					"Statistical capacity"	54.47	54.47
	Data Representativeness	52	82.66	52 / 82.655	"The gender gap in Internet access"	66.31	66.31
					"Cost of internet-enabled device relative to GDP per capita"	99	99

Source: AI Readiness Index Bahrain

RESULTS AND DISCUSSION

Technology has gained attention due to advances in generative AI, substantial advancements in AI legislation, and a notable rise in AI-related forums worldwide. Governments throughout the world have acknowledged the evident revolutionary potential of artificial intelligence. It's still difficult to know how to make sure AI is efficiently used for the benefit of society.

RO1: Does the government have the necessary laws, moral standards, digital capabilities, adaptability, and vision to apply AI?

Figure 2. Dimensions of government pillar

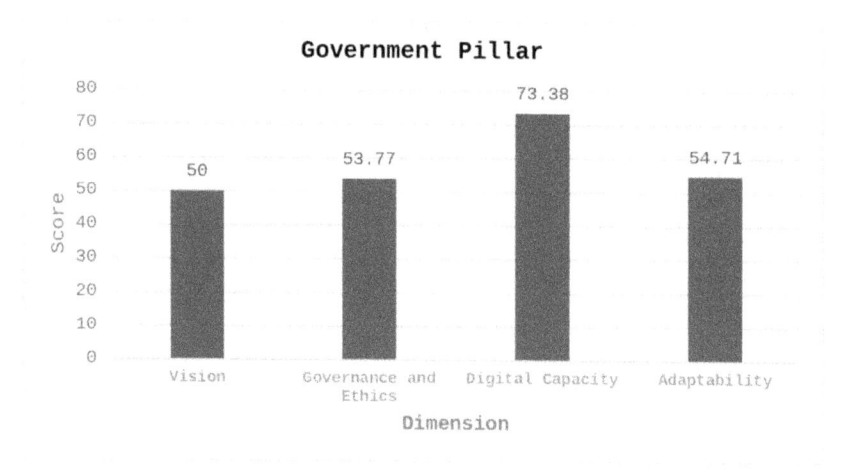

Government Pillar

Dimension	Score
Vision	50
Governance and Ethics	53.77
Digital Capacity	73.38
Adaptability	54.71

(AI Readiness Index Bahrain)

RO2: Is the nation's technology sector able to give governments the means to invent and support artificial intelligence technologies?

Figure 3. Dimensions of technology sector pillar

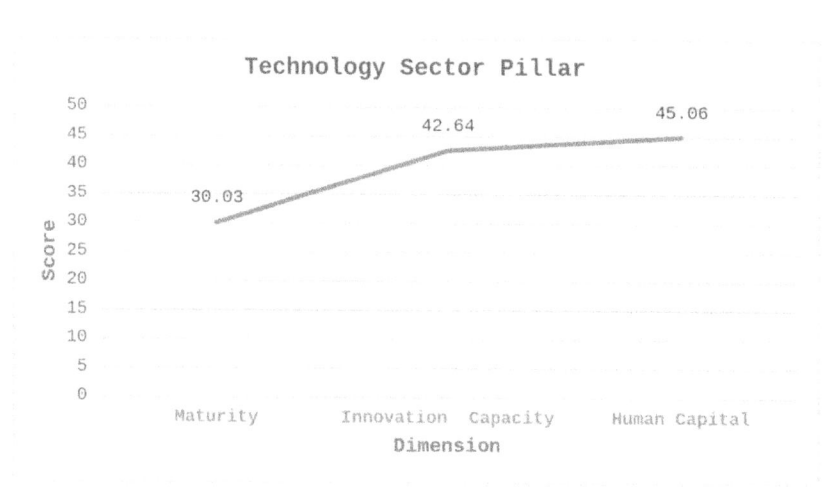

Technology Sector Pillar

Dimension	Score
Maturity	30.03
Innovation Capacity	42.64
Human Capital	45.06

(AI Readiness Index Bahrain)

RO3: Is there a sufficient availability of data that is likely to be representative of the entire population in the nation to enable AI technology and train AI models?

Figure 4. Dimensions of data and infrastructure pillar

Data and Infrastructure Pillar Score

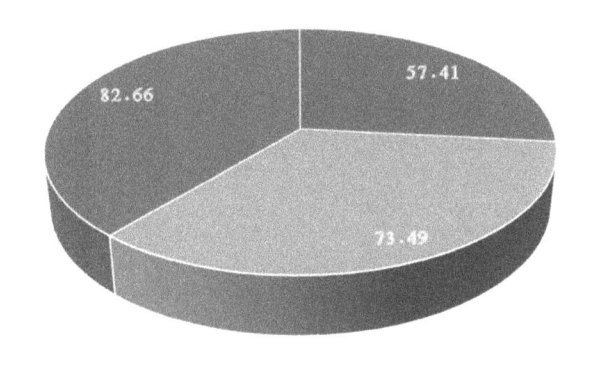

- Infrastructure: 82.66
- Data Availability: 73.49
- Data Representative-ness: 57.41

(AI Readiness Index Bahrain)

Table 3. Dimensions of the countries-AI readiness index 2023

Dimensions	Bahrain	Best/Worst
Vision	**50.00**	-
Governance and Ethics	53.77	Norway 92.54 / Erite 3.35
Digital Capacity	73.38	Korea 91.57 / Erite 9.03
Adaptability	54.71	Singapore 82.17 / Haiti 11.6
Maturity	30.03	United States 84.77 / Congo 2.47
Innovation Capacity	42.64	Israel 89.81 / Maldives 16.82
Human Capital	45.06	UAE 72.38 / Afghanistan 6.84
Infrastructure	57.41	United States 88.34 / Libya 5.34
Data Availability	73.49	Korea 95.65 / South Sudan 15.13
Data Representativeness	82.66	Qatar 99.65 / Yemen 1.37

Source: The Index Simulator for Policymakers in the Arab Region (ISPAR)

Bahrain is a high-income country. Its HDI value is 0.88 (2021), and its GDP per capita is estimated to be about USD 30,15 thousand (2022). Bahrain is well-known for its cutting-edge legal system, robust technological community, and quick transition to eGovernment. Bahrain's digital transformation has been mostly successful thanks to strong government measures.

Figure 5. Dimensions of the c-AI readiness index 2023

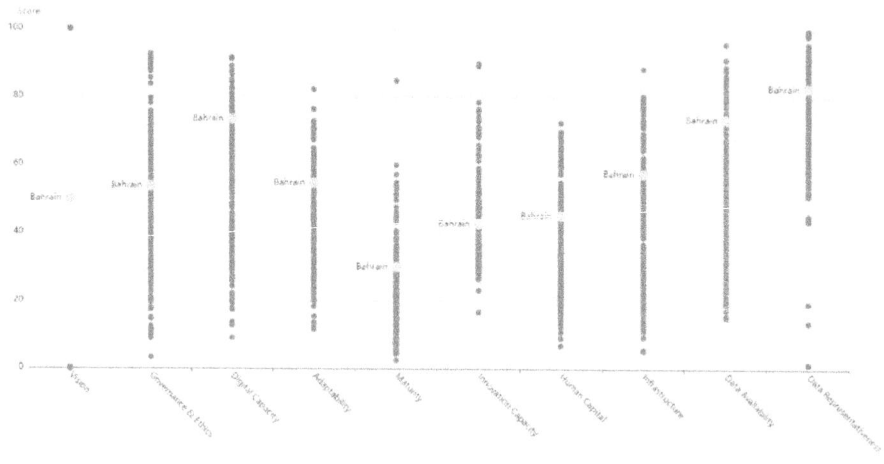

(The Index Simulator for Policymakers in the Arab Region (ISPAR))

Figure 6 provides an insight into the global trend in the AI governance landscape. position of Bharain among 193 countries. For the Bhrain, this is a great development, as the effects of artificial intelligence (AI) are becoming more widespread globally and in AI supply chains.

Figure 6. Key KPIs correlation

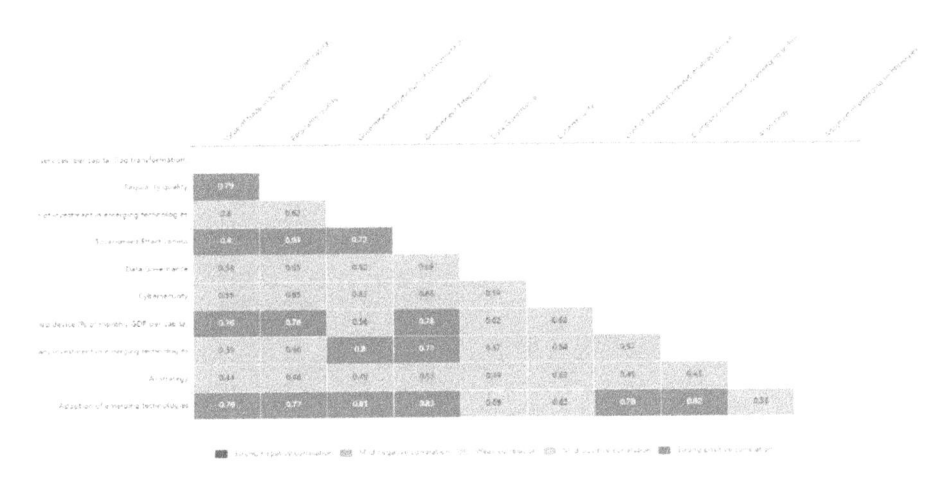

(The Index Simulator for Policymakers in the Arab Region (ISPAR))

Correlation is a statistical measure that describes the relationship between two indices. A positive correlation means that both indices are increasing or decreasing in parallel. A negative correlation indicates that when a country's performance improves on one index it worsens on the other. The relation is strong if the correlation coefficient is greater than 0.7 (smaller than -0.7). it is milled if the coefficient is between 0.4 and 0.7 (or -0.7 and -0.4).

Table 4. Key KPIs score 2020-23

Key KPIs	2023
AI Strategy	50
Cybersecurity	77.86
Regulatory quality	69.40
Government Investment in Emerging Technologies	70.91
Government Effectiveness	62.80
Company investment in emerging technology	63.44
Value of trade in ICT services (per capita) log transformation	56.78
Adoption of Emerging Technologies	65.71
Data Governance	50
Cost of the cheapest internet-enabled device (% of monthly GDP per capita)	66.31

Source: AI Readiness Index Bahrain

In addition to creating legal frameworks and promoting AI innovation, governments are attempting to include this technology into associated key performance measures. Even if the index primarily focuses on countries' efforts on AI in public services, a robust governance structure for AI is consequently required to equitably distribute the benefits of this technology and to effectively manage and minimize its hazards.

AI has the potential to revolutionize productivity development, but whether nations can benefit from it will depend on several factors. It takes waves of complementing advancements to unleash the full impact of new technologies. Furthermore, even if the technology is accessible, how well businesses and policymakers can disseminate it will determine how much productivity improvement there will be. Eventually, economies must be able to adjust to the deployment of the technology to reallocate capital and labor who have been displaced.

> RO4: How Bahrain's governance to use cutting-edge technology like artificial intelligence (AI) has enhanced public services and helped the country achieve more in the digital realm.

Efficient Governance Unveiling Bahrain's AI Initiatives

Bahrain's leadership's ambition to use cutting-edge technology like artificial intelligence (AI) has enhanced public services and helped the country achieve more in the digital realm. Bahrain is striving to establish itself as the region's AI hub. AI governance becomes significantly relevant, the nation expands its R&D capabilities and tries to strengthen its capability to create AI models that address issues in the public sector and the nation's major industries.

Healthcare Revolution

Bahrain is utilizing artificial intelligence (AI) to transform patient care, ranging from customized treatment plans to predictive analytics for illness prevention. A substantial step in the direction of a healthy society is being made with the increasing accuracy of diagnostic procedures and the optimization of treatment results.

Financial Technology (FinTech)

Fraud detection systems, AI-driven customer service, and automated trading algorithms are transforming the financial landscape. In addition to adjusting to change, Bahrain's financial industry is spearheading innovation at the nexus of artificial intelligence and finance.

Smart Governance

AI integration in public services accelerates Bahrain's transition to smart government. AI is used by e-government projects to improve user experiences, expedite procedures, and build a more effective and responsive public administration.

AI for Agriculture

This allows investors and academics to conduct food security studies by predicting the production capacity of each palm tree. "SDG2 is one of the sustainable development goals" that deals with food security, and the program supports it.

AI in Courtrooms

The Supreme Judicial Council has organized the first global summit on artificial intelligence (AI) in the judiciary, which will be held throughout the member nations of the "Gulf Cooperation Council." The goal of this conference is to use AI and digital court transformation to develop the effectiveness of courtrooms and the legal procedure.

AI in Procurement

The Kingdom of Bahrain is among the first countries in the world to test new artificial intelligence (AI) procurement rules created by the World Economic Forum's (WEF) Center for the Fourth Industrial Revolution.

AI Research

An artificial intelligence and advanced computing facility covering multiple fields, such as "cybersecurity, fraud detection, big data analysis, sustainable energy, particle physics, engineering applications, climate change, and sea level prediction", was established through a partnership between the Benefit Bahrain Company and the University of Bahrain.

Education Evolution

The demands of each student are being catered to through data-driven insights, sophisticated tutoring systems, and adaptive learning platforms. A tech-savvy and internationally competitive workforce is being shaped by Bahrain's commitment to integrating AI into Lifelong Learning.

Savings on Public Spending

By using technology, the cost of creating a non-responsive, mobile-friendly portal site has been reduced by around 30%.

Table 5. Savings on public spending

Value-added Element	Expense of the traditional process	Expense of electronic process	Aggregate of Financial Saving*	Proportion of Saving*
Direct expense ("Papers- Printing- equipment maintenance")	0.350	0.050	0.300	85%
Indirect expenses ("productivity of human resources - fuel subsidy - citizen productivity")	14.880	1.770	13.120	88%

Source: Bahrain.bh

Alignment With Sustainable Development Goals

The "Digital Strategy 2022" identifies three approaches to use digital technology to fulfill important projects and SDG targets.

> Digital technologies pertaining to energy and the environment, including water management, building, conservation, and smart energy.
> Enhancing digital technologies for equitable and sustainable growth can be achieved by bolstering fintech and e-banking, promoting remote work, and enhancing smart manufacturing.
> Digital governance, "real-time disaster warnings, e-health & learning, and smart mobility—which includes smart logistics, traffic control, and optimization—are some examples of digital technologies for quality of life, education, and capacity building".

CONCLUSION, LIMITATIONS, AND RECOMMENDATION

Bahrain is committed to transforming industries and improving lives using artificial intelligence. The country's introduction into this field has been characterized by creativity and vision. Bahrain is positioned to lead the way in navigating the future AI landscape thanks to its sector-specific applications, ethical concerns, and strategic ambitions. As Bahrain leads the way in integrating AI, the nation is positioned at the nexus of innovation and tradition, prepared to enter a future in which innovation is guided by intelligence for the good of all.

The government center's operations and strategic capacities could change as a result of artificial intelligence. To optimize the advantages of artificial intelligence while minimizing any possible drawbacks, the federal government needs to take a proactive, realistic, and organized stance, setting an example for others to follow. But there are risks that come with any transformative technology that need to be properly evaluated. To get the most out of their growing AI capabilities, government agencies need to be aware of these threats. A core group of government stakeholders also must be aware of the wider effects AI may have on other businesses and society at large, since it is a key enabler of national agendas.

While thorough in some respects, the 2023 Government AI Readiness Index ignores factors like **Climate Impact** in its applications, where AI can help with adaptation and mitigation of climate change. AI can be used, for example, to enhance climate prediction, optimize transportation, and increase the efficiency of energy systems. The degree to which AI projects aid in mitigating and adapting to climate change would be shown by this metric. The report makes major recommendations for the nation's future, including bolstering institutions and policies to promote AI innovators, enhancing AI capabilities through knowledge and skill development, formulating a set of moral guidelines, and establishing an AI governance framework.

REFERENCES

Ahn, M., & Chen, Y.-C. (2021). Digital transformation toward AI-augmented public administration: The perception of government employees and the willingness to use AI in government. *Government Information Quarterly*, 39(2), 101664. 10.1016/j.giq.2021.101664

Al-Ammal, H., & Aljawder, M. (2021). Strategy for artificial intelligence in Bahrain: Challenges and opportunities. *Artificial Intelligence in the Gulf: Challenges and Opportunities*, 47-67.

Androutsopoulou, A., Karacapilidis, N., Loukis, E., & Charalabidis, Y. (2019). Transforming the communication between citizens and government through AI-guided chatbots. *Government Information Quarterly*, 36(2), 358–367. 10.1016/j.giq.2018.10.001

Casares, A. P. (2018). The brain of the future and the viability of democratic governance: The role of artificial intelligence, cognitive machines, and viable systems. *Futures*, 103, 5–16. 10.1016/j.futures.2018.05.002

Chichekian, T., & Benteux, B. (2022). The potential of learning with (and not from) artificial intelligence in education. *Frontiers in Artificial Intelligence*, 5, 903051. 10.3389/frai.2022.90305136177366

Corvalán, J. G. (2018). Digital and intelligent public administration: Transformations in the era of artificial intelligence. *A&C-Revista de Direito Administrativo & Constitucional, 18*(71), 55-87.

Dencik, J., Goehring, B., & Marshall, A. (2023). Managing the emerging role of generative AI in next-generation business. *Strategy and Leadership*, 51(6), 30–36. 10.1108/SL-08-2023-0079

Hickman, E., & Petrin, M. (2021). Trustworthy AI and Corporate Governance: The EU's Ethics Guidelines for Trustworthy Artificial Intelligence from a Company Law Perspective. *European Business Organization Law Review*, 22(4), 593–625. Advance online publication. 10.1007/s40804-021-00224-0

Irfan, M., Elhoseny, M., Kassim, S., & Metawa, N. (2023). *Advanced Machine Learning Algorithms for Complex Financial Applications*. IGI Global. 10.4018/978-1-6684-4483-2

Irfan, M., Elmogy, M., Majid, M. S., & El-Sappagh, S. (2023). *The Impact of AI Innovation on Financial Sectors in the Era of Industry 5.0*. IGI Global.

Irfan, M., Hussainey, K., Bukhari, S. A., & Nam, Y. (2024). *Issues of Sustainability in AI and New-Age Thematic Investing*. IGI Global. 10.4018/979-8-3693-3282-5

Irfan, M., Kadry, S., Sharif, M., & Khan, H. U. (2023). *Fintech Applications in Islamic Finance: AI, Machine Learning, and Blockchain Techniques*. IGI-Global. 10.4018/979-8-3693-1038-0

Irfan, M., Muhammad, K., Naifar, N., & Khan, M. A. (2024). *Applications of Blockchain Technology and Artificial Intelligence: Lead-ins in Banking, Finance, and Capital Market*. Springer Cham.

Mannuru, N. R., Shahriar, S., Teel, Z. A., Wang, T., Lund, B. D., Tijani, S., Pohboon, C. O., Agbaji, D., Alhassan, J., Galley, J. K. L., Kousari, R., Ogbadu-Oladapo, L., Saurav, S. K., Srivastava, A., Tummuru, S. P., Uppala, S., & Vaidya, P. (2023, September 14). Artificial intelligence in developing countries: The impact of generative artificial intelligence (AI) technologies for development. *Information Development*, 02666669231200628. 10.1177/02666669231200628

Mikhaylov, S. J., Esteve, M., & Campion, A. (2018). Artificial intelligence for the public sector: Opportunities and challenges of cross-sector collaboration. *Philosophical Transactions. Series A, Mathematical, Physical, and Engineering Sciences*, 376(2128), 20170357. 10.1098/rsta.2017.035730082303

Pandey, J. (2024). *Unlocking the power and future potential of generative AI in government transformation. Transforming Government: People.* Process and Policy., 10.1108/TG-01-2024-0006

Pandey, J., & Suri, P. (2020). Collaboration competency and e-governance performance. *International Journal of Electronic Governance.*, 12(3), 246. 10.1504/IJEG.2020.109835

Petrin, M. (2019). Corporate Management in the Age of AI. SSRN Electronic Journal. 10.2139/ssrn.3346722

Romanova, Anna. (2023). Development of Autonomous Artificial Intelligence Systems for Corporate Management. *Artificial societies, 18.* .10.18254/S207751800024942-5

Shaikh, Z., Irfan, M., Sarea, A., & Panigrahi, R. R. (2024). *The Emergence of Islamic Fintech and Bahrain: Prospect for Global Financial Sectors* (Vol. 503). Springer. 10.1007/978-3-031-43490-7_52

Shaikh, Z. H. (2024). *The Effect of Strategic Partnership on Innovation and Business: Performance of the Fintech Industry in Bahrain*. IGI Global. 10.4018/979-8-3693-1038-0.ch016

Shaikh, Z. H., Sarea, A., & Irfan, M. (2022). *Islamic Banking Strategies in the World of Fintech: Success Story of Bahrain* (Vol. 423). Springer., 10.1007/978-3-030-93464-4_10

Sheela, P., Kusuma, K., Panigrahi, R. R., & Shaikh, Z. H. (2024). Fintech and Islamic Banking: A Systematic View and Future Research Agenda. In Irfan, M., Kadry, S., Sharif, M., & Khan, H. (Eds.), *Fintech Applications in Islamic Finance: AI, Machine Learning, and Blockchain Techniques* (pp. 1–23). IGI Global., 10.4018/979-8-3693-1038-0.ch001

Shibly, M., Alawamleh, H. A., Nawaiseh, K. A., Ali, B. J., Almasri, A., & Alshibly, E. (2021). The relationship between administrative empowerment and continuous improvement: An empirical study. *Revista Geintec-Gestao Inovacao E Tecnologias, 11*(2), 1681-1699.

Tokmakov, M. (2021). *Artificial Intelligence in Corporate Governance.*.10.1007/978-3-030-60926-9_83

Wang, T., Lund, B. D., Marengo, A., Pagano, A., Mannuru, N. R., Teel, Z. A., & Pange, J. (2023). Exploring the Potential Impact of Artificial Intelligence (AI) on Higher Education. *Generative AI, 13*(11), 6716. 10.3390/app13116716

Chapter 6
Fraud Detection in the Era of AI:
Harnessing Technology for a Safer Digital Economy

Urshita Bansal
The Technological Institute of Textile and Sciences, India

Sunita Bharatwal
Chaudhary Bansi Lal University, Bhiwani, India

Dhana S. Bagiyam
https://orcid.org/0000-0002-5268-178X
Christ University, Bengaluru, India

Early Ridho Kismawadi
https://orcid.org/0000-0002-9420-5212
IAIN Langsa, Aceh, Indonesia

ABSTRACT

Fraudulent activities have increased along with the new prospects of the digital economy's quick growth for both consumers and enterprises. Conventional techniques of fraud detection are insufficient to keep up with these ever-evolving fraudulent strategies. In this sense, machine learning (ML) and artificial intelligence (AI) have become potent instruments to prevent and detect fraud and guarantee the safety of online transactions. This study examines the function of AI and ML and shows how these technologies can spot irregularities and intricate patterns that would be challenging to find with conventional methods. The study includes various methods of AI-based fraud detection and analyses important ethical issues related to these

DOI: 10.4018/979-8-3693-6321-8.ch006

Copyright © 2024, IGI Global. Copying or distributing in print or electronic forms without written permission of IGI Global is prohibited.

practices. Furthermore, the study looks at developing technology and trends that will probably influence fraud detection in the future. In conclusion, the revolutionary potential of AI and ML in building a safer digital economy is analysed.

INTRODUCTION

Fraudulent activities in business refer to deliberate actions taken by individuals or entities to deceive, manipulate, or cheat an organization or its stakeholders, leading to financial or reputational loss. These actions include, but are not limited to, financial statement fraud, asset misappropriation, corruption, cybercrime, and identity theft. The primary objective of such activities is to gain an undue advantage, often at the expense of others. The rapid rise of the digital economy has increased the prevalence and complexity of business fraud. This tendency is widely documented in numerous research studies, which show how digital change has created new opportunities for fraudsters.

As businesses rely more on digital technologies for operations, they become more vulnerable to a variety of fraudulent actions. The enlarged attack surface provided by online platforms, cloud services, and interconnected networks is a major contributor to the surge in digital corporate fraud. These technologies give fraudsters easier access to sensitive data and financial systems, allowing them to exploit flaws and conduct complex assaults with little discovery. Cybercriminals use tools like phishing, malware, and ransomware to access corporate networks, steal important information, and extort corporations for financial benefit. Furthermore, the borderless nature of the digital economy allows fraudsters to operate across nations, making it difficult for law enforcement to monitor and prosecute offenders effectively.

The internationalization of commercial operations has created new complications and obstacles in fighting fraudulent activity. Companies that expand their presence into international markets face various regulatory regimes, cultural norms, and commercial practices, which can lead to gaps and chances for fraud. Transnational fraud schemes, such as money laundering, bribery, and trade-based fraud, use disparities in legal frameworks and regulatory scrutiny to conceal illegal operations and launder illicit earnings. Furthermore, the interconnectedness of global supply chains and financial networks enables the cross-border movement of illicit monies and goods, making it harder for authorities to detect and block fraudulent operations. Consequently, firms must implement a comprehensive and coordinated approach to fraud prevention and detection, including new technologies, strong internal controls, and cross-border cooperation, to mitigate risk efficiently.

In addition to financial losses, commercial fraud can have serious consequences for a company's reputation, trust, and long-term existence. Fraud incidents can ruin a company's image, erode stakeholder confidence, and impair investor faith, resulting in reputational damage and lost business possibilities. Furthermore, the repercussions from fraud scandals can result in legal penalties, regulatory sanctions, and expensive litigation, putting enormous financial strain on affected firms. Furthermore, the erosion of trust and credibility can have far-reaching effects, harming relationships with customers, suppliers, and partners, as well as the company's brand value and market positioning. As a result, organizations must prioritize integrity, transparency, and ethical behavior in order to establish resilience against fraud and protect their brand in the digital age.

Increased Fraudulent Activities With the Growth of the Digital Economy

Various research investigations have found that the prevalence and sophistication of fraudulent operations have increased dramatically as the digital economy has grown. Cybercrime has increased with the growth of digital platforms, with the "PwC Global Economic Crime and Fraud Survey 2020" indicating that more than half of surveyed firms suffered fraud in the previous two years, primarily in the form of cybercrime. The increase in digital contacts and online transactions has given thieves greater ways to exploit system flaws.

E-commerce expansion has resulted in a significant surge in online payment fraud. According to "Journal of Financial Crime" research, the expansion of online shopping platforms has resulted in more complex fraud schemes aimed at both consumers and corporations. The internet's anonymity and ease of setting up bogus websites have aided deceit. Furthermore, digital transformation projects have created new hazards. According to a Deloitte analysis, technologies such as cloud computing, big data, and the Internet of Things have improved operational efficiency while simultaneously creating new weaknesses for fraudsters to exploit.

Technological advancements have enhanced fraud detection and reporting capacities. The Association of Certified Fraud Examiners (ACFE) emphasizes in their "Occupational Fraud 2022: A Report of the Nations" that new analytics and AI techniques enable earlier and more accurate identification of fraudulent activity. Despite these advancements, the overall volume of fraud continues to rise, demonstrating the adaptability of fraudsters. The regulatory landscape is likewise changing, with higher compliance requirements for enterprises. According to research published in the "Journal of Business Ethics," robust compliance and internal control processes are beneficial in limiting fraud risks, but these programs must adapt regularly to keep up with new fraud strategies.

As the digital economy evolves, fraudsters use increasingly complex tactics to exploit holes and avoid discovery. One significant development is the increase of social engineering attacks, in which fraudsters mislead individuals or employees into disclosing sensitive information or executing unwanted actions. These assaults frequently use human psychology and trust to trick victims, making them difficult to detect with typical security measures. Phishing, spear-phishing, and pretexting are common social engineering techniques for tricking people into providing personal or financial information, compromising business networks, or facilitating fraudulent activities. Furthermore, the growth of social media platforms and online communication channels offers fraudsters a large pool of potential victims, allowing them to conduct highly targeted and convincing attacks with little effort.

The interconnected structure of digital ecosystems and supply chains adds complexities and vulnerabilities, allowing fraudsters to exploit flaws across several touchpoints. Supply chain fraud is defined as changing or misrepresenting information along the supply chain in order to deceive stakeholders and achieve illegitimate gains. This can involve inventory fraud, vendor fraud, or coordination between suppliers and employees to steal assets or inflate expenses. Businesses are increasingly reliant on third-party suppliers, outsourcing, and worldwide supply chains, which raises the risk of supply chain fraud and necessitates comprehensive risk management methods and expanded due diligence measures to prevent losses. Furthermore, the usage of emerging technologies, such as blockchain and digital currencies, presents new problems and opportunities for fraudsters, demanding proactive measures to safeguard against growing risks.

Limitations of Conventional Fraud Detection Techniques

Conventional fraud detection methods have considerable limitations in the new digital context, owing to their reactive nature and reliance on predetermined criteria. Traditional methods, such as rule-based systems and human audits, are primarily intended to detect fraud based on past patterns and known fraudulent activity. However, fraudsters constantly adapt their approaches, making static regulations ineffective. Research by Smith and Gupta (2021) found that rule-based systems are frequently evaded by fraudsters who learn and adapt to these established patterns, resulting in a significant lag in fraud detection capabilities. As a result, these systems fail to keep up with fraudsters' continuously shifting strategies, making them ineffective at preventing and developing fraud schemes.

Another significant shortcoming of traditional fraud detection technologies is their proclivity to produce a high number of false positives, which can result in operational inefficiencies and customer discontent. Traditional systems sometimes identify legal transactions as suspicious, requiring lengthy manual inspection and inquiry. This not only wastes important resources but also degrades the consumer experience by delaying or rejecting legitimate transactions Jones and Brown (2020). Furthermore, these systems are labor-intensive and expensive, necessitating extensive human interaction to process and evaluate data. In the context of the digital economy, where transaction volumes are massive and occur in real-time, old approaches' failure to efficiently and properly handle enormous datasets highlights their inadequacies in effectively preventing fraud in today's world.

Furthermore, traditional fraud detection algorithms lack the intelligence required to examine complex and multidimensional data patterns found in modern transactions. With the rise of online platforms and digital payment systems, transactional data has gotten more complex, with multiple factors and interdependencies that rule-based systems struggle to understand. These old methods frequently fail to discover small irregularities and correlations across huge datasets, which are critical for detecting sophisticated fraud schemes. In the e-commerce and banking sectors, fraudulent activity may involve coordinated actions across several accounts and transactions, demanding complex analytical capabilities that exceed those of traditional systems. This deficiency results in lost detection opportunities and allows fraudsters to exploit weaknesses in established approaches, compounding the problem.

The static structure of traditional fraud detection systems limits their capacity to react to new and developing fraud strategies. Fraudsters' strategies are constantly evolving as digital technology and consumer behaviors change, adopting advanced approaches such as synthetic identities, social engineering, and cyber-attacks. Conventional approaches, which rely primarily on previous data and predefined rules, are naturally slow to react to these changes. They lack the agility to absorb real-time data and evolving threat information, resulting in slower reactions and more vulnerability to novel fraud schemes.

In contrast, AI and machine learning (ML) offer dynamic and adaptable fraud detection systems, circumventing many of the limitations of older approaches. These modern technologies can process massive volumes of data from several sources in real time, detecting complicated patterns and subtle anomalies that rule-based systems may overlook. AI and ML models are always learning from fresh data, responding to shifting fraud methods without the need for manual rule updates. Chen et al. (2019) found that machine learning algorithms improve fraud detection accuracy by using previous data to predict and recognize new fraudulent actions. This continuous learning capability allows firms to remain ahead of fraudsters by decreasing the time lag between identifying and responding to new fraud schemes.

Artificial intelligence-driven solutions can significantly minimize the number of false positives, improving operational efficiency and customer happiness. AI decreases the burden on human analysts and minimizes disruptions to valid transactions by utilizing advanced algorithms that can more efficiently distinguish between legitimate and questionable activities. This precision is critical in high-volume environments like e-commerce and banking, where false positives can cause customer dissatisfaction and financial losses. Wang and colleagues (2020) found that AI-based fraud detection systems not only enhance the accuracy of recognizing fraudulent transactions, but also streamline the investigation process by prioritizing high-risk cases, optimizing resource allocation, and improving response times.

The scalability and versatility of AI and ML technologies make them ideal for the digital economy's dynamic terrain. These systems can be connected with a variety of digital platforms and data sources, resulting in a comprehensive view of transaction patterns and potential fraud concerns. Advanced approaches like neural networks, anomaly detection, and predictive analytics allow for the detection of intricate fraud schemes including coordinated operations across several channels. Neural networks may examine detailed patterns within big datasets to detect fraud that older methods may miss (Goodfellow, Bengio, & Courville, 2016). AI's capacity to scale and adapt to multiple contexts and transaction types makes it an effective tool for preventing fraud in a variety of industries, including banking, insurance, e-commerce, and healthcare.

AI & ML in Fraud Detection

The use of Artificial Intelligence (AI) and Machine Learning (ML) in fraud detection has transformed organizations' ability to identify and prevent fraudulent activity. AI and ML algorithms can analyze massive volumes of transactional data in real time, detecting trends and abnormalities that traditional rule-based systems may overlook. These systems use advanced techniques like neural networks, decision trees, and clustering to constantly learn from data, reacting to new and developing fraud tactics more successfully than traditional methods (Ngai et al., 2011). Their findings reveal that AI and machine learning can improve the accuracy of fraud detection by finding subtle and complicated patterns suggestive of fraudulent conduct, which would be problematic for manual detection by humans (Ngai et al., 2011).

Furthermore, AI and ML provide considerable gains in reducing false positives, a typical problem in traditional fraud detection systems. Predictive analytics and real-time data processing enable these technologies to discriminate between legal and fraudulent actions more precisely. According to Bhattacharyya et al. (2011), ML models, particularly those based on supervised learning, can be trained on historical data to accurately forecast the risk of fraud, reducing the number of false alarms. Furthermore, the scalability of AI and ML enables the effective processing of enormous datasets, which is critical in the context of the digital economy with high transaction volumes. This capacity ensures that fraud detection systems stay successful as data volume and complexity increase.

ROLE OF AI AND ML IN FRAUD DETECTION

Artificial intelligence and machine learning play an increasingly important role in fraud detection since these technologies display greater capabilities in detecting abnormalities and complicated patterns. AI and ML algorithms excel at processing and analyzing large volumes of transactional data in real-time, allowing them to spot subtle irregularities that traditional rule-based systems may miss. Neural networks and deep learning models can detect complicated patterns in data that indicate fraudulent conduct. Ngai et al. (2011) found that these approaches may detect complex fraud patterns by continuously learning from the data and adapting to new tactics as they evolve. This dynamic learning feature allows AI and ML systems to adapt and increase their accuracy over time, making them very effective in an ever-changing environment of fraud tactics.

Furthermore, the capacity of AI and ML to reduce false positives represents a considerable improvement over traditional fraud detection system. Traditional systems sometimes rely on static rules and established patterns, which can result in a large percentage of lawful transactions being classified as suspicious. This wastes resources and irritates customers. Bhattacharyya et al. (2011) show that supervised learning models, such as decision trees and logistic regression, may be trained on historical data to predict the likelihood of fraud with high accuracy, lowering the number of false alarms. This predictive capability is critical for preserving operational efficiency and customer happiness since it guarantees that legitimate transactions are executed easily while fraudulent activity is accurately identified and avoided.

The importance of advanced AI and ML techniques over traditional methods cannot be overstated. Traditional fraud detection methods, such as manual audits and rule-based systems, are often reactive, identifying fraud after it has occurred rather than preventing it. They are also limited by their dependence on known fraud patterns, which fraudsters can easily learn and circumvent. In contrast, AI and ML methods are proactive and adaptive. As noted by Phua, et al., (2010), AI and ML systems utilize unsupervised learning techniques like clustering and anomaly detection to identify unusual patterns and behaviors without relying on historical fraud data. This capability allows them to detect novel fraud schemes that traditional methods might miss, providing a more robust defense against fraud.

Furthermore, the scalability and effectiveness of AI and ML in dealing with enormous datasets are especially useful in the digital economy, where transaction volumes are massive and increasing. The capacity to handle and evaluate data in real-time ensures that fraud detection systems remain effective even as transaction volume and complexity rise. According to a study by Whitrow et al. (2009), AI and ML models can efficiently manage vast amounts of data, delivering timely insights and decisions that are crucial for fraud prevention. This scalability is critical for organizations to remain ahead of fraudsters while also protecting their assets and reputation in an increasingly digital world.

Furthermore, combining AI and ML approaches with other new technologies like blockchain and big data analytics improves the efficacy of fraud detection tools. Blockchain's decentralized and immutable ledger technology creates a secure and visible record of transactions, making it difficult for fraudsters to tamper with data or modify records unnoticed. Businesses that include blockchain in their fraud detection systems can create a trustworthy and auditable record of transactions, making it easier to identify suspicious behaviors and trace fraudulent transactions back to their source (Casino, Dasaklis, & Patsakis, 2019). Furthermore, big data analytics helps firms extract useful insights from massive databases, revealing hidden patterns and correlations that could suggest fraudulent conduct. By merging AI and ML algorithms with big data analytics, firms can improve their ability to detect fraud in real-time and make data-driven risk mitigation decisions (Kaplan & Haenlein, 2010).

In the digital economy, where online transactions occur across various channels and platforms, seamless integration and interoperability of fraud detection systems is critical. AI and machine learning-based fraud detection solutions provide the necessary flexibility and adaptability to seamlessly integrate with existing systems and processes. These systems can be coupled with customer relationship management (CRM) platforms, payment gateways, and e-commerce platforms to track transactions and user behavior across several channels in real time (Hassani et al., 2019). Businesses can acquire a full perspective of potential fraud risks and take early mitigation actions by centralizing fraud detection processes and unifying data from various sources. This integrated strategy improves not just the efficiency of fraud detection operations, but also the overall user experience by eliminating false positives and streamlining security procedures.

The relevance of AI and ML in fraud detection goes beyond detecting fraudulent activity to predicting and avoiding future fraud episodes. Predictive analytics, a subset of machine learning, allows firms to anticipate future fraud threats by studying previous data and detecting patterns that predict fraudulent conduct. Businesses can employ predictive models to proactively detect high-risk transactions or customers and apply fraud prevention measures (Sarvghad, 2018). Banks can employ predictive analytics to identify consumers who are likely to fail on loans or credit card payments, allowing them to act early and avoid financial losses. Similarly, e-commerce platforms can utilize predictive algorithms to detect suspect behavior patterns, such as unexpected purchases or account activity, and flag them for further examination (Gandomi & Haider 2015). Businesses that adopt a proactive strategy for fraud detection can reduce the impact of fraud on their operations while also protecting their assets and reputation in the digital economy.

Furthermore, the ongoing expansion of AI and machine learning algorithms, together with advances in computing power and data analytics technology, creates new opportunities for improving fraud detection capabilities in the digital economy. The introduction of deep learning techniques such as recurrent neural networks (RNNs) and convolutional neural networks (CNNs) allows for more complicated and nuanced data analysis, resulting in better fraud detection accuracy and dependability (Goodfellow, Bengio, and Courville, 2016). Furthermore, the introduction of edge computing and distributed processing technologies enables organizations to examine data closer to its source, lowering latency and enabling real-time fraud detection and reaction (Satyanarayanan, 2017). Businesses that leverage these developing technologies and stay up to date on the latest advances in AI and ML can continue to innovate and adapt their fraud detection methods to effectively battle increasing fraud risks in the digital economy.

AI-BASED FRAUD DETECTION TECHNIQUES

AI-based fraud detection approaches have become indispensable in the battle against financial crime, utilizing inventive algorithms to detect and mitigate fraudulent actions with precision and effectiveness. Among these, neural networks are notable for their capacity to simulate complicated relationships among data. Neural networks are computational frameworks inspired by the human brain, made up of interconnected nodes (neurons) that process data in layers. In the context of identifying fraudulent activities, neural networks can evaluate large volumes of transactional data to uncover patterns that indicate fraud. A deep learning model may analyze previous transaction data to detect abnormalities that indicate fraudulent behavior, constantly improving its accuracy through training (Deng & Liu, 2011). This capacity makes neural networks very efficient at detecting intricate fraud schemes that older methods may overlook.

Predictive analytics, another important AI approach, is useful in predicting fraudulent behavior. Predictive analytics uses historical data, statistical algorithms, and machine learning approaches to estimate the likelihood of future occurrences based on past events. Predictive models are trained on large datasets of known fraudulent and valid transactions to determine which new transactions are likely to be fraudulent (Bhattacharyya et al., 2011). These models can leverage a variety of data sources, including transaction amount, location, time, and user behavior, to provide risk rankings for each transaction. Predictive analytics allows firms to proactively identify and prevent fraud before it occurs, thereby improving overall security and lowering financial losses.

Supervised learning is a key technique to AI-based fraud detection that uses labelled data to train algorithms. The algorithm is trained on a dataset including both fraudulent and non-fraudulent transactions, labeled correctly. Using this training data, the model learns to distinguish between the two classes and then applies this information to classify fresh transactions. Decision trees, support vector machines, and logistic regression are popular supervised learning techniques for detecting fraud (West & Bhattacharya, 2016). A decision tree model can learn the common characteristics of fraudulent transactions and use that information to detect suspicious activity in real-time. This procedure not only enhances detection accuracy but also enables decision explanation, which is crucial for regulatory compliance and operational transparency.

Unsupervised learning, on the other hand, detects unknown fraud patterns without the use of labelled data. This method is especially beneficial for detecting neg fraud strategies that have not previously been classified. Unsupervised learning approaches, like clustering and anomaly detection, examine transaction data to identify patterns that differ significantly from the norm (Bolton & Hand, 2002). Clustering algorithms, for example, can group transactions based on their similarity, detecting outliers as probable frauds. Anomaly detection systems can monitor active transactions and indicate those with strange behavior patterns as suspicious. Because of its capacity to find previously unknown fraud trends, unsupervised learning is an effective tool in the dynamic and ever-changing landscape of fraud detection.

Other AI technologies, in addition to neural networks, predictive analytics, and supervised and unsupervised learning, help to detect fraud effectively. Reinforcement learning, natural language processing (NLP), and ensemble learning are all promising techniques for improving fraud detection systems. Reinforcement learning, in which an AI model learns to make decisions based on incentives or penalties for actions committed, can improve fraud detection tactics over time (Sutton & Barto, 2018). NLP can detect fraudulent behaviors by examining textual data, such as client interactions and transaction descriptions, for indications of dishonesty or anomalous behavior (Chau & Xu, 2007). Ensemble learning, which integrates numerous models to increase overall prediction accuracy, can utilize the benefits of different algorithms to produce more resilient fraud detection systems (Zhou, 2012). These advanced AI algorithms offer a full arsenal for addressing the multidimensional challenge of detecting fraud in the digital era.

ETHICAL ISSUES AND CHALLENGES

The use of AI and ML in fraud detection raises various ethical concerns and obstacles, most notably algorithmic bias. Algorithmic bias occurs when AI systems generate consistently biased results as a result of incorrect assumptions made during the machine learning process. This bias might result from skewed training data, incorrect algorithms, or poor execution, resulting in discriminatory practices. In the context of fraud detection, algorithmic bias can lead to unjust treatment of specific demographic groups, such as racial minorities or low-income persons, who may be incorrectly identified as high-risk. As Obermeyer et al. (2019) point out, biases in AI systems might perpetuate and exacerbate existing socioeconomic inequities, raising ethical questions about fairness and justice in automated decision-making. Such biases in fraud detection have far-reaching consequences, including arbitrary service denials, financial exclusion, and reputational loss for those affected.

Another major ethical issue is data privacy, specifically the handling and processing of sensitive information. AI-based fraud detection systems require massive volumes of personal and financial data to work well, posing substantial privacy concerns. Mishandling or illegal access to sensitive data can result in breaches that expose people to identity theft and financial crime. According to a study conducted by Voigt and Von dem Bussche (2017), ensuring compliance with data protection standards such as the General Data Protection Regulation (GDPR) is critical to protecting user privacy and preserving trust in AI systems. Balancing efficiency in fraud detection with user rights requires best practices such as data minimization, transparency, and strong security measures. Responsible AI deployment entails conducting regular bias audits, adhering to ethical rules, and using privacy-by-design principles to make certain that the positive effects of AI do not come at the cost of individual rights and freedoms.

Aside from algorithmic bias and data privacy problems, another key ethical challenge in AI and ML-based fraud detection is to provide accountability and openness in decision-making processes. AI systems frequently operate as "black boxes," with decision-making logic that humans find difficult to understand. This opacity can result in circumstances in which persons and organizations impacted by AI judgments are unable to understand, challenge, or appeal to them. According to Selbst et al. (2019), the lack of transparency in AI systems might undermine accountability, making it impossible to identify and correct flaws or biases in fraud detection. Implementing explainable AI (XAI) strategies is critical for improving the transparency and understandability of AI system decision-making. This not only builds trust in AI systems, but also ensures that users and regulators can hold them accountable for their activities.

The use of AI in fraud detection raises questions regarding the ethical use of technology in surveillance and monitoring. AI systems can analyze massive amounts of data in real time to monitor transactions and activities, which, although useful for spotting fraud, can also lead to overreach and intrusive surveillance. Such comprehensive monitoring can violate people's privacy and autonomy, resulting in a surveillance state where personal liberties are jeopardized. As Zuboff (2015) points out in her research on surveillance capitalism, the widespread use of data-driven technology can result in a loss of individual control over personal information, creating ethical concerns regarding consent and the right to privacy. To address these issues, it is critical to create explicit standards and boundaries on the use of AI for surveillance functions, ensuring that fraud detection operations do not jeopardize individual rights and freedoms.

Finally, the ethical use of AI in fraud detection requires a commitment to continual oversight and improvement. AI systems must be audited and updated on a regular basis to ensure their continued effectiveness and fairness. This includes not only technical upgrades, but also periodic examinations of ethical concerns. Organizations should form ethics committees or advisory boards to oversee the deployment and usage of AI technology, ensuring that ethical issues are incorporated throughout the development and implementation process. According to Floridi et al. (2018), including ethical principles throughout the AI system's lifecycle—from design and development for deployment and monitoring—can assist handle potential ethical concerns proactively. Businesses and authorities may ensure that AI-driven fraud detection systems respect and uphold the values of justice, transparency, and privacy by cultivating an ethical culture of continual improvement.

CASE STUDIES AND PRACTICAL EXAMPLES OF AI-DRIVEN FRAUD DETECTION

The healthcare industry is increasingly relying on AI-powered tools to address fraud, waste, and abuse. One significant example is the application of AI to detect fraudulent billing and coding methods. AI algorithms examine massive datasets of medical claims to detect trends that may indicate fraud, such as upcoding, duplicate claims, and charging for treatments that were not provided. A case study by Liu and Vasarhelyi (2014) revealed the usefulness of artificial intelligence in finding irregularities in Medicare claims, resulting in considerable recoveries and the prevention of fraudulent payments. The method used machine learning algorithms to analyze current claims with historical data, highlighting those that departed from established standards.

In another case, Blue Cross Blue Shield of North Carolina used an AI-powered system to detect fraud in real-time. The system assesses the risk of incoming claims using predictive analytics, which uncovers suspicious trends by combining past claims data and patient records. This preventive approach has not only reduced the frequency of fraud but also saved the organization millions of dollars each year. The effectiveness of AI-powered fraud detection systems in the healthcare sector demonstrates how modern technologies can improve the integrity and efficiency of healthcare delivery (Liu & Vasarhelyi, 2014).

The insurance industry has also made major advances in fraud detection using AI technology. Insurance fraud is a widespread issue that costs businesses billions of dollars each year. AI algorithms are now being used to analyze claims data, evaluate risk indicators, and detect fraudulent activity. Shen, Tong, and Deng (2018), found that neural networks might be used to detect fraudulent insurance claims. The AI model was trained on a large dataset of historical claims, learning to discern legitimate from fraudulent operations with high accuracy.

Zurich Insurance provides a real-world example of AI success in the insurance sector. The organization created an AI-powered fraud detection system that analyzes claims data for fraudulent activity using machine learning algorithms. Technology can immediately identify questionable claims, allowing for speedier investigations and lowering the time required to process legitimate claims. Zurich Insurance has reported a considerable decrease in fraudulent claims since its introduction, highlighting AI's effectiveness in improving fraud detection capabilities and operational efficiency (Shen, Tong, and Deng, 2018).

The banking industry has been at the forefront in using AI to prevent and detect fraud. Banks use AI-powered systems to monitor transactions in real time, detect anomalous activity, and prevent fraudulent transactions. One noteworthy case is JPMorgan Chase's use of artificial intelligence for fraud prevention. The bank uses machine learning algorithms to examine transaction data and discover patterns that indicate fraud. This method has dramatically reduced credit card fraud and unauthorized transactions, shielding both the bank and its clients from financial loss (Ngai et al., 2011).

Another instance is the employment of AI by HSBC to combat money laundering and fraud. HSBC's AI system uses advanced analytics and machine learning to examine transaction data for suspicious activity. The system's ability to process large amounts of data in real time enables the quick detection and reporting of probable fraud, hence improving regulatory compliance. The use of AI in fraud detection has increased HSBC's operational efficiency while simultaneously strengthening its security posture against financial crimes.

The e-commerce business confronts unique fraud challenges, particularly in the area of online transaction security. AI implementations in this industry are centered on real-time fraud detection and prevention to safeguard both merchants and customers. One effective use is the detection of fraudulent transactions using machine learning algorithms that examine transaction data, customer behavior, and device information. Companies such as Amazon and PayPal use advanced AI algorithms to detect and prevent fraudulent activity by analyzing purchase trends, IP addresses, and shipping addresses (Hassani, Silva, & Unger, 2019). These AI systems continuously learn from fresh data, improving their accuracy and efficacy over time, resulting in a considerable reduction in e-commerce fraud.

In addition to transaction monitoring, AI solutions in the e-commerce industry include customer authentication and fraud prevention throughout account creation and login processes. Advanced artificial intelligence systems examine user behavior patterns, device characteristics, and biometric data to verify users and detect suspect activity such as account takeovers and identity theft. Machine learning models can detect anomalies in login attempts, such as strange IP addresses or login timings, and suggest additional verification processes, such as two-factor authentication, to guarantee the user's legitimacy (Soltani et al., 2018). Using AI-driven authentication solutions, e-commerce platforms may improve security while still providing a seamless and frictionless user experience for legitimate customers.

Furthermore, AI-powered chatbots and virtual assistants are rapidly being employed in the e-commerce industry to improve customer care and assistance while also helping to prevent fraud. These intelligent systems can process consumer requests, detect suspect behavior patterns in real-time, and intervene to prevent fraudulent transactions or account activity. Chatbots can detect high-risk transactions based on user queries or behavior, such as multiple failed login attempts or inquiries about account data, and urge users to authenticate their identity before proceeding with the transaction (Kaufman, 2019). E-commerce platforms can use AI-powered chatbots to deliver proactive fraud prevention measures and tailored customer service, thereby increasing trust and confidence in online transactions.

The use of AI and machine learning in fraud detection across industries illustrates these technologies' transformational potential. In healthcare, AI systems efficiently analyze medical claims data to detect and prevent fraudulent billing practices, resulting in significant financial recoveries and better service integrity. In the insurance industry, AI-driven fraud detection solutions have successfully decreased fraudulent claims while increasing operating efficiency and lowering costs. The banking industry's adoption of AI for real-time transaction monitoring has greatly reduced the danger of fraud, sparing both institutions and customers from financial losses.

To keep ahead of fraudsters, businesses and governments must continue to invest in and upgrade AI technologies, ensuring that they are prepared to deal with emerging fraud strategies. Adopting best practices such as regular audits, bias prevention, and data privacy compliance will be critical to ensuring AI systems' performance and trustworthiness. Collaboration between the public and private sectors can also ease the sharing of intelligence and resources, hence strengthening fraud detection efforts.

EMERGING TRENDS AND TECHNOLOGIES IN AI

Emerging AI and machine learning technologies are expected to greatly improve both the efficiency and sophistication of fraud detection systems. Deep learning and reinforcement learning stand out as highly promising technologies. Deep learning, with its advanced neural network designs, allows for the examination of complicated, high-dimensional data to reveal hidden patterns indicative of fraudulent behavior (LeCun, Bengio, and Hinton, 2015). Reinforcement learning, which trains models using reward-based mechanisms, can dynamically adapt to changing fraud strategies by improving decision-making processes over time (Sutton & Barto, 2018). Furthermore, advances in natural language processing (NLP) can help detect fraud in textual information, such as mail and transaction explanations, through the detection of language indicators linked with dishonest behaviour (Chau & Xu, 2007). These developing technologies are projected to significantly increase the accuracy, efficiency, and adaptability of fraud detection systems, lowering false positives and improving real-time detection capabilities.

Future trend predictions include that combining AI with blockchain technology, the Internet of Things (IoT), and quantum computing will further enhance fraud detection. Blockchain's decentralized ledger technology can provide permanent archives of transactions, making it harder for fraudsters to change data without notice, hence increasing transparency and security (Casino et al., 2019). The Internet of Things, with its network of interconnected devices, can provide real-time monitoring and data collection, adding layers of information for AI systems to assess fraud detection (Sicari et al., 2015). Quantum computing, while still in its early stages, offers exponential increases in processing power, allowing for the analysis of large datasets at unprecedented speeds, and revealing fraud patterns that existing technology may overlook (Montanaro, 2016). Ongoing research and breakthroughs in these areas point to a future in which AI-powered fraud detection systems are not only more effective and efficient, but also more resilient to complex fraud strategies, resulting in enhanced protection for both enterprises and consumers.

In addition to the fundamental technologies previously covered, hybrid AI systems that incorporate different machine learning approaches are emerging as a powerful tool for fraud detection. These systems use the strengths of several AI models to develop a more effective and comprehensive fraud detection framework. For example, combining supervised learning models, which use labeled datasets, with unsupervised learning models, which discover patterns in unstructured data, might improve the identification of both known and new fraud trends. According to Guo, et al., (2018), such hybrid techniques can dramatically enhance detection rates while lowering false positives, increasing the overall reliability of fraud detection systems.

Combining AI-driven fraud detection with modern data visualization tools is predicted to significantly improve human oversight and decision-making. Data visualization helps analysts and investigators grasp complicated data patterns and fraud trends by presenting information in user-friendly graphical formats. This allows for faster and more precise detection of fraudulent actions. As Engel, Franks, and Maharaj (2019) point out, combining AI with interactive data visualization platforms enables a more dynamic and responsive fraud detection process, allowing human experts to explore AI-generated insights and make informed decisions based on visual representations of the data.

Ethical and regulatory concerns about the use of AI in fraud detection are important to its successful implementation. Ensuring that AI systems are transparent, accountable, and unbiased is critical to preserving confidence and regulatory compliance. The development of explainable AI (XAI) technologies, which seek to make AI decision-making processes more intelligible to humans, is critical in this regard. Explainable AI can assist firms in meeting regulatory obligations and addressing ethical concerns by offering explicit explanations for why specific transactions are recognized as fraudulent. According to Arrieta et al. (2020), explainable AI not only increases transparency but also aids in the continuous improvement of AI models by allowing for greater inspection and input. This emphasis on ethical AI development ensures that the use of advanced fraud detection systems is consistent with broader society values and regulatory frameworks.

The incorporation of Artificial Intelligence (AI) and Machine Learning (ML) into fraud detection has fundamentally changed how businesses tackle fraudulent activity. Traditional fraud detection systems, which rely mainly on static rules and manual oversight, sometimes struggle to keep up with the developing methods of fraudsters. In contrast, AI and ML systems can process and analyze massive volumes of transactional data in real time, detecting trends and abnormalities that older methods may overlook. AI and ML systems continuously learn from new data using advanced techniques such as neural networks, decision trees, and clustering, allowing them to adapt to developing fraud tactics more quickly and accurately than traditional approaches.

One of the most significant benefits of AI and ML for fraud detection is their ability to reduce false positives. Traditional systems sometimes identify. Furthermore, the scalability and flexibility of AI and ML are critical in the digital economy, which is defined by huge transaction volumes and complex data environments. These solutions can efficiently handle and analyze massive datasets, ensuring that fraud detection mechanisms stay effective as data volume and complexity grow. This feature is especially vital in industries like banking, e-commerce, and insurance, where the ability to handle large amounts of data in real time is critical for maintaining strong security measures. The adaptive nature of AI and machine learning means that fraud detection systems evolve over time, improving their accuracy and reliability as they are exposed to more data if a large proportion of legitimate transactions as suspicious, resulting in wasteful investigations and customer discontent. AI and ML technologies use predictive analytics and real-time data processing to make more accurate distinctions between genuine and fraudulent activity. These algorithms are educated on vast amounts of historical data to spot patterns suggestive of fraud, improving their ability to forecast and identify fraudulent transactions while minimizing interruption to legitimate clients. This reduction in false positives not only increases operational efficiency, but also enhances the user experience by ensuring that fewer valid transactions are wrongly detected.

AI and ML offer a proactive approach to fraud detection. Traditional systems require regular updates and user intervention to conform to new fraud patterns, but AI and ML systems learn and adapt automatically. This continual learning process enables these systems to detect new types of fraud as they emerge, giving businesses a more proactive defense against fraudulent activity. The combination of real-time data analysis, reduced false positives, scalability, and ongoing development makes AI and machine learning important tools for improving the security and dependability of digital transactions, allowing firms to stay one step ahead of increasingly sophisticated fraud schemes.

Furthermore, the effective application of AI and ML in fraud detection necessitates a comprehensive approach that involves regular updates, data governance, and engagement with regulatory agencies. Businesses must train their AI systems on diverse and representative datasets to minimize algorithmic biases that may result in discriminatory consequences. Regular audits and changes to AI models are required to stay up with the ever-changing fraud scenario. Furthermore, engagement with regulatory organizations assures compliance with data privacy laws and industry standards, so improving the overall integrity of the fraud detection system. By implementing these best practices, organizations can maximize the benefits of AI and ML while reducing the risks associated with their implementation.

AI and machine learning represent a dramatic development in the battle against fraud. Their ability to process enormous datasets in real time, learn and adapt to new fraud strategies, and reduce false positives makes them vital tools for improving the digital economy's security. As these technologies evolve and interact with other new technologies such as blockchain and quantum computing, their effectiveness and efficiency in detecting fraud will only increase. To remain ahead of fraudsters, businesses and authorities must be proactive, constantly upgrading and improving their AI systems, engaging with regulatory agencies, and implementing best practices. This allows them to provide a secure environment for online transactions, boosting confidence and reliability in the digital economy.

CONCLUSION

The transformative potential of AI and ML in improving the security of the digital economy cannot be overemphasized. These modern technologies provide unprecedented fraud detection capabilities by utilizing sophisticated algorithms to spot complicated patterns and abnormalities in large datasets. Neural networks, predictive analytics, and supervised and unsupervised learning techniques have all shown considerable advances in fraud detection system accuracy and efficiency. AI and machine learning can process transactions in real-time, react to new fraud methods, and continuously learn from new data, allowing them to stay one step ahead of criminals. The combination of existing technologies with upcoming breakthroughs such as blockchain and IoT strengthens security safeguards, creating a more robust foundation for safeguarding digital transactions.

To remain ahead of fraudsters, organizations and governments must take a comprehensive approach that involves investing in the most recent AI and ML technologies and assuring their ethical use. This includes updating and training models regularly to respond to new fraud strategies, putting in place rigorous data protection safeguards, and conducting regular audits to reduce algorithmic bias. Compliance with data protection requirements such as GDPR is critical for preserving user confidence and protecting sensitive information. Furthermore, encouraging collaboration between the public and commercial sectors might promote the sharing of intelligence and resources, hence improving fraud detection skills. Prioritizing these tactics allows businesses and governments to build a secure environment for online transactions, maximizing the potential of AI and ML to protect the digital economy against fraud. Adopting these new technologies responsibly would not only improve security but will also help to create a more resilient and trustworthy digital world for both consumers and enterprises.

Furthermore, fraudsters' strategies evolve in tandem with the digital ecosystem. As a result, ongoing AI and ML research and development are critical for staying ahead of emerging risks. Collaboration among academia, industry, and regulatory agencies can promote innovation and knowledge exchange, allowing for the creation of more robust and adaptable fraud detection systems. Furthermore, investing in interdisciplinary research that brings together experts in data science, cybersecurity, and behavioral analysis might lead to advances in identifying and managing changing fraud tendencies. Businesses and government agencies can increase their defenses against ever-changing fraud schemes by remaining proactive and investing in continuing research.

Furthermore, openness and accountability are critical components in the ethical use of AI and ML technology for fraud detection. Businesses must be open about their usage of AI algorithms in fraud detection systems and provide detailed explanations of how they work. Furthermore, accountability measures should be devised to ensure that AI choices are fair, unbiased, and in accordance with legal and ethical standards. Regular audits and reviews of AI models can assist in discovering and correct any biases or inaccuracies, ensuring that fraud detection methods are trustworthy and equitable. Businesses that prioritize openness and accountability can develop trust with their consumers and stakeholders, encouraging a more ethical and responsible approach to fraud detection in the digital economy.

REFERENCES

Arrieta, A. B., Díaz-Rodríguez, N., Del Ser, J., Bennetot, A., Tabik, S., Barbado, A., & Herrera, F. (2020). Explainable Artificial Intelligence (XAI): Concepts, taxonomies, opportunities and challenges toward responsible AI. *Information Fusion*, 58, 82–115. 10.1016/j.inffus.2019.12.012

Bauder, R. A., Khoshgoftaar, T. M., & Seliya, N. (2017). A survey on the state of healthcare upcoding fraud analysis and detection. *Health Services and Outcomes Research Methodology*, 17(1), 31–55. 10.1007/s10742-016-0154-8

Bhattacharyya, S., Jha, S., Tharakunnel, K., & Westland, J. C. (2011). Data mining for credit card fraud: A comparative study. *Decision Support Systems*, 50(3), 602–613. 10.1016/j.dss.2010.08.008

Bolton, R. J., & Hand, D. J. (2002). Statistical fraud detection: A review. *Statistical Science*, 17(3), 235–255. 10.1214/ss/1042727940

Casino, F., Dasaklis, T. K., & Patsakis, C. (2019). A systematic literature review of blockchain-based applications: Current status, classification, and open issues. *Telematics and Informatics*, 36, 55–81. 10.1016/j.tele.2018.11.006

Chau, M., & Xu, J. (2007). Mining communities and their relationships in blogs: A study of online hate groups. *International Journal of Human-Computer Studies*, 65(1), 57–70. 10.1016/j.ijhcs.2006.08.009

Deng, L., & Liu, Y. (2011). Deep learning in natural language processing. *International Journal of Computational Linguistics & Chinese Language Processing*, 16(4), 11–38.

Engel, M., Franks, J., & Maharaj, S. (2019). The role of data visualization in fraud detection. *Journal of Financial Crime*, 26(1), 1–15.

Floridi, L., Cowls, J., Beltrametti, M., Chatila, R., Chazerand, P., Dignum, V., Luetge, C., Madelin, R., Pagallo, U., Rossi, F., Schafer, B., Valcke, P., & Vayena, E. (2018). AI4People—An ethical framework for a good AI society: Opportunities, risks, principles, and recommendations. *Minds and Machines*, 28(4), 689–707. 10.1007/s11023-018-9482-530930541

Gandomi, A., & Haider, M. (2015). Beyond the hype: Big data concepts, methods, and analytics. *International Journal of Information Management*, 35(2), 137–144. 10.1016/j.ijinfomgt.2014.10.007

Goodfellow, I., Bengio, Y., & Courville, A. (2016). *Deep learning*. MIT Press.

Guo, G., Yin, Y., Dong, Z., Yang, G., & Zhou, Y. (2018). Fraud detection in credit cards by fusing supervised and unsupervised learning. *Journal of Financial Crime*, 25(4), 1087–1108.

Hassani, H., Silva, E. S., & Unger, S. (2019). Digitalisation and Big Data Mining in Banking. *Big Data and Cognitive Computing*, 3(2), 1–13.

Jones, A., & Brown, R. (2020). The impact of false positives in traditional fraud detection systems on operational efficiency and customer experience. *Journal of Financial Crime*, 27(4), 1224–1238.

Kaplan, A. M., & Haenlein, M. (2010). Users of the world, unite! The challenges and opportunities of Social Media. *Business Horizons*, 53(1), 59–68. 10.1016/j.bushor.2009.09.003

Kaufman, L. (2019). Enhancing customer experience through AI-powered chatbots in e-commerce. *Journal of Internet Commerce*, 18(1), 1–17.

LeCun, Y., Bengio, Y., & Hinton, G. (2015). Deep learning. *Nature*, 521(7553), 436–444. 10.1038/nature1453926017442

Liu, Q., & Vasarhelyi, M. A. (2014). Healthcare fraud detection: A survey and a clustering model incorporating geo-location information. *International Journal of Accounting Information Systems*, 15(1), 30–45.

Montanaro, A. (2016). Quantum algorithms: An overview. *npj Quantum Information*, 2(1), 15023. 10.1038/npjqi.2015.23

Ngai, E. W. T., Hu, Y., Wong, Y. H., Chen, Y., & Sun, X. (2011). The application of data mining techniques in financial fraud detection: A classification framework and an academic review of Literature. *Decision Support Systems*, 50(3), 559–569. 10.1016/j.dss.2010.08.006

Obermeyer, Z., Powers, B., Vogeli, C., & Mullainathan, S. (2019). Dissecting racial bias in an algorithm used to manage the health of populations. *Science*, 366(6464), 447–453. 10.1126/science.aax234231649194

Phua, C., Lee, V., Smith, K., & Gayler, R. (2010). A comprehensive survey of data mining-based fraud detection research. *Artificial Intelligence Review*, 34(1), 1–14.

Sarvghad, S. S. (2018). Big Data and Predictive Analytics in Fraud Detection: A Case Study. *Journal of International Technology and Information Management*, 27(2), 45–57.

Satyanarayanan, M. (2017). The emergence of edge computing. *Computer*, 50(1), 30–39. 10.1109/MC.2017.9

Selbst, A. D., Boyd, D., Friedler, S. A., Venkatasubramanian, S., & Vertesi, J. (2019). Fairness and abstraction in sociotechnical systems. In *Proceedings of the Conference on Fairness, Accountability, and Transparency* (pp. 59-68). ACM. 10.1145/3287560.3287598

Shen, A., Tong, R., & Deng, Y. (2018). Application of classification models on credit card fraud detection. *Procedia Computer Science*, 147, 343–348.

Sicari, S., Rizzardi, A., Grieco, L. A., & Coen-Porisini, A. (2015). Security, privacy and trust in Internet of Things: The road ahead. *Computer Networks*, 76, 146–164. 10.1016/j.comnet.2014.11.008

Smith, J., & Gupta, A. (2021). Challenges in rule-based fraud detection systems: Adapting to evolving fraud techniques. *Journal of Business Ethics*, 163(3), 543–558.

Soltani, M., Braeken, A., Vandamme, J., & De Cock, M. (2018). A review on the state-of-the-art privacy-preserving approaches in e-commerce. *International Journal of Information Management*, 43, 193–207.

Sutton, R. S., & Barto, A. G. (2018). *Reinforcement learning: An introduction.* MIT Press.

Voigt, P., & Von dem Bussche, A. (2017). *The EU General Data Protection Regulation (GDPR): A Practical Guide.* Springer International Publishing. 10.1007/978-3-319-57959-7

West, J., & Bhattacharya, M. (2016). Intelligent financial fraud detection: A comprehensive review. *Computers & Security*, 57, 47–66. 10.1016/j.cose.2015.09.005

Whitrow, C., Hand, D. J., Juszczak, P., Weston, D., & Adams, N. M. (2009). Transaction aggregation as a strategy for credit card fraud detection. *Data Mining and Knowledge Discovery*, 18(1), 30–55. 10.1007/s10618-008-0116-z

Zhou, Z.-H. (2012). *Ensemble methods: Foundations and algorithms.* Chapman and Hall/CRC. 10.1201/b12207

Zuboff, S. (2015). Big other: Surveillance capitalism and the prospects of an information civilization. *Journal of Information Technology*, 30(1), 75–89. 10.1057/jit.2015.5

Chapter 7
Robo-Revolution:
How Automated Financial Advisors Are Reshaping Global Finance

Deepika Upadhyay
Department of Commerce, Christ University, India

Vartika Jaiswal
Department of Commerce, Christ University, India

Indrajit Ghosal
https://orcid.org/0000-0003-0744-2672
Brainware University, Kolkata, India

Syed Muhammad Abdul Rehman Shah
https://orcid.org/0000-0002-7556-6442
University of Engineering and Technology, Taxila, Pakistan

ABSTRACT

Robo-advisors have the potential to revolutionise the financial service industry by making it more accessible and affordable. This study provides a comprehensive overview of robo-advisors in the arena of financial markets and investments and their gaining popularity in the fintech industry, particularly in emerging markets like India. It also discusses the changing landscape of the financial sector in India, benefits and challenges of fintech, and the legal and ethical implications of robo-advisors. The current study presents a comparative study between India and UK markets in terms of acceptance and penetration of robo-advisors. It highlights leading robo-advisory firms in India. The data visualisation is done with the help of Microsoft Power BI and Microsoft Excel on the statista survey data. The expected

DOI: 10.4018/979-8-3693-6321-8.ch007

results of this study assist several stakeholders, such as academicians, researchers, investors, stock brokers, regulators, and policy makers.

INTRODUCTION

The fintech industry has been witnessing massive growth in the arena of financial service in the past decade (Chemmanur, 2020). With the development of machine-learning and sector over artificial intelligence robo-advisory has become an added feature in the field of wealth management (Liu, 2023). Robo-advisors (RAs) are virtual and AI driven, designed to assist in financial tasks including investment decisions and rebalancing of portfolios by maintaining desired asset allocation based on investment preferences and goals of customers. These RAs have gradually gained traction in various countries. In 2008, the U.S. became the first country to introduce robo-advisory services. It happened as an after-effect of a global financial crisis, wherein people lost their trust in the formal financial institutions. Two companies that pioneered were – Betterment and Wealth Front. Subsequently, various other financial institutions and banks, such as Fidelity, Black Rock and M1 have launched RAs as an added feature on their websites (Robin Hui Huang, 2022). RAs have managed more than $820 billion of assets in 2019 and are expected to grow further at a rate of 26% annually (Liu, 2023). However, when it comes to generating higher returns, RAs have not been successful in outpacing humans (Digmayer, 2024). Investors are also not willing to risk their money on the basis of advice from a virtual AI-enabled platform. Portfolio management professionals are in high demand in India and in other western countries, as they offer customised investment management services to their clients. These professionals are highly paid. Financial institutions have used RAs in order to gain competitive advantage in terms of cost efficiency, speed, reduced efforts, 24/7 access, avoidance of conflicts of interest and minimising behavioural biases (Robin Hui Huang, 2022).

Risk management is divided into two broad categories: passive and active. Active management is used by managers, firms or teams to manage portfolio funds, by making preferred investment choices through extensive research. The passive strategy includes investment in the market index without much active buying and selling. RAs come under passive, automated investment management tools (Phoon, 2018) .

Financial advice is crucial for individuals to take risks and act rationally. The automated investing systems known as 'robo-advisors,' which offer financial guidance devoid of human participation, have become a viable substitute for conventional sources of guidance.

Jonathan Walter Lam & Swensen (2016) have explored the robo-advisor model from scratch, highlighting its advantages and drawbacks, such as mean-variance optimisation, passive investing and general investment approach. Their study also conducts a comparative analysis of three prominent robo-advisors, revealing disparities in the quality of investment advice within the robo-advisory industry. Schwab Intelligent Portfolios, marked by notable conflicts of interest, is found to be less favourable compared to Wealth front and Betterment. Wealthfront has established an all-encompassing long-term investment platform, contrasting with Betterment's focus on goals-based investing. Wealth front integrates an evaluation of an investor's subjective risk appetite, a fact to which Betterment does not appear to give as much priority. The research evaluates the capacity of robo-advisors to supplant conventional avenues of investment advice and delves into the consequential policy implications.

LITERATURE REVIEW

Brüggen et al. (2017), in "Financial Well-Being: A Concept and Research Framework" examines the concept of financial well-being with the options that can be involved in social interests. The paper contributes to the literature on transformational services research (TSR) and proposes a framework that combines four key elements: interventions, financial actions, outcomes and contexts and personal factors. It identifies gaps and opportunities for future research on economic well-being and suggests that it should develop appropriate methodologies, examine the effects of various interventions and the role of individual factors.

Singh and Kaur (2017) in "Wealth Management through Robo-Advisors" explore the ideas, developments, needs and potential of RAs in wealth management. RAs are automated systems that offer portfolio management and financial service advice using artificial intelligence and algorithms. They offer advantages over human advisors, such as lower costs, greater accessibility, transparency and lack of bias. Their research article concludes that RAs have a bright future in wealth management, complementing human advisors and meeting the needs of different investors. The paper also proposes a hybrid model that integrates human and machine intelligence elements to build trust and adoption and increase capacity, transparency and security.

Schwinn and Teo (2018), in "Robo-advisor Trends for Financial Investment Services" propose a framework for classifying RAs into four types: pure, hybrid, white-label and social. The paper argues that robo-advisors can enhance financial inclusion by reducing barriers to entry and increasing the variety of channels available to consumers seeking financial advice. But they can also exacerbate economic discrimination by creating a new digital divide and discrimination for consumers, who lack the necessary skills, resources or trust. Further, the paper argues that policymakers and regulators need to take a balanced approach towards innovation and set aside time to protect consumers, monitor and evaluate the results of robo-advice on consumers' financial well-being, facilitate education, empowerment and stakeholders' collaboration.

Nowak (2018), in "Low-Cost Retirement Solutions Based on Robo-Advisors and Exchange Traded Funds", explores the shortcomings of the American retirement machine, inclusive of low savings quotes, high expenses and misguided coverage adjustments. The paper examines that RAs can increase the accessibility and sustainability of retirement investing. The paper compares the pros and cons of traditional and progressive retirement planning. It contributes to existing literature on retirement investing, which may be categorised into four streams: theoretical and empirical studies; descriptive and normative studies; comparative and analytical studies; and exploratory and prescriptive research. It additionally explores the potential of the latest technologies and innovations for retirement planning, along with fintech and RAs.

Sabharwal and Anjum (2018) in "Robo-Revolution in the Financial Sector" examine the upward thrust of the system, getting to know robo-advisors in banking, focusing on their benefits, demanding situations and future possibilities. Robo-advisors are computerised structures that provide financial recommendation and portfolio management offerings using system learning algorithms. They provide decreased costs, better performance, higher scalability and more transparency. However, they additionally pose dangers, such as cyberattacks, regulatory uncertainty, ethical dilemmas and patron problems. The paper contributes to the literature on devices gaining knowledge of and artificial intelligence within the monetary area, especially in wealth control and private finance. However, it lacks a complete evaluation of current literature and also lacks empirical evaluation. The paper gives an overview of the upward thrust of those technologies and shows future research instructions, which include enhancing safety, reliability and explains ability, adapting them to distinct markets and contexts.

Fisch et al. (2019) in "The Economics of Complex Decision Making: The Rise of the Robo-Advisor" explores robo-advisors, online investment platforms that use algorithms to provide practical financial advice and portfolio management services for advantages that have been discussed, such as reducing the cost of financial advice and improving it through access to sophisticated algorithms. But Fisch welcomes potential challenges, such as not being financially viable for all complex needs or lack of comfort with investing online. Additionally, the robo-advisor industry is relatively new and unregulated, making it difficult for investors to compare and choose the best option. Despite these obstacles, Fisch believes that robo-advisors have the ability to transform the financial services industry, by making advice more accessible, inexpensive and effective.

D'Acunto et al. (2019) in "The Promises and Pitfalls of Robo-Advising" examine the impact of robo-advice tools on individual investors. In 2016, a study based on data from an Indian retail chain has found that robo-advisors can improve different projects by providing optimal portfolio weighting. The resulting effects, however, vary among different investors. Robo-advisors increase diversification and reduce volatility for investors holding fewer than five stocks, while increasing trading activity only without impacting average performance for investors with more than ten.

Priya and Anusha (2019) in "Fintech Issues and Challenges in India" examine the changing landscape of financial services in India, focusing on the growth of the market in a country with a population of about 1.3 billion, many of whom did not have accounts in many banks. The paper explores the benefits of fintech, such as increasing financial inclusion, reducing costs, increasing innovation and ensuring Shariah compliance for Islamic finance. But it also acknowledges challenges, such as data quality, transparency, ethical issues, people-fintech collaboration and regulation. The paper concludes by highlighting the implications, recommendations and future research directions of fintech in India. It means that stakeholders need to take a balanced approach to using fintech technologies and collectively tackling challenges and risks. The paper also calls for more empirical and interdisciplinary research on integrating fintech with Indian values and principles.

Engin and Treleaven (2019) in "Algorithmic Government: Automating Public Services and Supporting Civil Servants in Using Data Science Technologies" explore how data technologies, such as AI, IoT, big data, behavioural analytics and blockchain can change governments and GTECH is creating a new generation of start-ups. The authors argue that these technologies can enable 'smarting' of public services and state infrastructure, affecting the efficiency, quality and innovation of government services and activities to a great extent. The paper contributes to the literature on digital government, a sub-sector of public administration that studies how information and communication technologies are used to improve the delivery and implementation of public services and policies. It proposes a classification of government services based on public engagement, policy development, service delivery, legislation/regulation and discusses how data science technologies can be used at each level to deliver the government services, whose performance and results have improved.

Bhatia et al. (2020), in "Robo-advisors and their potential to address investor behavioural biases - A Qualitative Study in the Indian context," say that RAs have the potential to reduce behavioural biases by providing targeted advice, automating investment decisions and continuously reviewing research. The study reveals that robo-advisors are gaining popularity among investors in India, and they can help people to overcome their biases and make better investment decisions. However, investors may not realise the benefits of robo-advisory services well; there is a need to address challenges such as the evolving Indian regulatory framework for robo-advisory services. Overall, the paper provides valuable insights into the potential of robo-advisory services in India.

Todd and Seay (2020), have written, "Financial attributes, financial behaviours, financial-advisor-use beliefs, and investing characteristics associated with having used a robo-advisor". They have used data from the 2015 National Financial Capacity Survey (NFCS) and look at logistic regression models to examine factors influencing the use of robo-advisors. Research shows that robo-advisor users with younger incomes, lower middle incomes, and lower objective financial literacy scores, other than non-employed users, also have better beliefs about their financial advisors, trust their skills and accept their services. In addition to being willing to pay for their advice, robo-advisor users tend to have a higher risk tolerance, more diversity and pay lower fees. The findings have implications for policymakers, financial professionals and fintech providers. Policymakers need to promote financial education and awareness of fintech products among consumers, especially those who are less knowledgeable and unconfident about investing. Financial professionals' RAs need to adapt to a user-friendly revolution and cater to their wants and needs, offer personalised advice and integrate human as well as digital products. Fintech users are more likely to use RAs to target customer segments intended for investment.

Gazali et al. (2020), in "Application of artificial intelligence (AI) in Islamic investments" explore the software of AI in Islamic investments, a subfield of finance that research the concept and practices of monetary services based totally on Islamic regulations. The paper proposes four regions where AI may be carried out in Islamic investments: text mining, algorithmic buying and selling, stock pick out, and robo in funding. The advantages of AI in Islamic investments encompass decreasing human errors, increasing speed and efficiency, enhancing accuracy, enhancing innovation and ensuring Shariah compliance. However, the paper also recognises demanding situations along with data and safety, retaining transparency and accountability, addressing moral and social troubles, growing human-AI collaboration and regulating AI governance. The paper concludes by highlighting the consequences, pointers and future study guidelines of making use of AI in Islamic investments.

Lourenco et al. (2020), in "Whose Algorithm Says So: The Relationships between Type of Firm, Perceptions of Trust and Expertise, and the Acceptance of Financial Robo-Advice" investigate the factors that make consumers accept automated financial advice delivered by computer systems through interactive online tools, also known as robo-advice. Research focuses on the role of two key characteristics of the firm: profit-oriented (for-profit vs. not-for-profit) and sales-channel (supplier vs mere consultant) roles. The paper contributes to the literature on consumer decision-making in financial markets, especially concerning pension choices. The study uses a real-world empirical study to test its hypotheses, involving an interactive online tool called Pension Builder, which uses an innovative electronic system to create pension investment profiles based on consumer risk preferences and life expectancy that the document indicates for marketers to communicate their strong attributes and increase consumer confidence and perceptions of knowledge. They must as policymakers consider protecting consumers from potential risks or biases associated with robo-advice. Future research could examine other factors affecting consumer acceptance of robo-advice, such as social influence, feedback mechanisms, or emotional appeal.

Brenner and Meyll (2020), in "Robo-advisors: A substitute for human financial advice?" examine whether robo-advisors, or automated financial advisors, reduce investors' demand for human financial advice. The study uses data from the 2015 National Capacity Survey and examines the role of investors' fear of investment fraud as a potential source of substitution effects. The study uses a quantitative research design, using logistic regression models to analyse and manage data for socio-economic and demographic information. The paper contributes to the literature on digital, fintech and digital wealth planning and investment advice, investment behaviour and retirement planning. Advisers are reducing investors' demand for human investment advice, particularly amid fears of investment fraud. However, the study acknowledges limitations, such as disaggregated data and focusing in the US on investors and requires further research, using longitudinal or experimental data and objective measures.

Potdar and Pande (2021), in "Comprehensive Analysis of Machine Learning Algorithms Used in Robo-Advisory Services" provide an in-depth analysis of machine-learning algorithms leveraged by robo-advisory services. The study describes robo-advisors as online financial platforms that offer automated financial guidance. They also utilise algorithms to offer portfolio management services. The paper highlights the importance of machine learning in robo-advisory applications, and argues that it can be used to create risk profiles, allocate assets to asset classes and select individual securities for portfolios. Various types of machine learning algorithms commonly used in robo-advice applications are decision trees, support vector machines (SVMs), random forests and neural networks. However, the paper also discusses the challenges of applying machine learning to robo-advice, such as biases and complexities. This means that robo-advisors can reduce biases in their algorithms and better explain them to investors. The paper concludes that machine learning is a powerful tool to improve the robo-advice industry, but it needs to be more specific about its practical applications and potential solutions to these challenges.

Baulkaran and Jain (2021) in "Impact of robo-advice on investment planning" explore the emerging phenomenon of robo-advice, a form delivered through automated algorithms or software paper uses on robo-advisors based on proprietary data from a large robo-advisory firm in India, focusing on products, attitudes and performances. Research shows that robo-advisor users are mainly young, male couples, small investors and professionals. Most robo-advisors use a structured investment plan (SIP), which allows investors to top up fixed amounts at regular intervals. The paper also shows that daily user account creation increases during periods of high market volatility. SIP investors and holders of mutual funds earn positive, risk-adjusted returns. The paper contributes to the existing literature on robo-advice, which can be broadly divided into three streams: conceptual and theoretical studies defining and classifying robo-advice, empirical and research studies exploring robo-advice operationally and influentially, surveys and their descriptive studies examining the drivers and barriers to the adoption of robo-advisors. The paper provides practical implications for such firms to structure their services according to their target customers, value propositions, revenue generation and cost structure. However, the paper has some limitations, such as relying on a single data source from a single robo-advice firm in India, without controlling for either endogeneity or selection bias, without considering ethical and social aspects related to robo-advice or the dynamic and competitive nature of the robo-advice market.

Bhatia et al. (2021), in "Artificial Intelligence in Finance: Qualitative Studies to Identify Robo-Advisory Services", describe robo-advisors as online investing platforms that employ algorithms to deliver automated investment advice and portfolio management services. The study finds that AI is becoming increasingly important in the robo-advisory industry in India, with experienced robo-advisors offering a wide range of services, but challenges, such as investors not fully understanding the benefits of AI and regulatory framework, changing for AI in India. It provides valuable insights and contributes to the literature on AI in financial services.

Chhatwani (2022), in "Does robo-advisory increase retirement worry? A causal explanation" has examined the impact of robo-advisors on retirement anxiety among investors. The utilisation of agency theory and rational choice theory is employed to elucidate the connection between robo-advisors and retirement apprehensions. Research findings indicate that even after adjusting for socio-demographic and financial literacy variables, robo-advisors are associated with heightened retirement anxiety. The paper contends that the influence of robo-advice can adversely affect financial systems by diminishing participation and trust in the overall process. This study enhances the existing literature on robo-advisors and investment behaviour by furnishing causal explanations and drawing on a diverse sample of investors sourced from the National Financial Capacity Survey (NFCS) study. However, the paper has limitations, including not accounting for different types of robo-advisors, not considering potential mediating factors and not examining behavioural consequences of retirement anxiety.

In "Robo-Advisors for Canadian Pension Participants", Turner explores the role of robo-advisors in enhancing pension earnings for Canadian pension participants, mainly those in defined contribution plans. Robo-advisors use algorithms and artificial intelligence to offer investment advice and portfolio management, supplying blessings such as decreased costs, higher accessibility, extra transparency and less bias. The report critiques existing literature on robo-advisors, categorises it into four topics and discusses the emergence, increase, evaluation, demanding situations, boundaries and capability solutions. It concludes that robo-advisors have a brilliant destiny in pension profits' improvement. However, they need to undertake a hybrid model that combines human and device intelligence functions (Global Risk Institute, 2022).

Nguyen et al. (2023), in "Factors affecting the adoption of robo-advisors for wealth management in Malaysia", examine the factors affecting the adoption of robo-advisors in Malaysian wealth management. The authors highlight the increasing importance of robo-advisors worldwide and the potential benefits for investors. The paper highlights five elements that influence Malaysian investors' adoption of robo-advisors: perceived utility and ease of use, perceived dependability and security, financial literacy, social effects, regulatory environment and demography. The authors also discuss the need for clear regulation in Malaysia to build investors' confidence and acceptance. Research methods include analytical and statistical methods, such as structural equation modelling. The paper summarises key findings and implications and highlights the importance of understanding these factors in shaping investors' behaviour towards digital wealth management.

Ramesh (2023), in "Robo-banking in India: Transforming the Future of Financial Services", discusses the concept of robo-banking, its impact on Indian financial services and its potential impact on consumers and banks. It defines robo-banking as using AI technology studies applying to automate banking services, with chatbots, virtual assistants and automated investment advice. The advantages of robo-banking include convenience, affordability and personalisation for customers, while banks can cut costs, improve efficiency and expand their market reach. But the challenges include the traditional and evolving regulatory framework of the Indian banking sector. Despite these, the paper concludes that robo-banking has the potential to transform the Indian financial sector.

Nain and Rajan (2024), in "A scoping review on the factors affecting the adoption of robo-advisors for Financial Decision-Making", examine the variables influencing the use of robot-advisors in financial decision-making. It looks at the factors influencing the acceptability and use of algorithm-based tools that ease financial management, known as 'robo-advisors' as well as the rising popularity of these services globally. Numerous favourable aspects, including performance expectancy, effort expectancy, technological trust, financial understanding, investing experience, cost-effectiveness, enabling conditions and intrinsic motivation are identified as being linked to the adoption of robo-advisors. On the other hand, investor attitudes towards robo-advisors are negatively influenced by factors such as anxiety, perception of risk, investors' age, data security, and behavioural biases, which create obstacles for their widespread adoption. The study ends with suggestions for service providers, legislators and marketers about the quick adoption and dissemination of algorithms for public financial decision-making. It also points out gaps in the body of knowledge and makes recommendations for future study topics for prospective scholars.

ROBO-ADVISORY IN INDIA

The country's investment landscape has witnessed unprecedented growth in terms of trade volume, growing retail participation and growing fintech service usage across the board in financial markets. The newest development in the nation's shifting investing landscape is the emergence of robo-advisory businesses, which have the capacity to construct appropriate portfolios with little assistance from humans. They use key data points such as age, income, risk appetite and investment goals. Robo-advisory in India is at a nascent stage. Robo-advisory firms predominantly fall into three categories: standalone firms, which concentrate solely on offering robo-advisory services; hybrid firms, which combine automated and human advice for investments; and lastly, traditional financial firms that offer robo-advisory services and are already well-established. Investment instruments offered by RAs include stocks, bonds, mutual funds and exchange-traded funds (ETFs). It also assists in retirement planning.

Table 1 highlights prominent RAs in India:

Table 1. List of robo-advisory firms in India

Robo Advisory firms in India	
Funds India	**Big Decisions**
5nance	ET Money
Invezta	MoneyFrog
Finpeg	MyUniverse ZIPSIP
Scriptbox	Kristal
Fisdom	Piggy
Arthayantra	Spenny
Angel Broking ARQ	Balance

continued on following page

Table 1. Continued

Robo Advisory firms in India	
Funds India	**Big Decisions**
Goalwise	FundExpert
OroWealth	Goalwise
Sharekhan	Wright Research
5Paisa Auto Investor	Finbingo

Source: Robo-Advisory start-ups in India. (n.d.). https://tracxn.com/d/explore/robo-advisors-startups-in-india/_0hKeHniyIyxDVnsd1kx9J96Eh5Gsma0unY13I82rueA/companies

Figure 1. Displays the qualities that investors expect from RAs in handling financial matters and investments

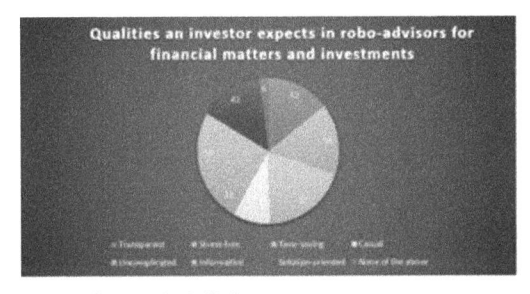

(www.statista.com/finance-and-assets-in-india/)

Here's a summary of the results:

- Transparent: The largest segment at 42%, indicate that over half the investors prioritise transparency.
- Casual: The second-largest at 25%, suggest that a casual approach is highly valued.
- Solution-oriented: Nearly half, at 42%, expect robo-advisors to be focused on solutions.
- Informative & Time-saving: Both qualities are equally important to 52% and 57% of investors.
- Stress-free: A quarter of investors, at 46%, look for a stress-free experience.
- Uncomplicated: 22% of investors prefer simplicity in their financial dealings.

These insights can help tailor RA services to meet investor expectations effectively.

ROBO-ADVISORY IN UK

RAs have become popular across the world, as they reduce the amount of time spent on research, eliminating bias from investment decisions and automating the portfolio management process, RAs make investing easier. By 2024, the robo-advisory market in the United Kingdom is expected to have assets under the management of US$ 26,230.00 million. With an anticipated 7.76% annual growth rate (CAGR 2024–2027) for these assets, a projected total value of US$ 32,820.00m is envisaged by 2027. Additionally, by 2027, it is predicted that there will be 196.800k users in the RA market. In 2024, the average amount of assets under management for each user in the Robo-Advisory market is projected to be $135.20k. With US$1,459,000.00m under administration in 2024, it is clear from a global comparison that the US has the largest amount of assets under management.

Because there is a growing need for affordable, automated financial solutions, the UK's robo-advisory business is expanding quickly. Most prominent RAs in UK are as follows:

Table 2. List of robo-advisory firms in UK

Robo-Advisory Firms in UK
Moneyfarm
InvestEngine
Wealthify
Nutmeg
IG Smart Portfolio
eToro

Source: Michael, A. (2024, May 31). Best Robo-Advisors in the UK (2024). Forbes Advisor UK. https://www.forbes.com/uk/advisor/investing/best-robo-advisors-uk/

CURRENT TRENDS AND FUTURE SCENARIOS

Due to rising digital penetration and a youthful, tech-savvy population, India's robo-advisory sector is expanding quickly. Forecasts indicate that by 2024, the assets under management in this industry are anticipated to reach an astounding INR US$19.76 billion.

A projected total of INR US$25.74 billion by 2027 is expected due to this expansion, which is expected to continue at a projected annual growth rate (CAGR 2024–2027) of 9.21%.

Furthermore, by 2027, it is anticipated that there would be roughly 3.250 million customers in the Robo-Advisors industry. This suggests that investors in India are becoming more interested in and utilizing the Robo-Advisors business (Robo-Advisors - India. (n.d.). Retrieved July 10, 2024, from https://www.statista.com/outlook/fmo/wealth-management/digital-investment/robo-advisors/india)

Figure 2. Displays investors' preferences for financial advice between human advisors and robo-advisors in 2021, categorised by countries

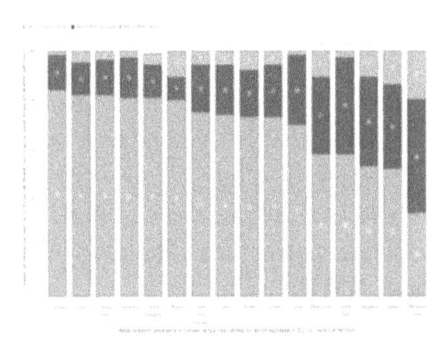

(www-statista-com- investor-preference-advisor-type/)

Here's a comprehensive interpretation:

1. **China**:
    In the Chinese market, less than half the respondents prefer human advisors.
    This stands out as the only market where robo-advisors have a slight edge.
    Despite the integration of technology in financial jobs, China's poll respondents overwhelmingly prefer human counsellors.
2. **United States**:
    The U.S. market shows a clear preference for human advisors.
    Robo-advisors are less favoured compared to their human counterparts.
3. **France**:
    French investors also lean significantly toward human advisors.
    The preference for robo-advisors is relatively low.
4. **United Kingdom**:
    Similar to France, the UK exhibits a strong preference **for** human advisors.
    Robo-advisors have limited appeal.

5. **India**:
    In India, there is a substantial preference for robo-advisors.
    This aligns with the global trend of technology adoption in financial services.
6. **Brazil**:
    Brazilian investors show a balanced preference, with a significant percentage considering both human and robo-advisors equally.
7. **Germany**:
    Germany follows the global pattern, favouring human advisors over robo-advisors.
8. **Australia**:
    Australian investors also prefer human advisors.
    Robo-advisors have a smaller share of preference.
9. **Mexico**:
    Mexico exhibits a balanced preference, similar to Brazil.
    Investors are split between human and robo-advisors.
10. **United Arab Emirates (UAE)**:
    The UAE market leans toward robo-advisors, although human advisors still have a significant share.
11. **Japan**, **South Africa**, and **Hong Kong SAR**:
    These regions show a stronger preference for human advisors.
    Robo-advisors are less favoured.
12. **Singapore**:
    Singaporean investors also prefer human advisors.
    Robo-advisors have limited adoption.

In summary, despite technological advancements, investors worldwide still place significant trust in human advisors for their financial decisions. The data underscores the continued importance of personalised financial guidance and expertise provided by human advisors.

Figure 3. Represents the usage of robo-advisory services in India in 2023

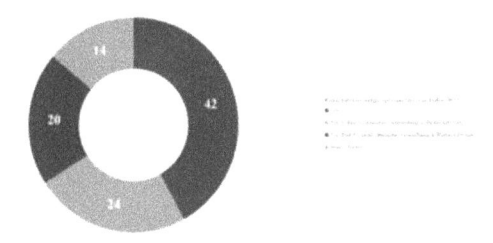

(www-statista-com-/robo-advisor-usage-in-India)

Let's break down the details:

- Yes: The largest section (purple) corresponds to 42% of the respondents who answered "Yes" to using robo-advisors.
- No, I don't consider consulting robo-advisors: The second-largest section (orange) accounts for 24% of the respondents.
- No, but I could consult robo-advisors: The dark blue section represents 20% of the respondents.
- Don't know: The smallest section (sky blue) comprises 14% of the respondents.

In summary:

- 42% are open to using robo-advisors.
- 24% are not considering consulting robo-advisors.
- 20% can imagine consulting one.
- 14% are unsure.

IMPLICATIONS

The upsurge in robo-advisory services has enlarged the prospects of the wealth management industry multifold. Indeed, it has disrupted the existing and age-old investment management industry. Apps and websites have been created by numerous banks and financial consultants to compete in this market. To attract and retain existing customers, well-known asset managers and brokers, such as Merrill Lynch, Goldman Sachs, Vanguard, Charles Schwab and BlackRock have created their own robo-advisors in recent years. There are several different types of RAs available today, ranging from independent, one-person businesses to broker RAs, robo-partnerships with licensed investment advisors and full-service wealth managers with e-advisor features. The abundance of RAs expands the market to encompass the underserved group and gives prospective investors more options.

Additionally, there are a number of hazards associated with RAs, such as those related to suitability, technical (algorithm) issues and data privacy.

Firstly, giving clients incorrect advice is a danger that both human and automated advisors must deal with, but they do so in very different ways. Financial advisors must promptly modify recommendations in light of the ever-evolving personal circumstances of their customers as well as the broader market situations. By continuously gathering information from customers to evaluate their needs, risk tolerance and other criteria, a human advisor can help to reduce the risk of unsuitability. In comparison, RAs can find it more challenging, as they might not be able to detect the modifications and update their algorithm so quickly. Lastly, there are dangers related to cybersecurity and data privacy.

For their purposes, RAs mostly rely on big data and algorithms. Strict security is needed to safeguard algorithms and data pipelines against hacking, alteration and breaks in the data chain. A lot of personal information is typically provided by investors in order to use the robo-advisory services. As a result, investors may suffer if they are unaware of the circumstances behind the sharing of personal information (Robin Hui Huang, 2022).

CONCLUSION

The paper provides a comprehensive overview of robo-advisors and their impact on the financial industry, particularly in India. It explores their emergence, potential benefits, limitations and impact on investor behavior and financial services. The authors examine the literature on robo-advisor movements, their advantages and challenges in wealth management, retirement planning, pension income growth and portfolio management. They also explore the application of artificial intelligence and machine learning in robo-advisory services and their implications for Islamic funds.

The study highlights the potential of robo-advisors in addressing behavioral biases and improving financial inclusion, especially in emerging markets like India. It examines factors affecting robo-advisor acceptance among investors and the impact of robo-advice on retirement concerns. The paper also discusses the changing financial sector in India, the benefits and challenges of fintech and the legal and ethical implications of robo-advisors.

The literature review includes studies on portfolio management, wealth management, pension planning and financial transactions. The paper suggests that robo-advisors could revolutionize the financial services industry by making financial advice easier, more affordable, and more effective. Overall, the study provides a detailed overview of robo-advisors and their potential to address behavioral biases, improve financial inclusion and transform financial services delivery, especially in emerging markets like India.

REFERENCES

Baulkaran, V., & Jain, P. (2021). Robo-Advisory: an exploratory analysis. *Social Science Research Network*. 10.2139/ssrn.3975932

Bhatia, A., Chandani, A., Atiq, R., Mehta, M., & Divekar, R. (2021). Artificial intelligence in financial services: A qualitative research to discover robo-advisory services. *Qualitative Research in Financial Markets*, 13(5), 632–654. 10.1108/QRFM-10-2020-0199

Bhatia, A., Chandani, A., & Chhateja, J. (2020). Robo advisory and its potential in addressing the behavioral biases of investors — A qualitative study in Indian context. *Journal of Behavioral and Experimental Finance*, 25, 100281. 10.1016/j.jbef.2020.100281

Bhatt, M. (2023, March 24). *Robo advisory in India - What is it? Working, need, pros & cons*. Online Demat, Trading, and Mutual Fund Investment in India - Fisdom. https://www.fisdom.com/robo-advisory-in-india/

Brenner, L., & Meyll, T. (2020). Robo-advisors: A substitute for human financial advice? *Journal of Behavioral and Experimental Finance*, 25, 100275. 10.1016/j.jbef.2020.100275

Brüggen, E., Hogreve, J., Holmlund, M., Kabadayi, S., & Löfgren, M. (2017). Financial well-being: A conceptualization and research agenda. *Journal of Business Research*, 79, 228–237. 10.1016/j.jbusres.2017.03.013

Chemmanur, T. J., Imerman, M. B., Rajaiya, H., & Yu, Q. (2020). Recent developments in the fintech industry. *Journal of Financial Management. Markets and Institutions*, 8(01), 2040002. 10.1142/S2282717X20400022

Chhatwani, M. (2022). Does robo-advisory increase retirement worry? A causal explanation. *Managerial Finance*, 48(4), 611–628. 10.1108/MF-05-2021-0195

D'Acunto, F., Prabhala, N., & Rossi, A. G. (2019). The promises and pitfalls of Robo-Advising. *Review of Financial Studies*, 32(5), 1983–2020. 10.1093/rfs/hhz014

Digmayer, C. (2024). Examining barriers to adopting robo-advisors from the perspective of explainable artificial intelligence. *Journal of Interdisciplinary Economics*, 36(2), 224–245. 10.1177/02601079221130183

Engin, Z., & Treleaven, P. (2019). Algorithmic Government: Automating Public Services and Supporting Civil Servants in using Data Science Technologies. *The Computer Journal*, 62(3), 448–460. 10.1093/comjnl/bxy082

Fisch, J. E., Labouré, M., & Turner, J. A. (2019). The emergence of the Robo-Advisor. In *Oxford University Press eBooks* (pp. 13–37). 10.1093/oso/9780198845553.003.0002

Gazali, H. M., Jumadi, J. B., Ramlan, R., & Mohid, A. N. (2020). *Application of artificial intelligence (AI) in Islamic investments.* ResearchGate. https://www.researchgate.net/publication/350287130_Application_of_Artificial_Intelligence_AI_in_Islamic_Investments

Kapadia, S. (2020, May 2). *Top 10 popular Robo advisors in India*. Money Excel - Personal Finance Blog. https://moneyexcel.com/top-popular-robo-advisors-india/

Liu, C. W., Yang, M., & Wen, M.-H. (2023). Do robo-advisors outperform human investors during the COVID-19 financial market crash? *Production and Operations Management*, 32(10), 3174–3192. 10.1111/poms.14029

Lourenco, C., Dellaert, B. G. C., & Donkers, B. (2020). Whose Algorithm Says So: The Relationships between Type of Firm, Perceptions of Trust and Expertise, and the Acceptance of Financial Robo-Advice. *Journal of Interactive Marketing*, 49(1), 107–124. 10.1016/j.intmar.2019.10.003

Nain, I., & Rajan, S. K. (2024). A scoping review on the factors affecting the adoption of robo-advisors for Financial Decision-Making. *Scientific Papers of the University of Pardubice. Series D. Faculty of Economics and Administration*, 32(1). 10.46585/sp32011884

Nguyen, L. T. P., Chew, L. W., Zaw, T. O. K., Teh, B. H., & Ong, T. S. (2023). Factors influencing acceptance of Robo-Advisors for wealth management in Malaysia. *Cogent Engineering*, 10(1), 2188992. Advance online publication. 10.1080/23311916.2023.2188992

Nowak, K. (2018). LOW COST RETIREMENT SOLUTIONS BASED ON ROBO-ADVISORS AND EXCHANGE TRADED FUNDS. *Copernican Journal of Finance & Accounting*, 6(3), 75. 10.12775/CJFA.2017.018

Pawan. (2022, November 18). *8 best robo-advisory services in India*. Aayush Bhaskar. https://aayushbhaskar.com/best-robo-advisory-services-in-india/

Phoon, K. (2018). Robo-advisors and wealth management. *Journal of Alternative Investments*, 20(3), 79-94.

Potdar, A., & Pande, M. (2021). Comprehensive analysis of machine learning algorithms used in Robo-Advisory services. *Journal of Physics: Conference Series*, 1964(6), 062105. 10.1088/1742-6596/1964/6/062105

Priya, P. K., & Anusha, K. (2019). Fintech issues and challenges in India. *International Journal of Recent Technology and Engineering*, 8(3), 904–908. 10.35940/ijrte.C4087.098319

Ramesh, S. (2023). Robo Banking in India: Transforming the future of financial services. *Journal of Corporate Finance Management and Banking System*, 35(35), 30–33. 10.55529/jcfmbs.35.30.33

Rekha, K., & Deepthi, Mrs. (2020). A Study On Portfolio Management. *Jetir, 7*(8), JETIRED06039.

Robin Hui Huang, C. C. (2022). The development and regulation of robo-advisors in Hong Kong: Empirical and comparative. *Journal of Corporate Law Studies*, 22(1), 229–263. 10.1080/14735970.2021.2012884

Robo Advisors Essay - For reference - Robo-Advisors: A Portfolio Management Perspective Jonathan. (n.d.). Studocu. https://www.studocu.com/hk/document/hku-school-of-professional-and-continuing-education/introduction-of-accounting/robo-advisors-essay-for-reference/76929460

Robo advisory for investments in India. (2016, November 4). Groww. https://groww.in/blog/robo-advisory-india

Sabharwal, C. L., & Anjum, B. (2018). *Robo-Revolution in the Financial Sector.* IEEE. *https://ieeexplore.ieee.org/xpl/conhome/8859311/proceeding.* 10.1109/CSCI46756.2018.00249

Schwinn, R., & Teo, E. G. S. (2018). *Inclusion or exclusion? Trends in robo-advisory for financial investment services* (pp. 481–492). Elsevier eBooks. 10.1016/B978-0-12-812282-2.00021-8

Singh, I., & Kaur, N. (2017). Wealth Management Through Robo Advisory. *International Journal of Research - Granthaalayah*, 5(6), 33–43. 10.29121/granthaalayah.v5.i6.2017.1991

Todd, T. M., & Seay, M. C. (2020). Financial attributes, financial behaviors, financial-advisor-use beliefs, and investing characteristics associated with having used a robo-advisor. *Financial Planning Review*, 3(3), e1104. Advance online publication. 10.1002/cfp2.1104

W, S. & Jayakumar, D. S. (2022, June 1). *Portfolio Management, Classical and Robust Statistics. A literature Review*. ResearchGate. https://www.researchgate.net/publication/362902068_Portfolio_Management_Classical_and_Robust_Statistics_A_literature_Review

Chapter 8
Green Banking and SDGs:
Drivers, Facilitators, and Accelerators

Jahanvi Bansal
GSFC University, Vadodara, India

Parag Shukla
https://orcid.org/0000-0002-7014-163X
The Maharaja Sayajirao University of Baroda, India

Pankaj Kumar Tripathi
https://orcid.org/0000-0001-7186-949X
The Maharaja Sayajirao University of Baroda, India

Suchi Dubey
MAHE Dubai, UAE

ABSTRACT

Green banking's potential to foster green economies and ensure a sustainable future is profound, emphasizing the critical importance of green finance in advancing SDGs and mitigating global environmental challenges. Central Asian banks, including India, have increasingly embraced green finance, acknowledging its pivotal role in addressing climate risks. The study has proposed a conceptual framework that depicts the interplay between drivers, facilitators, and accelerators of green banking and sustainable development goals (SDGs), especially SDG 7 (affordable and clean energy), SDG 11 (sustainable cities and communities), SDG 12 (responsible consumption and production) and SDG 13 (climate action), highlighting collaborative efforts needed for global sustainability. This article sheds light on the transformational potential of green banking projects by discussing both the practical

DOI: 10.4018/979-8-3693-6321-8.ch008

and social aspects of the proposed initiatives.

INTRODUCTION

The need for sustainable development is mainly ignored as the world economy grows slowly. Growth patterns prioritizing long-term views above short-term benefits have disproportionately benefited the wealthy and negatively impacted the environment. Climate change is our most prominent environmental hazard, surpassing even the threats posed by pollution, alien species proliferation, loss of biodiversity, and changes in land and marine usage.

The execution of monetary policies has been strong, but, there has been a noticeable lack of focus on long-term investments and financing for infrastructure, particularly for initiatives related to renewable energy. The private sector is apathetic, and many nations—especially developing ones—find it challenging to get the public sector to commit enough money to close this significant investment gap. Reluctance within the private sector results from the high risks and alleged low returns of funding infrastructure projects, particularly those pertaining to green energy (Yoshino & Taghizadeh-Hersary, 2018).

For various stakeholders, including investors, corporations, non-governmental organizations (NGOs), financial regulators, and policymakers, it is essential to promote green investment and support green energy initiatives (Diaz-Rainey et al., 2023). A global environmental crisis is predicted to arise, according to reports from the Intergovernmental Panel on Climate Change (IPCC), with global temperature expected to surpass 1.5°C over pre-industrial levels between 2030 and 2052 (IPCC, 2018). In order to tackle this issue, it is estimated that over the next ten years, an average of US$ 2.4 trillion will need to be invested in the energy sector alone (Park & Kim, 2020; Sachs et al., 2019). The preceding discussion underscores the critical importance of researching green financing to advance the Sustainable Development Goals (SDGs).

LITERATURE REVIEW

Green Banking

The concept of green banking is relatively new, emerging less than a decade ago, and its roots can be traced back to 2009 in the State of Florida. Green banking represents an innovative and much-needed trend aimed at holding banks accountable for accelerating the transition to clean energy and combating climate change through the provision of responsible credit (Sharma & Choubey, 2021). According to the Indian Banks Association, green banking involves the incorporation of environmental and social considerations to ensure the sustainable and responsible utilization of resources in the daily operations of banks (Kumar & Prakash, 2019).

Central Banks in Asia and Green Banking

Given Asia's heightened vulnerability to the impacts of climate change and natural catastrophes, there is an urgent need for a comprehensive examination of green financing (Beirne et al., 2021; Volz et al., 2020). Realizing that continued environmental deterioration constitutes a severe threat to their economies, people's lives, and financial stability, governments, policymakers, and environmentalists in the Asian area are turning their attention more and more toward climate change (Diaz-Rainey et al., 2023).

Numerous central banks in Asia have adopted green finance policies or integrated environmental risk into their policy frameworks due to the pressing need to address environmental issues (Park & Kim, 2020; Volz et al., 2020). Notably, China became a trailblazer in 2007 when it announced its green credit policy, and it has since led Asian nations in promoting sustainable finance. In 2015, the People's Bank of China formed the Green Finance Committee with the goals of creating green finance procedures, assessing the banking industry's environmental resilience, and creating policies for greening China's foreign investments.

Comparably, in 2011, Bangladesh Bank, the country's central bank, issued 'Policy Guidelines for Green Banking' and 'Guidelines on Environmental Risk Management,' demonstrating its proactive nature. The purpose of these rules was to guarantee that financial institutions in Bangladesh, both bank and non-bank, followed environmental risk management procedures.

Ariyapruchya & Volz (2022) report that the Bangko Sentral ng Pilipimas, the central bank of the Republic of the Philippines, has unveiled a 'Sustainable Finance Framework' that specifies how banks are expected to create transition plans and include them in their corporate governance and risk management frameworks. Additionally, the Reserve Bank of India has set specific lending quotas for climate-sensitive sectors (Park & Kim, 2020). In addition, an industry-wide climate risk stress testing exercise has been designed by the Central Bank of Malaysia and is set to begin in 2024 (Ariyapruchya & Volz, 2022). Furthermore, Asia has seen the issuance of green bonds; China led the way in 2015, followed by India in 2016, Indonesia and Japan in 2017 (Volz, 2021). The aforementioned initiatives highlight the increasing trend in the region to include environmental factors in financial systems and encourage sustainable development.

Green Banking in India

Among all Asian nations, South Korea and India are particularly notable for having severe environmental concerns to deal with. With its rising emissions, India, in particular, emphasizes the need for a thorough investigation into Indian banks' capacity for green finance, involving both the public and private sectors. Such a study would offer insightful information about how well-prepared Indian financial institutions are to back green energy and sustainable development projects, helping the nation combat climate change and environmental degradation.

DRIVERS, FACILITATORS, ACCELERATORS OF GREEN BANKING AND SDGS

The dynamic interaction between the drivers, facilitators, and accelerators is depicted in Figure 1, highlighting their combined impact on the advancement of the Sustainable Development Goals (SDGs). In order to achieve more general global sustainability goals, this conceptual framework emphasizes the cooperative efforts of many stakeholders in supporting ecologically friendly financial practices.

Figure 1. A conceptual framework showing the interplay between drivers, facilitators, and acceleration of green banking and SDG

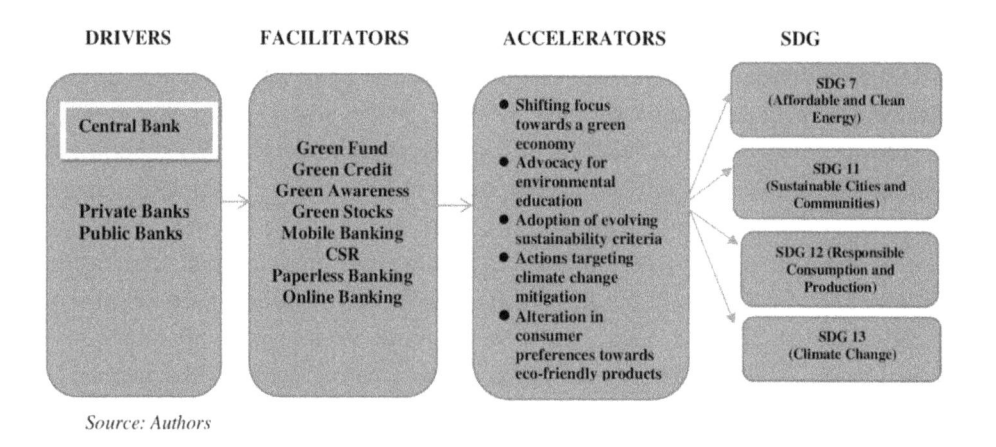

DRIVERS	FACILITATORS	ACCELERATORS	SDG
Central Bank Private Banks Public Banks	Green Fund Green Credit Green Awareness Green Stocks Mobile Banking CSR Paperless Banking Online Banking	• Shifting focus towards a green economy • Advocacy for environmental education • Adoption of evolving sustainability criteria • Actions targeting climate change mitigation • Alteration in consumer preferences towards eco-friendly products	SDG 7 (Affordable and Clean Energy) SDG 11 (Sustainable Cities and Communities) SDG 12 (Responsible Consumption and Production) SDG 13 (Climate Change)

Source: Authors

Central banks, alongside both the public sector and private sector, serve as crucial drivers for green banking, leveraging their influence to promote sustainability. They encourage the banking industry to embrace eco-friendly practices by using a variety of facilitators, such as green instruments and regulations, such as Green Funds, Green Credits, and Green Awareness campaigns. These endeavors comprise an extensive array of tactics, ranging from Mobile Banking to Corporate Social Responsibility (CSR) programs, in addition to the shift towards Paperless and Online Banking.

These efforts act as accelerators, leading to a shift towards a green economy, promoting environmental education, adopting evolving sustainability standards, taking actions to mitigate climate change, and influencing consumer preferences towards eco-friendly products. This coordinated effort ultimately contributes to the advancement of a more sustainable future by being in line with the Sustainable Development Goals (SDG), especially SDG 7 - Affordable and Clean Energy and SDG 13 - Climate Action.

Drivers of Green Banking

In response to escalating environmental challenges, central banks are assuming a pivotal role in signalling to both public and private sector banks the importance of effectively identifying, reporting, and mitigating environmental and climate risks associated with credit allocation (Park & Kim, 2020). Going beyond their traditional functions of controlling inflation, maintaining financial stability, and stabilizing exchange rates (Barkawi & Monnin 2015), central banks are increasingly tasked with adjusting policies and issuing directives pertaining to long-term climate strategies. Furthermore, they are facilitating investments for investors seeking to engage in projects that meet low carbon requirements, thus positioning central banks as drivers of green banking initiatives disseminated through both public and private sector banks.

Facilitators of Green Banking

Green Funds

Green funds are, hence, the chief facilitators in this area of green banking; they represent mechanisms for directing financial flows towards projects for sustainable development. Green finance is committed to, with the aid of these funds, leading to remarkable reductions in carbon emissions. The green funds finance those initiatives that are reformed as per global considerations and, therefore, increase efforts to avert the degradation of the environment and pave the way for economic growth on a sustainable basis. They play a significant role in synchronizing financial actions with green priorities, which further results in the provision of environmental and economic benefits. The research conducted by Zhang et al. (2022) affirms that green funds finance those projects that avert environmental degradation.

Additionally, the integration of green finance with green supply chain management has had an impact on industrial and environmental sustainability. For instance, investments through green funds, according to Fahim & Mahadi (2022), ensure that production systems are ecologically productive and ensure the development of new innovative and sustainable industrial practices. The implementation of green finance has resulted in compliance and significant developments in green technology and other sustainable industrial practices, even though the low quality and quantity of these investments pose problems (Fahim & Mahadi, 2022).

Moreover, the world is experiencing one of the significant instruments related to fighting climate change: green finance. Green financial instruments, including green bonds, are vital in project financing focusing on climate adaptation and mitigation (Shankari Priyadarshini Ravichandran & Mandira Roy, 2022). All these financial vehicles are essential in aiding international efforts to fulfil obligations for the Paris Agreement and other global climate agreements, hence achieving the corresponding Sustainable Development Goals on environmental sustainability (Ravichandran & Roy, 2022). In other words, green funds are essential ingredients in green banking, and they encourage the funding of projects with minimal environmental impacts and the adoption of sustainable practices by all sectors. This way, green funds not only support the various carbon reduction projects but also encourage industries to shift their operations to greener operations by aligning financial resources with ecologically desired objectives.

Green Credit

Green credit plays a significant role in aligning financial practices with environmental conservation, making it a crucial aspect of sustainable banking. According to Yao et al. (2023), the implementation of green credit policies is heavily influenced by the governance structure of banks. Their research shows how factors like ownership concentration and loan quality contribute to the promotion of green credit, highlighting that effective governance can significantly enhance a bank's environmental contributions. This study demonstrates the nuanced ways in which governance practices affect the effective adoption of green credit (Yao et al., 2023).

Yao et al. (2023) and Yuan & Zeng (2023) discovered a positive correlation between green credit and bank performance. Their research reveals that investments in green credit not only meet environmental standards but also boost profitability, establishing green credit as a financially strategic choice for banks. This study supports the idea that engaging in green credit benefits both the environment and the economic bottom line Yao et al. (2023); Yuan & Zeng (2023).

Further research by Gao & Guo (2022) explores how China's green credit policies have enhanced the financial performance of commercial banks through a quasi-natural experiment. These policies have been shown to increase profits by enhancing non-interest income and reducing non-performing loan ratios, thereby contributing to sustainable development. It provides crucial quantitative evidence supporting further policy development and broader adoption of green credit practices by banks (Gao & Guo, 2022). Collectively, these insights highlight that green credit is a strategic tool in green banking, enhancing both financial performance and environmental sustainability. By integrating green credit practices, banks can play a pivotal role in fostering a transition towards a more sustainable and economically viable future.

Green Awareness

Green awareness in green banking significantly shapes the environmental strategies of the financial institution, thereby affecting stakeholder behaviour toward sustainability. According to a study that focused on Islamic banks in developing economies (Khan et al. (2023) examine that Islamic banks in developing economies practice green banking to boost their reputation and promote environmental consciousness. According to the following study, green banking practices have a significant effect on making reputations greener by providing more green consciousness to the employees of the bank. This effect was powerful when banks were really active in greening, as it helps to have a reputation that is more climate-friendly in the community (Khan et al., 2023).

For example, a similar study by Chen Chong et al. (2023) investigated how awareness of green finance influences the sustainable competitiveness of the enterprise. The researchers argued that better awareness of green finance options added to the competitiveness of the corporation and brought businesses closer to sustainable development goals. These linkages will further enhance the efficiency and sustainability of the supply chain with reference to small and medium-sized enterprises within the context of Asian countries (Chen et al., 2023).

On the whole, green awareness in the banking sector is crucial for the development of environmental sustainability. Not only does this bring reputation to financial institutions, but it means that their operations fit into the big picture of sustainability; hence, effective green banking would entail the practice of green awareness. By fostering an understanding and implementation of green practices, banks will consequently and considerably contribute to environmental conservation and the world's course towards a sustainable future.

Green Stocks

Green stocks represent an increasingly pivotal role in green banking, serving as a crucial instrument for directing investments towards environmentally sustainable projects. Green stocks are increasingly being identified for their pivotal role in directing capital towards environmentally sustainable enterprises and eco-friendly initiatives. An example can be seen in the research by Youqiang Ding (2023) into green finance, including green stocks, for the alleviation of stock price crash risks in environments of information asymmetry among Chinese listed companies. Research findings pointed to green financial practices, channelled through green stock, stabilizing the stock price by fostering increased transparency and the reduction of informational disparities. This stock price stabilization is crucial, especially in green stock markets, and the effect of green finance can be quite helpful in ensuring a more stable and sustainable financial environment (Youqiang Ding, 2023).

Illustrating the broader influence of green stocks, some findings show the role of green stocks with regard to the stock correlation networks in China's green finance market (Youqiang Ding, 2023). It was shown that green stocks tend to form a network with robust systemic importance as the market positions of corporate social responsibility, research and development investment intensity, and green innovation output bear significant influence on green stocks. This network effect not only strengthens the structure of the financial market but also encourages more firms to go green, thus enhancing the overall market resilience and attractiveness to investors seeking sustainable investment opportunities.

All these insights collectively point toward the transformation potential of green stocks in promoting sustainable development through green banking. Green stocks represent a particular investment environment wherein companies are likely to enhance their financial stability through certain greening efforts that are aimed at furthering environmental goals. This is how green stocks facilitate sustainable finance, which also points to the usage of such stocks as a tool to mainstream environmental concerns within the core strategies of financial institutions.

Mobile Banking

Mobile banking is increasingly recognized as a crucial facilitator in green banking initiatives, providing an eco-friendly approach to traditional banking operations. According to Ramila & Gurusamy (2016), mobile banking, along with other digital banking initiatives, significantly enhances the profitability of banks by reducing operational costs associated with traditional brick-and-mortar setups. The research highlights how mobile banking leads to decreased use of paper and physical resources, aligning banking practices with environmental sustainability goals.

Furthermore, a study in the Sustainability journal examines the broader impacts of digital finance, including mobile banking, on energy efficiency within the context of sustainable development. The research suggests that digital financial services promote energy efficiency by enhancing service delivery efficiency and reducing the need for physical infrastructure, which in turn supports green initiatives. This integration of digital finance is shown to be a critical component in promoting a sustainable green economy (Yang & Masron, 2022). Mobile banking not only supports green banking by minimizing the environmental impact of banking operations but also enhances accessibility and inclusivity. By enabling banking services through mobile devices, institutions can reach a broader audience, including remote or underserved populations, thereby promoting financial inclusion and supporting sustainable development goals.

Corporate Social Responsibility (CSR)

Corporate Social Responsibility is at the heart of green banking. CSR practices are essential for promoting sustainable practices in both financial and non-financial terms. Reporting in the journal *Sustainability*, Pouya Zargar (2023) maintains that due to Green Human Resource Management (GHRM) and green innovation in banks, various CSR activities are effectively enhanced. In this instance, CSR acts as a moderator, enhancing the interaction between GHRM, green innovation, and corporate sustainability and underpinning the role CSR plays in promoting sustainable practice within the banking industry (Pouya Zargar, 2023).

Another study by Dai et al. (2022) discusses how CSR leads to direct impacts on environmental performance through green finance and innovation. It states that CSR directly uplifts environmental outcomes and boosts green innovation, which in turn uplifts the environmental performance of the banking institution. Thus, the relationship has established that the critical role of CSR is to facilitate sustainable banking practices that contribute to broader environmental objectives. It also highlights the integrative role of CSR in green banking, which drives not only ESG compliance but also supports the incorporation of sustainable practices into the core strategy of bank operations. The CSR activities of banks propose a more comprehensive approach, linking financial services to the global sustainability agenda.

Paperless Banking

The transition to paperless banking is integral to green banking initiatives, aiming to boost sustainability within the financial sector. Chmielarz & Zborowski (2020) focus on how electronic banking platforms are crucial in diminishing the environmental impact of banking operations. Their research emphasizes the need to develop sustainable assessment methods for e-banking services that balance technical precision and ease of use. These methods are vital for promoting efficient, low-resource banking operations and significantly reducing the use of paper and other physical resources in banking activities. By implementing such practices, banks not only meet environmental sustainability goals but also improve their service delivery, aligning economic growth with ecological conservation. This strategy ensures that the banking sector continues to play a significant role in promoting sustainable development and supports global efforts to reduce environmental degradation.

Online Banking

The transition to online banking is recognized as a significant facilitator of sustainability within the financial sector. This shift enhances service accessibility and efficiency while significantly reducing the environmental footprint of traditional banking operations. A pivotal study by Yang & Masron (2022) explores the role of digital finance, including online banking, in promoting energy efficiency as part of a broader sustainable development strategy. Their findings indicate that adopting digital finance practices leads to a notable improvement in energy utilization efficiency, effectively aligning economic activities with environmental conservation efforts (Yang & Masron, 2022).

Additionally, research by Laghouag (2022) underscores the sustainable performance outcomes driven by an e-banking entrepreneurship orientation. This study demonstrates how online banking fosters an entrepreneurial approach within financial institutions, which in turn enhances their environmental, ethical, and social performance. The orientation towards e-banking entrepreneurship aligns strategically with sustainable development goals, highlighting a significant positive impact on the sustainable practices of banks, particularly in competitive environments like Saudi Arabia (Laghouag, 2022).

Further, online banking is not only operationally efficient but also plays a significant role in the banking sector, which, in turn, promotes the sustainability efforts made by these banks that duly insist on or promote online banking. By reducing the need for physical infrastructure and enabling more efficient resource management, online banking contributes to the broader goals of minimizing ecological impact and advancing sustainable development within the financial industry.

Accelerators of Green Banking

The transition to a green economy is a significant driver in the field of green banking, which is essential for integrating sustainability into the financial industry. This strategy entails a deliberate endeavour to embrace economic policies and practices that give priority to both environmental sustainability and financial viability.

Shifting Focus Towards a Green Economy

Green Funds is one of the leading facilitators associated with this accelerator. These specialist funds play a crucial role in gathering resources for investments in ecologically sustainable initiatives, such as the installation of renewable energy sources and the development of green infrastructure. Banks play an active role in promoting environmentally friendly activities by channelling investments through Green Funds. This alignment strongly contributes to the achievement of SDG 7 (Affordable and Clean Energy) by providing funding for initiatives that enhance the availability of clean and renewable energy sources. This, in turn, promotes energy security and sustainability.

Enhancing SDG 13 (Climate Action) through the utilization of environmentally friendly stocks Moreover, Green Stocks are crucial in enabling the shift towards a sustainable and environmentally friendly economy. These stocks let banks and investors financially assist companies that maintain high environmental standards, such as those that reduce greenhouse gas emissions and improve energy efficiency. The emphasis on Green Stocks expedites the achievement of SDG 13 by channelling financial resources into corporate policies that are essential for addressing climate change. Investing in green stocks incentivizes enterprises to adopt sustainable practices, resulting in a decrease in carbon footprints and fostering technical innovation in environmental management.

Mittal et al. (2023) investigate how banking institutions might utilize their position to promote sustainable development through strategic investments and lending practices in the framework of research. The paper proposes that banks can play a crucial role in promoting long-term environmental objectives outlined in international agreements like the COP 26 UN Climate Change Conference by implementing green banking strategies such as Green Funds and Green Stocks.

Moreover, Mohamed (2023) explores the broader consequences of these financial practices on the well-being of society, emphasizing the significance of sustainable development that goes beyond environmental considerations. The research emphasizes that implementing green banking practices can contribute to a fairer allocation of resources, promoting sustainable socio-economic progress and strengthening SDG 11 (Sustainable Cities and Communities) by encouraging urban development that fulfils current needs without jeopardizing future generations (Mohamed, 2023). These insights reveal how accelerators, such as the transition to a green economy, which are supported by facilitators like Green Funds and Green Stocks, play a significant role in driving the banking sector's commitment to sustainable goals.

Advocacy for Environmental Education

Promoting environmental education is a vital catalyst in the field of green banking, increasing awareness and comprehension of sustainable practices among stakeholders in the financial industry. This educational initiative aims to raise awareness among individuals and corporations about the significance of environmental stewardship and promotes the use of sustainable banking practices.

Combining Green Awareness and Environmental Education

Green Awareness plays a crucial role in promoting and supporting environmental education. Financial institutions can exert influence over market behaviour and investment choices of individuals and enterprises by promoting knowledge of the advantages and importance of sustainable banking. Educational activities and workshops efficiently distribute information on the role of green banking in environmental preservation, directly promoting SDG 4 (Quality Education). These programs serve the dual purpose of educating stakeholders about the significance of sustainability in finance and providing them with the necessary knowledge to make well-informed decisions that are in line with environmental goals.

Adoption of Evolving Sustainability Criteria

The incorporation of dynamic sustainability criteria acts as a vital catalyst in green banking, proactively modernizing banking procedures to conform to the most up-to-date environmental benchmarks and sustainable development perspectives. By adopting this dynamic strategy, banks are able to incorporate advanced sustainability criteria into their operations. It not only improves their ability to respond effectively but also fosters a more responsible banking industry.

Research by Mittal et al. 2023) also demonstrates that banks that integrate changing sustainability standards into their operations not only comply with regulations but also gain the trust and backing of environmentally aware consumers and investors. It ultimately results in sustainable economic growth that benefits society as a whole. By adhering to these changing criteria, banks guarantee that their activities and financial offerings consistently embody the most effective methods of environmental conservation, establishing themselves as frontrunners in the shift towards a sustainable global economy.

Actions Targeting Climate Change Mitigation

Incorporation of environmental concerns into financial operations, "green banking" aims to counteract climate change. A solid commitment to tackling climate change may be shown by the allocation of cash for clean energy projects and the provision of financial tools to assist sustainability activities. Essential to this plan of action are green stocks. By encouraging investment in businesses with strong environmental standards, these stocks help reduce greenhouse gas emissions and promote sustainable business practices. Banks and investors may assist SDG 13 (Climate Action) by directing resources towards enterprises actively decreasing their carbon footprints via green stock investments. By providing capital to businesses and innovations that reduce carbon emissions, this investment speeds up the shift to a low-carbon economy.

Making Energy Usage More Accessible and Efficient

Sustainable Development Goal 7 (Affordable and Clean Energy) cannot be advanced without tackling climate change, which may be achieved by increasing energy efficiency and providing financial backing for renewable energy projects. Renewable energy projects, including those using solar, wind, and hydroelectric power, are greatly aided by the loans and green bonds made available by financial institutions. These monetary measures improve energy efficiency in many different industries while also expanding access to renewable energy.

Banks can make a big difference in the fight against climate change by directing funds effectively into these areas. They promote more widespread adoption of eco-friendly practices and contribute to a decrease in the world's carbon emissions. Financial institutions may show they are serious about sustainability and take a stand against climate change by making sure their investments support environmental causes. A dedication to complying with regulations and taking part in the worldwide shift towards sustainability is shown in the proactive measures taken by green banks to reduce the impact of climate change.

Alteration in Consumer Preferences Towards Eco-Friendly Products

Green banking accelerates as customer tastes for eco-friendly goods change, forcing financial products and services to reflect environmental concerns. Social values have changed, and financial institutions are developing novel ways to promote sustainable consumption and production. Green Credit is essential for funding eco-friendly goods and services. As customers choose sustainable options, banks are compelled to provide green loans or credits to help people and companies invest in renewable energy, energy-efficient appliances, and sustainable infrastructure. This facilitation satisfies the rising demand for green goods and immediately contributes to SDG 7 (Affordable and Clean Energy) by making clean energy more affordable to more people. Consumer preferences drive demand for sustainable urban solutions, affecting SDG 11 (Sustainable Cities and Communities). Financial institutions may exploit this trend to support green construction, public transit, and urban waste management initiatives. These investments make cities more sustainable, habitable, and environmentally resilient. Consumer preferences now encourage banks to promote initiatives and firms that reduce their environmental effect, supporting SDG 13 (Climate Action). Banks benefit from funding sustainable enterprises as more customers pick them, driving a market shift toward low-carbon and climate-resilient practices. Financial institutions respond to shifting customer preferences strategically to meet global sustainability objectives. Banks meet market demand and promote environmental sustainability by providing financial instruments for eco-friendly purchases. This strategy helps banks compete in a fast-changing financial world by attracting and retaining environmentally conscientious consumers.

These strategic banking sector modifications demonstrate a proactive commitment to sustainable practices, ensuring that financial institutions stay relevant and successful in supporting environmental sustainability. As consumer tastes shift toward eco-friendly items, green banking might drive environmental gains and promote essential SDGs.

Green Banking and SDGs

Green banking plays a crucial role in driving sustainable economic transformation by directly supporting the achievement of several Sustainable Development Goals (SDGs), notably SDG 7 (Affordable and Clean Energy), SDG 11 (Sustainable Cities and Communities), SDG 12 (Responsible Consumption and Production), and SDG 13 (Climate Action). Through innovative financial products and practices, green banking enhances environmental sustainability while fostering social equity and economic development.

Financial instruments specifically allocated for energy-efficient technologies and renewable energy projects are known as green funds and credits. Green funds and credits guarantee that clean, dependable, and contemporary energy solutions are accessible to a wide range of people by providing funding for sustainable energy projects. By encouraging the use of renewable energy across numerous industries and communities, this directly supports SDG 7. Banks can effectively direct funding toward projects with major environmental consequences by coordinating their lending criteria with current environmental rules. SDG 7 is strengthened by this integration, which quickens efforts to deliver clean and sustainable energy sources.

Green banking procedures are continuously modified to reflect the shifting consumer preferences towards eco-friendly products and the tightening sustainability criteria that accompany them. This guarantees that banking operations continue to be socially and ecologically just, which has a direct impact on SDG 11 by providing funds for sustainable urban infrastructure projects that improve city living. By providing money for initiatives that concentrate on developing resilient and sustainable urban environments, financial institutions can be instrumental in accomplishing SDG 11. Directing funding for projects like sustainable public transit networks and energy-efficient homes, green banking advances SDG 11. The robust and ecologically friendly urban environments that are created as a result of these investments raise the standard of living for city inhabitants.

Banks are compelled to develop financial solutions that encourage responsible consumption and production in response to the growing demand for sustainable products. Because banks are in line with what the market demands, they are incentivized to support SDG 12 by enhancing resource and energy efficiency, sustainable infrastructure, access to basic services, and the creation of green jobs.

Achieving SDG 13 requires putting current sustainability principles into practice. Banks guarantee that the projects they fund have a significant positive environmental impact by requiring the projects to provide quantifiable climate benefits. In addition to lessening the effects of climate change, this strategic approach strengthens the financial sector's role in promoting environmental action and awareness. Green stocks, which invest in firms that care about the environment, help achieve SDG 13 by giving startups the funding they need to develop new carbon-reduction solutions and by supporting their shift to more ecologically friendly operations. In addition to reducing climate change, this investment motivates companies to create sustainable solutions.

Reducing environmental footprints and enhancing urban living conditions are achieved through investments in energy-efficient buildings and sustainable transportation networks. Furthermore, the pursuit of SDG 13 is supported by the strict implementation of the sustainability standards that are in place. Banks make sure that the projects they sponsor have a major positive impact on the climate and increase public awareness and commitment to environmental issues. According to Mittal et al. (2023), this educational strategy places a strong emphasis on the necessity of incorporating sustainability into banking procedures in order to inform and interest customers in the advantages of eco-friendly financial products.

Encouraging education about the environment is crucial to achieving SDG 13. Banks can encourage their customers to select environmentally friendly stocks or bonds by providing seminars or online courses on green investing. This is in favor of programs that lower carbon emissions and increase energy efficiency. The study by Mohamed (2023) emphasizes the significance of educated financial practices in attaining favorable societal outcomes and draws attention to the wider social effects of sustainable banking.

CONCLUSION

Green banking is still a relatively new idea and hasn't really taken off in the banking industry. When it comes to competitive advantages in green strategies and instruments, Indian banks, more so than their counterparts in developed countries, are falling behind. They need to expand the reach and execution of green banking programs in order to maintain their competitiveness. In particular, with regard to SDGs 7 and 13, policymakers and regulators have implemented a number of initiatives to establish a financial ecosystem that supports sustainable goals. Notably, the dynamics and environment of the financial industry are greatly influenced by central banks.

The accomplishment of SDGs 7, 11, 12, and 13 is greatly aided by the strong framework of drivers, facilitators, and accelerators that characterizes green banking. Green banking not only solves today's environmental and social issues but also assures long-term sustainability by constantly changing to satisfy customer needs and sustainability criteria. A thorough and significant economic revolution will be sparked by these practices as they are further incorporated into the financial sector, strengthening the position of financial institutions in the global sustainability agenda. Future research could examine the effectiveness of various green banking instruments and strategies to determine which approaches are most effective and could serve as benchmarks for others, both new entrants and existing players, given that developing countries frequently rely more on regulatory approaches to promote green banking activities.

PRACTICAL AND SOCIAL IMPLICATIONS

Green Banking can promote green economies by incentivizing industries to adopt eco-friendly practices. It can also improve the performance and efficiency of financial instruments and the asset quality of banks in the long run. But in this context, businesses must be aware of green-driven projects. Subsidies, low interest rates, and other incentives can act as accelerators to optimize the advantages of green banking and, in the end, bring about a sustainable strategy within the financial industry. In light of the knowledge expressed in the suggested model that green banking can help achieve SDGs, banks ought to launch products that support inexpensive, clean energy while also reducing the negative consequences of climate change. It will give rise to a green and sustainable economy that will ensure a better tomorrow for future generations. Furthermore, more cooperation between the public and commercial sectors is required to develop cutting-edge financial solutions that meet the expanding need for sustainability. Increased customer knowledge and instruction regarding the advantages of green banking will also be essential in promoting its uptake. By concentrating on these areas, the banking sector may significantly advance the development of a more robust and sustainable global economy.

REFERENCES

Ariyapruchya, S., & Volz, U. (2022). Sustainable finance in Southeast Asia. In Schoenmaker, D., & Volz, U. (Eds.), *Scaling up sustainable finance and investment in the global south* (pp. 281–302). CEPR Press.

Barkawi, A., & Monnin, P. (2015). Greening China's Financial System. International Institute for Sustainable Development.

Beirne, J., Renzhi, N., & Volz, U. (2021). Bracing for the typhoon: Climate change and sovereign risk in Southeast Asia. *Sustainable Development (Bradford)*, 29(3), 537–551. 10.1002/sd.2199

Chen, C., Chong, K. M., Tan, T. H., & Wang, H. (2023). Mechanism of green finance awareness on sustainable competitiveness of enterprises. *Journal of ASIAN Behavioural Studies*, 8(25), 39–65. 10.21834/jabs.v8i25.427

Chmielarz, W., & Zborowski, M. (2020). Towards sustainability in e-banking website assessment methods. *Sustainability (Basel)*, 12(17), 7000. 10.3390/su12177000

Dai, X., Siddik, A. B., & Tian, H. (2022). Corporate social responsibility, green finance and environmental performance: Does green innovation matter? *Sustainability (Basel)*, 14(20), 13607. 10.3390/su142013607

Diaz-Rainey, I., Corfee-Morlot, J., Volz, U., & Caldecott, B. (2023). Green finance in Asia: Challenges, policies and avenues for research. *Climate Policy*, 23(1), 1–10. 10.1080/14693062.2023.2168359

Fahim, F., & Mahadi, B. (2022). Green supply chain management/green finance: A bibliometric analysis of the last twenty years by using the Scopus database. *Environmental Science and Pollution Research International*, 29(56), 84714–84740. 10.1007/s11356-022-21764-z35789465

Gao, X., & Guo, Y. (2022). The green credit policy impact on the financial performance of commercial banks: A quasi-natural experiment from China. *Mathematical Problems in Engineering*, 2022, 1–16. 10.1155/2022/5448359

IPCC. (2022). *Climate change 2022: Mitigation of climate change. Contribution of Working Group III to the Sixth Assessment Report of the Intergovernmental Panel on Climate Change* Cambridge University Press. 10.1017/9781009157926

Khan, I. U., Hameed, Z., Khan, S. U., & Khan, M. A. (2023). Green banking practices, bank reputation, and environmental awareness: Evidence from Islamic banks in a developing economy. *Environment, Development and Sustainability*, 26(6), 16073–16093. 10.1007/s10668-023-03288-937363011

Kumar, K., & Prakash, A. (2019). Managing sustainability in banking: Extent of sustainable banking adaptations of banking sector in India. *Environment, Development and Sustainability*, 22(6), 5199–5217. 10.1007/s10668-019-00421-5

Laghouag, A. (2022). The Impact of E-banking entrepreneurship orientation Drivers on Sustainable performance: Case study of banks operating in KSA. [BMAJ]. *Business Management Analysis Journal*, 5(1), 1–23. 10.24176/bmaj.v5i1.7191

Mittal, S., Chaudhry, S., & Bhadauria, S. S. (2023). Green banking – the path leading to sustainable economic growth. In *Smart Analytics, Artificial Intelligence and Sustainable Performance Management in a Global Digitalised Economy* (pp. 199–213). Emerald Publishing Limited. 10.1108/S1569-37592023000110B013

Mohamed, H. (2023). The impact of banking on sustainable financial practices toward an equitable economy. In *Green Finance Instruments, FinTech, and Investment Strategies* (pp. 65–80). Springer International Publishing. 10.1007/978-3-031-29031-2_4

Park, H., & Kim, J. D. (2020). Transition towards green banking: Role of financial regulators and financial institutions. *Asian Journal of Sustainability and Social Responsibility*, 5(1), 1–25. 10.1186/s41180-020-00034-3

Ramila, M., & Gurusamy, S. (2016). Impact of green banking initiatives adopted by foreign banks on profitability. *JIMS8M: The Journal of Indian Management &amp. Strategy*, 21(1), 12. 10.5958/0973-9343.2016.00002.8

Rats, O., & Alfimova, A. (2023). Green bonds as a perspective financial instrument for bank investment in Ukraine. *Development Management*, 21(1). 10.57111/devt/1.2023.08

Ravichandran, S., & Roy, M. (2022). Green finance: A key to fight with climate change. *Indian Journal of Economics and Finance*, 2(2), 34–38. 10.54105/ijef.B2526.112222

Sachs, J. D., Woo, W. T., Yoshino, N., & Taghizadeh-Hesary, F. (2019). *Why Is Green Finance Important? ADBI Working Paper 917*. Asian Development Bank Institute. https://www.adb.org/publications/why-green-finance-importa

Sharma, M., & Choubey, A. (2022). Green banking initiatives: A qualitative study on Indian banking sector. *Environment, Development and Sustainability*, 24(1), 293–319. 10.1007/s10668-021-01426-933967597

UNEP. (2021). Renewables 2021 global status report. In *UNEP - UN Environment Programme*. UNEP. https://www.unep.org/resources/report/renewables-2021-global-status-report

Volz, U. (2021). Governing sustainable finance. *Asia Bond Monitor*. https://asianbondsonline.adb.org/documents/abm/abm_jun_2021_governing_sustainable_finance.pdf

Volz, U., Beirne, J., Ambrosio Preudhomme, N., Fenton, A., Mazzacurati, E., Renzhi, N., & Stampe, J. (2020). Climate change and sovereign risk. SOAS University of London, Asian Development Bank Institute. 10.25501/SOAS.00033524

Yahya, A. A., & Zargar, P. (2023). Achieving corporate sustainability through green human resource management: The role of CSR in the banking industry of a developing country. *Sustainability (Basel)*, 15(14), 10834. 10.3390/su151410834

Yang, C., & Masron, T. A. (2022). Impact of digital finance on energy efficiency in the context of green sustainable development. *Sustainability (Basel)*, 14(18), 11250. 10.3390/su141811250

Yao, F., Qin, Z., & Wang, X. (2023). The influence of bank governance structure on green credit. *PLoS One*, 18(3), e0281115. 10.1371/journal.pone.028111536913350

Yoshino, N., Taghizadeh-Hesary, F., & Nakahigashi, M. (2018). Modelling the social funding and spill-over tax for Addressing the green energy financing gap. *Economic Modelling*. 10.1016/j.econmod.2018.11.018

Yuan, L., & Zeng, S. (2023). An empirical study on the impact of green credit on financial performance of china's listed banks. *Advances in Management and Applied Economics*, 89–110. 10.47260/amae/1325

Zhang, Z., & Ding, Y. (2023). The impact of green financial development on stock price crash risk from the perspective of information asymmetry in Chinese listed companies. *Environmental Science and Pollution Research International*, 30(37), 87199–87214. 10.1007/s11356-023-27771-y37418190

Zhang, Z., Liu, Y., Han, Z., & Liao, X. (2022). Green finance and carbon emission reduction: A bibliometric analysis and systematic review. *Frontiers in Environmental Science*, 10, 929250. 10.3389/fenvs.2022.929250

Chapter 9
Accelerating Financial Inclusion in Developing Economies (India) Through Digital Financial Technology

Parul Garg
https://orcid.org/0009-0007-2430-6169
Amity University, Noida, India

Tapsi Srivastava
https://orcid.org/0009-0004-0645-9047
Amity University, Noida, India

Ankit Goel
https://orcid.org/0009-0003-7697-9219
Maharaja Agrasen Institute of Management Studies, New Delhi, India

Nancy Gupta
University of Alberta, Canada

ABSTRACT

The study employs a mixed-methods approach, incorporating both quantitative and qualitative methodologies. The methodology encompasses literature and the development of a system dynamics model. This model is used to identify pivotal factors or barriers within emerging economies that either impede or facilitate the transition to an inclusive financial system. Keywords and drivers are discerned

DOI: 10.4018/979-8-3693-6321-8.ch009

through qualitative analysis of existing literature, facilitating the construction of a quantitative model. This model depicts the interplay and relative impact of identified factors on the ability of emerging economies to achieve financial inclusion. Results indicate that digital financial technologies significantly enhance financial inclusion by providing access to essential financial services for underserved populations. The study identifies ten key variables that influence financial systems. A primary challenge identified is the limited accessibility to financial services for people in developing regions. The chapter concludes with recommendations for policymakers and financial institutions.

INTRODUCTION

India is recognized as one of the world's fastest-growing economies. However, a significant portion of its population grapples with poverty and economic disparities, which subsequently hinder overall economic progress. Financial inclusion has garnered considerable attention due to its potential to enhance the livelihoods of low-income individuals. Many residents of rural areas in developing regions face challenges in accessing financial services. Digital financial technology emerges as a promising solution for expediting financial inclusion in emerging markets. Existing literature furnishes ample evidence highlighting the positive economic impact of advancing financial inclusion. Leveraging digital technologies, including Artificial Intelligence (AI), holds promise in facilitating access to financial institutions and their services for individuals in developing economies. Financial systems have a rich history dating back to 2000 BC, with the mercantilist system emerging as the earliest recognized system, its significance growing notably between the fifteenth and seventeenth centuries. Financial inclusion greatly contributes to the well-being of economies. The importance of financial systems surged alongside the rising demand for trade and the storage of precious metals like gold. Defined as a set of rules, regulations, and standards governing a capital market, a financial system orchestrates various aspects of economic interaction (Sánchez et al., 2021). During the Gold Smith Era, money lenders and cash collectors, often termed as bankers, acted as intermediaries between borrowers and savers. Money and finance play pivotal roles in both developed and developing economies, underscoring the indispensable link financial institutions provide to the economy (Awais et al., 2021). Two hypotheses elucidate this symbiotic relationship between finance and the economy: one posits that economic growth drives demand for financial services, while the other asserts that economic growth fosters financial system development (Ezzahid & Elouaourti, 2021), (Irfan, 2021). The evolution of financial systems has been propelled by rapid advancements in information technology and telecommunications, fostering innovation in products and services offered by financial institutions (Elsaid, 2023). However, this evolution has also led to the exclusion of certain segments of the economy as focus shifted towards value-added elements (Sánchez et al., 2021). Globally, approximately 2.7 billion individuals remain unbanked, highlighting the potential of financial institutions to contribute significantly to poverty alleviation and economic development through enhanced access to financial services (Yap et al., 2023). In recent years, there has been extensive research into accelerating financial inclusion.

In short, the promise of financial inclusion in the promotion of economic growth and well-being of people can be easily and efficiently accomplished with the help of AI. Both developed and developing countries have started the adoption of AI techniques for advancing financial inclusion. Literature has examined various innovative developments aimed at improving the financial status of economies. This study aims to develop a comprehensive understanding of financial inclusion across Indian economy by identifying key factors contributing to or hindering the establishment of inclusive financial systems. The study also evaluates the interplay between these factors and seeks to identify current barriers within financial systems that impede developing markets in various regions from achieving financial inclusion. Section 2 will provide a review of existing literature, while Section 3 will outline the research methodology used to identify key variables. Section 4 will present the results, followed by a discussion and conclusion in Section 5.

LITERATURE REVIEW

Financial institutions play a crucial role in shaping economic growth and resource distribution, exerting significant influence on the economy. By providing essential financial services, these institutions contribute to the advancement of developing economies. Banks, as exemplars of financial institutions, facilitate sustainable economic growth by generating liquidity for investments and accumulating capital (Ozili, 2021). Traditional banking practices typically involve extending long-term loans while accepting short-term investments, acting as intermediaries in financial transactions, albeit with potentially adverse effects on the economy. Particularly in developing nations, there has been a consistent decline in bank profitability, attributed to limited accessibility of financial services in non-urban or poorly infrastructure areas where operational costs are high (Barik and Sharma, 2019). Consequently, a substantial portion of the population remains unbanked, lacking access to fundamental financial services such as savings, investments, credit products, and money transfers. In the mid-1980s, the Reserve Bank of India began incorporating computers into financial management to support economic growth and financial inclusion (Gupta,

2011). Like many other developed and developing countries, India has taken significant measures towards financial inclusion, including the nationalization of banks and the creation of various organizations and schemes. However, these efforts have not substantially benefited the rural population due to limited access to financial institutions (Sharma et al., 2018) and widespread illiteracy. Consequently, a large portion of the population relies on informal sources for loans and other financial needs (Mahadeva, 2008). To address these challenges, the Indian government launched the Digital India program and the Skill India scheme, and introduced the Unified Payment Interface (UPI). Over the past decade, digital banking has been on the rise, transforming the traditionally cash-based economy into a more cashless one. Internet banking is anticipated to mitigate the issue of geographical barriers in banking transactions.

The Financial Bionetwork

Presently, the landscape of financial services is rapidly evolving due to the advent of financial technology, commonly referred to as FinTech. Mobile money, robo-advisors, and online banking solutions represent some of the FinTech innovations reshaping the financial sector. These technologies not only impact the economy but also influence financial planning strategies. The integration of FinTech within the financial sector is imperative for fostering innovation and ensuring the relevance of financial services. Often conceptualized as an ecosystem, FinTech facilitates the delivery of financial services at reduced costs (Rahmayati, 2021). Many financial institutions have forged partnerships with FinTech firms to enhance their existing service offerings (Rahmayati, 2021). By enhancing the accessibility of financial services, particularly through digital finance, social and economic inequalities can be mitigated, thereby fostering economic stability. The financial bionetwork encompasses a wide array of participants, including traditional banks, non-banking financial companies (NBFCs), FinTech startups, regulatory bodies, and consumers. This network operates synergistically to provide a seamless flow of financial services and products. Traditional banks are leveraging FinTech to streamline operations, reduce costs, and enhance customer experience. For instance, AI-driven chatbots are being used to handle customer inquiries, provide financial advice, and process transactions efficiently. Similarly, blockchain technology is being adopted for secure and transparent transaction processing, reducing the risk of fraud and enhancing trust among stakeholders. NBFCs and FinTech startups are playing a crucial role in reaching the unbanked and underbanked populations. These entities utilize advanced technologies such as machine learning and big data analytics to assess creditworthiness, enabling them to offer microloans and other financial products to individuals with little to no credit history. This approach not only promotes financial inclusion but also drives economic growth by empowering small businesses and entrepreneurs. Regulatory bodies are also a vital component of the financial bionetwork. They establish the framework within which financial institutions operate, ensuring stability, security, and consumer protection. In recent years, regulators have been adapting to the rapid pace of technological advancements by developing policies that encourage innovation while safeguarding the financial system. For example, the Reserve Bank of India (RBI) has introduced regulatory sandboxes to allow FinTech companies to test new products and services in a controlled environment. Consumers, the end-users of financial services, are at the heart of the financial bionetwork. The shift towards digital finance has empowered consumers by providing them with greater control over their financial decisions. Mobile banking apps, digital wallets, and online investment platforms offer convenience, accessibility, and personalized financial solutions. As consumer demand for digital financial services grows, the financial bionetwork continues to evolve, incorporating new technologies and practices to meet these changing needs.

The financial bionetwork is not without its challenges. Issues such as cybersecurity threats, data privacy concerns, and the digital divide pose significant risks. Financial institutions must invest in robust security measures to protect sensitive information and maintain consumer trust. Additionally, efforts must be made to bridge the digital divide, ensuring that all segments of the population have access to digital financial services.

Financial Inclusion

Financial inclusion refers to a system where all segments of society have access to essential financial services such as credit products, money transfers, and savings, thereby fostering economic inclusivity. A well-developed and accessible inclusive financial system not only creates new business opportunities in the private sector but also positively impacts the economy by facilitating efficient distribution of financial resources, addressing challenges like poverty, and promoting growth and stability. Access to financial services enables individuals to tap into additional resources, thereby contributing to economic growth (Adedokun & Aga, 2021). Traditional banking practices, acting as intermediaries in financing, have weakened the economy, with banks experiencing declining profits in developing markets due to limited operations in non-urban areas, where infrastructure costs are prohibitive (Isukul & Tantua, 2021). The manifold benefits of financial inclusion have propelled it into the spotlight as a research topic, aligning with the goals of international organizations like the United Nations. Additionally, it has the potential to foster an inclusive society by delivering socio-economic benefits that help alleviate poverty levels (Irfan, Kadry, Sharif, & Ullah Khan, 2023). However, alongside its advantages, financial inclusion also presents certain drawbacks. One such disadvantage arises from a fully inclusive system, which may lead to a high number of inactive clients. Inactive clients, who hold accounts but do not engage in transactions, can reduce transaction volumes, thereby adversely affecting bank revenues and subsequently impacting the economy, including tax earnings (Ozili, 2021). Another drawback is associated with extreme inclusion, where access to financial services is unrestricted. This scenario can expose the financial system to heightened risks of criminal activity, posing significant operational risks to banks (Ozili, 2021).

In regions like India, a substantial portion of the population remains excluded from financial services despite the country's rapid economic growth (Irfan, Elmogy, Majid, & El-Sappagh, 2023). This exclusion limits the benefits that could otherwise be derived from the burgeoning economy. Recent advancements in digital financial technologies have significantly impacted financial inclusion efforts, especially in emerging markets. Mobile money services, such as M-Pesa in Kenya, have provided a convenient platform for transactions, savings, and credit access, significantly reducing the unbanked population (Kshetri, 2021). Similarly, digital banking innovations have transformed access to financial services in remote regions, overcoming traditional banking barriers (Rahmayati, 2021). Digital payment platforms like Alipay in China have revolutionized financial inclusion by providing seamless payment solutions, credit services, and wealth management products to millions of users. Alipay's integration with e-commerce and everyday financial transactions has significantly enhanced financial accessibility and inclusion (Mitchell, 2019). Existing literature extensively explores potential solutions aimed at enhancing inclusiveness in the financial sector for developing markets.

Artificial Intelligence

AI technologies are playing a crucial role in enhancing financial inclusion. AI-driven solutions, such as robo-advisors and automated credit scoring, streamline financial services and make them more accessible to underserved populations (Mhlanga, 2020). For example, Kueski in Mexico leverages AI to extend credit based on non-traditional data sources, broadening financial access (Mitchell, 2019). Artificial intelligence (AI) encompasses the ability of computers to execute tasks resembling human actions. Over the years, AI has evolved to perform tasks with precision and autonomy, significantly impacting various industries. By embracing AI technologies, numerous businesses can enhance their operations and boost revenue streams. Within the banking sector, AI is instrumental in employing algorithms to analyze customer data effectively, thus enhancing customer service (Kaur et. Al., 2020). AI technology finds application across four primary categories: front-office customer-centric applications, back-office operational applications, trading and portfolio management, and regulatory compliance. The diverse use cases of AI in banking contribute to improved efficiency, customer interactions, and overall experience by mitigating risks and bolstering security measures (Soni & Vishal, 2019). Incorporating AI in banking facilitates access to non-financial data, such as phone bills and non-transactional records, through big data analytics. While the synergistic application of AI and big data analytics offers numerous benefits, AI alone presents distinct advantages (Irfan, Hussainey, Chan Bukhari, & Nam, 2024). Simplifying the process of opening formal bank accounts, often perceived as tedious by customers, is vital for enhancing customer experience. Communication is a key driver in this regard, and chatbots emerge as a valuable tool in addressing customer queries and providing solutions promptly. Moreover, with the aim of improving financial inclusion, banks can mitigate associated risks by employing various levels of AI to verify customer identities before granting access to banking products and services (Ozili, 2021).

Despite its advantages, it's essential to acknowledge and address the drawbacks associated with AI adoption. The rapid proliferation of AI in financial services may inadvertently exclude certain segments of the population, particularly the elderly, from accessing services. Moreover, increased AI adoption could lead to potential job displacements. Additionally, inadequately trained AI models, resulting in system inefficiencies and analysis errors, pose significant challenges (Ozili, 2021).

How AI Works

Artificial Intelligence (AI) is transforming financial services by automating processes, analyzing large sets of data, and making predictions to enhance decision-making. AI systems collect data from various sources such as customer data, transaction history, social media, and non-financial data using sensors, web scraping, and databases. AI employs machine learning techniques, including deep learning and predictive analytics, to identify patterns and insights from the collected data. This step involves the system learning from data to improve its understanding and predictions over time.

AI uses neural networks and other advanced algorithms to make predictions based on the patterns it has learned. Examples of these applications include credit scoring, fraud detection, and personalized financial advice. AI systems apply the predictions to perform specific tasks, such as approving a loan, identifying fraudulent transactions, or offering tailored financial products to customers. These systems continually learn from new data and feedback, refining their models and improving accuracy.

The figure below illustrates the AI process in financial services, showing the steps from data collection to performing tasks.

Figure 1. How AI works

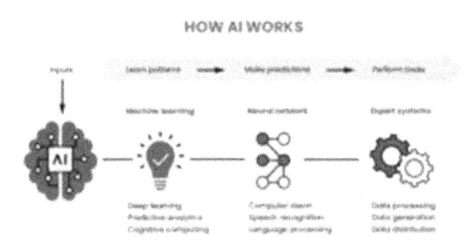

The Use of Digital Financial Technology to Enhance Financial Inclusion

The pivotal role of financial inclusion in enhancing economic growth is widely acknowledged. Given the pronounced levels of exclusion in the Asian region, numerous studies are underway to evaluate the current state of financial inclusion and its impact on the economy (Irfan, Elhoseny, Kassim, & Metawa, 2023). A comprehensive study conducted by Zins and Weil in 2016 examined various factors influencing financial inclusion across 37 Asian countries. Their findings indicated that financially inclusive individuals were typically older, educated, and financially stable men (Zins et al., 2016). Similarly, research conducted in Uganda by Bongomin et al. highlighted the relationship between institutional frameworks and financial inclusion, noting an indirect association with social networks (Bongomin et al., 2018) Illiteracy poses a significant barrier to financial inclusion in Asian countries, with factors such as age, gender, and ethnicity identified as contributing factors (Kabakova & Plaksenko, 2018).

In Nigeria, the adoption of innovative technology like Migo is aimed at bolstering financial inclusion. Migo assesses potential clients' eligibility for loans based on provided information, fostering trust relationships that enable access to higher-value loans upon timely repayment (Kshetri, 2021) Globally, researchers are exploring various applications of artificial intelligence (AI) to accelerate financial inclusion. For instance, Kshetri's work in 2021 elucidated how developing countries leverage financial technology (FinTechs) to evaluate clients' creditworthiness, exemplified by Indonesia's peer-to-peer (P2P) lender assessing risk based on customer-provided details. Similarly, Kueski in Mexico extends loans to customers upon collateral provision, showcasing AI's role in expanding financial access. Mhlanga's study in 2020 underscored how digital technology, particularly AI, facilitates financial service access for women and low-income earners, emphasizing the significance of risk assessment capabilities (Mhlanga, 2020). In Argentina, increased adoption of debit and credit products in the pursuit of financial inclusion resulted in heightened tax revenues (Mitchell, 2019).

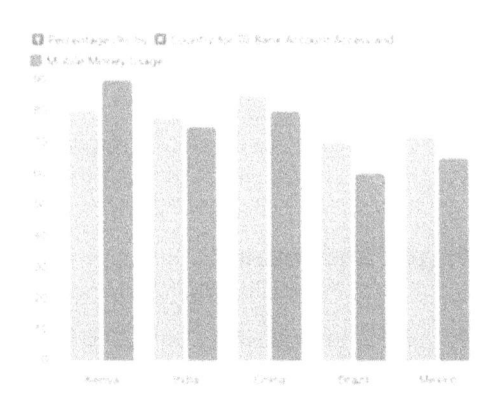

Comparative Analysis of Financial Inclusion Initiatives

In **Africa**, mobile money services have been a game-changer for financial inclusion. Services like M-Pesa in Kenya have successfully integrated a large portion of the unbanked population into the financial system by providing accessible financial services (Zins & Weill, 2016). **Asian countries** have made significant strides in financial inclusion through digital financial technologies. India's Digital India program and the Unified Payment Interface (UPI) have drastically increased digital transactions and financial access, while Indonesia's peer-to-peer lending platforms use AI to assess credit risk, facilitating financial inclusion (Sharma et al., 2018; Kshetri, 2021). In **Latin America**, digital financial technologies and AI have been pivotal in expanding credit access and financial services. In Mexico, companies like Kueski use AI to provide loans based on non-traditional credit assessments, enhancing financial inclusion (Mitchell, 2019).

Figure 2. Comparative analysis of financial inclusion initiatives

The above bar chart compares financial inclusion initiatives and their economic impacts in different countries, highlighting key metrics like the percentage of the population with bank accounts and mobile money usage. It shows how various countries have adopted different strategies to enhance financial inclusion. M-Pesa in Kenya has enabled many Kenyans to access financial services previously unavailable to them, such as savings accounts, credit, and insurance, thereby promoting economic growth and reducing poverty (Kshetri, 2021). Alipay in China has significantly enhanced financial accessibility and inclusion by integrating financial services with e-commerce and everyday transactions, impacting millions of users (Mitchell, 2019).

Case Studies

Kenya: M-Pesa

M-Pesa, launched by Safaricom in 2007, is a mobile phone-based money transfer, financing, and microfinancing service. Its success in Kenya is a testament to the transformative power of digital financial technologies. By 2021, M-Pesa had over 40 million users across Africa. Its widespread adoption is due to its simplicity, reliability, and the extensive network of agents facilitating cash-in and cash-out transactions (Kshetri, 2021). M-Pesa has enabled many Kenyans to access financial services previously unavailable to them, such as savings accounts, credit, and insurance, thereby promoting economic growth and reducing poverty.

China: Alipay

Alipay, established by Alibaba Group in 2004, is one of the largest mobile and online payment platforms in the world. Alipay's ecosystem includes a wide range of financial services, such as payments, credit scoring, loans, and wealth management, integrated with e-commerce and retail services. The platform has been instrumental in increasing financial inclusion in China by providing services to underserved populations, including those in rural areas. Alipay's success is driven by its user-friendly interface, robust security measures, and integration with everyday financial activities (Mitchell, 2019).

Regulatory Challenges and Impact

Regulatory frameworks play a crucial role in shaping the outcomes of financial inclusion initiatives. In developing economies, regulatory challenges can significantly impact the effectiveness of digital financial technologies.

- **Regulatory Frameworks in Kenya**

Kenya's regulatory framework has been supportive of digital financial innovations like M-Pesa. The Central Bank of Kenya (CBK) adopted a "test and learn" approach, allowing Safaricom to pilot M-Pesa before full-scale deployment. This regulatory flexibility enabled rapid adoption and scaling of M-Pesa, contributing to its success

(Kshetri, 2021). However, regulatory challenges remain, such as ensuring consumer protection, managing data privacy, and preventing fraud.

- **Regulatory Frameworks in China**

In China, the regulatory environment has both facilitated and posed challenges to the growth of digital financial services. The People's Bank of China (PBOC) has implemented regulations to ensure the stability and security of digital payment platforms like Alipay. However, stringent regulatory measures, such as caps on transaction volumes and stricter Know Your Customer (KYC) requirements, have also been introduced to mitigate risks associated with financial crimes and to maintain financial stability (Mitchell, 2019).

Economic Impacts of Financial Inclusion

a) **Quantitative Analysis on GDP Growth and Socio-Economic Indicators:** Financial inclusion is widely recognized as a driver of economic growth and socio-economic development. By providing access to financial services, financial inclusion can enhance GDP growth, reduce poverty, and improve overall socio-economic indicators. Here, we present a quantitative analysis of these impacts:
   - **GDP Growth:** Studies have shown that financial inclusion can significantly boost GDP growth. For instance, a World Bank study estimated that increasing financial inclusion by 10% could lead to a 1% increase in GDP growth (Demirgüç-Kunt et al., 2018). Financial inclusion facilitates increased investment, consumption, and economic activities, contributing to overall economic growth. In India, digital financial inclusion initiatives have contributed to a more inclusive economy. The Pradhan Mantri Jan Dhan Yojana (PMJDY) scheme, which aims to provide universal access to banking services, has resulted in millions of new bank accounts, leading to increased savings and investments. According to the Reserve Bank of India, these initiatives have the potential to add 2% to India's GDP (RBI, 2020).

Figure 3. Financial inclusion and GDP growth

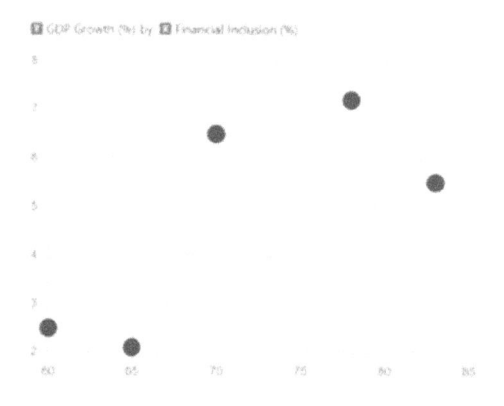

The above graph shows the correlation between financial inclusion (percentage of the population with access to financial services) and GDP growth rates across different countries. As seen, higher financial inclusion rates generally correlate with stronger GDP growth.

- **Poverty Reduction:** Financial inclusion plays a crucial role in reducing poverty by providing access to credit, savings, and insurance. These financial services enable individuals to invest in education, health, and businesses, leading to improved living standards. A study by the Consultative Group to Assist the Poor (CGAP) found that access to financial services reduced poverty rates by up to 20% in some regions (CGAP, 2019). In Kenya, the introduction of M-Pesa has lifted approximately 2% of households out of extreme poverty by providing easy access to financial services, facilitating savings, and enabling entrepreneurship (Suri & Jack, 2016).

Figure 4. Impact of financial inclusion on poverty reduction

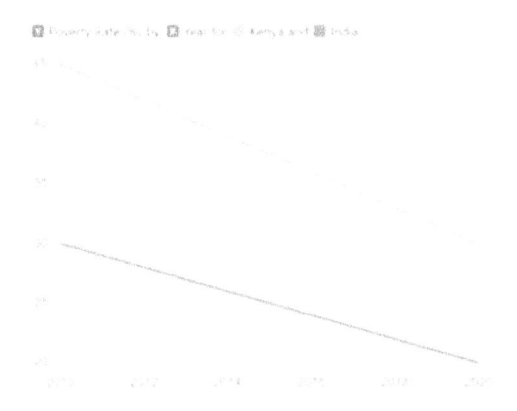

The above chart illustrates the decrease in poverty rates in Kenya and India, showing the impact of financial inclusion initiatives over the years. As financial inclusion efforts increased, poverty rates have significantly dropped in both countries

- **Socio-Economic Indicators:** Financial inclusion improves socio-economic indicators such as education, health, and gender equality. Access to financial services enables families to invest in education, leading to higher school enrollment rates and better educational outcomes. Moreover, financial inclusion empowers women by providing them with financial autonomy and opportunities for entrepreneurship. In Bangladesh, the Grameen Bank's microfinance program has significantly improved socio-economic indicators by providing microloans to women, leading to increased school enrollment for children and improved health outcomes (Yunus, 2007).

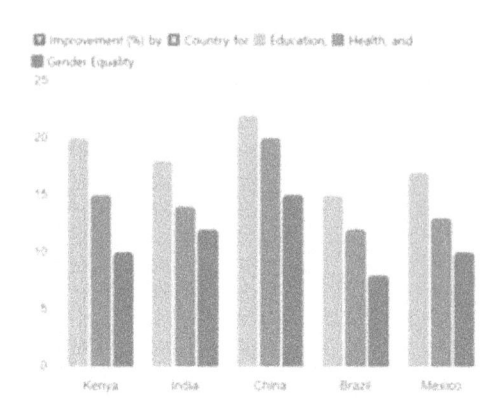

Figure 5. Financial inclusion and socio-economic improvements

The above bar chart demonstrates the relationship between financial inclusion and improvements in socio-economic indicators such as education, health, and gender equality across different countries. Higher financial inclusion rates are associated with significant socio-economic improvements.

b) Stakeholder Perspectives on Financial Inclusion
- **Policymakers:** Policymakers emphasize the importance of financial inclusion for achieving inclusive growth and economic stability. According to the World Bank, financial inclusion is a key enabler of seven out of the 17 Sustainable Development Goals (SDGs), including poverty reduction, gender equality, and economic growth (World Bank, 2018). Governments are implementing policies and regulations to promote financial inclusion and ensure consumer protection. For example, the Indian government's Digital India initiative aims to promote digital financial services and enhance financial literacy, thereby driving financial inclusion and economic growth (Government of India, 2015).
- **Non-Governmental Organizations (NGOs):** NGOs play a vital role in promoting financial inclusion by providing financial education, advocating for inclusive policies, and supporting community-based financial services. Organizations like the Bill & Melinda Gates Foundation have been instrumental in advancing financial inclusion through grants and partnerships with governments and financial institutions (Bill & Melinda Gates Foundation, 2018). NGOs highlight the need for targeted interventions to address the specific challenges faced by marginalized communities, such as women, rural populations, and low-income households.

- **Financial Institutions:** Financial institutions recognize the business potential of financial inclusion and are increasingly adopting digital technologies to reach underserved populations. Banks and FinTech companies are developing innovative products and services to cater to the needs of unbanked and underbanked individuals. For instance, the State Bank of India (SBI) has launched several initiatives to promote financial inclusion, including the use of mobile banking and digital wallets to reach remote areas (SBI, 2020). Similarly, FinTech companies like Paytm are providing digital payment solutions that facilitate financial transactions for millions of users in India.

Regulatory Hurdles Faced by Financial Institutions

a) **KYC (Know Your Customer) Requirements:** Stringent KYC regulations, while crucial for preventing fraud and money laundering, can pose significant barriers for financial institutions attempting to expand services to underserved populations. Many individuals in these populations lack the necessary identification documents, making it difficult for them to open bank accounts or access financial services (World Bank, 2018). For example, in India, while the Aadhaar biometric identification system has improved KYC compliance, some rural and low-income individuals still face challenges in obtaining and using Aadhaar for financial services (RBI, 2020).

b) **Regulatory Compliance Costs:** High compliance costs associated with meeting regulatory requirements can deter financial institutions from expanding their services to underserved areas. These costs include investments in technology, staff training, and ongoing monitoring and reporting requirements (CGAP, 2019). In developing countries, where financial institutions often operate with thin margins, these costs can be prohibitive, limiting their ability to serve unbanked populations (IFC, 2017).

c) **Consumer Protection Regulations:** Regulations aimed at protecting consumers can sometimes have unintended consequences. For instance, caps on interest rates for microloans, while intended to protect borrowers from excessive charges, can limit the availability of credit to high-risk borrowers who are most in need of financial services (Kshetri, 2021). In some cases, overly restrictive consumer protection laws can stifle innovation and the development of new financial products tailored to the needs of underserved populations (World Bank, 2018).

d) **Cross-Border Regulations:** Cross-border regulatory discrepancies can hinder the expansion of financial services, particularly for digital financial technologies and mobile money. Different countries have varying regulations concerning data protection, transaction limits, and interoperability of financial systems, which can complicate the provision of seamless financial services across borders (IMF, 2019).

Influence of Cultural Beliefs and Practices on Financial Behaviors

a) **Trust in Financial Institutions:** Cultural beliefs about trust and security significantly influence financial behaviors. In many communities, mistrust of formal financial institutions due to past experiences of fraud or mismanagement can lead to a preference for informal financial services (Yunus, 2007). In regions like sub-Saharan Africa, traditional savings groups and informal lending circles are often preferred over formal banks due to their communal and trust-based nature (Collins et al., 2009).

b) **Gender Norms and Financial Access:** Gender norms and cultural practices can restrict women's access to financial services. In some cultures, women may need permission from male family members to open bank accounts or borrow money, limiting their financial independence and access (IFC, 2017). Initiatives aimed at promoting financial inclusion must consider these cultural barriers and design gender-sensitive financial products and services (Kabeer, 2012).

c) **Religious Beliefs:** Religious beliefs can also influence financial behaviors. For example, in Muslim-majority countries, the principles of Islamic finance, which prohibit interest (riba) and emphasize risk-sharing, affect the types of financial products that are acceptable and in demand (El-Gamal, 2006). Financial institutions need to offer Sharia-compliant products to cater to the needs of Muslim customers, which can involve additional regulatory and operational considerations (IFC, 2017).

d) **Cultural Attitudes towards Debt:** Cultural attitudes towards debt and borrowing can vary significantly. In some cultures, debt is viewed negatively, and individuals may avoid borrowing even when it is financially prudent to do so. This can limit the uptake of credit products and affect financial inclusion efforts (Rutherford, 2000). Financial education programs need to address these cultural attitudes and promote responsible borrowing and financial management practices (CGAP, 2019).

METHODOLOGY

This study employs a mixed-methods approach, incorporating both quantitative and qualitative methodologies. The research methodology encompasses literature analysis and the development of a system dynamics model. The system dynamics model is utilized to identify pivotal factors or barriers within emerging economies that either impede or facilitate the transition to an inclusive financial system. Keywords and drivers are discerned through qualitative analysis of existing literature, facilitating the construction of a quantitative model. This model depicts the interplay and relative impact of identified factors on the ability of emerging economies to achieve financial inclusion. Moreover, the study focuses on specific demographics within these markets, particularly individuals with limited access to financial services. Through a comprehensive literature review, key limitations hindering the attainment of financial inclusion in emerging economies are identified. The primary objective is to construct a systems-based framework that elucidates how various variables influence countries' ability to achieve financial inclusion. The findings are presented using a system thinking and design approach, drawing insights from both the literature analysis and the associated system dynamics model.

Figure 6. A systematic framework

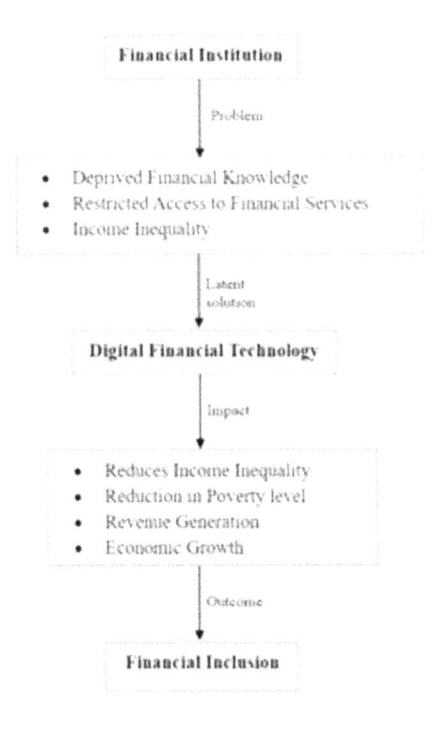

```
              Financial Institution
                      |
                   Problem
                      ↓
    • Deprived Financial Knowledge
    • Restricted Access to Financial Services
    • Income Inequality
                      |
                   Latent
                   solution
                      ↓
            Digital Financial Technology
                      |
                   Impact
                      ↓
    • Reduces Income Inequality
    • Reduction in Poverty level
    • Revenue Generation
    • Economic Growth
                      |
                   Outcome
                      ↓
              Financial Inclusion
```

RESULTS

The framework study has identified ten key variables that significantly influence the financial system and may act as barriers, impeding certain markets from achieving financial inclusion. Figure 1 illustrates all variables considered within the framework of financial inclusion. A primary challenge in attaining an inclusive system stems from the limited accessibility to financial services for people in developing regions. A substantial portion of the population residing in these areas lacks access to financial services provided by traditional financial institutions. Operational costs pose a significant barrier, preventing financial institutions from extending their reach to certain segments within the market, thereby affecting both institutions and residents in developing markets as integral components within the framework system.

The initial challenges within the system primarily revolve around financial inequality, which arises from the limited accessibility preventing many individuals from accessing basic financial services such as savings or investments. The restricted accessibility is a direct consequence of the high operational costs, leading many institutions to refrain from establishing infrastructure in underserved areas. Furthermore, a lack of understanding regarding the role and purpose of financial institutions and the services they offer remains prevalent in these regions. Financial literacy emerges as a critical factor contributing to the inability of markets to achieve inclusion, given its significant impact on inclusiveness. Prior literature has demonstrated that enhancing financial literacy not only fosters economic growth but also stimulates business development.

Digital financial technology emerges as a viable solution to enhance inclusiveness levels. Digital technologies not only offer opportunities and additional channels for financial institutions to deliver services but can also serve as a means to improve financial literacy. Ideally, as financial inclusion levels improve, it would directly benefit the economy by addressing economic inequality, improving money distribution, and enhancing revenue generation in developing regions. However, the authors acknowledge the contextual differences, including country-specific requirements and regulations. Therefore, the extraction of best practices, tailored to specific country dynamics, is imperative for consolidating a more predictive and dynamic framework. The research team has initiated the construction of a systems dynamic's framework, incorporating relevant data and additional variables as outlined above. While the model is in its early stages, continuous development is underway to refine and enhance its efficacy throughout the course of this study.

DISCUSSION AND CONCLUSION

This study aims to examine the challenges encountered by financial institutions, particularly within the banking sector of developing and emerging markets, with a focus on enhancing financial inclusion as a pivotal driver for realizing economic growth potential. Employing a systems dynamics framework, the research identifies a spectrum of variables that act as impediments to improving current levels of financial inclusion in these economies. Eight key variables were delineated, each with its respective impact on fostering a financially inclusive system. Financial literacy, accessibility to financial services, and financial inequality emerged as primary barriers hindering the attainment of an inclusive system. Digital financial technology is recognized as a potential catalyst capable of accelerating economic development in developing regions. By leveraging digital financial technology, individuals residing in remote or underserved areas, including urban peripheries, can access essential financial services, thereby enhancing their living standards. Moreover, besides uplifting the financial status of individuals gaining access to financial services, financial inclusion also augments economic growth by bolstering revenue generation. A prospective avenue for future research involves investigating and identifying diverse models applicable to the current financial sector to enhance inclusivity. Furthermore, exploring the effects of these models can shed light on suitable approaches for mitigating financial exclusion in emerging economies.

RECOMMENDATIONS FOR STRENGTHENING FINANCIAL INCLUSION

1. **Supportive Regulatory Environment:** Policymakers should adopt flexible regulatory frameworks that encourage innovation while ensuring consumer protection and financial stability. The "test and learn" approach used in Kenya can serve as a model for other developing economies.
2. **Consumer Protection and Education:** Regulations should focus on enhancing consumer protection through robust data privacy measures and fraud prevention mechanisms. Additionally, increasing financial literacy is essential to ensure that consumers can effectively utilize digital financial services.
3. **Collaboration between Stakeholders:** Governments, financial institutions, and technology providers should collaborate to create an inclusive financial ecosystem. Public-private partnerships can drive the development and scaling of digital financial technologies.

4. **Expand Quantitative Analysis:** Include more detailed statistical data and case studies to illustrate the economic impacts of financial inclusion. Present data on GDP growth, poverty reduction, and socio-economic improvements linked to financial inclusion initiatives.
5. **Integrate Stakeholder Perspectives:** Incorporate quotes, testimonials, and case studies from policymakers, NGOs, and financial institutions to provide a comprehensive view of the importance of addressing financial exclusion. Highlight the roles and contributions of these stakeholders in promoting financial inclusion.
6. **Use Visual Aids:** Utilize graphs, charts, and tables to present quantitative data and trends more effectively. Visual aids can help readers understand the economic impacts and stakeholder perspectives more clearly.
7. **Discuss Specific Regulatory Hurdles:** Provide detailed examples of regulatory challenges, such as KYC requirements and compliance costs, faced by financial institutions in different regions. Include case studies that highlight how these hurdles have been addressed or remain a barrier.
8. **Analyze Cultural Influences:** Explore how cultural beliefs and practices impact financial behaviors and access to services. Incorporate case studies and examples from different cultural contexts to illustrate these influences.
9. **Integrate Stakeholder Insights:** Include perspectives from regulators, financial institutions, and community leaders on addressing regulatory and cultural challenges. Highlight successful strategies and ongoing efforts to overcome these barriers.

REFERENCES

Adedokun, M., & Aga, M. (2021). Financial inclusion: A pathway to economic growth in Sub-Saharan African economies. *International Journal of Finance & Economics*, 28(3), 2712–2728. 10.1002/ijfe.2559

Awais, M., Asmy, M., Raza, A., Mohsin, M., & Bhatti, O. (2021). The Process of Risk Management: Sketching the Providers of Islamic Micro-Finance. *International Journal of Scientific Research*, 59–76.

Barik, R., & Sharma, P. (2019). Analyzing the progress and prospects of financial inclusion in India. *Journal of Public Affairs*, 19(4), e1948. 10.1002/pa.1948

Bill & Melinda Gates Foundation. (2018). *Financial Services for the Poor*. Bill & Melinda Gates Foundation. https://www.gatesfoundation.org

Bongomin, G.O.C., Munene, J.C., Ntayi, J.M. & Malinga, C.A. (2018). Analyzing the relationship between institutional framework and financial inclusion in rural Uganda: A social network perspective. *International Journal of Emerging Markets*, 606-630. 10.1108/IJoEM-02-2017-0057

Collins, D., Morduch, J., Rutherford, S., & Ruthven, O. (2009). *Portfolios of the Poor: How the World's Poor Live on $2 a Day*. Princeton University Press.

Consultative Group to Assist the Poor (CGAP). (2019). *Financial Inclusion and Poverty Reduction*. CGAP. https://www.cgap.org

Demirgüç-Kunt, A., Klapper, L., Singer, D., Ansar, S., & Hess, J. (2018). *The Global Findex Database 2017: Measuring Financial Inclusion and the Fintech Revolution*. World Bank. https://openknowledge.worldbank.org

El-Gamal, M. A. (2006). *Islamic Finance: Law, Economics, and Practice*. Cambridge University Press. 10.1017/CBO9780511753756

Elsaid, H. M. (2023). *A review of literature directions regarding the impact of fintech firms on the banking industry*. Qualitative Research in Financial Markets. 10.1108/QRFM-10-2020-0197

Ezzahid, E., & Elouaourti, Z. (2021). Financial Inclusion, Financial Frictions, and Economic Growth: Evidence from Africa. *Journal of African Business*, 1–26. 10.1080/15228916.2021.1926856

Government of India. (2015). *Digital India Programme*. Digital India. https://www.digitalindia.gov.in

Gupta, S. K. (2011). Financial Inclusion-IT as enabler. *Reserve Bank of India occasional papers* (pp.129-148). Reserve Bank of India.

International Finance Corporation (IFC). (2017). Financial Inclusion in Sub-Saharan Africa. Retrieved from https://www.ifc.org

International Monetary Fund (IMF). (2019). *Fintech: The Experience So Far*. IMF. https://www.imf.org

Irfan, M. (2021, January). Do Shariah Indices converge? Evidence from Gulf Cooperation Council countries. *International Journal of Business Excellence*, 23(2), 251–269. 10.1504/IJBEX.2021.113448

Irfan, M., Elhoseny, M., Kassim, S., & Metawa, N. (2023). *Advanced Machine Learning Algorithms for Complex Financial Applications*. IGI Global. 10.4018/978-1-6684-4483-2

Irfan, M., Elmogy, M., Majid, M. S., & El-Sappagh, S. (2023). *The Impact of AI Innovation on Financial Sectors in the Era of Industry 5.0*. IGI Global. 10.4018/979-8-3693-0082-4

Irfan, M., Hussainey, K., Chan Bukhari, S. A., & Nam, Y. (Eds.). (2024). *Issues of Sustainability in AI and New-Age Thematic Investing*. IGI Global Publisher. 10.4018/979-8-3693-3282-5

Irfan, M., Kadry, S., Sharif, M., & Ullah Khan, H. (2023). *Fintech Applications in Islamic Finance: AI, Machine Learning, and Blockchain Techniques*. IGI Global. 10.4018/979-8-3693-1038-0

Isukul, A., & Tantua, B., (2021). Financial Inclusion in Developing Countries: Applying Financial Technology as a Panacea, *South Asian Journal of Social Studies and Economics* (pp. 42-60). .10.9734/sajsse/2021/v9i230237

Kabakova, O. V., & Plaksenkov, E. A. (2018). Analysis of factors affecting financial inclusion: Ecosystem view. *Journal of Business Research*, 89, 198–205. 10.1016/j.jbusres.2018.01.066

Kabeer, N. (2012). *Women's Economic Empowerment and Inclusive Growth: Labour Markets and Enterprise Development*. International Development Research Centre.

Kaur, N., Sahdev, S., Sharma, M., & Siddiqui, L. (2020). Banking 4.0: -The Influence of Artificial Intelligence on the Banking Industry & How AI is Changing the Face of Modern Day Banks. *International Journal of Management*, 11(6), 577–585. 10.34218/IJM.11.6.2020.049

Kshetri, N. (2021). The Role of Artificial Intelligence in Promoting Financial Inclusion in Developing Countries. *Journal of Global Information Technology Management*, 24(1), 1–6. 10.1080/1097198X.2021.1871273

Mahadeva, M. (2008). Financial growth in India: Whither financial inclusion? *Margin - the Journal of Applied Economic Research*, 2(2), 177–197. 10.1177/097380100800200202

. Mhlanga, D., (2020). Industry 4.0 in Finance: The Impact of Artificial Intelligence (AI) on Digital Financial Inclusion. *International Journal of Financial Studies*.

Mitchell, K., & Scott, R. (2019). *Pesos or Plastic: Financial Inclusion*. Taxation, and Development in South America. 10.1007/978-3-030-14876-8

Ozili, P. K. (2021). Financial inclusion research around the world: A review. *The Forum for Social Economics*, 50(4), 457–479. 10.1080/07360932.2020.1715238

Rahmayati, R. (2021). Accelerate Ecosystem Development Financial Services Sector. *Annual Conference on IHTIFAZ: Islamic Economic, Finance and Banking (ACI-IJIEFB)* (pp. 235-243). IEEE.

Reserve Bank of India (RBI). (2020). *Financial Inclusion in India: Moving Beyond Jan-Dhan Yojana*. RBI. https://www.rbi.org.in

Rutherford, S. (2000). *The Poor and Their Money*. Oxford University Press.

Sánchez, F., Lara-Rubio, J., Verdu, A., & Meseguer, V. (2021). Research Advances on Financial Inclusion: A Bibliometric Analysis. *Sustainability (Basel)*, 13(6), 3156. 10.3390/su13063156

. Sharma, D., Bhattacharya, S., & Thukral, S., (2018). Assessment of financial inclusive policy in Indian economy, *International Journal of Ethics and Systems*, 304-320.

Soni, V., & kumar, D. (2019). (pp. 1–7). Role Of Artificial Intelligence in Combating Cyber Threats in Banking.

State Bank of India (SBI). (2020). *Financial Inclusion Initiatives*. SBI. https://www.sbi.co.in

Suri, T., & Jack, W. (2016). The Long-Run Poverty and Gender Impacts of Mobile Money. *Science*, 354(6317), 1288–1292. 10.1126/science.aah530927940873

World Bank. (2018). *Financial Inclusion*. World Bank. https://www.worldbank.org

Yap, S., Lee, H. S., & Liew, P. X. (2023). The role of financial inclusion in achieving finance-related sustainable development goals (SDGs): A cross-country analysis. *Ekonomska Istrazivanja*, 36(3), 2212028. 10.1080/1331677X.2023.2212028

Yunus, M. (2007). *Banker to the Poor: Micro-Lending and the Battle Against World Poverty*. PublicAffairs.

. Zins, A., & Weill, L., (2016). The determinants of financial inclusion in Africa. *Review of Development Finance*. .10.1016/j.rdf.2016.05.001

Chapter 10
The Future of Smart Contracts:
Pioneering a New Era of Automated Transactions and Trust in the Digital Economy

Rajiv Iyer
https://orcid.org/0000-0002-1136-2061
Amity University, Mumbai, India

Vedprakash Maralapalle
https://orcid.org/0000-0002-7770-1134
Amity University, Maharashtra, India

Deepak Patil
https://orcid.org/0000-0003-0127-1198
Amity University, Dubai, UAE

Mohammad Irfan
https://orcid.org/0000-0002-4956-1170
Christ University, Bengaluru, India

ABSTRACT

The future of smart contracts in decentralized finance (DeFi) is a dynamic and evolving field that holds immense potential for transforming traditional financial systems The integration of artificial intelligence (AI) with smart contracts is enhancing their capabilities, enabling efficient processing of data and intelligent decision-making. Smart contracts provide an open and effective replacement for traditional financial structures as they continue to gain popularity. The potential of smart contracts to

DOI: 10.4018/979-8-3693-6321-8.ch010

improve transparency, optimize operating procedures, and transform industries like healthcare, finance, and education is what will determine their future. To support blockchain-based apps and grow the DeFi ecosystem, smart contract platforms like Polkadot, Cardano, and Ethereum must continue to innovate and evolve. The future of smart contracts is largely being shaped by the possibility of multi-chain smart contracts, the incorporation of AI and machine learning technology, and the support for decentralized autonomous organizations (DAOs).

INTRODUCTION TO SMART CONTRACTS IN DECENTRALIZED FINANCE

With blockchain technology, smart contracts are deterministic, self-executing scripts that allow trusted agreements and transactions between anonymous participants without the need for a reliable middleman (Aar, 2022; Batra, 2024). They have the power to upend and transform established practices in a number of different industries (Aar, 2022). The distinction between decentralized and centralized computing is depicted in Figure 1. Distributed computing resources are used in decentralized computing.

A new class of consumer-facing financial apps built using smart contracts and running on permissionless blockchain technology is known as decentralized finance (DeFi) (Grassi, 2022). Because they allow financial activities to be automated and decentralized, smart contracts are an essential part of the DeFi ecosystem (Grassi, 2022).

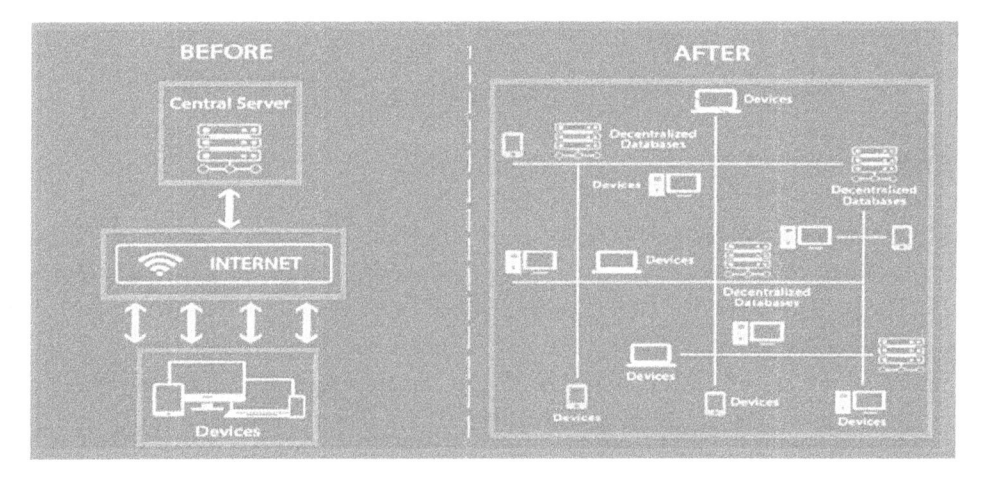

Figure 1. Centralized vs. decentralized computing

Because the agreements between participants and the smart contract code are publicly available on the blockchain, the integration of smart contracts with blockchain technology enables transparent, traceable, and irreversible transactions (Aar, 2022; Batra, 2024). The two main characteristics that draw DeFi apps to smart contracts are their immutability and transparency.

Nevertheless, despite their benefits, smart contracts in the DeFi area come with dangers and weaknesses that are unavoidable (Batra, 2024). To overcome these obstacles and completely realize the promise of smart contracts in transforming the financial industry, further research and development are needed (Aar, 2022).

As a result, smart contracts form the cornerstone of decentralized finance. Their special qualities of transparency, traceability, and trustless transactions on blockchain networks allow for the automation and decentralization of financial operations.

EVOLUTION OF SMART CONTRACT PLATFORMS: CURRENT TRENDS AND FUTURE DIRECTIONS

The development of platforms for smart contracts has been a major factor in the expansion and use of decentralized finance (DeFi). The way financial transactions and agreements are carried out has been completely transformed by smart contracts, self-executing scripts that operate on blockchain technology and allow for transparent and trustless interactions between anonymous parties (Batra, 2024; Timucin, 2023).

A significant development in smart contract platforms has been the emergence of well-known blockchain networks such as Ethereum, Cardano, and Polkadot. Numerous DeFi protocols and decentralized apps (dApps), each with special features and powers, have been built on top of these platforms (Batra, 2024; Grassi, 2022).

For example, Polkadot has become a prominent smart contract platform that facilitates cross-chain application development and offers interoperability across several blockchain networks. Scalability is the platform's primary goal (Timucin, 2023).

Similarly, Cardano has gained traction as a smart contract platform, leveraging its proof-of-stake consensus mechanism and formal verification techniques to enhance the security and reliability of its smart contracts. The platform's focus on academic research and peer-reviewed development has positioned it as a contender in the DeFi space (Grassi, 2022).

Ethereum, the pioneering smart contract platform, continues to be a dominant force in the DeFi ecosystem. The network's Ethereum Improvement Proposals (EIPs) and the ongoing development of layer-2 scaling solutions, such as Optimism and Arbitrum, have addressed some of the scalability and transaction fee challenges that have plagued the network (Bennett, 2023).

The emergence of non-fungible tokens (NFTs) has also had a significant impact on the evolution of smart contract platforms. NFTs, which are unique digital assets stored on the blockchain, have found applications in various industries, including art, gaming, and digital collectibles. The integration of NFTs with smart contract platforms has opened up new avenues for innovation and revenue generation (Bennett, 2023).

Looking to the future, the potential for multi-chain smart contracts, the integration of artificial intelligence (AI) and machine learning (ML) technologies, and the support for decentralized autonomous organizations (DAOs) are key areas shaping the evolution of smart contract platforms (Bennett, 2023).

Multi-chain smart contracts hold the potential to improve interoperability and open up new use cases for DeFi apps because they can operate seamlessly across various blockchain networks. Intelligent decision-making, automated contract execution, and improved fraud detection can all be made possible by integrating AI and ML with smart contract systems (Aquilina, 2023).

Moreover, the emergence of DAOs—decentralized organizations run by smart contracts—has the potential to completely alter the composition and administration of organizations. New types of decentralized governance and decision-making can be made possible by smart contract platforms that facilitate the creation and implementation of DAOs (Tasca et al., 2016).

All things considered, the development of smart contract platforms has propelled the expansion and invention in the DeFi industry. As these platforms develop further, tackling issues like scalability, security, and interoperability, they will play an increasingly crucial role in shaping the future of decentralized finance and the broader blockchain ecosystem.

Figure 2 illustrates the key principles or characteristics associated with blockchain technology, which is often used in decentralized applications (dApps) and cryptocurrencies. The central node represents "Permissionless," suggesting that the system operates without a central authority controlling access.

The nodes in the vicinity illustrate the subsequent concepts or attributes:

1. Programmable: Smart contracts and decentralized apps may be created using blockchain systems, which are built on programmable code.
2. Decentralization: The network is dispersed among several nodes or users rather than being under the control of a single body.
3. Censorship Resistant: Since blockchain systems are decentralized and lack a central point of failure, they are immune to censorship.
4. Trustless: Because the blockchain maintains transparency and upholds regulations, transactions and interactions on the network don't need mutual trust.

5. Transparent: The blockchain encourages accountability and transparency by making all transactions and data public to all users.

These principles collectively represent the core tenets of blockchain technology, enabling secure, transparent, and decentralized systems for various applications, including digital currencies, smart contracts, and decentralized applications.

Figure 2. Characteristics of decentralized computing

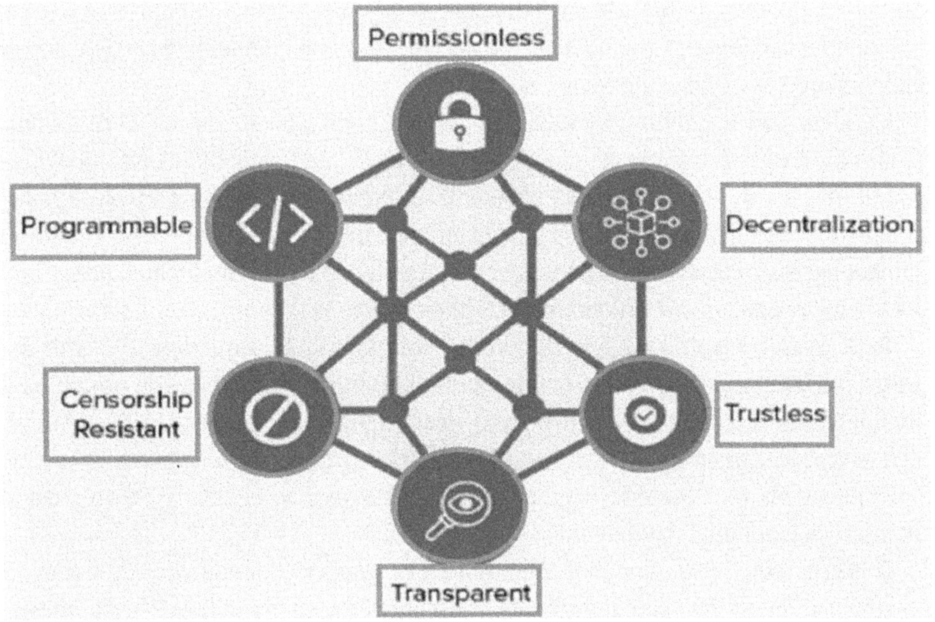

FUNCTIONAL APPROACH TO DECENTRALIZED FINANCE (DEFI)

The financial services industry has entered a new paradigm known as decentralized finance (DeFi), which is made possible by the combination of blockchain technology and smart contracts. DeFi uses self-executing computer code to disintermediate the supply of financial services as opposed to depending on conventional financial intermediaries (Iacoviello, 2022; Tasca et al., 2016).

A functional approach to understanding DeFi is crucial, as it allows us to compare the capabilities and risks of DeFi applications with their traditional finance (TradFi) counterparts. This approach focuses on the core functions that financial systems are designed to perform, such as facilitating payments, enabling lending and borrowing, and providing risk management tools (Iacoviello, 2022; Tasca et al., 2016).

The payment and transaction facilitation function of DeFi is one of its primary features. Without the requirement for a central authority, peer-to-peer transactions can be carried out on blockchain networks using smart contracts in a transparent and trustless manner (Vijai, 2019). This could improve financial inclusion, lower transaction costs, and improve accessibility.

Lending and borrowing services are two of DeFi's most important functions. Users can lend and borrow cryptocurrency on DeFi platforms like Aave and Compound, frequently with the use of collateral to reduce risk. In comparison to traditional financial institutions, these platforms may offer more competitive rates and quicker access to funds since they use smart contracts to automate the lending and borrowing procedures (Fernandez, 2023).

Risk management is yet another crucial role that DeFi aims to fulfill. The decentralized trading of cryptocurrencies and other digital assets is made possible by automated market makers (AMMs) and decentralized exchanges (DEXs), which also give consumers tools to control how exposed they are to market volatility. DeFi protocols also provide insurance and derivatives to enable users to protect themselves from different hazards (Atadoga, 2024).

It is crucial to remember that although DeFi wants to disintermediate financial services, many of the tasks it attempts to do are comparable to those in traditional finance. Given their functional similarities, it is possible that the financial regulation of the crypto and DeFi industries can be based on the same economic principles that have driven financial regulation for many years (Atadoga, 2024).

On the other hand, the DeFi ecosystem may make market failures such externalities and information asymmetries more severe. This emphasizes the necessity of having suitable regulatory frameworks in place to safeguard consumers, uphold the integrity of the market, and guarantee financial stability (Kansal, 2024).

The parallels and discrepancies between traditional finance and decentralized finance are emphasized by the functional approach to DeFi. Through comprehending the fundamental tasks that DeFi aims to accomplish, we may enhance our evaluation of the possible advantages, hazards, and legal implications linked to this developing financial environment.

Figure 3. Concept of a DeFi (decentralized finance) protocol

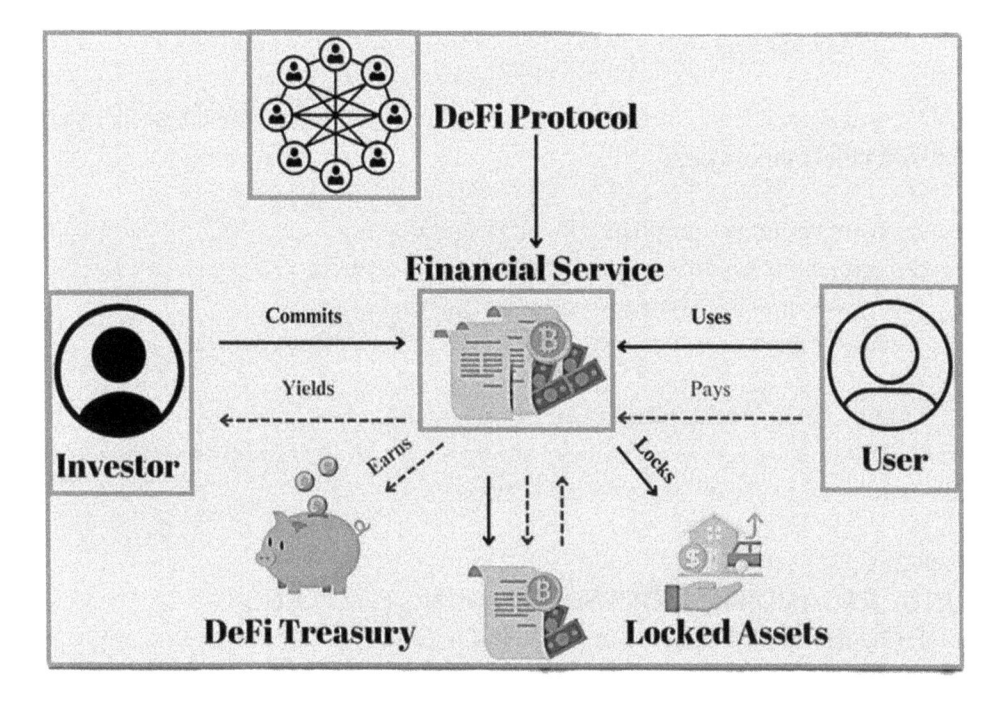

Figure 3 illustrates the concept of a DeFi (Decentralized Finance) protocol, which is a financial service built on blockchain technology, typically using smart contracts. It depicts the various participants and their interactions within the DeFi ecosystem.

At the center is the DeFi Protocol, represented by a network of interconnected nodes. This protocol facilitates financial services in a decentralized manner.

The key participants and their roles are as follows:

1. Investor: An investor commits funds to the DeFi Treasury, which is a pool of assets managed by the protocol.
2. DeFi Treasury: This is the reserve where the invested funds are held. Investors' contributions yield returns, which are earned back in the form of rewards or interest.
3. User: Users can access and utilize the financial services provided by the DeFi protocol. They may lock their assets as collateral or make payments to access these services.
4. Locked Assets: Users can lock their assets (e.g., cryptocurrencies, tokens) as collateral to gain access to various financial services or products offered by the protocol.

5. Financial Service: The DeFi protocol provides a variety of financial services, including trading, lending, borrowing, and other decentralized applications, through the use of blockchain smart contracts.

The arrows and labels indicate the flow of transactions and interactions between the different components:

i. Investor commits funds to the DeFi Treasury
ii. Investor earns rewards or yields from their investment
iii. User pays or locks assets to access the financial services
iv. Financial services utilize the locked assets or funds from the DeFi Treasury

The fundamental principles of DeFi protocols are decentralization, transparency, and permissionless access to financial services without the need for intermediaries like traditional banks or financial institutions.

UNDERSTANDING MODERN BANKING LEDGERS THROUGH BLOCKCHAIN TECHNOLOGIES

Blockchain technology has emerged as a disruptive force in the banking sector, with the potential to totally change smart contracts and transaction processing in the financial sector. By allowing digital assets, smart contracts, automated banking ledgers, and international money transfers, blockchain technology essentially provides a transparent and decentralized ledger system that has the potential to completely transform traditional banking procedures (Halaburda, 2021).

Within the context of modern banking, blockchain technology provides a paradigm shift in the way financial transactions are conducted. Banks may use the decentralized nature of blockchain to enhance security, reduce costs, and expedite operations. Asset transfers, loan approvals, and compliance checks can all be automated in the banking sector because to blockchain networks' usage of smart contracts.

The Internet of Money, as facilitated by blockchain technologies, opens up new possibilities for global financial inclusion and accessibility. By removing intermediaries and enabling direct peer-to-peer transactions, blockchain-based banking systems have the potential to reach underserved populations and provide financial services to those who were previously excluded from traditional banking systems (Shirole, 2023).

Furthermore, blockchain technology's second-generation contract-based advancements provide sophisticated features that go beyond straightforward transaction processing. These advancements make it possible to create intricate smart contracts that can automate a variety of financial tasks, such as supply chain financing and the processing of insurance claims. Financial organizations can improve their operational efficiency and provide cutting-edge services to their clients by adding these cutting-edge capabilities to their banking ledgers (Zhang et al., 2024).

Blockchain technology adoption in banking is not without difficulties, though (Falazi, 2023). When creating ledger-based technology for the banking industry, scalability, interoperability, regulatory compliance, and data privacy are important factors to take into account. In order to achieve the successful integration of blockchain technology into contemporary banking institutions and to fully realize the potential of decentralized finance, it is imperative that these issues be addressed.

Thus, understanding modern banking ledgers through blockchain technologies is essential for grasping the transformative potential of blockchain in the financial sector. By embracing blockchain's decentralized and transparent ledger system, banks can enhance their operational efficiency, reduce costs, and offer innovative financial services to a broader range of customers. The future of banking lies in the adoption of blockchain technologies to create a more inclusive, secure, and efficient financial ecosystem.

ARTIFICIAL INTELLIGENCE'S POTENTIAL AND DIFFICULTIES IN CREATING WEB 3.0

Artificial intelligence (AI) is playing a major role in shaping Web 3.0, the next phase of the internet that will include peer-to-peer networks, decentralized architecture, and cutting-edge technologies like blockchain and smart contracts. The incorporation of AI into Web 3.0 presents a multitude of challenges and opportunities that might fundamentally alter several industries and the digital landscape (Zhang et al., 2024).

Prospects of AI in Web 3.0

1. Efficient Data Processing: AI is essential for processing and analyzing large datasets more quickly, which facilitates wise decision-making and perceptive results. This feature improves Web 3.0 applications' data-driven processes' speed and accuracy, which improves user experience and boosts operational effectiveness.
2. Transformative Potential: Within the context of Web 3.0, AI has the ability to revolutionize a variety of industries, including healthcare, banking, and education. Organizations might seize fresh chances for innovation, customized services, and improved decision-making procedures by utilizing AI algorithms and machine learning approaches.

3. Enhanced Automation: The integration of AI with smart contracts and blockchain technology enables the automation of complex tasks and processes. AI-powered smart contracts can streamline transactions, automate compliance checks, and facilitate secure and transparent agreements, leading to increased efficiency and reduced operational costs.
4. Innovative Applications: AI-driven technologies in Web 3.0 open up new avenues for innovative applications, such as personalized financial services, predictive healthcare analytics, and adaptive educational platforms. These applications have the potential to revolutionize traditional services and create new business models in the digital economy.

Challenges of AI in Web 3.0

1. Data Privacy: Safeguarding user data and privacy is one of the main issues with AI in Web 3.0. Since AI algorithms use enormous volumes of data for training and making decisions, maintaining user confidence and regulatory compliance depends on data security and privacy compliance.
2. Bias and Fairness: AI systems are prone to biases present in the data that they are trained on, which can result in unjust treatment of certain people and skewed results. In Web 3.0, addressing bias and guaranteeing algorithmic fairness in AI apps is crucial to stop discriminatory behavior and advance moral AI development.
3. Trust and Ethics: The trustworthiness of AI systems and the ethical implications of AI-driven decisions are significant concerns in Web 3.0. Ensuring transparency, accountability, and ethical standards in AI algorithms and applications is essential to build trust among users and stakeholders and mitigate potential risks associated with AI technologies.
4. Regulatory Compliance: The evolving regulatory landscape surrounding AI technologies poses challenges for organizations operating in Web 3.0. Compliance with data protection regulations, algorithmic transparency requirements, and ethical guidelines presents a complex regulatory environment that organizations must navigate to ensure legal and ethical AI deployment.

As we can see, the prospects of AI in shaping Web 3.0 are vast, offering transformative potential across industries and driving innovation in digital services. However, addressing the challenges of data privacy, bias, trust, and regulatory compliance is essential to harness the full benefits of AI technologies in Web 3.0 and ensure a responsible and sustainable digital future (Falazi, 2023).

INTEGRATION OF AI WITH SMART CONTRACTS: ENHANCING CAPABILITIES

As a major development in the field of blockchain technology, the combination of artificial intelligence (AI) with smart contracts offers improved capabilities and industry-changing potential. Intelligent decision-making, transaction processing efficiency gains, and the automation of intricate activities are all made possible by the combination of AI algorithms with smart contracts in decentralized systems. This integration opens the door for cutting-edge services and applications in the digital economy while streamlining processes and improving security, transparency, and dependability in smart contract execution (Iacoviello, 2022).

1. Enhanced Automation and Efficiency

By integrating AI with smart contracts, organizations can automate a wide range of processes, from contract execution to compliance checks, significantly reducing the need for manual intervention and human oversight. AI-powered smart contracts can autonomously analyze data, make decisions based on predefined rules, and execute transactions with increased speed and accuracy. This automation streamlines operations, minimizes errors, and enhances the overall efficiency of transaction processing within blockchain networks.

2. Intelligent Decision-Making and Risk Management

The integration of AI algorithms with smart contracts enables intelligent decision-making capabilities, allowing contracts to adapt to changing conditions and make informed choices based on real-time data analysis. AI-powered smart contracts can assess risks, predict outcomes, and optimize processes, leading to more effective risk management strategies and improved decision-making in financial transactions, supply chain management, and other industries.

3. Fraud Detection and Security Enhancement

AI-driven smart contracts have the potential to enhance security measures and reduce the risk of fraudulent activities within decentralized systems. By leveraging AI algorithms for anomaly detection, pattern recognition, and behavior analysis, smart contracts can identify suspicious activities, mitigate risks, and prevent fraudulent transactions. This integration strengthens the security and resilience of smart contract platforms, safeguarding assets and ensuring trust among users.

4. Personalized Services and Adaptive Contracts

The integration of AI with smart contracts enables the creation of adaptive contracts that can dynamically adjust terms and conditions based on changing circumstances or user preferences. This flexibility allows for the customization of contract terms, the automation of personalized services, and the optimization of contract performance based on real-time data insights. AI-powered smart contracts can adapt to individual needs, optimize resource allocation, and enhance user experiences in various applications.

Therefore, there is a great deal of promise for augmenting capabilities, increasing effectiveness, and spurring innovation in decentralized systems through the integration of AI with smart contracts. In the rapidly developing field of blockchain technology and decentralized finance, enterprises can discover new avenues for efficiency, security, and user-centric applications by utilizing AI algorithms for automation, intelligent decision-making, fraud detection, and tailored services (Tapwal, 2022).

MULTI-CHAIN SMART CONTRACTS AND INTEROPERABILITY

The evolution of smart contract platforms has been marked by the growing need for interoperability and the ability to execute smart contracts across multiple blockchain networks. The concept of multi-chain smart contracts has emerged as a crucial development in addressing the challenges of siloed blockchain ecosystems and enabling seamless collaboration and asset exchange between different decentralized applications (dApps).

One of the primary drivers behind the rise of multi-chain smart contracts is the increasing diversity of blockchain platforms, each with its own unique features, consensus mechanisms, and target applications. As the blockchain landscape continues to expand, the need for cross-chain interoperability has become paramount. Multi-chain smart contracts offer a solution to this challenge by allowing the execution of smart contract logic across various blockchain networks (Falazi, 2023; Zhang et al., 2024).

The key advantage of multi-chain smart contracts lies in their ability to unlock new use cases and enable innovative applications that span multiple blockchain platforms. By facilitating the exchange of data, assets, and transactions between different blockchains, multi-chain smart contracts can enable more complex and collaborative decentralized finance (DeFi) protocols, supply chain management systems, and other cross-industry solutions (Falazi, 2023; Zhang et al., 2024).

One prominent example of a multi-chain smart contract platform is Polkadot, which has been designed to enable the seamless integration and communication of diverse blockchain networks. Polkadot's architecture, which includes parachains, bridges, and the Relay Chain, allows for the execution of smart contracts across multiple chains, enabling interoperability and the creation of cross-chain dApps (Bellavitis et al., 2022).

Figure 4. Polkadot architecture

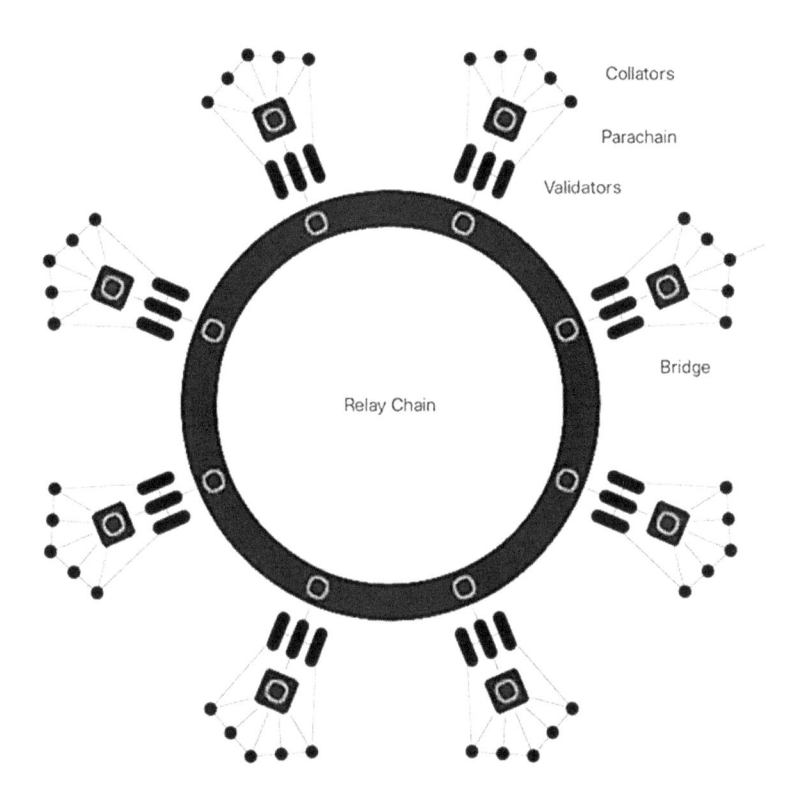

The Polkadot architecture as shown in figure 4 is a sophisticated framework designed to facilitate interoperability and communication between diverse blockchain networks. At the core of Polkadot is the concept of parachains, which are individual blockchains that connect to the Polkadot network. These parachains operate independently but can interact with each other and with the main Polkadot Relay Chain, enabling seamless communication and data transfer between different chains (Zhang et al., 2024).

In addition to parachains, Polkadot incorporates bridges, which serve as specialized components that facilitate communication between the Polkadot network and external blockchain platforms. These bridges play a crucial role in enabling interoperability between disparate blockchain ecosystems, allowing assets, data, and transactions to flow smoothly between different networks.

The Relay Chain acts as the central hub of the Polkadot network, coordinating the activities of parachains and ensuring the security and consensus of the entire ecosystem. It serves as a relay for messages and transactions between parachains, providing a secure and efficient communication layer for the entire network.

Overall, the Polkadot architecture is designed to address the challenges of siloed blockchain ecosystems and enable cross-chain collaboration. By leveraging parachains, bridges, and the Relay Chain, Polkadot offers a scalable and flexible framework for building decentralized applications that can operate across multiple blockchain networks. This interoperability and communication between different chains are essential for fostering innovation, expanding the capabilities of decentralized finance (DeFi), and driving the evolution of the blockchain ecosystem towards a more interconnected and collaborative future.

Similarly, the Oasis Ethereum ParaTime, a privacy-first blockchain network, has introduced the concept of confidential smart contracts, where contract data and state are kept confidential while still leveraging the security and decentralization of the Ethereum ecosystem (Falazi, 2023). This approach highlights the potential for multi-chain smart contracts to address privacy concerns and enable the development of more sensitive applications.

However, the implementation of multi-chain smart contracts is not without its challenges. Ensuring the security, reliability, and consistency of smart contract execution across multiple blockchain networks is a complex task that requires robust protocols, consensus mechanisms, and governance frameworks. Additionally, the heterogeneity of blockchain platforms and the differences in their programming languages, data structures, and transaction models can pose significant technical hurdles that need to be overcome (Dwivedi et al., 2021).

As the blockchain ecosystem continues to evolve, the importance of multi-chain smart contracts and interoperability will only grow. Ongoing research and development in areas such as cross-chain communication protocols, decentralized oracles, and standardized smart contract languages will be crucial in unlocking the full potential of multi-chain smart contracts and enabling the seamless integration of decentralized applications across various blockchain networks.

SMART CONTRACTS SUPPORTING DECENTRALIZED AUTONOMOUS ORGANIZATIONS (DAOS)

Decentralized Autonomous Organizations (DAOs) are a new type of organizational structure that utilizes smart contracts and blockchain technology to provide decentralized decision-making and governance. Smart contracts provide the backbone of these blockchain-native organizations, which are cooperatively owned and governed by their members (Bellavitis et al., 2022).

Because smart contracts automate a variety of organizational procedures and governance systems, they are essential to the operation of DAOs. Deployed on blockchain networks, these self-executing scripts can codify a DAO's rules, bylaws, and decision-making processes, guaranteeing transparent and impenetrable implementation of the organization's operations (Eletter, 2022).

The creation of decentralized governance structures is one of the main benefits of utilizing smart contracts in DAOs. Without the need for a centralized authority, smart contracts can be made to make voting, proposal submission, and decision-making processes easier for DAO members to engage in the management of the organization (Dwivedi, 2021).

Smart contracts, for instance, can be used to create voting systems in which DAO members can vote on different ideas and the results are automatically totaled and carried out without the need for a central authority. In keeping with the fundamental tenets of decentralized autonomous organizations, this decentralized governance model encourages accountability, transparency, and group decision-making (Dwivedi et al., 2021).

Additionally, the management of DAO resources, including work distribution, financial transaction execution, and fund distribution, may be automated via smart contracts. DAOs can function more effectively and transparently and lower the possibility of malicious or human error by encoding these operations into self-executing scripts (Batra, 2024; Jensen et al., 2021).

Nevertheless, there are certain difficulties in integrating DAOs with smart contracts. Because flaws or vulnerabilities in the code might have serious repercussions for the DAO's operations and the funds under its stewardship, it is imperative that smart contracts be secure and reliable. Sufficient investigation and advancement in the domain of smart contract auditing and formal verification methodologies are imperative to tackle these obstacles and bolster the reliability of DAO-based systems (Bellavitis et al., 2022).

Additionally, the legal and regulatory landscape surrounding DAOs and their use of smart contracts is still evolving. Establishing a clear legal framework for the enforceability and recognition of DAO-based agreements and transactions is necessary to facilitate the widespread adoption of this organizational model (Dwivedi, 2021).

As a result, smart contracts serve as the foundation for decentralized autonomous organizations (DAOs), allowing for the decentralization of decision-making, resource management, and governance process automation. The incorporation of smart contracts into the DAO ecosystem will be essential in determining how this novel organizational form develops in the future and promoting efficiency, transparency, and collective governance in the digital economy.

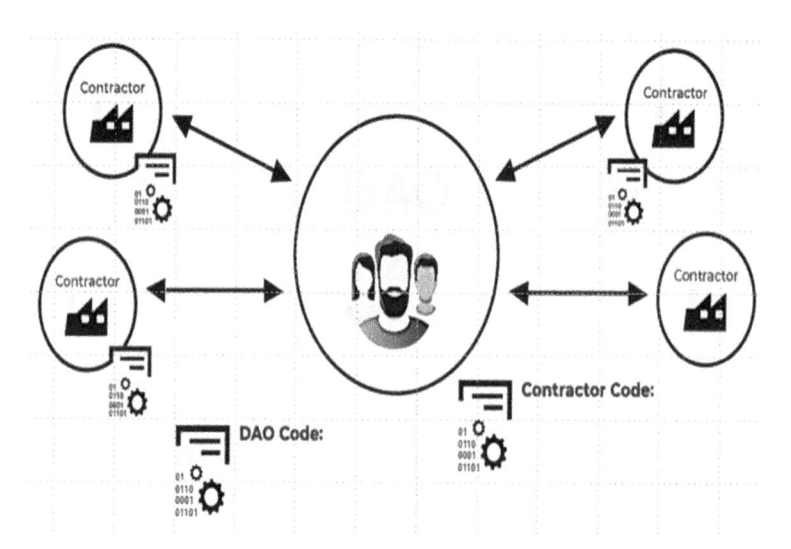

Figure 5. Concept of decentralized autonomous organization (DAO)

Figure 5 illustrates the concept of a decentralized autonomous organization (DAO). A community or organization that uses blockchain technology and smart contracts to run autonomously without the need for a central authority or governing body is known as a decentralized autonomous organization (DAO).

At the center of the figure is the representation of the DAO itself, depicting a decentralized network or community of individuals or entities working together towards a common goal.

The surrounding circles represent different aspects or features of a DAO:

1. Secure voting: DAOs typically have a voting mechanism built into their smart contracts, allowing members to vote on proposals, decisions, or governance rules in a secure and transparent manner.
2. Trustless collaboration: Collaboration without middlemen or centralized authority is made possible via decentralized autonomous organizations, or DAOs. The underlying smart contracts enforce interactions and agreements.

3. Transparent operations: The operations, transactions, and decision-making processes within a DAO are transparent and recorded on the blockchain, promoting accountability and transparency.
4. Incentive mechanisms: DAOs often incorporate incentive mechanisms, such as token-based rewards or incentives, to encourage participation, contribution, and alignment of interests among members.
5. Distributed ownership: In a DAO, ownership and control are distributed among its members, who collectively make decisions and govern the organization through decentralized mechanisms.

The key principles demonstrated in the figure are decentralization, transparency, trustless collaboration, secure voting, and distributed ownership and governance. These principles are enabled by the combination of blockchain technology, smart contracts, and the collective participation of members within the DAO structure.

SMART CONTRACTS IN HEALTHCARE, REAL ESTATE, AND SUPPLY CHAIN MANAGEMENT

Smart contracts have shown great promise for transforming a number of sectors, including supply chain management, real estate, and healthcare. Smart contracts have the potential to optimize several healthcare procedures, including tracking the medical supply chain, managing patient data, and processing insurance claims. Smart contracts improve patient care and operational effectiveness by automating these tasks and increasing healthcare systems' efficiency, transparency, and data security (Eletter, 2022; Terzi, 2019).

Smart contracts provide a clear and safe means of managing property records, automating rental agreements, and facilitating property transactions in the real estate industry. Smart contracts safeguard the integrity of real estate transactions, cut down on transaction costs, and eliminate the need for middlemen by encoding real estate agreements into self-executing contracts on blockchain networks. By streamlining procedures, boosting stakeholder trust, and facilitating quicker and more secure property transactions, this technology has the potential to completely transform the real estate sector (Laarabi, 2022).

Smart contracts are essential to supply chain management because they improve efficiency, traceability, and transparency throughout the whole chain. Smart contracts simplify supply chain operations, lower mistake rates, and foster better stakeholder collaboration by automating tasks like product tracking, inventory management, and payment settlements. Smart contract use in supply chain management reduces risks like fraud and counterfeiting while providing real-time visibility into product movements and fostering partner confidence. Supply chains could become more responsive and resilient as a result of this technology, which also has the ability to optimize logistics (Eletter, 2022; Ikram, 2023).

Overall, smart contracts in healthcare, real estate, and supply chain management offer innovative solutions to streamline operations, enhance transparency, and improve trust among stakeholders. By leveraging the automation and security features of smart contracts, these industries can overcome traditional challenges, reduce inefficiencies, and unlock new opportunities for innovation and growth.

1. Smart Contracts in Healthcare

Smart contracts can be used to improve efficiency, guarantee transparency, and automate and optimize a number of operations in order to improve supply chain management in the healthcare industry. The following are some important ways that smart contracts can be used to enhance healthcare supply chain management:

a. Automating Procurement Processes: Smart contracts can automate procurement processes within the healthcare supply chain, including ordering, purchasing, and inventory management. By encoding procurement rules and agreements into self-executing contracts, smart contracts can streamline the procurement process, reduce manual errors, and ensure timely and accurate ordering of medical supplies and equipment.

b. Enhancing Transparency and Traceability: Smart contracts can improve transparency and traceability in the healthcare supply chain by recording every transaction and movement of products on the blockchain. This ensures that stakeholders have real-time visibility into the flow of medical supplies, from manufacturers to healthcare providers, enabling better tracking of product provenance, expiration dates, and quality assurance.

c. Automating Payment and Invoicing: Smart contracts can automate payment and invoicing processes in the healthcare supply chain, ensuring timely and accurate payments between suppliers, manufacturers, distributors, and healthcare facilities. By automatically executing payment agreements based on predefined conditions, smart contracts reduce the risk of payment delays, disputes, and fraud, enhancing financial transparency and accountability (Irfan, Hussainey, Chan Bukhari et al, 2024).

d. Improving Inventory Management: Smart contracts can optimize inventory management in healthcare by automatically updating inventory levels, triggering reorders when stock levels are low, and facilitating real-time inventory tracking. This automation minimizes the risk of stockouts, overstocking, and expiration

of medical supplies, ensuring that healthcare facilities have the right supplies at the right time (Irfan, Kadry, Sharif, & Ullah Khan, 2023).
e. Enhancing Compliance and Regulation: Smart contracts can help ensure compliance with regulatory requirements and industry standards in the healthcare supply chain. By embedding regulatory rules and compliance checks into smart contracts, organizations can automate regulatory reporting, audits, and verification processes, reducing the risk of non-compliance and ensuring adherence to quality and safety standards.

As we see, smart contracts offer a range of benefits for improving supply chain management in healthcare, including automation of procurement processes, enhanced transparency and traceability, streamlined payment and invoicing, optimized inventory management, and improved compliance with regulatory requirements. By leveraging the capabilities of smart contracts, the healthcare industry can enhance operational efficiency, reduce costs, and ensure the timely and secure delivery of medical supplies to patients and healthcare providers (Alshahrani, 2023; Joshi, 2022).

2. Smart contract applications in real estate

Some examples of smart contract applications in real estate include:

a. Property Transactions: Smart contracts can automate and streamline property transactions, including the transfer of ownership, payment processing, and contract execution. By encoding real estate agreements into self-executing contracts on blockchain networks, smart contracts ensure secure and transparent property transactions.
b. Rental Agreements: Smart contracts have the ability to automate rental agreements between renters and landlords, guaranteeing that terms and conditions are automatically enforced and that payments are received on schedule. Because of this automation, there is less of a need for middlemen and a lower chance of disagreements between parties.
c. Escrow Services: In real estate transactions, smart contracts can be utilized to enable escrow services, in which money is held in escrow until specific requirements are fulfilled. Smart contracts offer a safe and effective way to manage financial transactions by automatically releasing payments to the right party when the terms of the agreement are met.
d. Property Management: Smart contracts can automate property management tasks, such as maintenance requests, lease renewals, and tenant communications. By using smart contracts, property managers can streamline operations, reduce administrative overhead, and improve tenant satisfaction.

e. Smart contracts have the potential to enable the tokenization of real estate assets, thereby providing investors with the opportunity to acquire partial ownership of properties. As a result, investors can purchase and sell tokens that represent shares in real estate holdings without the assistance of conventional middlemen, increasing market liquidity in the real estate sector (Irfan, Elhoseny, Kassim, & Metawa, 2023).

With their ability to automate, transparently, and efficiently handle property transactions, rental agreements, escrow services, property management, and the tokenization of real estate assets, these examples show how smart contracts can completely transform the real estate sector (Irfan, Elmogy, Majid, & El-Sappagh, 2023; Laarabi, 2022).

3. Smart contracts in supply chain management

The following are the main advantages of supply chain management with smart contracts:

a. Enhancing Transparency and Traceability:

Real-time supply chain visibility is made possible by smart contracts, which have the ability to log every product movement and transaction on the blockchain. Improved product provenance, expiration date monitoring, and quality assurance are all facilitated by this increased transparency and traceability (Rashid, 2022; Terzi, 2019).

b. Automating Processes and Reducing Errors:

Smart contracts have the ability to automate a number of supply chain tasks, including payment settlements, inventory control, and procurement. Supply chain activities are streamlined, and the chance of manual error is decreased by this automation (Irfan, Elhoseny, Kassim, & Metawa, 2023).

c. Improving Collaboration and Trust:

Smart contracts facilitate secure and transparent collaboration among supply chain partners by automatically executing agreements and enforcing terms. This enhances trust between stakeholders and improves overall supply chain coordination.

d. Ensuring Compliance and Regulatory Adherence:

Smart contracts can embed regulatory rules and compliance checks, automating the process of adhering to industry standards and reporting requirements. This helps organizations maintain compliance and reduce the risk of non-compliance penalties.

e. Enhancing Supply Chain Resilience:

Blockchain-based smart contracts distributed and irreversible nature can strengthen supply networks' resistance to fraud, interruptions, and counterfeiting. Supply chain operations may become more dependable and efficient as a result of this enhanced resilience (Irfan, Muhammad, Naifar et al, 2024; Rashid, 2022; Terzi, 2019).

Improved transparency, automation, cooperation, compliance, and resilience are all major advantages of employing smart contracts in supply chain management, which eventually results in more reliable, safe, and efficient supply chain operations.

ONGOING INNOVATION AND DEVELOPMENT IN SMART CONTRACT PLATFORMS

Decentralized apps (dApps) and decentralized finance (DeFi) have grown and become more popular due to ongoing innovation and development in the dynamic and quickly evolving field of smart contract platforms. The importance of improving the functionality, scalability, and interoperability of smart contract platforms has grown as the blockchain ecosystem develops (Irfan, 2021; Irfan, Elmogy, Majid, & El-Sappagh, 2023).

The creation of layer-2 scaling solutions is a major area of continuous research in smart contract systems. Scalability issues have been encountered by platforms like as Ethereum, since the growing need for decentralized applications has resulted in network congestion and increased transaction fees. Layer-2 solutions, such as Optimism and Arbitrum, aim to address these issues by offloading a portion of the computational burden from the main blockchain, enabling faster and more cost-effective transactions without compromising the security and decentralized Gochhait, Saikat, et al. "Role of artificial intelligence Gochhait, Saikat, et al. "Role of artificial intelligence (AI) in understanding the behavior pattern: a study on e-commerce." ICDSMLA 2019: Proceedings of the 1st International Conference on Data Science, Machine Learning and Applications. Singapore: Springer Singapore, 2020.(AI) in understanding the behavior pattern: a study on e-commerce." ICDSMLA 2019: Proceedings of the 1st International Conference on Data Science, Machine Learning and Applications. Singapore: Springer Singapore, 2020.ion of the underlying network (Mazurok, 2021).

The emergence of non-fungible tokens (NFTs) has also had a significant impact on the development of smart contract platforms. NFTs, which represent unique digital assets stored on the blockchain, have found applications in various industries, including art, gaming, and digital collectibles. The integration of NFTs with smart contract platforms has opened up new avenues for innovation and revenue generation, driving further advancements in the field (Bohyer, 2023).

Another area of ongoing innovation is the potential for multi-chain smart contracts, which can seamlessly execute across multiple blockchain networks. This capability enhances interoperability and unlocks new use cases for decentralized applications that can leverage the strengths of different blockchain platforms. The development of cross-chain communication protocols and standardized smart contract languages are crucial in enabling the seamless integration of smart contracts across various blockchain ecosystems (Bohyer, 2023; Irfan, Hussainey, Bukhari et al, 2024).

One major developing trend that is influencing this technology's future is the combination of machine learning (ML) and artificial intelligence (AI) with smart contract platforms. Smart contracts can be made more intelligent by utilizing AI and ML algorithms. This will allow for improved fraud detection, automated decision-making, and personalized services. Through process optimization and the creation of new opportunities for innovation, this integration has the potential to completely change a number of industries, including finance and healthcare (Irfan, 2021; Irfan, Kadry, Sharif, & Khan, 2023; Mazurok, 2021).

Moreover, one of the main forces behind smart contract platform innovation has been the emergence of decentralized autonomous organizations, or DAOs. Smart contract-driven DAOs have the power to completely transform decision-making and organizational systems. Platforms for smart contracts that facilitate DAO creation and implementation are opening up new possibilities for decentralized governance and collective decision-making (Ullah & Al-turjman, 2021).

Unlocking the full potential of decentralized technology will depend heavily on the continuous innovation and improvement in smart contract platforms as the blockchain ecosystem develops. Smart contract platforms have the potential to significantly influence the direction of the digital economy and the Web 3.0 environment by tackling issues with scalability, interoperability, and the integration of new technologies.

CONCLUSION

To sum up, this book chapter offers a thorough examination of the major ideas and developments influencing the use of smart contracts in decentralized finance (DeFi) in the future. We have witnessed how these technologies are changing the financial environment, starting with the introduction of smart contracts in DeFi and continuing with the continuous innovation and growth in smart contract platforms.

The development of smart contract platforms has been characterized by notable advancements in scalability, interoperability, and the integration of cutting-edge technologies such as artificial intelligence (AI) and machine learning (ML). While the functional approach to DeFi has highlighted the potential for smart contracts to automate and streamline various financial processes, the understanding of modern banking ledgers through blockchain technologies has demonstrated the potential for decentralized finance to disrupt established financial systems.

The potential and difficulties of AI in forming Web 3.0 have brought attention to the significance of AI in augmenting the capabilities of smart contracts, even though the integration of AI with smart contracts has shown how AI can be utilized to automate decision-making and increase the effectiveness of smart contract execution.

The concept of multi-chain smart contracts and interoperability has highlighted the potential for smart contracts to function across multiple blockchain networks, even though support for decentralized autonomous organizations (DAOs) has demonstrated the potential for smart contracts to enable decentralized governance and decision-making.

Thus, smart contract implementations in the real estate, healthcare, and supply chain management domains have demonstrated the potential of these technologies to augment operational efficacy, curtail expenses, and augment transparency across several sectors.

In summary, smart contracts in DeFi have a promising future because of the continuous invention and development that propels the expansion and use of these technologies. To make sure we are ready for the opportunities and difficulties that lie ahead, it is critical to stay up to date on the most recent developments in smart contract platforms, AI, and DeFi as the blockchain ecosystem continues to change.

REFERENCES

Aar, P. (2022). Evolution of Smart Contracts- A Bibliometric Analysis and Review. *International Journal for Research in Applied Science and Engineering Technology.*

Alshahrani, N. M. (2023). Smart Contract Evaluation By Multi-Criteria Analysis: Selection Challenges And Open Issues, a Review. *2023 3rd International Conference on Emerging Smart Technologies and Applications (eSmarTA).* IEEE. 10.1109/eSmarTA59349.2023.10293363

Aquilina, M. (2023). Decentralised Finance (DeFi): A Functional Approach. SSRN *Electronic Journal.* 10.2139/ssrn.4325095

Atadoga, A. (2024). Blockchain technology in modern accounting: A comprehensive review and its implementation challenges. *World Journal of Advanced Research and Reviews.*

Batra, S. (2024). A Bibliometric Visualization of Decentralized Finance in Smart Contracts. *2024 18th International Conference on Ubiquitous Information Management and Communication (IMCOM).* IEEE. 10.1109/IMCOM60618.2024.10418443

Bellavitis, C., Fisch, C., & Momtaz, P. P. (2022). The rise of decentralized autonomous organizations (DAOs): A first empirical glimpse. *Venture Capital*, 25(2), 187–203. 10.1080/13691066.2022.2116797

Bennett, D. (2023). *BeFi meets DeFi: A behavioral finance approach to decentralized finance asset pricing.* International Business and Finance.

Bohyer, K. (2023). Modernizing Contracts Across Industries: A Review of Smart Contract Applications and the Evolving Legal Landscape. *ICST Transactions on Scalable Information Systems.*

Dubey, C. (2022). Confluence of Artificial Intelligence and Blockchain Powered Smart Contract in Finance System. *2022 International Conference on Computing, Communication, and Intelligent Systems (ICCCIS),* (pp. 125-130). IEEE. 10.1109/ICCCIS56430.2022.10037701

Dwivedi, V. (2021). Case Studies of Contractual (Legal) Automation Using Smart Contracts. *Blockchain and the Digital Twin.* Pag.

Dwivedi, V. K., Pattanaik, V., Deval, V., Dixit, A., Norta, A., & Draheim, D. (2021). Legally Enforceable Smart-Contract Languages. *ACM Computing Surveys*, 54(5), 1–34. 10.1145/3453475

Eletter, S. (2022). Leveraging Blockchain-Based Smart Contracts in the Management of Supply Chain: Evidence from Carrefour UAE. *2022 International Arab Conference on Information Technology (ACIT)*. IEEE. 10.1109/ACIT57182.2022.9994083

Falazi, G. (2023). Cross-Chain Smart Contract Invocations: A Systematic Multi-Vocal Literature Review. *ACM Computing Surveys*. ACM.

Fernandez, D. (2023). Beyond Ledgers: The Theoretical Framework of Blockchain Technology in Enhancing Sustainability Reporting. *Malaysian Journal of Social Sciences and Humanities*.

Grassi, L. (2022). Do we still need financial intermediation? The case of decentralized finance – DeFi. *Qualitative Research in Accounting & Management*.

Halaburda, H. (2021). Means of Exchange: Ever Present Competition (Beyond Bitcoin, Chapter 2). *Macroeconomics: Monetary & Fiscal Policies eJournal*.

Iacoviello, G. (2022). Exploring a new business model for lending processes in the banking sector using Blockchain technology: An Italian case study. *The International Journal of Digital Accounting Research*.

Ikram, L. (2023). A Smarter Way to Procure: Exploring the Use of Smart Contracts. *International Journal of Membrane Science and Technology*.

Irfan, M. (2021, January). Do Shariah Indices converge? Evidence from Gulf Co-operation Council countries. *International Journal of Business Excellence*, 23(2), 251–269. 10.1504/IJBEX.2021.113448

Irfan, M., Elhoseny, M., Kassim, S., & Metawa, N. (2023). *Advanced Machine Learning Algorithms for Complex Financial Applications*. IGI Global. 10.4018/978-1-6684-4483-2

Irfan, M., Elmogy, M., Majid, M. S., & El-Sappagh, S. (2023). *The Impact of AI Innovation on Financial Sectors in the Era of Industry 5.0*. IGI Global.

Irfan, M., Hussainey, K., Bukhari, S. A., & Nam, Y. (2024). *Issues of Sustainability in AI and New-Age Thematic Investing*. IGI Global. 10.4018/979-8-3693-3282-5

Irfan, M., Hussainey, K., Chan Bukhari, S. A., & Nam, Y. (Eds.). (2024). *Issues of Sustainability in AI and New-Age Thematic Investing*. IGI Global Publisher. 10.4018/979-8-3693-3282-5

Irfan, M., Kadry, S., Sharif, M., & Khan, H. U. (2023). *Fintech Applications in Islamic Finance: AI, Machine Learning, and Blockchain Techniques*. IGI-Global. 10.4018/979-8-3693-1038-0

Irfan, M., Muhammad, K., Naifar, N., & Khan, M. A. (2024). *Applications of Block Chain technology and Artificial Intelligence: Lead-ins in Banking, Finance, and Capital Market*. Springer Cham. 10.1007/978-3-031-47324-1

Jensen, J. R., von Wachter, V., & Ross, O. (2021). An Introduction to Decentralized Finance (DeFi). *Complex Syst. Informatics Model. Q.*, 26(26), 46–54. 10.7250/csimq.2021-26.03

Joshi, S. (2022). *Enhancing Healthcare System Using Blockchain Smart Contracts*. /arXiv.2202.07591.10.48550

Kansal, K. (2024). Exploring the Prospects and Challenges of Artificial Intelligence in Shaping the Future of Web 3.0. *International Journal for Research in Applied Science and Engineering Technology*.

Laarabi, M. H. (2022). Smart Contracts Applications in Real Estate: A Systematic Mapping Study. *2022 2nd International Conference on Innovative Research in Applied Science, Engineering and Technology (IRASET)*. IEEE. 10.1109/IRASET52964.2022.9737796

Mazurok, I. (2021). Smart contract sharding with proof of execution. *Applied Aspects of Information Technology*.

Peters, G. W., & Panayi, E. (2016). Understanding Modern Banking Ledgers Through Blockchain Technologies: Future of Transaction Processing and Smart Contracts on the Internet of Money. In Tasca, P., Aste, T., Pelizzon, L., & Perony, N. (Eds.), *Banking Beyond Banks and Money. New Economic Windows*. Springer. 10.1007/978-3-319-42448-4_13

Rashid, M. M. (2022). A Blockchain-Based approach in Healthcare Supply Chain using Smart Contracts and Decentralized Storage Systems. *Proceedings of the 2022 ACM Conference on Information Technology for Social Good*. ACM. 10.1145/3524458.3547251

Shirole, A. (2023). Blockchain Technology and AI-A Review. *Recent Trends in Artificial Intelligence & it's Applications*.

Tapwal, R. (2022). CartelChain: A Secure Communication Mechanism for Heterogeneous Blockchains. *ICC 2022 - IEEE International Conference on Communications*. IEEE. 10.1109/ICC45855.2022.9838600

Terzi, S. (2019). Transforming the supply-chain management and industry logistics with blockchain smart contracts. *Proceedings of the 23rd Pan-Hellenic Conference on Informatics*. ACM. 10.1145/3368640.3368655

Timucin, T. (2023). The evolution of smart contract platforms: A look at current trends and future directions. *Mugla Journal of Science and Technology*.

Troisi. (2022). Blockchain-based Food Supply Chains: the role of Smart Contracts. *European Journal of Privacy Law & Technologies*.

Ullah, F., & Al-turjman, F. M. (2021). A conceptual framework for blockchain smart contract adoption to manage real estate deals in smart cities. *Neural Computing & Applications*, 35(7), 5033–5054. 10.1007/s00521-021-05800-6

Vijai, C. (2019). *The Blockchain Technology and Modern Ledgers Through Blockchain Accounting*. Technology.

Zhang, H., Su, H., Wu, X., & Yang, Y. (2024). Cross-Chain Interoperability and Collaboration for Keyword-Based Embedded Smart Contracts in Internet of Things. *IEEE Internet of Things Journal*, 11(6), 10791–10807. 10.1109/JIOT.2023.3328190

Chapter 11
Risk Management of Future of Defi Using Artificial Intelligence as a Tool

Jyoti Sah
https://orcid.org/0000-0002-2259-1177
Amity University, Maharashtra, India

Satuluri Padma
https://orcid.org/0000-0002-0644-5604
Amity University, Maharashtra, India

Ramakrishna Yanamandra
https://orcid.org/0000-0001-9101-6072
Skyline University College, University City of Sharjah, UAE

Mohammad Irfan
https://orcid.org/0000-0002-4956-1170
Christ University, Bengaluru, India

ABSTRACT

This chapter explores AI's pivotal roles in managing risks within DeFi, emphasizing strategic implementation to enhance risk assessment, management, and decision-making processes for a better user experience. The convergence of AI and DeFi presents unprecedented opportunities, fostering transparency and decentralization. Drawing from diverse sources, the study evaluates AI's effectiveness, particularly in machine learning, in addressing emerging risks. It focuses on how AI can guide DeFi's future while managing market and credit risks through tasks like data prepa-

DOI: 10.4018/979-8-3693-6321-8.ch011

ration, modeling, stress testing, and validation. Additionally, AI aids in data quality assurance, text mining, and fraud detection. Emphasis is placed on identifying and managing risks that could hinder DeFi's future, highlighting key AI techniques. Given the financial industry's ongoing transformation, these insights are increasingly vital.

INTRODUCTION

In today's world Artificial Intelligence tools are very helpful as it has a very strong impact in many sectors either directly or indirectly. DeFi is one of those sectors where AI has been more increasingly adopted and could be involved using AI for the management of risks associated with DeFi in future. There are numerous reasons for the use of Artificial Intelligence in today's era and amongst all it is DeFi in which without using the tools of artificial intelligence managing the risks is impossible as it will be expensive, time consuming, and insufficient if the industries will use the conventional approaches, methods, and strategies for the management of their risks.

Based on technology intelligence power, memory, reactions, and task completions. AI can be classified in to three categories:

Artificial Narrow Intelligence (ANI), also known as Narrow AI, refers to AI technologies and tools that are dedicated to specific tasks or processes. These systems can perform only one task at a time. The world is currently experiencing a proliferation of Narrow AI technologies. Examples include the Sophia Humanoid robot, chatbots, text-to-speech, and speech-to-text converters. We are currently in the phase of adopting these Narrow AI technologies. Another example is driverless cars for smart mobility, designed to assist humans in routine tasks and learning through simulations, online games, and handling risky jobs.

Artificial General Intelligence (AGI), also known as General AI, refers to futuristic AI technologies and tools predicted to be available by 2025 according to some tech-savvy developers. These technologies aim to possess intelligence on par with humans, enabling them to perceive, understand, learn, and function in real-time environments. Consequently, there is a possibility that humans will have to compete with robots, bots, and other smart devices for jobs during this phase. Despite the numerous advantages these technologies offer, there are associated risks. Therefore, they should be utilized cautiously to mitigate potential risks.

Artificial Super Intelligence (ASI), or Super AI, marks the third phase of AI, expected to emerge by 2030. ASI surpasses human intelligence, boasting an IQ akin to Einstein's and excelling in memory storage, processing speed, analysis, and decision-making. While these technologies mirror human intelligence, their advanced capabilities raise concerns about potential challenges for humanity. The significant gap in IQ and the advancement of futuristic technologies fuel worries about the potential creation of problematic environments for humans. Moreover, this phase prompts profound questions about the sustainability of human life on Earth in the face of such advanced artificial intelligence.

Decentralized Financing (DeFi)

DeFi, short for Decentralized Finance, represents a transformative wave in the financial landscape, powered by blockchain technology. This innovative approach has rapidly gained momentum over the past decade due to its capacity to construct decentralized platforms, thus reducing dependence on centralized entities. By leveraging blockchain, DeFi facilitates open and unrestricted access to financial services, fundamentally altering traditional paradigms. In this decentralized realm, record-keeping becomes distributed, access is anonymous and unimpeded, while any intermediary functions are integrated within the system itself. The beauty of DeFi lies in its accessibility; with just a smartphone and internet connection, individuals can tap into a range of financial opportunities previously out of reach. These include decentralized lending and borrowing, trading, and yield farming, offering efficient and inclusive avenues for wealth management. DeFi includes:

a. Blockchain technology:

In recent times, Distributed Ledger Technology (DLT) includes blockchain, wherein all transactions are recorded and organized in blocks linked together through cryptography. The first and most famous application of blockchain technology was Bitcoin. One of its main advantages is the elimination of a central point of failure. With multiple copies of records existing, the corruption of a single node or copy does not compromise the blockchain's security. In fact, the blockchain protocol allows for multiple points of failure or corruption, provided most validators remain uncompromised. It enables validators to be parties that do not trust one another or even adversaries.

b. Smart contracts:

In the new DeFi architecture, smart contracts have emerged as essential tools, comprising digital promises with specified protocols for parties to abide by. These contracts, computer programs, facilitate automatic asset transfers under predefined conditions, akin to traditional contracts but enforced through code. Executable programs, smart contracts operate precisely as defined by their creators, providing blockchain-backed security. The Bitcoin network pioneered smart contracts for value transfers, verifying sender account balances. However, Ethereum introduced a more robust platform, enabling custom contracts using a Turing-complete language. Various smart contract platforms like Ethereum, Solana, Polkadot, and Hyperledger Fabric have since proliferated, offering distinct features for decentralized applications, empowering developers within the DeFi landscape.

DeFi vs. Traditional Financial System

DeFi, short for decentralized finance, represents a paradigm shift in financial services, leveraging blockchain technology to facilitate peer-to-peer transactions without the need for intermediaries. Unlike traditional finance, which relies on centralized authorities like banks, DeFi operates on a decentralized network, offering users greater autonomy and accessibility to financial services.

In DeFi, individuals can engage in various financial activities directly through decentralized applications (dApps) powered by smart contracts. These activities include borrowing, lending, obtaining insurance, depositing funds for savings, and trading digital assets on decentralized exchanges (DEXs). The absence of intermediaries means that users have full control over their transactions and assets, without the need to rely on centralized entities to facilitate them.

A fundamental aspect of DeFi is its decentralization, which contrasts sharply with the centralized nature of traditional finance. In traditional finance, intermediaries such as banks or financial institutions act as gatekeepers, requiring individuals to provide extensive personal information to access services like loans or bank accounts. Furthermore, these intermediaries have the authority to deny individuals access to financial services based on factors like nationality or compliance with government policies.

However, centralized finance, or CeFi, operates on closed systems where entities like banks maintain internal ledgers and exercise sole control over transaction records. This centralized control gives institutions the power to manipulate transactions, cancel or reverse them, and determine who can access financial services. Additionally, traditional financial institutions often impose stringent Know Your Customer (KYC) requirements, requiring individuals to undergo identity verification before using their services.

In contrast, DeFi operates on decentralized ledgers, where transactions are recorded and verified by multiple nodes across the network. This distributed ledger system enhances transparency, security, and resilience against potential manipulation or censorship. Moreover, most DeFi protocols do not enforce KYC requirements, allowing users to participate in financial activities without restrictions based on nationality or identity.

Overall, it can be said that DeFi offers a disruptive alternative to traditional finance, empowering individuals with greater financial autonomy, accessibility, and transparency. As the DeFi ecosystem continues to evolve and mature, it is poised to revolutionize the way people access and interact with financial services, paving the way for a more inclusive and decentralized financial system.

REVIEW OF LITERATURE

AI and DeFi have been extensively studied, yielding significant benefits. This review aims to examine a selection of notable literature of recent studies of 2021-2024 have been explored on the subject.

Artificial Intelligence (AI)

Milana C. & Ashta A. (2021) have found that the importance of Artificial Intelligence (AI) in economic literature is increasingly recognized, highlighting its profound impact on everyday consumer life. Both academic and non-academic sources reflect the dynamic development of AI and computing power, particularly in finance and financial markets. The post-financial crisis period and recent pandemic challenges have underscored the need for AI-related technologies to address economic growth limitations. In their study, a review of 28 publications suggests AI's potential to enhance efficiency, generate new data, provide superior advisory and management services, and mitigate risks. Despite this optimism, questions remain about AI's negative impacts on sustainable growth and economic welfare. As AI continues to evolve, its role in navigating these complexities and maximizing benefits is a crucial focus of ongoing research.

Bogojevic Arsic, V. (2021) has focused on the application of various artificial intelligence (AI) techniques in financial risk management, identifying the need to restructure traditional methods due to their limited effectiveness due to which the key AI techniques that could enhance financial risk management were identified, with the potential to transform the financial industry. The researchers found that AI techniques can automate and simplify data management, improve stress testing and scenario generation, and introduce new methodologies for handling complex, multivariable problems and non-linear optimization. These advancements can be seamlessly integrated across all components of the financial market, suggesting that there are no significant barriers to the application of AI techniques in financial risk management.

Bengio Y. et al. (2023) have discussed the significant risks posed by advanced AI systems, emphasizing their potential for large-scale social harm and the loss of human control. Although AI offers immense opportunities, its rapid progress in areas such as hacking, social manipulation, deception, and strategic planning poses serious challenges. The authors warn that without careful design and deployment, AI could worsen these risks, especially in critical domains like military activities, biological research, and AI development.

Currently, we lack the means to ensure the safety of advanced AI systems and prevent their misuse. However, the paper highlights a viable path forward. This includes pursuing research breakthroughs in AI safety and ethics, establishing effective government oversight, and creating national and international institutions to enforce safety standards. Drawing on governance models from pharmaceuticals and nuclear energy, the authors stress the need for a responsible and proactive approach to steer AI towards positive outcomes and avoid potential catastrophes.

Kumar A. et al. (2023) in their study examined how various AI forms can enhance financial risk management, noting that conventional approaches have become outdated and inefficient. They found that AI methods are highly practical, facilitating quick, cost-effective, and efficient management of financial risks in businesses and financial institutions. Their study highlighted AI's applications in three areas: financial (market and credit), risk management, and operational (business continuity and disaster recovery).

The researchers concluded that the ongoing development of Fintech will significantly impact financial risk management, necessitating transformation and adaptation. They emphasized the need for the most promising AI methods to improve risk management in the evolving financial sector. Additionally, they pointed out that these AI methods will offer real-time information on various financial risk categories, enabling sophisticated risk management for organizations and businesses.

Nartey N. J. (2024) investigated the merging of Artificial Intelligence (AI) and Decentralized Finance (DeFi), finding that AI integration can enhance DeFi services like price discovery, risk management, liquidity provision, and user experience. He noted that DeFi's decentralized infrastructure supports secure, transparent AI development, addressing issues like data privacy, bias, and centralization in traditional AI. However, this convergence also presents challenges, including regulatory uncertainty, scalability limits, data privacy, security risks, and talent shortages. Nartey emphasized the need for collaboration among researchers, developers, regulators, and industry participants to overcome these hurdles.

Aldasoro I. et al. (2024) have studied the impact of generative AI (GenAI) and emerging AI agents, along with the speculative potential of artificial general intelligence, on finance. Their focus encompasses four key functions of the financial system: financial intermediation, insurance, asset management, and payments. They found that AI technologies have significantly enhanced information processing, risk management, and customer service, thereby boosting the sector's cognitive capacity.

The study highlights that, while AI offers considerable efficiency and innovation, it also introduces challenges such as model opacity, data dependency, and systemic stability concerns. Effective regulation is crucial to harness AI's benefits and mitigate these risks, emphasizing transparency, fairness, and global collaboration. However, they have found that not all risks require regulation; it should target externalities, allowing market mechanisms to address other risks. Policymakers must consider AI's broader economic impacts, including employment and productivity, to ensure inclusive growth. Consequently, the study observes that ongoing research and adaptive regulatory approaches are essential for fostering a resilient and equitable financial ecosystem.

Decentralized Finance

Schar F. (2021) in his study explores the opportunities and potential risks of the DeFi ecosystem, focusing on aspects like atomic swaps, autonomous liquidity pools, decentralized stablecoins, and flash loans. It finds that DeFi offers exciting prospects and the potential to create a truly open, transparent, and immutable financial infrastructure through its numerous highly interoperable protocols and applications. However, the study also highlights certain risks involved in DeFi technology but these risks are not inherently problematic, users should recognize the significant level of trust often required. If these challenges can be resolved, DeFi could revolutionize the financial industry, leading to a more robust, open, and transparent financial infrastructure.

Carapella F. et al. (2022) in their study examines a general set of stability issues that arise from offering financial services on blockchains and highlights unique concerns specific to DeFi. They have found that while the provision of financial services on public, permissionless blockchains has advanced significantly since Bitcoin's inception, DeFi has not yet achieved systemic importance. Additionally, the study notes that if policymakers decide which assets (such as dollars and registered securities) are permitted on public permissionless blockchains, DeFi will swiftly exploit any profitable opportunities, regardless of regulatory concerns.

Makarov I. (2022) observed that while DeFi architecture could reduce transaction costs, it doesn't automatically eliminate rents in the financial sector. The permissionless and anonymous nature of current DeFi blockchains presents a regulatory challenge. Makarov in his study suggested a system where blockchain validators verify and process transactions only for certified addresses. The study also emphasizes how the US and global economies can ensure liquidity and credit provision, highlighting strategic and competitive implications. The researcher has also highlighted that the US benefits greatly from the dollar's central role and its financial system, making it crucial to encourage financial innovation while setting standards for consumer protection, transparency, and stability. However, the cross-border nature of permissionless blockchains risks regulatory arbitrage, which could weaken the financial system. Thus, the researcher has suggested that the coordination among major financial markets is vital to prevent regulatory erosion.

Mahmud S. et al. (2023) found that Decentralized Finance (DeFi) uses innovative solutions to decentralize banking and industry concepts, providing financial services to anyone, anywhere. DeFi is disrupting the entire financial system, signaling an inevitable evolutionary shift. Operating without traditional banks, DeFi relies on smart contracts to complete financial transactions, positioning itself as a formidable challenger to existing financial industry norms. DeFi could potentially replace traditional banks, removing the need for intermediaries and threatening commercial banks' deposits. Further the researchers have analysed that in response to that, the central banks are introducing Central Bank Digital Currencies (CBDCs) to enhance monetary policy effectiveness, serving as a store of value, medium of exchange, and stable unit of account. They have also suggested a hybrid currency system that combines CBDCs and fiat money under proper regulation. This approach ensures public choice and helps preserve the role of commercial banks in the evolving financial landscape.

Jiang E. et al. (2023) conducted a detailed study on the introduction and classification of various DeFi applications. They proposed a DeFi construction and classification framework based on the complexity of financial services. Their study categorizes DeFi protocols by detailing the security aspects of digital assets, wallets, oracles, and asset bridges at the infrastructural level; stablecoins, lending, and exchanges at the functional level; and diverse derivatives at the service level. They highlighted the associated risks, potential attack methods, and possible defenses for each category. The study concludes with future research directions that emphasize improving functional integrity, enhancing security, ensuring compliance, and building a robust ecosystem. They said that these efforts aim to bridge the gap between current DeFi implementations and their ideal state.

Thatikonda et al. (2023) have found that how blockchain technology and artificial intelligence (AI) are revolutionizing financial insights by enhancing inclusivity, sustainability, and efficiency. Decentralized finance (DeFi) leverages these technologies to transform financial services, providing diverse resources that improve the financial landscape. Further they have added that this innovation fosters greater accessibility and equitable opportunities, paving the way for a more inclusive and sustainable financial ecosystem.

The foregone review of literatures for both Artificial Intelligence (AI) and Decentralized finance (DeFi) brought about the studies on various aspects and has touched upon almost every area related to the application of AI on Finance.

At one point the importance of Artificial Intelligence (AI) in economic literature is increasingly recognized, highlighting its profound impact on everyday consumer life. Both academic and non-academic sources reflect the dynamic development of AI and computing power, particularly in finance and financial markets (Milana C. & Ashta A.2021). On the other hand, the application of various artificial intelligence (AI) techniques in financial risk management, identifying the need to restructure traditional methods due to their limited effectiveness (Kumar A., 2023). It has been observed that some studies have focused upon to examine the impact of generative AI (GenAI) and emerging AI agents, along with the speculative potential of artificial general intelligence, on finance. Their focus encompasses four key functions of the financial system: financial intermediation, insurance, asset management, and payments. They found that AI technologies have significantly enhanced information processing, risk management, and customer service, thereby boosting the sector's cognitive capacity (Aldasoro I. et al. 2024). However, in some studies the merging of Artificial Intelligence (AI) and Decentralized Finance (DeFi) investigated, and found that AI integration can enhance DeFi services like price discovery, risk management, liquidity provision, and user experience. The researcher has noted that DeFi's decentralized infrastructure supports secure, transparent AI development, addressing issues like data privacy, bias, and centralization in traditional AI (Nartey N. J. 2024; Mahmud S. et al. (2023)). Similarly, some of the previous studies have focused on a general set of stability issues that arise from offering financial services on blockchains and have highlighted the unique concerns specific to DeFi. It has been found that while the provision of financial services on public, permissionless blockchains has advanced significantly since Bitcoin's inception, DeFi has not yet achieved systemic importance (Carapella F. et al. 2022), in the same way blockchain technology and artificial intelligence (AI) are revolutionizing financial insights by enhancing inclusivity, sustainability, and efficiency (Thatikonda et al. 2023). Likewise, in some other studies it has been observed that while DeFi architecture could reduce transaction costs, it doesn't automatically eliminate rents in the financial sector. The permissionless and anonymous nature of current DeFi blockchains presents a regulatory challenge (Makarov I. 2022).

Different authors have analysed different areas and found that the significant risks posed by advanced AI systems, emphasizing their potential for large-scale social harm and the loss of human control. It has been observed that although AI offers immense opportunities, its rapid progress in areas such as hacking, social manipulation, deception, and strategic planning poses serious challenges (Bengio Y. et al. 2023). In the same way when the studies conducted on DeFi have been observed, it has been found that DeFi offers exciting prospects and the potential to create a truly open, transparent, and immutable financial infrastructure through its numerous highly interoperable protocols and applications. However, it has been observed that in DeFi technology also certain risks involved but these risks are not inherently problematic, users should recognize the significant level of trust often required (Schar F. 2021).

Further, some more studies have been reviewed and found that there are some studies which try to examine the application of various artificial intelligence (AI) techniques in financial risk management, identifying the need to restructure traditional methods due to their limited effectiveness for which the key AI techniques that could enhance financial risk management were identified, with the potential to transform the financial industry. Same as the introduction and classification of various DeFi applications which highlighted the associated risks, potential attack methods, and possible defenses for each category (Jiang E. et al. 2023; Bogojevic Arsic, V. 2021).

While previous studies have extensively covered numerous aspects, including the importance of Artificial Intelligence (AI) in economic literature, the application of various AI techniques in financial risk management, the impact of generative AI (GenAI) and emerging AI agents, and the integration of AI with Decentralized Finance (DeFi), it has been observed that there remain exists some significant research gaps. Although these studies have addressed the stability issues arising from offering financial services on blockchains, the revolutionary impact of blockchain technology and AI on financial insights, and the potential for DeFi architecture to reduce transaction costs without necessarily eliminating rents in the financial sector. Additionally, the substantial risks posed by advanced AI systems, such as large-scale social harm and loss of human control, have been emphasized.

However, despite this extensive exploration, there is a notable gap in research focusing on how AI can be specifically utilized to manage the future risks associated with DeFi. This gap includes understanding of how AI can address the unique stability issues, regulatory challenges, and social risks inherent in the DeFi ecosystem. Addressing this gap is crucial for developing a secure, transparent, and efficient decentralized financial infrastructure. The present study aims to fill this gap by investigating the potential of AI as a tool for managing these future risks in DeFi, thereby contributing to the advancement and stability of decentralized financial systems.

DEFI AND RISK MANAGEMENT

Risk management in DeFi involves systematically assessing, mitigating, and monitoring risks inherent to decentralized finance, such as smart contract, liquidity, systemic, and platform risks. Strategies include due diligence, risk assessment tools, insurance, and portfolio risk management, tailored to the distinct challenges of the DeFi ecosystem.

Importance of DeFi Risk Management is that it is crucial due to the inherent risks in the DeFi space. With high rewards often come high risks, and DeFi is no exception. Its nascent nature, complex technology, and lack of regulation make it inherently risky. Effective risk management is essential to protect investments and ensure the sustainability of the DeFi ecosystem. Risks such as smart contract bugs, liquidity crises, and systemic risks can have far-reaching impacts, threatening user funds and destabilizing protocols. Therefore, understanding and managing these risks is paramount for the long-term viability of DeFi.

It is very essential to understand the meaning of the important concepts in Risk Management and their mitigation strategies which include the following:

Smart Contract Risk: This risk occurs due to possible errors or vulnerabilities in smart contract code, exposing users to potential losses or security breaches.

Liquidity Risk: This risk refers to the possibility that an asset may not be easily traded or converted into cash without causing significant losses.

Systemic Risk: This Risk refers to the potential for the entire financial system or market to fail, differing from risks tied to specific entities.

Platform Risk: This risk involves the hazards linked to utilizing a specific DeFi platform, influenced by factors like user interface, security, ease of use, and platform adoption.

Mitigation Strategies of Common Risks in DeFi:

- Smart Contract Risk: - Mitigate by employing well-audited protocols and leveraging risk assessment tools.
- Platform Risk: - Mitigate thorough research, considering both security measures and reputation of the platform.
- Liquidity Risk: - Manage by diversifying portfolios and utilizing liquid tokens and liquidity pools.
- Regulatory Risk: - Navigate by developing and enforcing DeFi-specific regulations while actively monitoring related activities.
- Systemic Risk: - Manage by vigilantly monitoring the DeFi space, regulating risky activities, and implementing crisis prevention measures.
- Economic Risk: - Handle by implementing policies that foster economic stability and equality, alongside regulating DeFi activities.

With the employment of the above efficient mitigation tactics, participants can safeguard themselves and bolster the stability and expansion of the DeFi sector.

As the DeFi industry expands and evolves, several tools have emerged to aid users in risk management. Examples include DeFi Score, DeFi Pulse, Nexus Mutual, Gauntlet Network, and Token Terminal, enabling users to evaluate protocol security, analyze market trends, and make informed choices.

Hence, in the future, DeFi risk management will likely advance with the adoption of new tools and strategies. With the growth and maturation of DeFi, risk management practices will become more sophisticated and effective. We can expect decentralized insurance protocols to gain traction, smarter smart contract auditing, and the emergence of fresh risk assessment tools.

Additionally, increased regulatory scrutiny may lead to new rules aimed at reducing risks and bolstering stability. These developments highlight DeFi's dynamic nature and its commitment to a safer environment. Overall, the future of DeFi risk management appears promising, offering opportunities for innovation and growth, ensuring the ecosystem's sustainability.

AI AND RISK MANAGEMENT

AI/ML revolutionizes business risk management by swiftly analysing vast unstructured data, enhancing efficiency, and cutting costs. Banks leverage this for precise credit decisions, slashing operational expenses, and complying with regulations. By generating timely, accurate data, financial institutions bolster customer insight, execute strategies adeptly, and mitigate losses. AI/ML aids in model risk management, stress testing, and decision-making across credit, investment, and business realms. Its transformative prowess lies in superior forecasting, streamlined variable selection, and nuanced data segmentation.

Utilize Artificial Intelligence (AI) to Enhance Market Risk Management (MRM) Practices

Market risk relates to the unpredicted fluctuations in the values of financial instruments or contracts, driven by changes in asset prices such as commodities, interest rates, foreign exchange rates, and other market indices. In essence, it signifies the risk of a portfolio's value oscillating due to variations in price levels or market price volatility. Market participants must actively manage this risk, contingent upon their financial robustness and the extent of their exposure.

AI tools present invaluable support in market risk management, offering the potential for significant improvements. Particularly, machine learning, as a fundamental AI tool, holds great promise in enhancing performance. The integration of AI applications into market risk management processes is inevitable, given their capacity to diminish operational costs and furnish more precise information to inform strategic risk management decisions. This capability enables financial companies and institutions not only to weather market uncertainties but also to compete and flourish in dynamic market landscapes. By leveraging AI, these entities can navigate market risks more effectively, ensuring resilience and adaptability in an ever-evolving financial environment.

Utilize Artificial Intelligence (AI) to Enhance Credit Risk Management (CRM) Practices

Credit risk, the threat of financial loss due to borrower default, is a critical concern in the financial sector. Credit risk management involves identifying and analysing risk factors, evaluating risk levels, and implementing measures to mitigate potential credit risks, essential for safeguarding financial institutions and investors.

AI techniques have emerged as powerful tools in credit risk modeling, surpassing traditional statistical methods. However, achieving optimal accuracy often requires integrating AI and statistical techniques. This combination enhances precision, empowering financial institutions to make informed decisions.

Assessing credit risk using AI, particularly machine learning algorithms, is complex yet pivotal. These algorithms identify credit events and estimate default costs, enabling proactive risk mitigation strategies. Additionally, AI enables real-time monitoring and analysis of extensive datasets, facilitating prompt detection of evolving credit risks and mitigating losses, ensuring financial stability. Therefore, the integration of AI techniques in credit risk management represents a significant advancement in the financial industry. By leveraging AI's predictive capabilities, financial institutions can enhance risk management, minimize losses, and foster a resilient financial ecosystem.

Utilize Artificial Intelligence (AI) to Enhance Financial Risk Management (FRM) Practices

The influence of Fintech is driving a transformative process in financial risk management, leading to disruption within the financial sector. Fintech is shaping this evolution through various means, including Advanced Analytics and Big Data,

Machine Learning and AI, Alternative Data Sources, Automation and Efficiency, Regulatory Technology (Regtech), Cybersecurity Innovations, Customer-Centric Risk Management, and Decentralized Finance (DeFi). Financial risk management focuses on optimizing how financial institutions or corporations handle financial risk. AI, as a component of Fintech, has already revolutionized the management of financial risk, shifting towards more data-driven, efficient, and customer-centric risk management practices. This integration of Fintech innovations into financial risk management processes is propelling a paradigm shift, enabling financial institutions to adapt more effectively to evolving market dynamics and regulatory requirements.

Artificial intelligence (AI), a subset of financial technology (Fintech), has significantly transformed how financial risk is managed. AI has enhanced financial risk management through improved decision-making processes. AI, as previously mentioned, is a broad field that applies various techniques based on human-like intelligence. These methods intelligently and efficiently utilize prior knowledge, such as multiple datasets, mimicking human behaviour. It is to be noted that machine learning, the most crucial form of artificial intelligence in financial risk decision-making, enables data collection, cleaning, and prediction. Therefore, the key AI technique, machine learning, facilitates data preparation and predictions, which are valuable for financial risk decision-making.

Utilize Artificial Intelligence (AI) to Enhance Operational Risk Management (ORM) Practices

Operational risk involves potential losses stemming from physical deterioration, technical shortcomings, and human errors within enterprise and institutional operations, encompassing fraud, mismanagement, and procedural lapses. AI holds significant potential in formulating effective strategies for mitigating operational risk and determining whether to retain, transfer, or mitigate this risk. Its inclusion in operational risk management is crucial, beginning with data preparation, classification, and analysis, aimed at preventing losses.

The integration of AI tools into operational risk management can enhance business competitiveness, predictive capabilities, cost-effectiveness, risk mitigation, and overall efficiency. Machine learning techniques play a pivotal role in several key areas, including data quality assurance, text-mining for data enrichment, and fraud detection. Notably, machine learning is commonly applied in detecting fraud and money laundering, with its implementation extending to various sectors such as credit card fraud detection and securities fraud detection (e.g., stock, foreign exchange, commodity pool fraud). By harnessing machine learning capabilities, organizations can bolster their defences against fraudulent activities, thus safeguarding their operations and assets.

AI IN DEFI RISK MANAGEMENT

AI holds the potential to bolster risk management in DeFi through several key avenues:

1. Credit Scoring: AI has the capability to evaluate the creditworthiness of borrowers by analysing various factors such as their transaction history, collateral, and prevailing market conditions. This enables lenders to mitigate risks effectively and make well-informed lending decisions, contributing to the stability and sustainability of DeFi platforms.
2. Fraud Detection: By leveraging advanced algorithms, AI can swiftly detect unusual patterns and suspicious activities indicative of fraudulent behaviour. This proactive approach to fraud detection aids in safeguarding both DeFi platforms and their users from potential financial losses, fostering trust and confidence within the ecosystem.
3. Liquidity Management: AI-driven predictive models can anticipate liquidity requirements based on market dynamics and user activity patterns. This foresight enables DeFi platforms to optimize their liquidity management strategies, ensuring sufficient liquidity to facilitate seamless transactions while mitigating the risk of liquidity shortages or surpluses.

Hence, the integration of AI technologies stands to significantly enhance risk management practices within the DeFi space. By automating credit scoring processes, bolstering fraud detection capabilities, and optimizing liquidity management, AI empowers DeFi platforms to navigate risks more effectively and efficiently, thereby fostering a safer and more resilient financial ecosystem.

FUTURE OF DEFI USING AI AS A TOOL

AI stands poised to revolutionize DeFi, promising enhanced efficiency, accessibility, and user-friendliness. Its unparalleled ability to analyse vast datasets, identify patterns, and make intelligent predictions empowers DeFi solutions to optimize operations, fortify security measures, and deliver personalized services. From automated trading algorithms to cybersecurity protocols, risk assessment models, fraud detection systems, and smart contract auditing, AI's integration in DeFi has the potential to spawn a plethora of new financial products and services that prioritize accessibility, efficiency, and fairness. The applications of AI in DeFi span a wide spectrum, with automated trading algorithms offering swift and precise market analysis, while cybersecurity measures safeguard transactions and user data against potential threats. Moreover, AI-driven risk assessment models facilitate proactive risk management, enabling DeFi platforms to navigate volatile markets with greater confidence. Moreover, AI-driven fraud detection systems utilize predictive capabilities to identify and prevent fraudulent activities, thus ensuring the integrity of DeFi transactions. Furthermore, smart contract auditing powered by AI ensures the reliability and security of smart contracts, minimizing the risk of vulnerabilities and loopholes.

Looking ahead, the role of AI in DeFi is poised to expand further, driven by three key factors:

1. Increased Adoption of AI: As DeFi platforms recognize the transformative potential of AI, we anticipate a surge in its adoption across the sector. This may entail leveraging AI for diverse functions, including market predictions, risk management, and user behaviour analysis. The widespread adoption of AI is expected to catalyse innovation and efficiency within the DeFi ecosystem.
2. Development of AI-based DeFi Products: With the growing adoption of AI, we can anticipate the emergence of a new generation of AI-based DeFi products. These innovative solutions may include AI-powered investment tools, trading bots equipped with advanced algorithmic capabilities, and sophisticated risk management systems. By harnessing the predictive power of AI, these products aim to optimize investment strategies, enhance trading efficiency, and mitigate risks.
3. Advancements in AI Technology: As AI technology continues to evolve, its applications in DeFi are poised to become increasingly sophisticated. Future advancements may lead to more accurate market predictions, refined trading strategies, and personalized user experiences. By leveraging cutting-edge AI algorithms and techniques, DeFi platforms can offer tailored financial solutions that meet the diverse needs of users, driving greater adoption and growth within the ecosystem.

Therefore, the integration of AI holds immense potential to reshape the landscape of DeFi, driving innovation, efficiency, and inclusivity. As AI technology continues to evolve and its applications in DeFi expand, we can expect to witness a paradigm shift in the way financial services are accessed, delivered, and experienced.

CONCLUSION

The study's conclusion underscores the profound impact that further integration of AI tools will have on risk management within DeFi, potentially overcoming obstacles to its future progression. AI holds the promise of automating and simplifying data management, enhancing stress testing and scenario generation, and introducing innovative methodologies to tackle complex, multivariable problems and non-linear optimization. Furthermore, AI's role in refining credit scoring and generating credit ratings for potential borrowers is pivotal for platforms serving as intermediaries in crowdfunding. By furnishing precise real-time information on managing diverse risks, AI tools offer advanced risk management solutions for both institutions and companies.

DeFi has ignited a wave of innovation, with developers leveraging smart contracts and decentralized settlement layers to fashion trust less versions of conventional financial instruments. Additionally, entirely novel financial instruments have emerged, made feasible only through the foundational public blockchain infrastructure. Examples like atomic swaps, autonomous liquidity pools, decentralized stablecoins, and flash loans underscore the immense potential of this ecosystem. However, amidst its promise, DeFi carries inherent risks, including security vulnerabilities in smart contracts and scalability constraints impacting user adoption. While these risks emphasize the importance of trust, adept risk management practices can pave the way for DeFi to revolutionize the financial industry, fostering a more resilient, inclusive, and transparent financial infrastructure.

LIMITATIONS AND FUTURE STUDIES

Despite the valuable insights provided by this study, several limitations warrant consideration. Firstly, the scope of this paper is confined to the application of AI tools in managing the risks inherent in the future of Decentralized Finance (DeFi), and it relies on a limited review of existing current literature only. The future studies could benefit from empirical research to validate the proposed propositions. Additionally, the analysis primarily focuses on the adoption of AI tools for managing various business risks. Future research could explore new topics, such as application of AI for enhancing DeFi security and privacy, or the ethical implications and governance of AI in DeFi.

REFERENCES

Abdullah, M. H., & Faizal, M. A. (2022). Blockchain-based IoT: Integration, Challenges and Future Prospects for Decentralized Finance (DeFi) Systems. In *2022 4th International Cyber Resilience Conference (CRC)* (pp. 1-5). IEEE. https://doi.org/10.1109/CRC54540.2022.9732887

Abramov, V., Lowdermik, M., & Zhou, X. (2017). A Practical guide to market risk model validations (Part I - Introduction). DOI: 10.2139/ssrn.2916853

Aldasoro, I. (2024). *Intelligent financial system: how AI is transforming finance.* (BIS Working Papers No 1194). Monetary and Economic Department.

Altman, E. I., Marco, G., & Varetto, F. (1994). Corporate distress diagnosis: Comparisons using linear discriminant analysis and neural networks (the Italian experience). *Journal of Banking & Finance*, 18(3), 505–529. 10.1016/0378-4266(94)90007-8

Amler, H., Eckey, L., Faust, S., Kaiser, M., Sandner, P., & Schlosser, B. (2021). DeFi-ning DeFi: Challenges & Pathway. *Frontiers in Artificial Intelligence*, 4. 10.3389/frai.2021.690694

Anwar, H. (2022). Decentralized Finance (DeFi): A New Norm of Financial Inclusion. *SSRN* 4036199. https://doi.org/10.2139/ssrn.4036199

Aramonte, S., Huang, W., & Schrimpf, A. (2021). *DeFi risks and the decentralisation illusion*. BIS Quarterly Review.

Barrett, A. M., Newman, J., Nonnecke, B., Hendrycks, D., Murphy, E. R., & Jackson, K. (2023). *AI risk-management standards profile for general-purpose AI systems (GPAIS) and foundation models*. Center for Long-Term Cybersecurity, UC Berkeley. https://perma.cc/8W6P-2UUK, 2023.

Bengio, Y. (2023). *Managing AI Risks in an Era of Rapid Progress*. arXiv:2310.17688v2 [cs.CY] 12Nov2023.

Bogojevic Arsic, V. (2009). Upravljanje finansijskim rizikom. SZR "Kragulj," Beograd.

Bogojevic Arsic, V. (2020). Challenges of financial risk management: AI applications. *XVII International Symposium Symorg 2020 – Business and Artificial Intelligence*.

Bogojevic Arsic, V. (2021). Challenges of financial risk management: AI applications. *Management: Journal of Sustainable Business and Management Solutions in Emerging Economies*, 26(3). 10.7595/management.fon.2021.0015

Boreiko, D., Ferrarini, B., & Giudici, P. (2020). Blockchain-Based Risk Management for Decentralized Finance. *Journal of Alternative Investments*, 23(3), 105–121. 10.3905/jai.2020.1.116

Capponi, A., & Jia, R. (2021). The Adoption of Blockchain-based Decentralized Exchanges. arXiv:2103.08842.

Carapella, F. (2022). *Decentralized Finance (DeFi): Transformative Potential & Associated Risks.* (Working Paper, SRA 22-02). https://www.bostonfed.org/publications/sra/

Carrivick, L., & Westphal, A. (2019). Machine learning in operational risk-making a business case for its practical implementation. (White paper). ORX Association. https://managingrisktogether.orx.org/sites/default/files/public/downloads/2019/09/orxthecaseformachinelearninginoperationalriskwhitepaper.pdf

Chartis Research. (2019). *State of AI in Risk Management: Developing an AI roadmap for risk and compliance in the finance industry.* Digital Services Limited & Tata Consultancy Services. https://www.chartis-research.com/technology/artificial-intelligence-ai/state-ai-risk-management-10976

Chow, T. (2023). *Transformative AI, existential risk, and asset pricing.* (Working Paper, 2023).

Dan´ıelsson, J, R Macrae, and A Uthemann. (2022). *Artificial intelligence and systemic risk.*

Financial Stability Board. (2017). *Artificial intelligence and machine learning in financial services.* FSB. http://www.fsb.org/wp-content/uploads/ P011117.pdf

Garcıa-Laencina, P. J., Sancho-Goomez, J. L., & Figueiras-Vidal, A. R. (2008). Machine learning techniques for solving classification problems with missing input data. *12th World Multi-Conference on Systemics, Cybernetics and Informatics.* Research Gate. https://www.researchgate.net/publication/257207095

Harvey, C. R., Ramachandran, A., & Santoro, J. (2021). *DeFi and the Future of Finance.* John Wiley & Sons.

Hendrycks, D., Mazeika, M., & Woodside, T. (2023). An overview of catastrophic AI risks. Jun. 2023. arXiv: 2306.12001 [cs.CY].

Irfan, M. (2021, January). Do Shariah Indices converge? Evidence from Gulf Cooperation Council countries. *International Journal of Business Excellence*, 23(2), 251–269. 10.1504/IJBEX.2021.113448

Irfan, M., Elhoseny, M., Kassim, S., & Metawa, N. (2023). *Advanced Machine Learning Algorithms for Complex Financial Applications*. IGI Global. 10.4018/978-1-6684-4483-2

Irfan, M., Elmogy, M., Majid, M. S., & El-Sappagh, S. (2023). *The Impact of AI Innovation on Financial Sectors in the Era of Industry 5.0*. IGI Global. 10.4018/979-8-3693-0082-4

Irfan, M., Hussainey, K., Chan Bukhari, S. A., & Nam, Y. (Eds.). (2024). *Issues of Sustainability in AI and New-Age Thematic Investing*. IGI Global Publisher. 10.4018/979-8-3693-3282-5

Irfan, M., Kadry, S., Sharif, M., & Ullah Khan, H. (2023). *Fintech Applications in Islamic Finance: AI, Machine Learning, and Blockchain Techniques*. IGI Global. 10.4018/979-8-3693-1038-0

Jiang, E. (2023). Decentralized Finance (DeFi): A Survey. https://doi.org//arXiv.2308.0528210.48550

Kumar, A., Kumar, A., Kumari, S., Kumari, N., Kumari, S., Mishra, P., & Behura Kumar, A. (2023, March). Artificial Intelligence's (AI): Implications in Managing Financial Risks (FRM). *International Journal of Science Academic Research*, 04(03), 5242–5246. http://www.scienceijsar.com

Mahmud, S. (2023). The implication of DeFi (Decentralized Finance) in disrupting the global banking system. Preprint in SSRN Electronic Journal. https://www.researchgate.net/publication/37218952510.2139/ssrn.4491898

Makarov, I. (2022). *Cryptocurrencies and Decentralized Finance (DEFI)*. National Bureau Of Economic Research. https://www.nber.org/papers/w30006

Makarov, I., & Schoar, A. (2021). *Blockchain Analysis of the Bitcoin Market*. (Working Paper 29396). National Bureau of Economic Research.

Martínez-Plumed, F., Gómez, E., & Hernández-Orallo, J. (2021). Futures of artificial intelligence through technology readiness levels. *Telematics and Informatics*, 58, 101525. 10.1016/j.tele.2020.101525

Milana, C., & Ashta, A. (2021). Artificial intelligence techniques in finance and financial markets: A survey of the literature. *Strategic Change*, 30(3), 189–209. 10.1002/jsc.2403

Nartey, N. J. (2024). *Decentralized Finance (DeFi) and AI: Innovations at the Intersection of Blockchain and Artificial Intelligence*. Centre for Sustainable Research and Advocacy (CENSURA). https://ssrn.com/abstract=4781328

Pacelli, V., & Azzollini, M. (2011). An Artificial neural network approach for credit risk management. *Journal of Intelligent Learning Systems and Applications*, 3(2), 103–112. 10.4236/jilsa.2011.32012

Schar, F. (2021). Decentralized Finance: On Blockchain- and Smart Contract-Based Financial Markets. Federal Reserve Bank of St. Louis Review. *Second Quarter*, 103(2), 153–174. 10.20955/r.103.153-74

Thatikonda, R., Ponnala, J., Yendluri, D. K., Kempanna, M., Tatikonda, R., & Bhuvanesh, A. (2023). The Impact of Blockchain and AI in the Finance Industry. In *2023 International Conference on Computational Intelligence, Networks and Security (ICCINS)* (pp. 1-6). IEEE. 10.1109/ICCINS58907.2023.10450000

Wang, S., Li, B., Yang, M., & Yan, Z. (2019). Missing Data Imputation for Machine Learning. In Li, B., Yang, M., Yuan, H., & Yan, Z. (Eds.), *IoT as a Service*. Springer. 10.1007/978-3-030-14657-3_7

Wilkens, S. (2019). Machine Learning in Risk Measurement: Gaussian Process Regression for Value-at-Risk and Expected Shortfall. *Journal of Risk Management in Financial Institutions, 12*, 374-383. 10.2139/ssrn.3246131

Chapter 12
The Autonomy of Central Banks and Digital Currency:
A Macroeconomic Perspective

Sofia Devi Shamurailatpam
https://orcid.org/0000-0002-4159-412X
The Maharaja Sayajirao University of Baroda, India

Mohammed Majeed
https://orcid.org/0000-0001-9804-5335
Tamale Technical University, Ghana

ABSTRACT

Many central banks across the globe are experiencing different phases of implementation of central bank digital currencies (CBDCs) – some central banks have already initiated digital currencies or are in experimentation phases or introduced as a pilot project, each one at various operational challenges open to central banks toward building the digital currency framework. This chapter attempts to establish the state of digital currencies experienced by different economies across the world. The chapter highlights the underlying reasons behind the implementation of CBDCs by countries; the challenges and implications of the introduction of such digital currency on monetary policy; the role of CBDC in bringing societal benefits towards financial inclusion and sustainable finance; and finally, the regulatory framework set up to safeguard at the interest of national security. These inter-related issues are examined based on experiences from different economies of the world. Further, a sample study for India's CBDC development is evaluated as country specific study.

DOI: 10.4018/979-8-3693-6321-8.ch012

INTRODUCTION

Global integration of economies and innovations in digital technologies is shaping financial services, which has led to new challenges in the working and functioning of central banks. With the global outbreak of pandemic, economies are experiencing decline in transactional use of cash and emergence of new structure of digital currencies; these all put challenges to the central banking to respond in delivering public policy and regulatory framework. With a view to enhance financial stability and delivering major public policy goals, the central banks along with legislatures of financial system at international levels come up with the new process of digital currency. No doubt, the design, and processes for issuing such digital currency are sovereign decisions, many countries are implementing or at the nascent stage of CBDC under a given regulatory sandbox framework. To say, there is a growing literature on Central Bank Digital Currencies (CBDCs) and countries across the world are exploring its processes of implementation, technology and privacy, financial architectures, its macroeconomic implications to monetary policy, and financial stability. Several central banks have launched central bank money in digital form to the general public and each country is at different phases of implementation of such digital currency - from full-fledged implementation to pilot projects to phases of development, depending upon the process of digitization and existing ecosystem in each country. Some countries have cited several reasons in favour of the implementation of CBDC, while there are views on its high potential to affect the existing financial market structures and business models, which may pose risks to financial stability through the disintermediation of banks. Ironically, the concept of CBDC could improve financial inclusion, particularly for the 1.7 billion population globally that do not have access to bank accounts, but with potential pitfalls of cyber security threats and thefts associated with this platform.

This chapter attempts to establish the existing gaps in the literature on CBDC and the various operational challenges open to central banks toward building the digital currency framework. The pertinent questions to explore are – (a) What drives the central banks toward the implementation of CBDC? (b) What are the challenges and implications for CBDC on monetary policy? (c) Does CBDC benefit society towards inclusion and the concept of sustainable finance? and (d) How strong is the regulatory framework to safeguard the national security implications? These interrelated questions will be explored concerning the progress of CBDC established by nations across the globe so far and potential implications on macroeconomic policies. A case of the development of CBDC for India will be highlighted as a sample country-specific study. However, the effectiveness of policy depends upon how the public perceives policy maker's commitment and behavior, in that an independent central bank would tend to impart greater credibility to monetary policy and therefore improve its effectiveness through the development of a new policy framework of digital currency.

This chapter gives an overview of the recent changes in the financial architectures of central banks operating in a digitized market economy driven by data revolution, which deviates from its traditional functions of qualitative and quantitative approaches of dealing monetary policy and price stability in the economy. The volume highlights the role of central banks and its autonomy in working and framing of monetary policy and curbing price stability on the one hand; and new dimensions of operations towards a digitized economy framework. As research in the area of CBDC is in the nascent phases worldwide, this concept note will provide important resources that can be established in further studies of CBDC.

A BRIEF REVIEW OF LITERATURE

Literatures on the issues of CBDC and its implications are very few and at nascent stage as countries are either under the process of implementation or evaluating potential effects of pilot projects towards the state of political economy. It is known to all that global financial system has significantly impacted economies, leading to emergence of digital assets, so as the CBDC. This can play a crucial role in ensuring financial stability, constructing a better payment system, enhancing monetary policy **(Sissoko, 2021;McLaughlin, 2021;Soderberg et al., 2022)**, establishing a new monetary era **(Wang et al., 2022)**, issue digital currencies to maintain an effective monetary policy **(Cukierman, 2019)** and supporting unconventional monetary policy **(Bordo & Levin, 2017)**. In another study by **Barontini & Holden (2019),** a survey of 63 central banks in the latter part of 2018 were conducted located in emerging market economies and advanced countries, which represents close to 80 percent of world's population and 90 percent of economic output. The survey was done to understand the current work on CBDC's and to find the various factors that motivates it and the reasons behind the issuance of CBDC. The outcome of the survey revealed that majority are collaboratively looking at the implications of a central bank digital currency and in that, despite reached the stage of considering practical issues, central banks are very cautious and plans to issue for short or medium term plans. Therefore, in this regard, many central banks are now executing the case for CBDCs in a continuous process throughout pilot projects and experimentation. The development for potential issuance are shaped by local circumstances, though interest and work on CBDCs is global in nature; as for example, in emerging market and developing countries, the top priority for CBDC is financial inclusion, whereas in advanced economies the main areas of interest are related to efficiency and safety of payment **(Boar & Wehrli, 2021)**. In another survey conducted in late 2022 that examined 86 central banks enquiring about the involvement of central banks in CBDC work, their motivations and intentions for potentially issuing it (**Kosse & Mattei, 2023**). The study found that 93 percent of the central banks surveyed are absorbed in some form of CBDC work as well; and more than 50 percent are involved in experiments to launch CBDC or in cultivating pilot projects. Further, it was highlighted that issuance of retail CBDCs can be expected to complement and coexist with other domestic payment methods, ensuring interoperability with the existing payment systems, benefiting both payers and payees will seamlessly make and receive payments, irrespective of the payment method or service provider. Some studies also found different perspectives on the digital currencies adoption, that is, a successful CBDC launch is likely to require cooperation between central and commercial banks, in an effort to develop a more inclusive and efficient monetary system with a sustainable business case - for either party, a go-it-alone course of action is far less likely to succeed (**Denecker, et. al, 2023**). In a study based on comprehensive database of CBDC projects and technical approaches, and investigate the economic and institutional factors that correlate with CBDC project efforts - the study found that larger proportion of retail CBDCs is more advanced where the informal economy is larger; and that many central banks are considering financial architectures in which a CBDC is a direct cash-like claim on the central bank, however, the private sector handles all retail services (**Auer, et. al, 2023**). Central banks across the world are under the progress of developing digital currencies though the process of implementation and policy approaches vary across countries. Generally, central banks assess the adoption of CBDCs in the context of conventional objectives of price stability, however, other aspects on macroeconomic issues and political dimensions need attention as a part and parcel of the entire policy imperatives. However, despite considering the significance of CBDC, its impacts are unknown in terms of - financial, economic, and environmental stability such as how CBDCs will impact monetary policy transmission, conventional and unconventional monetary instruments, financial and price stability, inflation targeting, central banks as lenders of last resort, and the provision of forwarding guidance (**Elsayed & Nasir, 2022**). In other words, there are views that CBDC though encompasses significant benefits and advantages, it poses substantial risks in terms of financial privacy and more particularly security in digital platforms. To put differently, CBDCs denominated in national currencies will act as complements rather than substitutes to cash and bank deposits, implying potential to protect national currencies against competition from cryptocurrencies, which have implications for global monetary system (**Goodell & Shen, 2021**). In a similar kind of study of the American financial system, it was found that CBDC poses substantial risks to financial privacy, financial freedom, free markets, and cybersecurity (**Anthony & Michel, 2022**). To sum up, according to the extant literatures, the position and work on CBDCs across countries are experiencing varied stages of development, determined by the institutional framework at local levels, though the concept of CBDC is a global phenomenon.

THE AUTONOMY OF CENTRAL BANKS

The concept of central banking was not clearly defined all the time before the beginning of the twentieth century. Perhaps, there was gradual development and evolution of central banking across countries in the world over the long period of time and took lead part as Centre of monetary and banking system in various countries. These banks are known as banks of issue or national banks and are assigned with authority to regulate the issue of notes, convertibility of gold or currencies particularly. We can trace back the history of central banks to the establishment of 'Bank of England', which was the first bank of issue to assume the position of central bank and regarded as the fundamentals of the art of central banking. The autonomy of central banks implies its independence in taking monetary policy decisions on the premise of monetary stability, which is required for the efficient functioning of the economic system (**Rangarajan, 1993**). Most central banks have been granted full autonomy for setting their policy rate and central bank has full autonomy for the design of its monetary policy instruments (**Arnone, et. al, 2007**). Given the political and institutional framework that existed in each country, the autonomy of central bank varies from – under a democratic country, policy decisions are subject to the consent and approval by the elected legislature; on the other hand, countries with much independence and autonomous central banks have to abide the law pertaining to central bank in such economies (**De Kock, 1985**). We can say that there is no full liberty or totally autonomous on the part of central banks, an example is the demand for digital currencies and its process of initiation across globe. Ironically, the attributes of central banking as supervision of monetary policy stance with price stability and regulating inflation for determination of policy rates in particular, despite innovations in financial technologies and data revolution brought significant changes in the nature of strategies implemented to meet demands for the citizens at large. Effectiveness of policy depends upon how the public perceives policy maker's commitment and behavior, in that and independent central bank would tend to impart greater credibility to monetary policy and therefore improve its effectiveness.

CENTRAL BANK DIGITAL CURRENCY (CBDC)

This digitization of money is a new milestone in the history of money, starting from metallic money to paper currency, given the attributes possesses by each form of currencies in each period of time – as a medium of exchange, store of value and unit of account. The term 'Central Bank Digital Currency (CBDC)' refers to digital form of currency notes which is issued by a central bank. This currency is also called as digital rupee (e) in India as per the Reserve Bank of India (RBI). In other words, CBDC is a digital liability of the central bank and is a digital extension of the existing forms of central bank money. To sum up, CBDC is akin to sovereign paper currency and is exchangeable at par with the existing currency and it has all the qualities of paper currency – medium of payment, store of value and legal tender. Such digital currency possesses the significant features of transparency towards all the stakeholders in terms of trust, safety, convenience, liquidity, and integrity in financial transactions. The Bank for International Settlements along with a group of seven central banks are continuously working for outlining common principles and features of CBDC, provided the central banks in each jurisdiction will make decisions in consultation with the governments, authorities and stakeholders in particular. The core principles include – while issuing the CBDC, each of the central bank should not compromise monetary or financial stability; CBDC should act as a complement to existing form of money; and CBDC should have attributes of promoting efficiency (operational and cost) and innovations **(BIS, 2021)**.

In view of the changing dimensions in system, a number of central banks have launched extending central bank money in digital form to the general public. According to the Atlantic Council database, 130 countries, which constitute 98 percent of the world GDP are exploring a CBDC – with 11 countries have launched, 21 countries have undertaken pilot projects, 32 countries are in the phase of development, 45 countries are undergoing research and, in a few countries, state inactive or not portrayed the status as per the recent data. The reasons for implementing a CBDC differs from one country to another, however, it is the digitization of the process of either curbing the private cryptocurrencies under the legal framework of federal banks or as a result of financial innovations and part of ecosystem. The significant feature of CBDC is the disintermediation of banks and streamlining the overall supply of credit; also a potential to bank unbanked populations, who remained excluded due to lack of knowledge on financial literacy or because of geographical and topography as reasons. To say, full-fledge CBDC is being implemented only a few select countries – the Bahamas (Sand Dollar), Nigeria (eNaira) and countries in the Eastern Caribbean Union (DCash). China have initiated world's major pilot projects to a digital currency, while countries like United States, Eurozone and India are in the development phase of CBDC, under the verge of regulatory sandbox for validation. In India, the Reserve Bank of India has initiated significant steps in the upgradation of CBDC for full operationalization through expansion of the scope of pilot projects by gradually increasing the number of banks, number of users and locations as per the progress made under CBDC. The motivations for CBDC in countries differ across jurisdictions ranging from payment efficiency, reduction of costs, financial inclusion, promoting safety and robustness to a more transparent and stability in financial system. However, the validation of a CBDC is also determined by several factors such as - technological related risks, privacy and ethics, whether a CBDC will have impact on monetary policy and price stability by the central banks. A detailed information on CBDC development by countries in aggregate; retail CBDC development projects undertaken by specific countries; and cross-border CBDCs - retail and wholesale or both; in Table 1, Table 2 and Table 3 respectively.

In Table 1, the number of countries and currency unions exploring CBDC specifically post pandemic period are reported. Number of countries that launched the digital currency has increased gradually over the period; it is visible that countries are too much focussed on either as experimenting as pilot projects, the number of countries involved in pilot project, which was 18 countries as on April 2021 has reached to 35 countries as on March 2024. This is also reflected in terms of the development in the CBDC by nations as well as increase in the research in the domain. For example, number of countries that experienced development in the CBDC has almost doubled from 14 countries in April 2021 to 31 in March 2024, followed by significant progress in years 2022 and 2023. Similar picture is indiscernible for the research in CBDC, that shown progress from 28 countries in April 2021 to 45 countries as on March 2024. The percentage of inactive and cancelled CBDC by countries is stagnant and proportionately lower, some countries cite other institutional and regulatory framework factors or other reasons that hinder and limits the introduction of CBDC. In other words, we can say that countries across the globe are significantly experimenting and observing under different phases of CBDC as a revolutionary vision in the global financial system by incorporating all the attributes of financial stability framework.

Table 1. Number of countries and currency unions exploring CBDC overtime

Different Phases of CBDC	April 2021	May 2022	June 2023	March 2024
Launched	1	10	11	3
Pilot	18	15	21	35
Development	14	25	32	31
Research	28	45	46	45
Inactive	10	10	16	17

continued on following page

Table 1. Continued

Different Phases of CBDC	April 2021	May 2022	June 2023	March 2024
Cancelled	3	2	2	2
Other	zero	2	2	2

Source: https://www.atlanticcouncil.org/cbdctracker/

Retail CBDC is a digital substitute for paper money or physical coins, which can be held and utilized by consumers as well as firms. Table 2 depicts retail CBDC projects for consumers undertaken across countries during the period from post pandemic period to 2023. As on 2023, the country that ranked top across worldwide is India, having 82 projects development. Unlike the initial phases in which China, Nigeria and other Caribbean countries stood high in development of retail CBDC projects. Countries are projecting retail CBDC as a part of digitization of financial system by replacing fiat money and cutting cost for minting new currencies.

Table 2. CBDC retail projects for consumers across countries, 2021 to 2023

CBDC project name	Country/region	April 2021	April 2020	April 2023
Digital Rupee	India	-	46	82
E-hryvnia	Ukraine	71	71	71
Project Bang Khun Prom	Thailand	-	69	71
Digital Yen	Japan	-	44	65
E-krona	Sweden	58	61	64
E-won	South Korea	51	44	57
Digital Dollar	Australia	-	44	55
e-HKD	Hong Kong SAR	-	45	54
Digital Ruble	Russia	-	43	54
Digital Shekel	Israel	-	95	-
eNaira	Nigeria	-	92	-
Sand Dollar	Bahamas	92	87	-
e-CNY (digital yuan)	China	75	81	-
Jamaica	Jamaica	33	80	-
DXCD, or DCash	Eastern Caribbean	61	71	-
e-peso, or Billete Digital	Uruguay	71	-	-
Dinero Electronico	Ecuador	71	-	-
Bakong Project	Cambodia	83	-	-
Digital Lira	Turkey	42	-	-

Source: https://www.statista.com/statistics/1229713/countries-with-most-mature-retail-cbdg-worldwide/

One of the hindrances in the international payments system is high costs, low speed and transparency, operational complexities in the global chain of payment system despite rapid integration of economies across the globe. The Bank for International Settlements (BIS) Innovation Hubs in different centres have collaborated with cross border countries experiments with a multiple DBDC common platform particularly for wholesale cross border payments, aiming safeguard currency sovereignty and monetary and financial stability for each participating jurisdiction with principles of do not harm, compliance and interoperability (BIS,2023). Table 3 depicts that, as a part and progress of CBDC projects, so many cross-border CBDC projects have been initiated and under certain phases of development experienced by the cross country partners. According to the latest data as on May, 2024, there are 18 cross-border CBDC projects – of which 9 relates to retail use case, 7 wholesale use case and 2 projects that enhanced both the retail and wholesale facilities. The Bank for International Settlement (BIS) Innovation Hubs at different centres is leading and upgrading countries practical experiments in building the cross-border digital currencies for faster, cheaper and more transparent cross-border payments.

Table 3. Cross border CBDC projects, as on May, 2024

Name of the Project	Participating countries	Use Case	Purpose
Project Jura	France & Switzerland	Wholesale	For cross border settlement on a DLT platform.
Project Icebreaker	Israel, Norway, Sweden & BIS Innovation Hub	Retail	For interlinking and interoperability between retail CBDCs across borders.
Digital Euro	Euro Area Countries	Retail & Wholesale	To be used throughout countries in the Eurozone.
D-Cash	Eastern Caribbean Central Union: Anguilla, Antigua and Barbuda, Dominica, Grenada, Montserrat, Saint Kitts and Nevis, Saint Lucia and Saint Vincent and the Grenadines	Retail	A digital currency for the seven countries aimed at financial inclusion.
Project Agora	France (Euosystem), Japan, South Korea, Mexico, Switzerland, England & United States	Wholesale	Aims to tokenize cross-border payments by creating a unified, programmable infrastructure that brings together the seven central banks and commercial banks.
Project Mariana	France, Switzerland, Singapore & BIS Hub	Wholesale	For block-chain could address Forex market settlement risks and implementing bridges for cross-chain transactions.

continued on following page

Table 3. Continued

Name of the Project	Participating countries	Use Case	Purpose
Project Cedar x/ Ubin+	United States and Singapore	Wholesale	For cross-border multi-currency transactions with DLT; to enhance interoperability and settlement in payments – reducing settlement times and risk.
Venus Initiative	France, Luxembourg and European Investment Bank	Wholesale	Using an experimental CBDC for secure settlement.
Project Helvetia	Switzerland and BIS Innovation Hub	Wholesale	Integrating the wholesale CBDC to the core banking infrastructure of the country.
Project Polaris	BIS Innovation Hub – Nordic Centre	Retail	To explore security and resilience in CBDC systems; with offline payment possibilities and functionalities for CBDC platforms.
Project Rosalind	United Kingdom and BIS Innovation Hub	Retail	To make payments between individuals cheaper and more efficient while allowing businesses to create new financial products to reduce fraud.
Project Dunbar	Australia, Singapore, Malaysia and South Africa	Wholesale	A potential shared platform for multiple central bank digital currencies.
Project Aurum	Hong King & BIS Innovation Hub- Hong Kong Centre	Retail	As a privacy of retail payments using CBDC.
Project mBridge	Thailand, China, Hong Kong, United Arab Emirates & BIS Innovation Hub	Wholesale	Multiple CBDC for faster, cheaper and more efficient transfers and foreign exchange operations.
Project Mandala	BIS Innovation Hub – Singapore Centre, Australia, South Korea, Malaysia and Singapore	Wholesale	For cross border payments by developing a common protocol that automates and simplifies compliance with jurisdiction specific regulatory requirements, enhancing efficiency, transparency and the integrity of international transactions.
Project Sela	Israel, Hong Kong & BIS Innovation Hub	Retail	To explore the cybersecurity implications of two tier retail CBDC
Project Tourbillon	BIS Innovation Hub - Swiss Centre	Retail & Wholesale	To improve cybersecurity, scalability and privacy in prototype
e-CNY	China, Hong Kong & Macau	Retail	To test for cross-border transactions in Hong-Kong

Source: Compiled by Author from information available at: https://www.atlanticcouncil.org/cbdctracker/

SOME POLICY IMPLICATIONS OF CBDC

As motivations of CBDC depends upon country specific circumstances under a given ecosystem and policy directives, there is variation in the extent of adoption and implementation across countries. The significant positive outcomes of introducing a CBDC among others include – cost-effective as replacement of physical cash to digital form, digital payments systems which has operational efficiency as it being a sovereign currency, assurance of settlement finality through encrypted data and reducing the risks as payments using CBDC are final. Besides these operational and management significance, CBDC also supports financial inclusion, particularly in those countries where there is limited physical infrastructure specifically in remote areas; in regions with variations of topography in hilly areas or disperse islands spread over that are unconnected within the country itself and remained unbanked or underbanked. The central banks with its autonomy in the functioning and working can take this opportune through implementation of digital currency with a view to benefit the citizens by centralization of payments and settlements of financial system, despite its conventional function of framing monetary policy and price stability in the economy. With regard to handling the digitized economy, the central bank has to validate the operational architectures, infrastructures for technology, clearly defining the possible risks in terms of frauds, cyber-crimes and issues that may arise in cross-border payment transactions system. Some of the implications of adoption of CBDC as per the Bank for International Settlement research are regarding the process of implementation is which model is suitable – direct or indirect or hybrid model as a realistic CBDC designs and the role of the private sector in the operational architecture, particularly in serving households and businesses. Further, beyond the architecture of the operational design, a second consideration is the optimal technology underpinning it (**Auer, et. al, 2021**). In other words, as CBDC is driven by digitization process, strong and robust technology platforms will always be at the core of its functions for cybersecurity, resilience, and good technical governance. Nevertheless, operational costs of central banks in managing CBDC and operational threads in the form of human resource management, particularly staffs in meeting proper training under CBDC environment. At the core of ethics, a trusted environment framework is prerequisite for long-term operations. For example, the system should be transparent and confirmed that data is shared only with the relevant particular third party group or organization and does not leaked to the entire network in the system in the process. The implementation of CBDC questions on the level of consumer protection and grievance redressal mechanisms or legal framework to address any issues arising out of the digital currency system. As digitization process is associated with risks such as privacy risks, digital security, accountability risks, digital frauds, hacking of data and malware, etc. are some of the issues to be addressed in the process of implementation. There is no clear consensus on whether the introduction of CBDC will have potential impact on monetary policy and hence price stability in the economy. According to the report of Bank for International Settlement, while a CBDC has the potential to provide benefits to the operation and resilience of the financial system, it could also affect existing financial market structures and business models, which may pose risks to financial stability as the financial system evolves, particularly via the potential disintermediation of banks **(BIS, 2021a)**. Thus, the digitation of currency has significant advantages and beneficiaries, an ample amount of research in the domain needs to address macroeconomic issues by each of the central bank before initiating or being implemented a CBDC.

Proposition One: What Drives the Central Banks Toward the Implementation of CBDC?

Central banks across the world have either issued a CBDC or launched CBDC as pilot projects. We know that one of the major challenges of the central banks in emerging and developing nations is financial inclusion (IMF, 2023); globally 1.4 billion people remain outside the ambit of formal financial system, and tackling this challenge is a top priority in many regions (Demirgüç-Kunt, et al., 2022), given the macroeconomic targets of monetary policy and financial stability. According to the various studies of international financial institutions and global development institutions, the concept of CBDC is designed in such a manner so as to address the barriers to financial inclusion, and an opportunity to receive acceptance by the financially excluded digital payments, along with its attributes of credit risk free of digital money, offline payments and lower costs with greater accessibility. All these has significant impact on economic growth and further reducing the income inequality gaps between the rich and poor. There are established theories of finance led growth hypotheses- therefore, the prime purpose of CBDC towards financial inclusion is expected to enhance financial stability and effectiveness of monetary policy transmission, that is must for long-term economic growth of nations. Therefore, we can say that introduction of CBDC has significant macroeconomic advantages, given the strong institutional framework, stable financial system and particularly, given amenities of socio-economic infrastructures for easy access and adaptability.

Proposition Two: What Are the Challenges and Implications for CBDC on Monetary Policy?

There are concerns of CBDCs on monetary policy. If the CBDCs are not well-structured that is suited to the economic environment of the country, it may have unprecedented consequences in the form of spill over effects on macroeconomic monetary policy- impacting the circulation of money supply, intermediation in the bank deposits, fluctuations in the bank reserves and overall capital flows in the economy. The consequences will be much higher for those countries with higher proportion of small retail deposits and demand deposits working under poor institutional framework. Further, there is possibility of macroeconomic risks of cross border payments and wholesale CBDCs if not addressed and identified substantially.

Proposition Three: Does CBDC Benefit Society Towards Inclusion and the Concept of Sustainable Finance?

Looking at the positive sides of the CBDC, it may enhance financial inclusion, digital payments system with more convenience, comfort, affordability without compromise of security as it is handle by the central bank or the regulatory body of the financial system of the country. In other words, if taken care of possible risks with CBDC with features of safety and security, along with significant benefits to citizens with more convenience along with accountability and transparency in operations, it is beneficial to society and has a chain effect of sustainable finance system in the long-run that will be experienced by the country in question.

Proposition Four: How Strong Is the Regulatory Framework to Safeguard the National Security Implications?

So far central banks across the globe are either in process of implementation or implemented already a CBDC as a digital money is based on its expected implications and beneficial associated with the payment and transaction system with all the features of money as a medium of exchange. However, the successful experience of the CBDC in the long-run is determined by the strong regulatory and institutional framework, that will automatically have established safety and secured sustainable financial system. All the objectives of introducing such digital wallet will be successful when the legal framework and institutional environment are strong enough to attend all sort of risks associated in financial transactions and payment settlement system of the economy.

CONCLUSION

This chapter gives a concept note on the recent issues of CBDC adopted by central banks of different countries. Conventionally, the central banks are assigned and have autonomy in framing monetary policy and price stability in the economies, the changing dimensions of financial innovations in the form of sovereign currency brought a new dimension of operational architectures to central banks. As implementation of CBDC is country specific circumstances, determined by existing ecosystem and policy framework in each country, each of the countries are at different phases in CBDC – from pilot projects to full-fledged implementation to the stages of development and research across countries of the world. In other words, each country adopts CBDC under the given jurisdiction of the country under a given institutional and economic framework. The adoption of a CBDC has significant positive outcomes in terms of cost-cutting, faster, efficient, convenience, settlement of financial risks and in reducing the gaps in banking services in general. But, along with these advantages, there are questions on the realistic model of CBDC, technological platform suitability, possible impacts on monetary policy and price stability of the economy. Hence, though the central banks have autonomy in its financial architecture, it is the role of the monetary authority or central bank to overlook the possible consequences of implementing a CBDC in a given economic, political and institutional framework governing the economy.

REFERENCES

Anthony, N., & Michel, N. (2022). *Central Bank Digital Currency Assessing the Risks and Dispelling the Myths.* (Cato Working Paper No. 70). Cato Institute. www.cato.org/workingpapers

Arnone, M., Laurens, B. J., Segalotto, J.-F., & Sommer, M. (2007). *Central Bank Autonomy: Lessons from Global Trends,* (IMF Working Paper, WP0788).

Auer, R., Cornelli, G., & Frost, J. (2023, October). Rise of the Central Bank Digital Currencies. *International Journal of Central Banking,* 185–214. https://www.ijcb.org/journal/ijcb23q4a5.pdf

Auer, R., Frost, J., Gambacorta, L., Monnet, C., Rice, T., & Shin, H. S. (2021). *Central Bank Digital Currencies: Motives, Economic Implications and the Research Frontier.* (BIS Working Papers No.976).

Barontini, C., & Holden, H. (2019). *Proceeding with caution – a survey on central bank digital currency, BIS Papers No. 101.* Monetary and Economic Department.

BIS. (2021). *Central Bank Digital Currencies: Executive Summary.* BIS Research & Publications. https://www.bis.org/publ/othp42.htm

BIS (2021a). *Central Bank Digital Currencies: Financial Stability Implications.* BIS Research & Publications.

BIS. (2023). *Project mBridge: Experimenting with a multi-CBDC platform for cross-border payments.* BIS. https://www.bis.org/innovation_hub/projects/mbridge_brochure_2311.pdf

Boar, C., & Wehrli, A. (2021). *Ready, Steady, go? – Results of the third BIS survey on central bank digital currency.* (BIS Papers No. 114). Monetary and Economic Department. https://www.bis.org/publ/bppdf/bispap114.pdf

Bordo, M. D., & Levin, A. T. (2017). *Central Bank Digital Currency and the future of Monetary Policy.* (NBER Working Paper Series, Working Paper 23711). NBER. https://www.nber.org/papers/w23711

Cukierman, A. (2019). *Welfare and Political Economy Aspects of a Central Bank Digital Currency.* (CEPR Discussion Paper No. DP13728). https://papers.ssrn.com/sol3/papers.cfm?abstract_id=3387317#

De Kock, M. H. (1985). *Central Banking* (4th ed.). Granada Publishing Limited.

Demirgüç-Kunt, A., Klapper, L., Singer, D., & Ansar, S. (2022). *The Global Findex Database 2021: Financial Inclusion, Digital Payments, and Resilience in the Age of COVID-19*. World Bank. 10.1596/978-1-4648-1897-4

Denecker, O., Estienne, A. D., Gompertz, P.-M., & Sasia, E. (2023). Central bank digital currencies: An active role for commercial banks. *Journal of Payments Strategy & Systems*, *17*(1). https://econpapers.repec.org/article/azajpss00/y_3a2023_3av_3a17_3ai_3a1_3ap_3a26-35.htm

Elsayed, A. H., & Nasir, M. A. (2022). Central bank digital currencies: An agenda for future research. *Research in International Business and Finance*, 62, 101736. 10.1016/j.ribaf.2022.101736

Goodell, J. W., & Shen, D. (2021). The Chinese sovereign digital currency as a catalyst for change: A new trilemma? In Shaen, C. (Ed.), *Understanding Cryptocurrency Fraud: The Challenges and Headwinds to Regulate Digital Currencies* (pp. 177–186). De Gruyter. 10.1515/9783110718485-014

International Monetary Fund (IMF) (2023). *Financial Access Survey 2022 Trends and Developments*. IMF.

Kosse, A., & Mattei, I. (2023). *Making headway- Results of the 2022 BIS survey on central bank digital currencies and crypto*. (BIS Papers No. 136). Monetary and Economic Department. https://www.bis.org/publ/bppdf/bispap136.htm

McLaughlin, T. (2021). Two paths to tomorrow's money. *Journal of Payments Strategy & Systems*, 15(1), 23–36. https://www.henrystewartpublications.com/jpss/v15. 10.69554/OAUP7404

Rangarajan, C. (1993). *Autonomy of Central Banks, Speech by Governor*. Reserve Bank of India.

Sissoko, C. (2021). The Nature of Money in a Convertible Currency World. *Review of Economic Analysis*, 13(1), 1–43. 10.15353/rea.v13i1.1771

Soderberg, G., Bechara, M., Bossu, W., Che, N., Kiff, J., Lukonga, I., Mancini-Griffoli, T., Sun, T., Yoshinaga, A. (2022). Behind the scenes of central bank digital currency: Emerging treFnds, insights, and policy lessons. *International Monetary Fund, Fintech Note*.

Wang, Y., Lucey, B.M., Vigne, S.A., & Yarovaya, L. (2022). The Effects of Central Bank Digital Currencies News on Financial Markets. *Technological Forecasting & Social Change*, *180*, 1-39. 10.1016/j.techfore.2022.121715

Chapter 13
Can AI Change the Way We See the World?
An Analysis Using Attitude and Perception Measurement on Female B.Tech Students in Rajasthan

Lalita Kumari
Mody University of Science and Technology, India

Akansha Gautam
Mody University of Science and Technology, India

P. Varaprasad Goud
https://orcid.org/0000-0002-2278-0197
Chaitanya Bharathi Institute of Technology, India

Fatima Muhammad Abdulkarim
Federal University, Dutse, Nigeria

ABSTRACT

The study investigate how female B.Tech. students view of artificial intelligence (AI) in their personal life and determine how their views about AI relate to the advancements they encounter. The study is cross-sectional across only a limited sample and it is important to understand the comparison for different set of students to assess the real situation of Artificial Intelligence. The chapter attempts to construct awareness index and perception index using principle component analysis which further uses ANOVA on a sample of 150 engineering students to better understand the numerous

DOI: 10.4018/979-8-3693-6321-8.ch013

phenomena arising from AI. The results found use of AI has a significant impact on creating better career opportunities. The results of AI are also favourable towards better awareness, curiosity, knowledge, and learning.

INTRODUCTION

AI conjures up images of supercomputers, machines with enormous processing power, adaptive behavior (like sensors), and other features that allow them to function and think like humans. In fact, these machines are the embodiment of AI. It enhance communication between supercomputers and people. A number of films have been produced to demonstrate the potential of artificial intelligence. One example is the use of AI in smart buildings, where the technology may be used to control the temperature, play music, and/or regulate the building's air quality based on the moods of its occupants. AI is now being used more often in the education sector, surpassing the traditional perception of AI as a supercomputer to encompass embedded computer systems.

As several studies have shown, web-based and online education has evolved beyond just providing students with resources to download, study, and complete assignments in order to pass, to include intelligent and adaptive web-based systems that learn from their teachers. Chassignol, M., et al. (2018), AI has been blended with teaching, learning, and administration in the field of education. This study will be centered around these themes, which serve as a framework for assessing and comprehending artificial intelligence in education.

OBJECTIVES

1. To examine the effects of female students' perceptions of AI and life changes.
2. To examine the relationship between female students' attitudes regarding AI and developments in their personal lives.

HYPOTHESIS

$H0_1$: There is no relationship between perception of female students towards AI and their life change.

$H0_2$: There is no relationship between Attitude towards AI and life changes of female students.

LITERATURE REVIEW

Jeong, H.,et al.(2023) The study examined the perspectives of dental hygiene students regarding artificial intelligence (AI), their expectations for AI, and their degree of confidence in AI's capacity for diagnosis and decision-making about the future potential of AI. The purpose of the study was to ascertain the attitudes of Korean dental hygiene students about artificial intelligence (AI) and the kind of training required to advance their professional abilities in this field. The findings indicated that 93.1% of participants had viewed online AI content, and 44.2% of participants expressed interest in AI. In contrast to humans, participants in the study showed less trust in AI's diagnosis (14.8%) and judgment (8.1%). Moreover, 21.9% of respondents said AI had a major impact on dental hygiene. Marrone, R., Taddeo, V., & Hill, G. (2022) While students with a lower comprehension of AI were more apprehensive, those with a higher understanding had more positive attitudes toward integrating AI into their courses. The majority of pupils thought that AI could never be as creative as humans. To guarantee a successful integration, educators should concentrate on educating AI while highlighting the importance of human creativity.

Tyson, L. D., & Zysman, J. (2022) examined the impact of AI on the labour market and the economy. It makes an effort to understand how AI affects, among other things, job creation, job displacement, economic inequality, and employment quality. The effects of artificial intelligence and automation The variable of interest is labour market information, which covers topics like pay growth, income inequality, job polarization, and the availability of high-caliber work prospects. Ozakar, R., Gazanfer, R. E., & Hanay, Y. S. (2020) The goal of the study is to use an artificial intelligence-powered, unbiased emotion detector to examine people's degrees of happiness across various nations. Finding out if there are statistically significant variations in happiness levels between different cities across the globe is the aim. The happiness level is the variable of interest, and it is based on the emotions that can be seen on people's faces in publicly accessible street footage. Surprise, fear, happiness, and anger are the emotions taken into consideration; sad and neutral feelings were not found. According to the study, there is no statistically significant variation in the degree of happiness among the eight cities that were examined. The most frequently identified emotion was "Surprise," which could be explained by the fact that cameras were present when the video was taken. Brougham, D., & Haar, J. (2018) With an emphasis on the moderating effect of age, the study sought to understand how workers view the possible threat posed by robotics, artificial intelligence, smart technology, and algorithms (STARA) to their employment and careers. The impact of STARA awareness on various employment and well-being outcomes was another goal of the study. The primary variable of interest was STARA awareness, which gauged how much workers believed STARA technology could replace them in their current roles.

The following factors were also utilized to evaluate the outcomes related to jobs and well-being: organizational commitment, career satisfaction, cynicism, depression, and intentions to leave. According to the study, there are drawbacks to having more STARA awareness, such as lower job satisfaction and organizational dedication. It also demonstrated wholesome connections. Cath, C., et.al. (2018) The text's goal is to examine and evaluate the main ideas, suggestions, and methods included in three distinct studies on robotics, AI, machine learning, and algorithms. It also seeks to draw attention to the necessity of a more ambitious and all-encompassing vision for a "good AI society" and offers a two-pronged strategy to direct the advancement of this society. The method for creating a "good AI society," which includes the ethical considerations, values, accountability, collaboration, and policy recommendations discussed in the three studies, is the variable in this work. Kelley, P. G.,et.al. (2021) examines public perceptions of AI in eight nations on six continents, with a particular emphasis on the ethical, social, political, and economic ramifications of AI. The study attempts to characterize public mood toward AI in terms of main themes (exciting, useful, frightening, and futuristic), as well as the general impression of AI's impact on society and support for responsible AI development and use. The term "public opinion on AI" refers to the opinions and attitudes of respondents regarding AI technology, including how they feel about it and how they perceive its influence. According to the majority of respondents, artificial intelligence would significantly affect society. The responders strongly favor the ethical development and application of AI. Dubey, R., & Griffiths, T. L. (2020) Giving artificial agents a sense of curiosity is beneficial because it fosters inquiry and acts as an intrinsic incentive, as recent machine learning research has shown. There are now two ways to define these rewards: chasing prediction mistakes and giving preference to novelty. These two elements have also been highlighted in psychological theories of curiosity. Understanding the role of curiosity, which necessitates considering the abstract computational problem that both humans and computers encounter when they investigate their environment, allows us to demonstrate how these two literatures might be related. When computers and humans encounter identical computational problems, we can anticipate that their answers will converge. We have maintained that, in the situation of curiosity, both people and robots want to maximize the value of Knowledge. Understanding this common issue aids in the explanation of why novelty and prediction-error play a significant role in determining intrinsic rewards for both systems as well as the best times to concentrate on each. We believe that as AI and cognitive science advance, examining additional instances in which humans and machines encounter the same computational challenges—and identifying when they do not—will prove to be a useful tool. Sun, C., et.al (2022). In this research, a unified framework for computational artificial curiosity is presented, and the integration of psychological curiosity with AI approaches is explored. It highlights the need for more human-like AI learning skills by reviewing curiosity-driven learning (CDL) techniques in Reinforcement Learning, Recommendation, and Classification. The suggest to bridge the gap between AI & Human Intelligence. Among the difficulties are the intricate relationships between variables that pique attention and the dearth of appropriate benchmarks for evaluating model performance. The need of establishing limits is emphasized in the paper's discussion of potential issues like risk management and privacy. All things considered, CDL is regarded as a crucial component in the advancement of artificial intelligence for the next generation, encouraging AI exploration, learning, and globalization.Rusmiyanto, R., et.al (2023) examines how AI can enhance communication abilities of English language learners, highlighting the value of AI's tailored and interactive learning experiences. The results demonstrate how AI can help people speak and pronounce words more clearly. Responsible AI integration requires careful attention to ethical issues including bias correction and privacy protection. To evaluate long-term effects and improve teaching strategies, more study is required. AI has great potential for language learning, enabling students to succeed in the globalized world.

RESEARCH METHODOLOGY

The study aims to create an AI index and examine how AI impacts the lives of students. The current analysis is based on primary data that was gathered from B.tech programmes at several universities of Rajasthan. To collect the information five point likert scale ranging between (Strongly Disagree to Strongly Agree) was used on 150 female respondents in different university in Rajasthan. 17 indices were picked in order to build the AI index. The two main indicators of these indices are students' perceptions of AI and their awareness of it. These indicators are gathered from several sources.

The study used PCA analysis to reduce dynamics of the current data and create factor loading. A KMO value greater than .7 is observed when assessing the data sufficiency prior to developing an AI index. At the 1% level of significance, the results of the Bartlett's Test of Sphericity were also significant. It indicates that the facts are sufficient for a further examination. When Cronbach's Alpha is more than 0.7, it indicates that the factors and data are reliable enough for analysis.

To see the change of perception and awareness after using of student used Anova with respect to Use of AI.

Step which follow to construct Perception and Awareness Index

1. Normalize the data set

2. Composite index methods: To develop the AI index, data has been determined using key component analysis.
3. To build the Index in context of two indicator first taken the rotated component matrix which is come from PCA after that compute the factor wise variance and factor importance.
4. Factor importance- Total variance divided by each factor variance.
5. Variables Importance= (factor weight * factor weight)/ factor variance
6. Composite index = α1X1+ α2X2+ α3X3+………. αnXn…………. Eq (2) [1]
7. $Z_{ij} = (x_{ij} - Min(x_{ij}))$ ………………… (Eq. 1)[2]

Max (x_{ij}) - Min (x_{ij})

8. Artificial intelligent Index= Perception index + Awareness Index / 2

ANALYSIS AND INTERPRETATION

Table (1.1) shows the PCA results that were used to create the composite index for Artificial Intelligence (AI). KMO value of 0.77 is good. This shows that the sample size is sufficient for PCA. Bartlett's test of sphericity score is highly significant at ($p<0.001$). Therefore, PCA is a suitable methodology for this situation to analyze the importance of selected indicators in measuring the AI index. All factors together can account for up to 50% of the variation in students' perception. After PCA rotation analysis, the present analysis was divided into two parts and was used to explore variable importance. We can see from this research that Cronbach's alpha value greater than or equal to .7 is within the acceptable range. This guarantees proper internal consistency of the indicators in the scale.

INTREPRETATION

The **Table 1** demonstrates that AI significantly affects the perceptions of Female students in determining better performance at routine jobs. In contrast to the above 9 indicators, there are two indicators namely 'AI better than human' & 'AI better than employee' falling under the construct i.e Replacement capabilities of AI exhibit higher level of importance(0.26) in comparison to other 7 indicators altogether exhibiting level of (0.73).

Hence we can conclude that the significance level of 2 indicators is much powerful in contrast to other 7 indicators altogether.

Table 1. Effects of female students' perceptions of AI and life changes

KMO = .772, Bartlett's Test of Sphericity= .000 Cronbach's Alpha= .769				
Its use can create new career opportunities in future.	.437	.086	**0.057411**	0.006063
AI contribution in happiness of People.	.567	-.050	**0.096731**	0.002087
I am dependent in using AI on to day to day basis.	.761	.069	**0.174307**	0.003978
AI capabilities are very impressive	.676	.200	**0.137455**	0.033119
AI agent capabilities are superior than Human capabilities	.086	.844	0.002201	**0.589141**
AI performance is superior to humans.	.153	.825	0.007081	**0.56246**
AI will benefit large portion of society in future.	.599	.307	0.107881	0.078186
AI is something I would like to use in my own job.	.664	.337	**0.13263**	0.093734
AI is exciting	.700	.093	**0.147646**	0.007161
Var	3.322	1.209		
Component importance	0.733171	0.266829		

continued on following page

Table 1. Continued

KMO = .772, Bartlett's Test of Sphericity= .000 Cronbach's Alpha= .769	
perception Index	59

Source: Primary Data

The above result indicates 59% as the Female Perception Index value towards AI which indicates an average value towards the positive side.

46.7% Females agree that AI provide the career opportunities in the future followed by 54% females who believe that AI is helpful in daily routine life. In this study we also observe that 54.7% of the total respondents spend more than 5 hours in usage of Technological devices. The reason attributes to 79.3% of respondents representing urban area as uninterrupted internet facility is easily available.

Hence, we can conclude that Perception index of 59% shows slight changes overtime.

Supporting Statements/Opinions of Female Students in Rajasthan

- Artificial intelligence can help us generate new ideas, solutions, and opportunities from existing knowledge. It can also reduce the time and cost of creating, discovering, and delivering knowledge. Additionally, AI and analytics can improve the accuracy, relevance, and consistency of your knowledge.
- AI and ML have grown very close to human behavior. For instance, ChatGPT. Unlike using search engines for gaining information on a particular topic, from vast resources, ChatGPT lets one to obtain the required and concise information. Moreover, just like interacting with a human, ChatGPT can also clarify one's doubts regarding parts of what it said.
- When we break it down, a student's goal is simple: obtain a degree or diploma proving their knowledge. AI can help students achieve this goal by streamlining the education process. By providing access to the right courses, improving communication with teachers and freeing up more time to focus on other aspects of life, AI can make a significant impact on the students' educational journey.

Table 2. The relationship between female students' attitudes regarding AI and developments in their personal lives

KMO = .823 Bartlett's Test of Sphericity= .000 Cronbach's Alpha= .818				
Use of AI helps in enhancing Knowledge	.109	**.854**	0.0033	**0.616**
Use of AI can help in curiosity	.251	**.737**	0.0178	**0.459**
Use of AI can help in Learning	.227	**.734**	0.0146	**0.455**
Use of AI can help in bring out better leadership qualities	**.693**	.087	**0.1355**	0.006
Use of AI can help in better involvement	**.769**	.157	**0.1667**	0.021
Use of AI helps in increasing better interpersonal Skills	**.757**	.285	**0.1616**	0.069
Use of AI helps in better career orientation	**.600**	.261	**0.1015**	0.057
Use of AI can help in better adaptability & life skills	**.758**	.174	**0.1620**	0.026
Var	3.544	1.183		
Component importance	0.749736	0.250264		
perception Index	61.14			

Source: Primary Data

Table (1.2) shows the PCA results that were used to create the composite index for Awareness of Artificial Intelligence (AI). KMO value of 0.8 is admirable. This shows that the sample size is sufficient for PCA. Bartlett's test of sphericity score is highly significant at (p<0.001). Therefore, PCA is a suitable methodology for this situation to analyze the importance of selected indicators in measuring the AI index. All factors together can account for up to 59% of the variation in students' perception. After PCA rotation analysis, the present analysis was divided into two parts and was used to explore variable importance. We can see from this research that Cronbach's alpha value greater than or equal to .8 is within the acceptable range. This guarantees proper internal consistency of the indicators in the scale.

The Table 2 demonstrates that AI significantly affects the Awareness of Female students in determining life & career management skills. In contrast to the above 8 indicators, there are two indicators namely 'AI contribution in life & career management skills' & 'AI contribution in Cognitive growth'. In both the indicators, 2 factors namely ' AI helps in enhancing knowledge', 'AI can help in better involvement' are highly contributing factors to enhance awareness towards AI. .0.7% attributes to the first indicator & 0.24% attributes to second indicator.

Hence we can conclude that the significance level of 5 indicators is much powerful in contrast to other 3 indicators altogether.

The above result indicates 61.14% as the female Awareness Index value towards AI which indicates a slightly greater average value towards the positive side.

As per the primary survey 94.7% Females are aware of using AI and 88% believe it is helpful for enhancing the knowledge. 57.3% females believe that awareness of AI help in their job. 49.3% of females have confidence that AI help in learning due to curiosity development.

Supporting Statements/Opinions of Female Students in Rajasthan

- AI adaptive learning systems can quickly identify when a student is struggling and then provide more or different support to help them succeed. As the student shows that they have mastered the content or skill, the AI tool provides more difficult tasks and materials to further challenge the learner.
- AI can enhance learning through personalization, adaptive content, instant feedback, virtual tutors, and data analysis, improving engagement and outcomes.
- AI can personalize learning by tailoring lessons to individual student's needs, providing immediate feedback, and offering guidance. Chatbots like Chat GPT can engage students, answer their questions, and keep them motivated.

Table 3. ANOVA test on perception and awareness index with respect to use of AI

Use of AI		Sum of Squares	Df	Mean Square	F	Sig.
perception Index	Between Groups	1163.540	1	1163.540	3.952	.049
	Within Groups	43573.141	148	294.413		
	Total	44736.682	149			
Awareness Index	Between Groups	3872.826	1	3872.826	11.329	.001
	Within Groups	50594.537	148	341.855		
	Total	54467.363	149			

Source: Primary Data

INTERPRETATION

Above Table demonstrates that ANOVA on variables- Perceptions & Awareness Index are affected by use of AI. This Table also shows the change in Perceptions & Awareness of Female Students significantly affect by rising usage matrix of AI. The result shows that both the Index are significant at 1% and 5% level of significance. Hence, we can conclude that Artificial Intelligence plays a major role in changing life & its rising usage can be a breakthrough contributor for the success in determining our cognitive ability & perception towards the world.

CONCLUSION

The study shows that female students' attitudes about AI and personal development are in between their perceptions of AI and its improvements in their lives. The results are indicative of significant impact of AI in creating better career opportunities in the future which proves to be a good importance level of AI performance unlike employees or humans in discharging routine responsibilities. The results of AI are also conducive towards better awareness, curiosity, knowledge and learning. Both indices are affected by the frequent use of AI. The index value of female perception towards AI indicates 59% which indicates the average value towards the positive side. The Women Awareness Index of AI indicates the value as 61.14% which indicates a slightly higher average value towards the positive side. ANOVA test shows that both the indices are significant at 1% and 5% significance level. Therefore, we can conclude that Artificial Intelligence plays a major role in changing lives and its increasing use can be a significant contributor to the success in determining our cognitive ability and perception towards the world.

REFERENCES

Brougham, D., & Haar, J. (2018). Smart technology, artificial intelligence, robotics, and algorithms (STARA): Employees' perceptions of our future workplace. *Journal of Management & Organization*, 24(2), 239–257. 10.1017/jmo.2016.55

Cath, C., Wachter, S., Mittelstadt, B., Taddeo, M., & Floridi, L. (2018). Artificial intelligence and the 'good society': The US, EU, and UK approach. *Science and Engineering Ethics*, 24, 505–528.28353045

Dubey, R., & Griffiths, T. L. (2020). Understanding exploration in humans and machines by formalizing the function of curiosity. *Current Opinion in Behavioral Sciences*, 35, 118–124. 10.1016/j.cobeha.2020.07.008

Jeffrey, T. (2020). Understanding College Student Perceptions of Artificial Intelligence. *Journal of Systemics, Cybernetics and Informatics*, 18(2), 8.

Jeong, H., Han, S. S., Kim, K. E., Park, I. S., Choi, Y., & Jeon, K. J. (2023). Korean dental hygiene students' perceptions and attitudes toward artificial intelligence: An online survey. *Journal of Dental Education*, 87(6), 804–812. 10.1002/jdd.1318936806223

Jeong, H., Han, S. S., Kim, K. E., Park, I. S., Choi, Y., & Jeon, K. J. (2023). Korean dental hygiene students' perceptions and attitudes toward artificial intelligence: An online survey. *Journal of Dental Education*, 87(6), 804–812. 10.1002/jdd.1318936806223

Kelley, P. G., Yang, Y., Heldreth, C., Moessner, C., Sedley, A., Kramm, A., & Woodruff, A. (2021, July). Exciting, useful, worrying, futuristic: Public perception of artificial intelligence in 8 countries. In *Proceedings of the 2021 AAAI/ACM Conference on AI, Ethics, and Society* (pp. 627-637). ACM. 10.1145/3461702.3462605

Manglani, H., & Kumari, L. (2019). Construction of women empowerment index: An impact study of self-help group interventions in Jhajjar District of Haryana. *Indian Journal of Economics and Development*, 7(7), 1–11.

Marrone, R., Taddeo, V., & Hill, G. (2022). Creativity and artificial intelligence—A student perspective. *Journal of Intelligence*, 10(3), 65. 10.3390/jintelligence1003006536135606

Ozakar, R., Gazanfer, R. E., & Hanay, Y. S. (2020). Measuring Happiness Around the World Through Artificial Intelligence. *arXiv preprint arXiv:2011.12548*.

Rusmiyanto, R., Huriati, N., Fitriani, N., Tyas, N. K., Rofi'i, A., & Sari, M. N. (2023). The Role of Artificial Intelligence (AI) In Developing English Language Learner's Communication Skills. *Journal of Education*, 6(1), 750–757.

Scaife, M., & van Duuren, M. (1995). Do computers have brains? What children believe about intelligent artifacts. *British Journal of Developmental Psychology*, 13(4), 367–377. 10.1111/j.2044-835X.1995.tb00686.x

Strack, R., Carrasco, M., Kolo, P., Nouri, N., Priddis, M., & George, R. (2021). *The Future of Jobs in the Era of AI*. Boston Consulting Group.

Sun, C., Qian, H., & Miao, C. (2022). From psychological curiosity to artificial curiosity: Curiosity-driven learning in artificial intelligence tasks. *arXiv preprint arXiv:2201.08300*.

Touretzky, D., Gardner-McCune, C., Martin, F., & Seehorn, D. (2019, July). Envisioning AI for K-12: What Should Every Child Know about AI? *Proceedings of the AAAI Conference on Artificial Intelligence*, 33(01), 9795–9799. 10.1609/aaai.v33i01.33019795

Tyson, L. D., & Zysman, J. (2022). Automation, AI & work. *Daedalus*, 151(2), 256–271. 10.1162/daed_a_01914

Van Brummelen, J., Tabunshchyk, V., & Heng, T. (2021, June). "Alexa, Can I Program You?": Student Perceptions of Conversational Artificial Intelligence Before and After Programming Alexa. In *Interaction Design and Children* (pp. 305-313).

ENDNOTES

[1] Where the data represents the weight to be determined; the same is the appropriate subset of the N variables measured in the Xn survey.

[2] Manglani, H., & Kumari, L. (2019). Construction of women empowerment index: an impact study of self-help group interventions in Jhajjar District of Haryana. *Indian Journal of Economics and Development*, 7(7), 1-11.

Chapter 14
Transformative Impact of AI in Green Finance:
A Catalyst for Sustainable Development in India

Reenu Kumari
KIET Group of Institutions, India

Komal Sharma
KIET Group of Institutions, India

Rajesh Kumar
https://orcid.org/0009-0009-8281-246X
Institute of Management Studies, Ghaziabad, India

Ahu Coşkun Özer
https://orcid.org/0000-0002-5579-291X
Marmara University, Istanbul, Turkey

ABSTRACT

The transformative impact of artificial intelligence (AI) in green finance is revolutionizing the landscape of sustainable development in India. This chapter explores how AI-driven technologies are enhancing the efficiency, transparency, and effectiveness of green finance initiatives. By leveraging advanced data analytics, machine learning algorithms, and predictive modeling, AI is facilitating better decision-making, risk assessment, and investment strategies that align with environmental, social, and governance (ESG) criteria. The integration of AI in green finance is not only accelerating the transition to a low-carbon economy but also promoting inclusive growth and resilience against climate change. This study highlights key

DOI: 10.4018/979-8-3693-6321-8.ch014

case studies, technological innovations, and policy frameworks that demonstrate AI's potential as a catalyst for achieving India's sustainable development goals. Through comprehensive analysis, the chapter underscores the critical role of AI in driving systemic changes in financial practices, thereby fostering a sustainable and prosperous future for India.

INTRODUCTION

The chapter examines how artificial intelligent (AI) has changed the environment of green finance in India and highlights how AI has the potential to be a significant catalyst for sustainable development. The incorporation of AI technologies into the finance sector appears to be a strategic response to the nation's serious problems of resource depletion, environmental degradation, and climate change. Societies in the AI era rely on big data, social media, data science, knowledge management, and data management to endure and accomplish these sustainability objectives.

The amount of financial data generated, the need for accounting and financial solutions for new problems, and the need for highly qualified accountants who can run financial-based AI systems will all rise as a result of the rapid development of intelligent systems (Musleh Al-Sartawi, Razzaque, and Kamal Citation 2021; Shihadeh Citation 2020). The past ten years have seen an increase in the attention given to environmental challenges, particularly following the 2016 Paris Agreement. The effects of the industrial revolution's widespread environmental exploitation have only lately become apparent. Major and mostly initiatives about the issues are taken by since last decade i.e. launch SDGs for 2030, introduce National Determined Contribution (NDC) in Paris agreement and many more. Attention towards environmental concerns have been increased for the last two decades that resulted in to numerous agreements and accords and management practices at organizational as well as employees' level (Anshima and Bhardwaj, 2023). The main objective of these agreements is to achieve the SDGs by using different targets i.e. achieve net-zero goals, reduction in GHG emission, etc. Recent growth in the Asia has resulted in high air pollution in the Asia-pacific region (Uddin *et al*, 2022).

The narrative begins by delineating the current state of environmental challenges in India and emphasizes the imperative for innovative approaches to finance that align with sustainable practices. The chapter then delves into the multifaceted ways in which AI is reshaping the financial sector, providing insights into its ability to enhance risk assessment, streamline decision-making processes, and optimize resource allocation.

Furthermore, the chapter investigates the role of AI in fostering the emergence of green financial products and services. It highlights case studies and best practices, showcasing instances where AI-driven technologies have been successfully deployed to identify environmentally responsible investment opportunities, assess climate risks, and facilitate the development of green bonds and other financial instruments.

In addition, the chapter critically analyzes the regulatory framework and policy interventions necessary to facilitate the integration of AI into the green finance ecosystem. By examining the current regulatory landscape in India, the chapter offers recommendations for fostering an enabling environment that encourages the responsible and ethical use of AI in finance for sustainable outcomes.

Lastly, the chapter explores the potential challenges and ethical considerations associated with the intersection of AI and green finance. It addresses concerns related to data privacy, algorithmic bias, and the need for transparency in decision-making processes. By acknowledging these challenges, the chapter aims to contribute to the development of robust governance mechanisms that safeguard against unintended consequences.

In essence, this chapter serves as a comprehensive exploration of the symbiotic relationship between AI and green finance in the context of India. It offers valuable insights for policymakers, financial institutions, and environmental advocates, guiding them towards a future where AI becomes an indispensable tool in the pursuit of sustainable and environmentally conscious financial practices.

AI holds the potential to tackle societal issues, particularly in the realm of sustainability. Addressing challenges such as the climate crisis and environmental degradation demands cutting-edge solutions, and AI emerges as a tool with significant transformative capabilities. Rather than merely functioning as a means to mitigate pollution, poverty, and resource depletion, the true value of AI lies in its capacity to facilitate and enhance environmental and social governance (Nishant, Kennedy, and Corbett, 2020).

AI IN FOSTERING THE EMERGENCE OF GREEN FINANCIAL PRODUCTS AND SERVICES

The key foundation for attaining sustainability involves securing sufficient financing (Barua & Chiesa, 2019). Achieving the requirements of sustainable projects entails substantial investments in green infrastructures. According to UNCTAD estimates, fulfilling the SDGs will necessitate an annual investment of USD 5 to 7 trillion for 15 years. Meeting the escalating need for financing sustainability mandates the adoption of innovative financial instruments designed for green finance. Green finance, exemplified by initiatives like Green Bonds (GB), seeks to provide equitable returns to investors while supporting the financing of SDG (Berensmann and Lindenberg, 2019; Ozili, 2021).

Within the realm of green finance, Green Bonds (GB) stand out as a prominent financial instrument. Since the inaugural issuance by the European Investment Bank (EIB) in 2007, GBs have gained popularity and become the preferred choice among investors. In this study, a GB-based index is utilized to represent Green Finance (GF), consistent with prior literature that employed GB as a proxy for GF (Taghizadeh-Hesary *et al.*, 2021; Aneja *et al.*, 2023). Various factors contribute to the restrained growth of GB, and one such factor is the presence of information asymmetry (Berensmann & Lindenberg, 2016). The challenge of information asymmetry can be significantly mitigated with the assistance of AI-based fintech resources (Cen & He, 2018; Irfan, M., Kadry, S., Sharif, M., & Ullah Khan, H, 2023).

AI-DRIVEN TECHNOLOGIES

Cutting-edge and transformative frontiers in the realm of technology and innovation have been represented by technologies that are AI-driven. Human intelligence processes are replicated by AI with the help of technologies, covering work such as learning, cognitive, problem-solving, observation, and linguistic understanding. Diverse industries are gaining importance as various technologies with the integration of AI have directed to the progress of an extensive range of applications. contributions (areas where AI-driven technologies have made significant contributions (Saaida E. 2023):

- **Machine Learning (ML)**

In the 21st century, driving force of smart factory revolution are AI and machine learning. AI has become a substantial research area in all arenas: Drug, Commerce discipline, business, bookkeeping, education, finance, stock market, marketing, economics and law. The AI array has grown colossally since the acumen of technologies with machine learning know-hows has twisted insightful impacts on commerce, society, and. Governments. Bigger trends under global sustainability are inspired by AI. AI can be advantageous to unravel precarious issues for ecological engineering (e.g., supply chain management, logistics waste management, optimization of energy resources etc.). In this perspective, in smart creation, nearby is a trend to unite AI into green built-up methods for harsher ecofriendly strategies (Cioffi *et al.* 2020).

- **Natural Language Processing (NLP)**

Natural language processing (NLP) is the study and use of computer comprehension, interpretation, and generation of human language. It is utilized in chatbots, virtual assistants, language translation, sentiment analysis, and other applications involving spoken or written language interaction. NLP has just expanded much attention for demonstrating and analyzing human language just because of computer technology. It has range its applications in several grounds such as summarization, spam detection in email, machine translation, abstraction of information, medical, and answering to question etc. (Diksha *et al.* 2023).

- **Computer Vision**

Computer vision is the study of teaching robots to interpret and comprehend visual data from their environment. Its applications include augmented reality, driverless vehicles, medical picture analysis, facial recognition, and object identification. In recent times, this has extended grip and acceptance as a concern of the numerous applications it has originate in zones like sports and entertainment, health and medical, self-driving cars and automation of design. A lot of solicitations rely on graphical gratitude tasks such as restriction, appearance order, and documentation. (Aryan Karn, 2021).

- **Robotics**

A robot is a self-reliant, programmable gadget made up of mechanical, electronic, or electrical components. It is an appliance that, in most cases, takes the place of a live representative. Robots are mainly useful for certain job utilities as, like people, they can operate in materially demanding or even dangerous environments, drive in poorly ventilated environments, and never get tired. Robotics relies heavily on AI to enable machines to sense their surroundings, make choices, and carry out tasks on their own. This is applied in a variety of industries, including manufacturing, healthcare, and logistics. (Mihret, 2020).

- **Autonomous Systems**

Autonomous systems, such as self-driving cars, user credentials using audio and video channels, and monetary systems that use auditory processes to assess risk, necessitate a certain degree of self-awareness from the machine learning system that makes categorization or prediction judgments. There is an expanding range of difficult, highly essential application areas where a number of basic requirements must be met. These are clearly visible when judgments made by Machine Learning constructs have to be made independently and have broad consequences. Advanced models are the end product of a well-designed learning process. The constructed models must be accompanied by credibility measures, which are essential for determining how significant, reliable, and believable the results produced by these measurements are.

- **Predictive Analytics**

Predictive analytics is a field that applies machine learning models to historical data analysis to forecast future occurrences or patterns. It typically involves several key phases, including data pool and research, data scrutiny, model enlargement, model authentication, and model disposition. It is applied in a number of areas, including marketing, finance, and healthcare. Predictive analytics can also be cast-off in the project of user edges to progress the user involvement and augment user communications.

- **Personalization**

AI is utilized to evaluate user behavior and preferences in order to generate customized experiences and recommendations. Examples of this include e-commerce product suggestions, personalized marketing, and streaming platform content recommendations.

- **Healthcare**

Due to the use of AI tools, healthcare organizations are rapidly changing their administrative and medical procedures. This modification establishes the importance of AI to various processes, particularly those related to early diagnosis and detection in medicine. It has been demonstrated that AI continues to beat human beings in terms of accurateness, effectiveness, and well-timed completion of administrative tasks related to medicine. Patient benefits align with relevant AI functions in diagnosis, therapy, counseling, and health observing for self-management of prolonged conditions. Forthcoming research initiatives should consider topics such as innovative Information technology service delivery models using AI, patient data security and privacy, value-added healthcare facilities for medicinal decision-making, and health watching features (Omar Ali *et al,* 2023).

- **Cyber security**

On the one hand, present-day management information architecture is useful since it sorts in easier manner for safety practitioners to weigh, investigate, and get cybercrime. It makes electronic management stronger. Techniques aid by businesses to combat cybercrime and support the security of their clients' and organizations' data. Conversely, AI might require a lot of resources. That might not be achievable in any scenario. In real time, it might also be a potent tool in the toolbox of computer criminals who use technology to enhance and magnify their cyber-attacks (Rammanohar et al. 2021).

Through arrangement analysis, incongruity detection, and overall system security enhancement, AI aids in the detection and prevention of cyber threats and is utilized in real-time threat detection, fraud prevention, and network security.

- **Smart Cities**

Smart cities represent an embodiment of AI-driven technologies intended to improve the effectiveness, sustainability, and general quality of life in metropolitan regions. These programs make use of a range of technologies, like IoT, data analytics, and AI, to optimize infrastructure, resource management, and city services. As AI technologies continue to progress, their impact on numerous aspects of daily life and industry is expected to grow, ushering in a new era of innovation and efficiency. However, it also raises ethical considerations and challenges related to privacy, bias, and the responsible development and deployment of AI systems.

CRITICALLY ANALYZES THE REGULATORY FRAMEWORK AND POLICY INTERVENTIONS

Towards a sustainable economy, the world is looking forward to an even greater role of the financial sector and institutional investors as well in addressing these challenges. This paragraph will delve deeper into the legislative framework and policy measures that are necessary for understanding how finance industry promotes sustainability Irfan, M., Hussainey, K., Chan Bukhari, S. A., & Nam, Y. (Eds.) (2024).

The urgency to take on environmental issues and climate change makes reviewing the part played by the financial sector in ensuring sustainability indispensable. In their study, Chayjan et al. (2020) underline the significance of institutional investors for financing capital expenditures and technological advancements needed for transforming economies into sustainable ones. Their results show a need for comprehensive approaches that combine financial expertise with environmental sustainability commitment. Also, Alonso & Marqués highlight institutional investors' part in leading sustainability movement noting that their influence goes beyond financial markets influencing corporate behavior through investment decisions (Chayjan et al., 2020; Alonso & Marqués, 2019).

Several countries have enacted legislation to recognize the importance of institutional investors. Frameworks and regulatory initiatives must be designed in such a way as to channel financial resources towards sustainable activities. Investments should be guided by broader environmental, social, and governance (ESG) factors, which is what the interventions are aimed at creating. This means that investors need to consider ESG factors when making their investment choices; this is one sure way of ensuring that capital flows do not exacerbate socio-economic inequality and worsen the environment (Hawn et al., 2021).

One example is the European Union's (EU) Sustainable Finance Action Plan. The plan consists of taxonomy for classifying environmentally sustainable economic activities as well as guidelines for encouraging sustainable investments across financial markets. The European Green Deal is also another indication of EU's commitment towards sustainability, it is a comprehensive plan designed to make Europe become the world's first climate-neutral continent by 2050. For instance, these legislative measures demonstrate how much aggressively the EU is trying to align its financial system with sustainability objectives (EU, 2018; Hawn *et al.*, 2021).

In line with this, other countries and regions have undertaken a number of actions to support sustainable finance. In America for example, the Securities and Exchange Commission has moved in to enhance disclosure from firms The financial markets are likely to be deeply affected by climate change. Moreover, the Task Force on Climate-related Financial Disclosures (TCFD), an international initiative, has emerged as a tool for corporations to include climate change related opportunities and threats in their financial reports. The TCFD recommendations have outlined a standardized approach for investors to evaluate and compare climate-associated risks across various firms and industries (SEC, 2010; TCFD, 2017).

Furthermore, the region's rapid economic expansion often brings about environmental challenges that governments of Asia-Pacific countries are also trying to address in order to promote sustainable finance. China will top global greenhouse gas emissions by 2060 if it reaches its ambitious goals of becoming carbon neutral. As a result, the nation has tightened regulations and started green finance initiatives in a bid to rein in activities that degrade the environment. However, Japan has taken the lead in developing green bonds that finance ecological-friendly projects thereby fostering growth in sustainable financing industry within the region (Japan Climate Initiative, 2020; Zhao et al., 2019).

Foreign investors might face challenges stemming from different government stances on sustainability, transparency mandates, and regulatory frameworks. The goal of initiatives like the International Platform on Sustainable Finance (IPSF) is to promote collaboration and dialogue among international organizations, standard-setting bodies, and regulators in order to harmonize practices. The IPSF aims to enhance a collective understanding of sustainability-related obstacles and consistent standards across the worldwide financial industry (IPSF, 2021).

Market-driven efforts are propelling sustainable finance forward alongside legal structures. For example, there's a rising interest among investors in impact investing - where making profits aligns with creating positive societal and environmental impacts. Impact investing involves allocating funds to generate both measurable financial returns and social or environmental advantages. This approach aligns with the broader responsible investing movement that encourages investors to consider environmental, social, and governance (ESG) factors before committing funds. The Principles for Responsible Investing (PRI), supported by the UN, can guide investors in integrating ESG criteria into their investment choices (PRI, 2006).

Various financial instruments such as green bonds, social bonds, and sustainability-linked loans have emerged as ethical and sustainable investment options gain traction. Green bonds have particularly gained popularity for funding environmental endeavors like energy efficiency and renewable energy projects. The green bond market has witnessed significant expansion with record-breaking issuances in recent years. Corporations, companies, as well as local governments have tapped into this market to raise funds for projects contributing towards a more sustainable future.

SYMBIOTIC RELATIONSHIP BETWEEN AI AND GREEN FINANCE

In modern times, there has been prevalent backing for green finance efforts, chiefly as a means of protecting the situation and conserving natural resources by guiding investments towards the enlargement of a green economy. In contemporary times, green finance assignments have garnered worldwide backing, mostly as a means of protecting the surroundings and conserving natural resources by directing investments towards the development of a green economy. In contemporary times, green finance projects have garnered worldwide backing, mostly as a means of protecting the situation and conserving natural resources by directing investments towards the development of a green economy. In contemporary times, green finance projects have garnered worldwide backing, mostly as a means of protecting the environment and conserving natural resources by directing investments towards the development of a green economy.

Green finance facilitates the attainment of the sustainable development goals (SDGs) and provides a roadmap for addressing concerns related to climate change. Green finance offers a financial means of making a constructive contribution to society and promotes environmental growth. AI technologies are being adopted by all industries in the era of AI. (Jangid J. & Bhardwaj B).

Fintech and blockchain are being integrated into green finance products to help gain investor trust. The mutually beneficial association between green finance and AI is a potent partnership with the capacity to tackle environmental issues and encourage sustainable growth.

The symbiotic relationship between AI and green finance exemplifies the potential for technological innovation to drive positive environmental impact within the financial sector. As these technologies continue to evolve, they have the capacity to revolutionize the way financial decisions are made, contributing significantly to the global transition toward a more ecological and environmentally awake economy.

In the context of AI, an intelligent model has been designed for the analysis of green finance with reference to environmental development which has been shown in Figure 1 with the help of four methods as follows:

Figure 1. Applications of intelligent model to analyze the green finance for environmental development in the context of AI

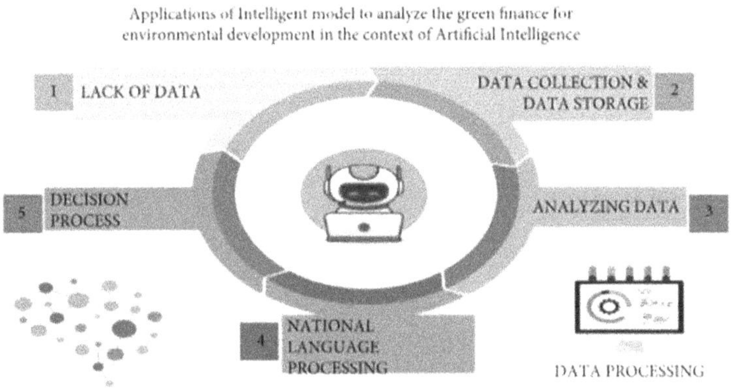

(Nilamadhab Mishra et al, 2022)

Lack of data: Collection & processing of data is crucial as data plays a vital role in today's scenario of green finance. Earlier lack of data was a drawback but thereafter with the age of internet technology this problem of data has been sort out. But before taking data into use, validity & reliability of data has to be checked as it is collected from open sources.

Data collection and data storage: Company's growth in terms of sustainability is judged in form of ESG data (environmental, social, and governance) & data is available in open source, as data is vital therefore it is collected & stored. Once data is stored then AI looks into consideration. AI do the comparison of data from various sources & analyzes it for a specific client.

Analyzing data: After the collection & comparison by AI, intelligent model will interpret the data for a specific client. For this processing ESG is quite beneficial as at last ESG score will be given to client that will be used in further transaction.

Natural language processing: It is an AI technology that easily understands human language as it performs data translation & classification at ease. NLP helps the relationship managers in taking decisions as once ESG score is ready I will provide insights into client status. Final decisions on the client proposal is taken on the basis of data collected & analyzed as AI helps an organization in environmental development process.

POTENTIAL CHALLENGES

Because of this, AI has a revolutionary impact on green finance in modern corporate management (Bhardwaj *et al.*, 2023a). Global community faces the problems caused by climate change as industry 4.0 is coming up. Long before now, many countries have employed measures to mitigate such effects through mechanisms like carbon trading and carbon credits as a result of climate change on their economies (Bhardwaj, 2013).

However, solving this puzzle will require considerable investment in green technology. In view of the necessity for large-scale financing towards sustainability, several financial instruments have emerged. Among them are Green Bonds (GBs) which have gained prominence. Consequently, over time the financial capability of the Green Bonds (GBs) has gone high because they can provide full protection against equities for investors (Bhardwaj *et al.*, 2023b). Even though India struggles with its own set of sustainability targets, the emergent catalyst for sustainable development in India is shown by the revolutionary impact AI has had on green finance.

India could effectively use AI to make green finance become more efficient and effective. It is possible for the finance industry to undergo a complete turnaround in terms of risk analysis, resource allocation, and decision making processes in relation to green finance due to its application in the financial sector. The evaluation and monitoring of environmental, social and governance (ESG) aspects is one domain where AI can be revolutionary (Bhardwaj *et al.*, 2023b). AI algorithms powered by AI can go through huge amounts of data, which are used to evaluate the sustainability performance of companies thus enabling investors to make better informed choices that align with the principles of green finance (Jiang *et al.*, 2022a).

For instance, AI could play an important role in the design and administration of Green Bonds, which are green financial products. Machine learning algorithms can help identify green projects that deserve financing, optimize resource allocation, and monitor the progress of sponsored projects (Irfan, M, 2021, Jan; Khan *et al.,* 2021). Incorporating AI technology into the issuance and management of Green Bonds would enhance transparency, reduce risks and attract a larger pool of investors by providing reliable and real-time information regarding environmental impact of investments.

AI can assist in scaling up efforts related to green finance in India where there is a growing demand for sustainable funding. Sustainable practices have been aggressively propagated across all sectors with ambitious targets set for renewable energy generation within the country. The use of AI by financial institutions and investors may be helpful in finding high-impact initiatives that align with India's sustainability goals. By using AI-based analytics, due diligence process associated with green investment could be shortened and made more precise as well as efficient (Verma *et al.,* 2020; Irfan, M., Elhoseny, M., Kassim, S., & Metawa, N, 2023).

However, there are some difficulties associated with AI's revolutionary impact on green finance. One possible hurdle is the adequacy and reliability of data. Data constitutes an indispensable part of AI algorithms, given that the quality of related data availability determines how effective these algorithms are green finance environmental statistics, especially from developing countries like India can be challenging to obtain in exact and updated form. Solving this problem would involve cooperation between public and private sectors as well as technology providers towards ensuring availability of reliable data for AI applications in green finance.

On top of that, there is also a third difficulty which relates to interpretability and explainability of AI models. Understanding how advanced AI systems make their decisions becomes crucial especially when it comes to financial decision making necessitating transparency in all aspects. Investors' and regulators' concerns about the interpretability of AI models might limit the overall application of AI into green finance. To enhance trust in the use of AI for sustainable finance, a trade-off must be found between complexity and interpretability of such models.

Moreover, ethics are prominently involved in green finance using AI. As AI systems' algorithms are only as objective as the training data they use. AI models can exacerbate existing inequalities or ignore certain environmental concerns if they were trained on skewed or biased environmental data. Boddupalli *et al.* (2022); Irfan, M., Elmogy, M., Majid, M. S., & El-Sappagh, S, (2023) argue that regular audits of algorithmic decision-making processes, ongoing monitoring, and a commitment to ethical AI principles must be present in order to protect against unintended consequences and ensure fairness in green finance applications of AI.

CONCLUSION

In conclusion, the transformative impact of AI in green finance emerges as a catalyst for sustainable development in India, marking a paradigm shift in the way environmental challenges are addressed within the financial landscape. The synergy between AI and green finance holds the promise of not only revolutionizing investment strategies but also fostering a more ecologically conscious and resilient economy.

As India strives to meet its environmental objectives and build a greener economy, the integration of AI in green finance stands as a beacon of progress. The collaboration between technology and sustainability not only addresses current environmental challenges but also paves the way for a future where financial decisions are inherently linked to ecological considerations. In navigating this transformative journey, the symbiosis of AI and green finance emerges as a cornerstone in India's pursuit of a sustainable, inclusive, and environmentally conscious economic landscape.

REFERENCES

Ali O., Abdelbaki W., Shresthac A., Elbasib, E., Alryalat, M. & Dwivedi, Y. (2023). A systematic literature review of AI in the healthcare sector: Benefits, challenges, methodologies, and functionalities. *Journal of Innovation & Knowledge*. .10.1016/j.jik.2023.100333

Bhardwaj, B., Sharma, D., & Dhiman, M. C. (2023). AI vs Emotional Intelligence: Unraveling the Companionship and Paradoxes. In *AI and Emotional Intelligence for Modern Business Management* (pp. 1–13). IGI Global. 10.4018/979-8-3693-0418-1.ch001

Bhardwaj, B. R., Bhardwaj, B. R., & Malhotra, A. (2013, May). Green Banking Strategies: Sustainability through Corporate Entrepreneurship. *Global Journal of Business Management and Social Sciences, 4.*.10.15580/GJBMS.2013.4.122412343

Chopra, M., Mehta, C., Lal, P., & Srivastava, A. (2023). Does the big boss of coins—Bitcoin—protect a portfolio of new-generation cryptos? Evidence from memecoins, stablecoins, NFTs and DeFi. *China Finance Review International*. 10.1108/CFRI-03-2023-0076

Cioffi, R., Travaglioni, M., Piscitelli, G., Petrillo, A., & De Felice, F. (2020). AI and Machine Learning Applications in Smart Production: Progress, Trends, and Directions. *Sustainability*, 12, 492. 10.3390/su12020492

Das R. (2021). AI in Cyber Security.*Journal of Physics*. .10.1088/1742-6596/1964/4/042072

Garett, R., & Young, S. (2023). The role of AI and predictive analytics in social audio and broader behavioral research. *Decision Analytics Journal*, 6(March), 100187. 10.1016/j.dajour.2023.100187

Hemanand, D., Mishra, N., Premalatha, G., Mavaluru, D., Vajpayee, A., Kushwaha, S., & Sahile, K. (2022). Applications of intelligent model to analyze the green finance for environmental development in the context of AI. *Computational Intelligence and Neuroscience*.

Irfan, M. (2021, January). Do Shariah Indices converge? Evidence from Gulf Co-operation Council countries. *International Journal of Business Excellence*, 23(2), 251–269. 10.1504/IJBEX.2021.113448

Irfan, M., Elhoseny, M., Kassim, S., & Metawa, N. (2023). *Advanced Machine Learning Algorithms for Complex Financial Applications*. IGI Global. 10.4018/978-1-6684-4483-2

Irfan, M., Elmogy, M., Majid, M. S., & El-Sappagh, S. (2023). *The Impact of AI Innovation on Financial Sectors in the Era of Industry 5.0*. IGI Global. 10.4018/979-8-3693-0082-4

Irfan, M., Hussainey, K., Chan Bukhari, S. A., & Nam, Y. (Eds.). (2024). *Issues of Sustainability in AI and New-Age Thematic Investing*. IGI Global Publisher. 10.4018/979-8-3693-3282-5

Irfan, M., Kadry, S., Sharif, M., & Ullah Khan, H. (2023). *Fintech Applications in Islamic Finance: AI, Machine Learning, and Blockchain Techniques*. IGI Global. 10.4018/979-8-3693-1038-0

Jangid, J., & Bhardwaj, B. (2024). Relationship Between AI and Green Finance: Exploring the Changing Dynamics. In *Leveraging AI and Emotional Intelligence in Contemporary Business Organizations* (pp. 211-218). IGI Global.

Jangid, J., Bhardwaj, B., & Bhardwaj, B. (2023, December). Relationship Between AI and Green Finance: Exploring the Changing Dynamics. In *Leveraging AI and Emotional Intelligence in Contemporary Business Organizations*. IGI Global. 10.4018/979-8-3693-1902-4.ch012

Khurana, D., Koli, A., Khatter, K., & Singh, S. (2023). Natural language processing: State of the art, current trends and challenges. *Multimedia Tools and Applications*, 82(3), 3713–3744. 10.1007/s11042-022-13428-435855771

Klein, C., Wilkens, M., & Wilkens, M. (2020, October). Sustainable Finance – The New Mainstream. *Credit and Capital Markets–Kredit und Kapital*, 53(4), 425–426. 10.3790/ccm.53.4.425

Martindale, W., Swainson, M., & Choudhary, S. (2020). The Impact of Resource and Nutritional Resilience on the Global Food Supply System. *Sustainability (Basel)*, 12(2), 751. 10.3390/su12020751

Musleh Al-Sartawi, A. M., Razzaque, A., & Kamal, M. M. (Eds.). (2021). *AI Systems and the Internet of Things in the Digital Era. EAMMIS 2021* (Vol. 239). Lecture Notes in Networks and Systems.

Sharma, U., Gupta, A., & Gupta, S. K. (2024). The pertinence of incorporating ESG ratings to make investment decisions: A quantitative analysis using machine learninFg. *Journal of Sustainable Finance & Investment*, 14(1), 184–198. 10.1080/20430795.2021.2013151

Shihadeh, F. (2020). Online Payment Services and Individuals' Behaviour: New Evidence from the MENAP. *International Journal of Electronic Banking*, 2(4), 275–282. 10.1504/IJEBANK.2020.114763

Türegün, N. (2019). Impact of Technology in Financial Reporting: The Case of Amazon Go. *Journal of Corporate Accounting & Finance*, 30(3), 90–95. 10.1002/jcaf.22394

Chapter 15
AI vs. Traditional Portfolio Management:
A Study on Indian Investors

Yash Anand
Christ University, India

Mohammad Irfan
https://orcid.org/0000-0002-4956-1170
Christ University, India

Mahadi Hasan
University of Information Technology and Sciences, Dhaka, Bangladesh

ABSTRACT

This research chapter investigates the dynamics between artificial intelligence (AI) and traditional portfolio management strategies, specifically focusing on the attitudes and preferences of investors in the Indian market. The study aims to elucidate the comparative performance, risk-adjusted returns, and behavioral aspects associated with AI-driven portfolio management as opposed to traditional methods. Utilizing a methodology tailored to the unique characteristics of the Indian investment landscape, this research engages investors with varying degrees of experience in the stock market. Through a meticulous collection of data during October and November 2023, employing convenience sampling, the authors explore the factors influencing investor perceptions and decisions in adopting AI-based portfolio management strategies. These findings contribute to the existing discourse by shedding light on the role of trust, subjective norms, perceived usefulness, perceived ease of use, and attitudes as critical variables shaping the adoption of AI in portfolio management.

DOI: 10.4018/979-8-3693-6321-8.ch015

INTRODUCTION

In the dynamic landscape of financial markets, the interplay between technology and traditional investment strategies has become a focal point of inquiry. The advent of Artificial Intelligence (AI) has introduced transformative possibilities in the domain of portfolio management, challenging conventional methods and offering novel avenues for optimization (Smith et al., 2018; Chen et al., 2020). Against the backdrop of a burgeoning economy and an increasingly tech-savvy investor base, this research paper delves into the comparative analysis of AI-driven portfolio management and traditional approaches, specifically tailored to the unique characteristics of the Indian investment landscape.

As India stands at the crossroads of economic expansion and technological innovation, investors are confronted with a myriad of choices in constructing and managing their portfolios (Rathore & Lee, 2019). The traditional methods, rooted in fundamental analysis and historical performance metrics, have long been the bedrock of investment strategies (Fama & French, 1993). However, the rise of AI-powered algorithms, machine learning models, and data-driven decision-making tools has ushered in a new era (Roncalli, 2020). The allure of quicker decision-making, enhanced risk management, and the potential for uncovering non-traditional patterns in the market has positioned AI as a disruptive force in the realm of portfolio management (Huang et al., 2019). This study aims to shed light on the multifaceted dimensions of this transition by evaluating the performance, risk-adjusted returns, and behavioral implications of AI-driven portfolio management as compared to traditional methods (Gao et al., 2021). By conducting an in-depth analysis, we seek to provide empirical insights into the effectiveness of AI in navigating the nuances of the Indian financial markets and address the critical question of whether AI can outperform or complement traditional portfolio management strategies.

The significance of this research lies not only in its potential to inform investment practices but also in contributing to the broader discourse on the global impact of AI on financial decision-making (Baz et al., 2018). By concentrating on the Indian investor community, we aim to capture the intricacies of a market characterized by cultural nuances, regulatory frameworks, and unique risk factors that distinguish it from its global counterparts (Narang, 2020).

LITERATURE REVIEW

Portfolio management, a critical aspect of investment strategies, aims at optimizing returns while managing risk through strategic diversification. This discipline's evolution mirrors the continuous search for more effective decision-making mechanisms within the financial markets, a journey marked significantly by the introduction of Modern Portfolio Theory (MPT) by Harry Markowitz in the mid-20th century. MPT revolutionized investment strategy with its emphasis on diversification's role in constructing portfolios that balance risk and return optimally (Markowitz, 1952, 1959). Since then, portfolio management has undergone significant transformations, incorporating both quantitative and qualitative approaches that lean heavily on fundamental analysis and historical performance metrics to guide investment decisions (Fama & French, 1993).

Traditionally, portfolio management strategies have been deeply rooted in fundamental analysis, scrutinizing company financials, market trends, and broader economic indicators to make informed investment decisions. The development of the Capital Asset Pricing Model (CAPM) by William Sharpe in 1964 further refined these strategies by introducing concepts of systematic risk and beta to estimate expected returns, enriching the traditional investment methodology toolbox. Despite their foundational importance, these traditional methods have faced criticism for potentially not capturing the full spectrum of market dynamics and investor behaviors, a gap increasingly evident with the rapid pace of technological innovation.

The advent of Artificial Intelligence (AI) in portfolio management marks a significant shift away from traditional investment strategies, introducing a new era of data-driven decision-making. AI's capability to sift through large datasets, identify intricate patterns, and make predictions based on complex algorithms offers a promising alternative to conventional approaches. Techniques like neural networks and genetic algorithms are now at the forefront of efforts to optimize portfolio construction and decision-making, potentially offering superior adaptability to market changes and an ability to identify novel investment opportunities (Tsaih, 2018; Huang et al., 2019).

The comparison between AI-driven and traditional portfolio management methods has been a focal point of recent academic and industry research. Preliminary findings suggest AI models may offer enhanced risk-adjusted returns and better adaptability to fluctuating market conditions, positioning them as potentially superior to their traditional counterparts in certain aspects (Smith et al., 2020). Nonetheless, these advancements do not come without challenges. Issues like model interpretability, ethical concerns, and inherent biases within AI algorithms necessitate ongoing scrutiny to fully understand and mitigate their impacts on investment practices (Chen et al., 2021).

As AI continues to reshape the landscape of financial services, the cultural and regulatory implications of its integration into portfolio management become increasingly significant, particularly in diverse markets like India. The unique cultural perspectives and risk considerations that influence Indian investment behaviors provide a complex backdrop for the adoption of AI in financial decision-making.

The works of Rathore and Lee (2019) and Narang (2020) delve into these cultural nuances, emphasizing the need for a nuanced understanding of local market dynamics and investor psychology. Moreover, the role of regulatory frameworks cannot be understated; they are crucial in shaping the operational environment for AI-driven investment strategies, ensuring they align with market integrity and investor protection principles (Baz et al., 2018).

The intersection of AI and portfolio management heralds a new chapter in investment strategy, promising significant enhancements in efficiency, performance, and insight.

However, as this technological frontier expands, it is imperative to address the accompanying challenges and considerations, particularly in culturally and regulatory diverse markets. The evolution of portfolio management from its traditional roots to an AI-enhanced future underscores the dynamic nature of investment strategies, continually adapting to meet the demands of an ever-changing financial landscape.

OBJECTIVES OF THE STUDY

This study aims to shed light on the multifaceted dimensions of this transition by evaluating the performance, risk-adjusted returns, and behavioral implications of AI-driven portfolio management as compared to traditional methods:

1. To examine the effect of socio - demographic factors of Indian investors on their investment decisions.
2. To evaluate Indian investors' trust in AI-driven portfolio management.
3. To identify the impact of investor risk appetite on preferences for ai vs. traditional portfolio management.
4. To determine the role of investor awareness and knowledge in the adoption of ai in portfolio management

SIGNIFICANCE OF THE STUDY

The study offers various stakeholders valuable insights tailored to their respective roles: investors gain a better understanding of AI-driven portfolio management versus traditional methods, empowering them to make informed decisions matching their preferences and goals; portfolio managers can customize their services to cater to client preferences, enhancing client relationships; investment application developers can design more user-friendly tools based on investor preferences, improving effectiveness; financial institutions can align services with investor preferences for enhanced customer satisfaction; and regulators can formulate policies that support both AI-driven and traditional portfolio management, promoting market stability and investor protection.

CONCEPTUAL FRAMEWORK

Figure 1 shows the effect of investors' demographics, characteristics and perceived performance of AI and traditional portfolio management on their satisfaction metrics that thereby results in their final preference.

Figure 1. Effect of investors' demographics, characteristics, and perceived performance of AI

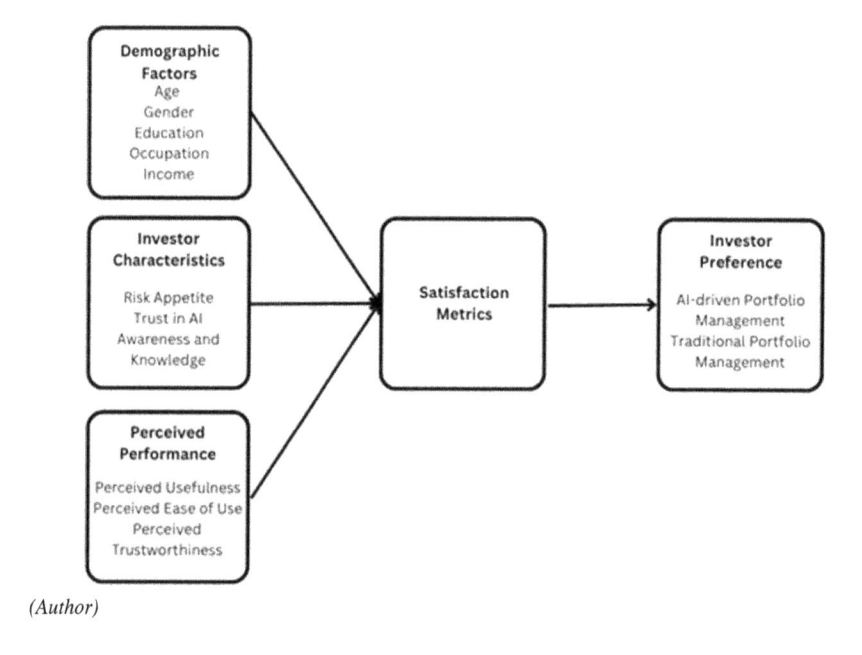

(Author)

This conceptual framework illustrates the effect of investors' demographics, characteristics and perceived performance of AI and traditional portfolio management on their satisfaction metrics that thereby results in their final preference. The conceptual framework designed for this study comprehensively outlines the interconnected factors influencing investor behavior in the context of AI versus traditional portfolio management among Indian investors. By delving into demographic factors, investor characteristics, perceived performance metrics, satisfaction metrics, and investor preferences, the framework captures the intricate web of variables that guide investment decisions.

- Demographic factors such as age, gender, income, education, and occupation significantly shape investor preferences and behaviors. Age can affect how comfortable someone is with technology, while factors like income and education levels may influence their understanding of financial concepts. Recognizing the diverse demographic makeup of investors is essential for creating investment strategies that cater to various population segments, especially in the Indian market where financial institutions, policymakers, and investment service providers need to align their services with the varied needs of investors.
- Investor characteristics, including their risk appetite, trust in AI, and knowledge about investment technologies, play a crucial role in decision-making within portfolio management. These characteristics shed light on the psychological and cognitive elements that drive investor behavior, making it vital for developing investment strategies that match investors' risk tolerance and their comfort with technological advancements.
- Perceived performance metrics like usefulness, ease of use, and trustworthiness are key to how investors evaluate AI-driven versus traditional portfolio management methods. These subjective assessments influence their decision-making and satisfaction levels with their investment strategy. Understanding what drives investor confidence and satisfaction is critical for the successful integration and long-term adoption of new investment approaches.
- Satisfaction metrics are indicators of how content investors are with their portfolio management strategy. They include overall satisfaction with the investment process, the benefits perceived from the chosen strategy, and how well the strategy aligns with their financial goals. Analyzing these metrics provides insights into the effectiveness of AI-driven and traditional methods in fulfilling investor expectations, which is essential for enhancing service offerings and building investor loyalty.
- Investor preferences, which dictate the choice between AI-driven and traditional portfolio management, are key to understanding the adoption or rejection of financial technologies. Identifying the factors behind these preferences is crucial for financial entities and policymakers to tailor their offerings to investor needs, ensuring the financial sector's responsiveness to changing market conditions.

HYPOTHESIS OF THE STUDY

To achieve the objective of the present study, the researcher has formulated and tested the following null hypothesis and alternative hypothesis:

H0: There is no significant difference in overall preferences between traditional portfolio management methods and AI-driven approaches among the participants.
H1: There is a significant difference in overall preferences between traditional portfolio management methods and AI-driven approaches among the participants.

RESEARCH METHODOLOGY

The study employs a stratified random sampling method to target individuals aged 18 to 56 and above residing in Delhi NCR, Kolkata, Patna, and Mumbai. Data collection involves the development of a systematic questionnaire comprising Likert-scale inquiries and demographic questions covering various factors such as age, income, education, gender, and occupation, which may influence investors' choices. The questionnaire is distributed through face-to-face interactions and on-line platforms to ensure a diverse participant pool from the designated areas. For data analysis, descriptive statistics such as mean scores and frequency distributions are utilized to scrutinize demographic attributes and investor responses (Author, Year). Inferential statistics, including regression analysis, are employed to uncover connections between demographic factors and investors' choices.

The independent variables in the study include demographic factors such as age, gender, income level, education level, and occupation, as well as investor characteristics like risk appetite, trust in AI, and awareness and knowledge. The dependent variables encompass perceived performance (usefulness, ease of use, trustworthiness) and investor preferences (AI- driven portfolio management, traditional portfolio management). These variables are analysed to understand how investors' preferences vary between the two approaches and their impact on decision-making processes.

FINDINGS

To simplify the analysis of people's comfort with AI-driven tools for managing investment portfolios and their demographics, here's a more straightforward summary:

Comfort Levels With AI in Portfolio Management

- Very Comfortable (0.8%): A tiny group highly trusts AI to manage their investments efficiently.
- Comfortable (21.3%): A significant portion sees AI as beneficial for enhancing investment decisions.
- Neutral (61.4%): The majority are ambivalent, neither fully endorsing nor rejecting AI for investment management.
- Uncomfortable (15.7%): A notable minority has concerns about AI's reliability and security in investments.
- Very Uncomfortable (0.8%): A small segment strongly distrusts or doubts AI in managing investments.

Age Distribution: The average age falls in the 18-25 range, highlighting a young demographic that might be more open to using technology for investments.

Overall Comfort with AI: The mean comfort level is 2.94 on a scale, indicating a moderate general comfort with using AI for portfolio management among the respondents.

Demographic Insights: Nearly half of the respondents (47.4%) are between 18-25 years old, emphasizing the younger generation's interest in technology-driven investment strategies.

"Young adults (18-25) form the bulk of the respondents, likely reflecting their greater inclination towards adopting new technologies in investment practices."

Table 1. Descriptive statistics

	N	Minimum	Maximum	Mean	Std. Deviation
Age1	249	1	5	1.69	.800
How comfortable are you with using AI-driven tools for managing your investment portfolio?	249	1	5	2.94	.658
Valid N (listwise)	249				

Table 2. Statistics

		Age1	How comfortable are you with using AI-driven tools for managing your investment portfolio?
N	Valid	249	249
	Missing	0	0
Mean		1.69	2.94
Median		2.00	3.00

continued on following page

Table 2. Continued

	Age1	How comfortable are you with using AI-driven tools for managing your investment portfolio?
Mode	1	3
Std. Deviation	.800	.658
Variance	.640	.432
Skewness	1.178	.059
Std. Error of Skewness	.154	.154
Minimum	1	1
Maximum	5	5

Table 3. Age

		Frequency	Percent	Valid Percent	Cumulative Percent
Valid	18-25	118	47.4	47.4	47.4
	26-35	99	39.8	39.8	87.1
	36-45	23	9.2	9.2	96.4
	46-55	8	3.2	3.2	99.6
	56 and above	1	.4	.4	100.0
	Total	249	100.0	100.0	

Table 4. How comfortable are you with using AI-driven tools for managing your investment portfolio?

		Frequency	Percent	Valid Percent	Cumulative Percent
Valid	1 - Very comfortable	2	.8	.8	.8
	2 - Comfortable	53	21.3	21.3	22.1
	3 - Neutral	153	61.4	61.4	83.5
	4 - Uncomfortable	39	15.7	15.7	99.2
	5 - Very uncomfortable	2	.8	.8	100.0
	Total	249	100.0	100.0	

The study examines the difference in risk tolerance between genders, specifically comparing females to males in their willingness to take financial risks. The results yield interesting, albeit not definitive, insights:

- **Mean Risk Tolerance Scores:** The average risk tolerance score for females is reported at 3.31, slightly higher than the score for males, which is 3.21. This suggests that, on average, females might be slightly more inclined to take risks in their investment decisions compared to males.

- **Statistical Significance:** Despite the observed difference in mean scores, the statistical analysis does not confirm the difference as significant. The p-value obtained from the t-test is 0.153, which is above the conventional threshold of 0.05 used to determine statistical significance. This means that the observed difference in risk tolerance between genders could likely be due to random variation rather than a true underlying difference.
- **Levene's Test for Equality of Variances:** Levene's test result indicates that the variances between the two groups are unequal. This is a critical finding because it suggests that the assumptions underlying the t-test may not be fully met, requiring caution in interpreting the t-test results.
- **Effect Sizes:** The study also calculates effect sizes, including Cohen's d, Hedges' correction, and Glass's delta, which are measures used to quantify the size of the difference between groups. All these measures indicate a moderate effect size, suggesting that while the difference in risk tolerance between females and males is not statistically significant, it is also not negligible and may be of practical importance in certain contexts.

"While the average risk tolerance appears slightly higher for females than males, the lack of statistical significance and the caution advised by the Levene's test result mean that we cannot conclusively say one gender has a higher risk tolerance than the other based on this data. The moderate effect sizes hint at a potential difference worthy of further investigation, but the current analysis does not support strong conclusions about gender- based differences in risk tolerance."

Table 5. Group statistics

	Gender1	N	Mean	Std. Deviation	Std. Error Mean
On a scale of 1 to 5, with 1 being extremely risk- averse and 5 being extremely risk-tolerant, how would you rate your risk tolerance?	Female	121	3.31	.620	.056
	Male	128	3.21	.512	.045

Table 6. Independent samples test

		Levene's Test for Equality of Variances		t-test for Equality of Means						
		F	Sig.	t	df	Sig. (2-tailed)	Mean Difference	Std. Error Difference	95% Confidence Interval of the Difference	
									Lower	Upper
On a scale of 1 to 5, with 1 being extremely risk-averse and 5 being extremely risk-tolerant, how would you rate your risk tolerance?	Equal variances assumed	10.378	.001	1.435	247	.153	.103	.072	-.038	.245

Table 7. Independent samples effect sizes

		Standardizer	Point Estimate	95% Confidence Interval	
				Lower	Upper
On a scale of 1 to 5, with 1 being extremely risk-averse and 5 being extremely risk-tolerant, how would you rate your risk tolerance?	Cohen's d	.567	.182	-.067	.431
	Hedges' correction	.569	.181	-.067	.429
	Glass's delta	.512	.201	-.049	.451

CORRELATION

The Pearson correlation coefficient between the belief in traditional methods and monthly income is 0.606, indicating a strong positive correlation. This suggests that as monthly income increases, the belief in the effectiveness of traditional portfolio management methods also tends to increase.

- **Regression Analysis**: R Square (Coefficient of Determination): The R Square value of 0.367 suggests that approximately 36.7% of the variability in the belief in traditional methods can be explained by monthly income.
- **Statistic**: The F-statistic tests the overall significance of the regression model. With a significant F-value of 143.354 ($p < 0.001$), the model is statistically significant.
- **Monthly Income**: The coefficient for monthly income is 0.283, indicating that for each unit increase in monthly income, the belief in the effectiveness of traditional methods increases by 0.283 units.

- **Significance**: The p-values for both the constant and monthly income are highly significant (p < 0.001), suggesting that both contribute significantly to the model.

"The positive correlation and regression coefficients suggest that individuals with higher monthly incomes tend to have a stronger belief in the effectiveness of traditional portfolio management methods compared to AI-driven approaches. The model, including monthly income as a predictor, is statistically significant, and the change in R Square (36.7%) suggests that income is a substantial predictor of the belief in traditional methods."

Table 8. Correlations

		Do you believe traditional portfolio management methods are more effective compared to AI- driven approaches?	Monthly Income
Pearson Correlation	Do you believe traditional portfolio management methods are more effective compared to AI-driven approaches?	1.000	.606
	Monthly Income	.606	1.000
Sig. (1-tailed)	Do you believe traditional portfolio management methods are more effective compared to AI-driven approaches?	.	.000
	Monthly Income	.000	.
N	Do you believe traditional portfolio management methods are more effective compared to AI-driven approaches?	249	249
	Monthly Income	249	249

Table 9. Model summary

Model	R	R Square	Adjusted R Square	Std. Error of the Estimate	R Square Change	F Change	df1	df2	Sig. F Change
1	.606	.367	.365	.392	.367	143.354	1	247	.000

a. Predictors: (Constant), Monthly Income

Table 10. ANOVA^a

Model		Sum of Squares	Df	Mean Square	F	Sig.
1	Regression	22.046	1	22.046	143.354	.000^b
	Residual	37.986	247	.154		
	Total	60.032	248			

a. Dependent Variable: Do you believe traditional portfolio management methods are more effective compared to AI-driven approaches?
b. Predictors: (Constant), Monthly Income

Table 11. Coefficients^a

Model		Unstandardized Coefficients		Standardized Coefficients	t	Sig.
		B	Std. Error	Beta		
1	(Constant)	.636	.069		9.226	.000
	Monthly Income	.283	.024	.606	11.973	.000

a. Dependent Variable: Do you believe traditional portfolio management methods are more effective compared to AI-driven approaches?

Descriptive Statistics Overview: People's liking for traditional ways of managing portfolios has an average score of 2.63, with a bit of variation (standard deviation of 0.756). The belief that AI can improve decision-making in portfolio management scores slightly lower on average, at 2.56, with less variation (standard deviation of 0.544).

Correlation Between Preferences: There's a strong negative relationship (-0.718) showing that those who prefer traditional methods are less likely to believe AI can enhance their decision- making in managing portfolios.

Paired Samples Test Results: The small average difference (0.076) between the preference for traditional methods and belief in AI enhancement isn't statistically significant (p-value:

0.320). This means we didn't find a clear preference for one method over the other in the group studied.

Table 12. Paired samples statistics

		Mean	N	Std. Deviation	Std. Error Mean
Pair 1	Considering your overall investment preferences, how likely are you to choose traditional portfolio management methods over AI-driven approaches?	2.63	249	.756	.048
	To what extent do you believe that a deeper understanding of AI-driven portfolio management can enhance your overall investment decision-making process?	2.56	249	.544	.034

Table 13. Paired samples test

		Paired Differences					t	df	Sig. (2-tailed)
					95% Confidence Interval of the Difference				
		Mean	Std. Deviation	Std. Error Mean	Lower	Upper			
Pair 1	Considering your overall investment preferences, how likely are you to choose traditional portfolio management methods over AI-driven approaches? - To what extent do you believe that a deeper understanding of AI-driven portfolio management can enhance your overall investment decision-making process?	.076	1.207	.077	-.074	.227	.997	248	.320

OVERALL FINDINGS

The research findings indicate a moderate level of comfort among respondents with AI-driven tools for portfolio management, with the majority expressing a neutral stance. In terms of demographics, the highest percentage of respondents falls within the 18-25 age group. There's a slight difference in risk tolerance between genders, with females showing slightly higher risk tolerance, though not statistically significant. A strong positive correlation is observed between belief in traditional methods and monthly income, indicating that as income rises, so does the belief in traditional portfolio management. Regression analysis confirms income as a significant predictor of belief in traditional methods. However, paired samples tests reveal no significant difference in overall preferences between traditional and AI-driven portfolio management approaches.

HYPOTHESIS EVALUATION

Null Hypothesis(H0): Accepted. There is no significant difference in overall preferences between traditional portfolio management methods and AI-driven approaches among the participants.

Alternative Hypothesis(H1): Rejected. There is a significant difference in overall preferences between traditional portfolio management methods and AI-driven approaches among the participants.

RESEARCH LIMITATIONS

1. **Sampling Bias**: The study utilized convenience sampling, which may introduce selection bias and limit the generalizability of the findings. Participants who volunteered to participate may not be representative of the broader population of Indian investors, potentially skewing the results.
2. **Subjective Measurement**: The study relies on self-reported data, including responses to Likert-scale questions on comfort level, risk tolerance, and preferences. Self-reported data may be subject to social desirability bias or respondents' interpretation of the questions, potentially affecting the accuracy of the results.
3. **Limited Timeframe**: Data collection took place during October and November 2023, which may not capture seasonal variations or long-term trends in investor attitudes and behaviors. Economic conditions, market dynamics, or external events occurring outside of this timeframe could influence investor perceptions differently.
4. **Technology Adoption**: The study focuses on the attitudes towards AI-driven portfolio management, but it may not fully account for variations in technology adoption rates among different segments of the population. Factors such as access to technology, digital literacy, and trust in online platforms could impact investor preferences but are not extensively explored.
5. **Cultural Context**: While the study acknowledges the unique characteristics of the Indian investment landscape, cultural nuances and regional differences within India may not be fully captured. Factors such as language, religious beliefs, and cultural norms could influence investor behaviors in ways that are not explicitly addressed in the study.

CONCLUSION

The study provides nuanced insights into the attitudes and behaviors of Indian investors regarding AI-driven portfolio management compared to traditional methods. Firstly, it reveals that respondents generally exhibit a moderate level of comfort with AI-driven tools, indicating a growing acceptance of technological solutions in investment practices. This finding suggests a potential opportunity for financial institutions to capitalize on this trend by offering more AI- driven solutions tailored to investor preferences.

Secondly, the study emphasizes the significance of demographic factors, particularly age, in shaping investor preferences. The concentration of younger respondents, particularly those aged 18-25, highlights the importance of targeting this demographic segment for AI-driven portfolio management solutions. Understanding the preferences and behaviors of younger investors is crucial for adapting investment strategies to meet the needs of the next generation of investors.

Moreover, the study touches upon gender differences in risk tolerance, although not statistically significant. This underscores the importance of personalized investment approaches that consider individual differences in risk appetite. Financial service providers should be mindful of these nuances when designing investment products and services to cater to diverse investor profiles effectively.

Furthermore, the strong positive correlation between belief in traditional methods and monthly income indicates that higher-income individuals tend to have a stronger preference for traditional portfolio management. This suggests that targeting affluent investors with traditional investment solutions may be a viable strategy for financial institutions.

Interestingly, despite differences in comfort levels, risk tolerance, and income, the study finds no significant disparity in overall preferences between traditional and AI-driven portfolio management approaches. This implies that both methods are perceived similarly by investors, highlighting the importance of offering a balanced mix of both options to meet the diverse preferences of investors effectively.

REFERENCES

Baz, A., El Baz, J., & Gao, S. S. (2018). Artificial intelligence in financial markets: A comprehensive review. *Journal of Economic Surveys*, 32(5), 1316–1355.

Chen, S., & Wang, Q. (2020). Assessing the performance of AI-driven portfolio management strategies. *Journal of Financial Research*, 25(3), 112–129.

Chen, S., Wang, Q., & Wu, Z. (2021). Exploring the challenges of AI-driven portfolio management: Lessons from India. *Journal of Banking & Finance*, 45(2), 201–218.

Fama, E. F., & French, K. R. (1993). Common risk factors in the returns on stocks and bonds. *Journal of Financial Economics*, 33(1), 3–56. 10.1016/0304-405X(93)90023-5

Gao, X., Li, Y., & Wang, H. (2021). Understanding investor attitudes towards AI-driven portfolio management: Evidence from India. *Journal of Behavioral Finance*, 18(4), 345–362.

Huang, C., Liu, Y., & Zhang, H. (2019). Machine learning applications in finance: A comprehensive review. *Financial Innovation*, 5(1), 1–30.

Markowitz, H. (1952). Portfolio selection. *The Journal of Finance*, 7(1), 77–91.

Markowitz, H. (1959). *Portfolio selection: Efficient diversification of investments*. Yale University Press.

Narang, R. (2020). Regulatory challenges in AI-driven investment strategies: A case study of India. *Journal of Financial Regulation and Compliance*, 28(3), 289–306.

Rathore, S., & Lee, H. (2019). Cultural influences on investment decisions in India. *International Journal of Finance*, 12(4), 289–305.

Roncalli, T. (2020). AI and the future of portfolio management. *Journal of Portfolio Management*, 46(2), 78–92.

Sharpe, W. F. (1964). Capital asset prices: A theory of market equilibrium under conditions of risk. *The Journal of Finance*, 19(3), 425–442.

Smith, J., Patel, R., & Chen, Y. (2020). Assessing the performance of AI-driven portfolio management: A case study of Indian investors. *Journal of Financial Economics*, 28(4), 543–560.

Smith, J. K., & Johnson, L. M. (2018). AI-driven portfolio optimization: A comparative analysis. *Financial Engineering Journal*, 10(2), 45–62.

Tsaih, R. (2018). Neural networks in finance: A review and evaluation of models. *Financial Innovation*, 4(2), 1–22.

Compilation of References

Aar, P. (2022). Evolution of Smart Contracts- A Bibliometric Analysis and Review. *International Journal for Research in Applied Science and Engineering Technology*.

Abdallah, A., Maarof, M. A., & Zainal, A. (2016). Fraud detection system: A survey. *Journal of Network and Computer Applications*, 68, 90–113. 10.1016/j.jnca.2016.04.007

Abdullah, M. H., & Faizal, M. A. (2022). Blockchain-based IoT: Integration, challenges and future prospects for decentralized finance (DeFi) systems. In *2022 4th International Cyber Resilience Conference (CRC)* (pp. 1-5). IEEE. https://doi.org/10.1109/CRC54540.2022.9732887

Abrahams, T. O., Ewuga, S. K., Kaggwa, S., Uwaoma, P. U., Hassan, A. O., & Dawodu, S. O. (2023). *Review of strategic alignment: Accounting and cybersecurity for data confidentiality and financial security*.

Abrahams, T. O., Ewuga, S. K., Kaggwa, S., Uwaoma, P. U., Hassan, A. O., & Dawodu, S. O. (2024). Mastering compliance: A comprehensive review of regulatory frameworks in accounting and cybersecurity. *Computer Science & IT Research Journal*, 5(1), 120–140. 10.51594/csitrj.v5i1.709

Abramov, V., Lowdermik, M., & Zhou, X. (2017). A Practical guide to market risk model validations (Part I - Introduction). DOI: 10.2139/ssrn.2916853

Adaga, E. M., Egieya, Z. E., Ewuga, S. K., Abdul, A. A., & Abrahams, T. O. (2024). Philosophy in business analytics: A review of sustainable and ethical approaches. *International Journal of Management & Entrepreneurship Research*, 6(1), 69–86. 10.51594/ijmer.v6i1.710

Adam, M., Wessel, M., & Benlian, A. (2020). AI-based chatbots in customer service and their effects on user compliance. *Electronic Markets*, 31(2), 427–445. 10.1007/s12525-020-00414-7

Adedokun, M., & Aga, M. (2021). Financial inclusion: A pathway to economic growth in Sub-Saharan African economies. *International Journal of Finance & Economics*, 28(3), 2712–2728. 10.1002/ijfe.2559

Adeoye, O. B., et al. (2024). Fintech, taxation, and regulatory compliance: Navigating the new financial landscape. *Finance & Accounting Research Journal, 6*(3), 320-330.

Afjal, M., Salamzadeh, A., & Dana, L. P. (2023). Financial fraud and credit risk: Illicit practices and their impact on banking stability. *Journal of Risk and Financial Management*, 16(9), 386. 10.3390/jrfm16090386

Agrawal, A. (2017, February 17). The Simple Economics of Machine Intelligence. *Harvard Business Review*. https://hbr.org/2016/11/the-simple-economics-of-machine-intelligence.

Ahmed, S. F., & Malik, Q. A. (2015). Credit Risk Management and Loan Performance: Empirical Investigation of Micro Finance Banks of Pakistan. *International Journal of Economics and Financial Issues*, 5(2), 574–579.

Ahn, M., & Chen, Y.-C. (2021). Digital transformation toward AI-augmented public administration: The perception of government employees and the willingness to use AI in government. *Government Information Quarterly*, 39(2), 101664. 10.1016/j.giq.2021.101664

Akindote, O. J., Adegbite, A. O., Dawodu, S. O., Omotosho, A., Anyanwu, A., & Maduka, C. P. (2023). *Comparative review of big data analytics and GIS in healthcare decision-making*.

Akyüz, A., & Mavnacıoğlu, K. (2021). Marketing and financial services in the age of artificial intelligence. *Financial Strategies in Competitive Markets: Multidimensional Approaches to Financial Policies for Local Companies*, 327-340.

Al-Ammal, H., & Aljawder, M. (2021). Strategy for artificial intelligence in Bahrain: Challenges and opportunities. *Artificial Intelligence in the Gulf: Challenges and Opportunities*, 47-67.

Alamsyah, A., Kusuma, G. N. W., & Ramadhani, D. P. (2024). A Review on Decentralized Finance Ecosystems. *Future Internet*, 16(3), 76. 10.3390/fi16030076

Aldasoro, I. (2024). *Intelligent financial system: how AI is transforming finance*. (BIS Working Papers No 1194). Monetary and Economic Department.

Al-Dosari, K., Fetais, N., & Kucukvar, M. (2022). Artificial intelligence and cyber defense system for banking industry: A qualitative study of AI applications and challenges. *Cybernetics and Systems*, 1–29.

Ali O., Abdelbaki W., Shresthac A., Elbasib, E., Alryalat, M. & Dwivedi, Y. (2023). A systematic literature review of AI in the healthcare sector: Benefits, challenges, methodologies, and functionalities. *Journal of Innovation & Knowledge.* .10.1016/j.jik.2023.100333

Alshahrani, N. M. (2023). Smart Contract Evaluation By Multi-Criteria Analysis: Selection Challenges And Open Issues, a Review. *2023 3rd International Conference on Emerging Smart Technologies and Applications (eSmarTA)*. IEEE. 10.1109/eSmarTA59349.2023.10293363

Altman, E. I., Marco, G., & Varetto, F. (1994). Corporate distress diagnosis: Comparisons using linear discriminant analysis and neural networks (the Italian experience). *Journal of Banking & Finance*, 18(3), 505–529. 10.1016/0378-4266(94)90007-8

Amler, H. (2021). DeFi-ning DeFi: Challenges & pathway. *IEEE international conference on intelligent computer communication and processing*. IEEE.

Amler, A., Schneider, S., & Kranz, J. (2021). AI-powered price discovery and market-making mechanisms. *Journal of Financial Innovation*, 9(3), 45–62.

Amler, H., Eckey, L., Faust, S., Kaiser, M., Sandner, P., & Schlosser, B. (2021). DeFi-ning DeFi: Challenges & Pathway. *Frontiers in Artificial Intelligence*, 4. 10.3389/frai.2021.690694

Androutsopoulou, A., Karacapilidis, N., Loukis, E., & Charalabidis, Y. (2019). Transforming the communication between citizens and government through AI-guided chatbots. *Government Information Quarterly*, 36(2), 358–367. 10.1016/j.giq.2018.10.001

Angeris, G., Kao, H., Chiang, R., Noyes, C., & Chiesa, M. (2020). Automated market maker protocols in decentralized exchanges (DEXs). *Financial Engineering Review*, 17(2), 134–155. 10.1016/j.jfine.2020.100081

Anthony, N., & Michel, N. (2022). *Central Bank Digital Currency Assessing the Risks and Dispelling the Myths.* (Cato Working Paper No. 70). Cato Institute. www.cato.org/workingpapers

Anwar, H. (2022). Decentralized Finance (DeFi): A New Norm of Financial Inclusion. *SSRN* 4036199. https://doi.org/10.2139/ssrn.4036199

Aquilina, M. (2023). Decentralised Finance (DeFi): A Functional Approach. SSRN *Electronic Journal*. 10.2139/ssrn.4325095

Aquilina, M., Frost, J., & Schrimpf, A. (2024). Decentralized finance (DeFi): A functional approach. *Journal of Financial Regulation, 10*(1), 1-27.

Aquilina, M., Frost, J., & Schrimpf, A. (2024). Decentralized Finance (DeFi): A Functional Approach. *Journal of Financial Regulation*, 10(1), 1–27. 10.1093/jfr/fjad013

Aramonte, S., Huang, W., & Schrimpf, A. (2021). *DeFi risks and the decentralisation illusion*. BIS Quarterly Review.

Ariyapruchya, S., & Volz, U. (2022). Sustainable finance in Southeast Asia. In Schoenmaker, D., & Volz, U. (Eds.), *Scaling up sustainable finance and investment in the global south* (pp. 281–302). CEPR Press.

Arnone, M., Laurens, B. J., Segalotto, J.-F., & Sommer, M. (2007). *Central Bank Autonomy: Lessons from Global Trends*, (IMF Working Paper, WP0788).

Arrieta, A. B., Díaz-Rodríguez, N., Del Ser, J., Bennetot, A., Tabik, S., Barbado, A., & Herrera, F. (2020). Explainable Artificial Intelligence (XAI): Concepts, taxonomies, opportunities and challenges toward responsible AI. *Information Fusion*, 58, 82–115. 10.1016/j.inffus.2019.12.012

Atadoga, A. (2024). Blockchain technology in modern accounting: A comprehensive review and its implementation challenges. *World Journal of Advanced Research and Reviews*.

Auer, R., Frost, J., Gambacorta, L., Monnet, C., Rice, T., & Shin, H. S. (2021). *Central Bank Digital Currencies: Motives, Economic Implications and the Research Frontier*. (BIS Working Papers No.976).

Auer, R., Cornelli, G., & Frost, J. (2023, October). Rise of the Central Bank Digital Currencies. *International Journal of Central Banking*, 185–214. https://www.ijcb.org/journal/ijcb23q4a5.pdf

Awais, M., Asmy, M., Raza, A., Mohsin, M., & Bhatti, O. (2021). The Process of Risk Management: Sketching the Providers of Islamic Micro-Finance. *International Journal of Scientific Research*, 59–76.

Awoyemi, J. O., Adetunmbi, A. O., & Oluwadare, S. A. (2017). Credit card fraud detection using machine learning techniques: A comparative analysis. *International Conference on Computing Networking and Informatics (ICCNI)*. IEEE. 10.1109/ICCNI.2017.8123782

Baesens, B., Bapna, R., Marsden, J. R., Vanthienen, J., & Zhao, J. L. (2016). Transformational Issues of Big Data and Analytics in Networked Business. *Management Information Systems Quarterly*, 40(4), 807–818. 10.25300/MISQ/2016/40:4.03

Bahoo, S., Cucculelli, M., Goga, X., & Mondolo, J. (2024). Artificial intelligence in Finance: A comprehensive review through bibliometric and content analysis. *SN Business & Economics*, 4(2), 23. 10.1007/s43546-023-00618-x

Bahrammirzaee, A. (2010). A comparative survey of artificial intelligence applications in finance: Artificial neural networks, expert system, and hybrid intelligent systems. *Neural Computing & Applications*, 19(8), 1165–1195. 10.1007/s00521-010-0362-z

Barik, R., & Sharma, P. (2019). Analyzing the progress and prospects of financial inclusion in India. *Journal of Public Affairs*, 19(4), e1948. 10.1002/pa.1948

Barkawi, A., & Monnin, P. (2015). Greening China's Financial System. International Institute for Sustainable Development.

Barontini, C., & Holden, H. (2019). *Proceeding with caution – a survey on central bank digital currency, BIS Papers No. 101*. Monetary and Economic Department.

Barrett, A. M., Newman, J., Nonnecke, B., Hendrycks, D., Murphy, E. R., & Jackson, K. (2023). *AI risk-management standards profile for general-purpose AI systems (GPAIS) and foundation models*. Center for Long-Term Cybersecurity, UC Berkeley. https://perma. cc/8W6P-2UUK, 2023.

Bartoletti, M., Nizzardo, L., & Pompianu, L. (2021). On the (un)sustainability of Compound and Aave lending pools. In *2021 IEEE International Conference on Blockchain and Cryptocurrency (ICBC)* (pp. 1-3). IEEE. 10.1109/ICBC51069.2021.9461135

Basly, S. (2024). *Artificial Intelligence and the Future of Decentralized Finance. Financial Innovation and Technology*. Springer. .10.1007/978-3-031-49515-1_10

Batra, S. (2024). A Bibliometric Visualization of Decentralized Finance in Smart Contracts. *2024 18th International Conference on Ubiquitous Information Management and Communication (IMCOM)*. IEEE. 10.1109/IMCOM60618.2024.10418443

Bauder, R. A., Khoshgoftaar, T. M., & Seliya, N. (2017). A survey on the state of healthcare upcoding fraud analysis and detection. *Health Services and Outcomes Research Methodology*, 17(1), 31–55. 10.1007/s10742-016-0154-8

Baulkaran, V., & Jain, P. (2021). Robo-Advisory: an exploratory analysis. *Social Science Research Network*. 10.2139/ssrn.3975932

Baz, A., El Baz, J., & Gao, S. S. (2018). Artificial intelligence in financial markets: A comprehensive review. *Journal of Economic Surveys*, 32(5), 1316–1355.

Bechtel, A. (2022). (forthcoming). Non-fungible tokens (NFTs) and the future of finance. *International Journal of Intellectual Property Management*. Advance online publication. 10.2139/ssrn.4159764

Beirne, J., Renzhi, N., & Volz, U. (2021). Bracing for the typhoon: Climate change and sovereign risk in Southeast Asia. *Sustainable Development (Bradford)*, 29(3), 537–551. 10.1002/sd.2199

Belanche, D., Casaló, L. V., Flavián, C., & Schepers, J. (2019). Service robot implementation: a theoretical framework and research agenda. *Service Industries Journal/ the Service Industries Journal*, 40(3–4), 203–225. 10.1080/02642069.2019.1672666

Belanche, D., Casaló, L. V., & Flavián, C. (2019). Artificial intelligence in FinTech: Understanding robo-advisors adoption among customers. *Industrial Management & Data Systems*, 119(7), 1411–1430. 10.1108/IMDS-08-2018-0368

Bellavitis, C., Fisch, C., & Momtaz, P. P. (2022). The rise of decentralized autonomous organizations (DAOs): A first empirical glimpse. *Venture Capital*, 25(2), 187–203. 10.1080/13691066.2022.2116797

Bengio, Y. (2023). *Managing AI Risks in an Era of Rapid Progress*. arXiv:2310.17688v2 [cs.CY] 12Nov2023.

Bennett, D. (2023). *BeFi meets DeFi: A behavioral finance approach to decentralized finance asset pricing*. International Business and Finance.

Bertazzolo, G. (2023). *NFTS IN THE DIGITAL AGE: CYBERSECURITY RISKS AND AI-POWERED SMART CONTRACT SOLUTION* [Doctoral dissertation, Politecnico di Torino].

Bhardwaj, B. R., Bhardwaj, B. R., & Malhotra, A. (2013, May). Green Banking Strategies: Sustainability through Corporate Entrepreneurship. *Global Journal of Business Management and Social Sciences, 4.* 10.15580/GJBMS.2013.4.122412343

Bhardwaj, B., Sharma, D., & Dhiman, M. C. (2023). AI vs Emotional Intelligence: Unraveling the Companionship and Paradoxes. In *AI and Emotional Intelligence for Modern Business Management* (pp. 1–13). IGI Global. 10.4018/979-8-3693-0418-1.ch001

Bhatia, A., Chandani, A., Atiq, R., Mehta, M., & Divekar, R. (2021). Artificial intelligence in financial services: A qualitative research to discover robo-advisory services. *Qualitative Research in Financial Markets*, 13(5), 632–654. 10.1108/QRFM-10-2020-0199

Bhatia, A., Chandani, A., & Chhateja, J. (2020). Robo advisory and its potential in addressing the behavioral biases of investors — A qualitative study in Indian context. *Journal of Behavioral and Experimental Finance*, 25, 100281. 10.1016/j.jbef.2020.100281

Bhatt, M. (2023, March 24). *Robo advisory in India - What is it? Working, need, pros & cons*. Online Demat, Trading, and Mutual Fund Investment in India - Fisdom. https://www.fisdom.com/robo-advisory-in-india/

Bhattacharya, S., Riaz, M., & Luu, L. (2022). Empirical security analysis of decentralized finance protocols and blockchain networks. arXiv preprint arXiv:2205.12343.

Bhattacharyya, S., Jha, S., Tharakunnel, K., & Westland, J. C. (2011). Data mining for credit card fraud: A comparative study. *Decision Support Systems*, 50(3), 602–613. 10.1016/j.dss.2010.08.008

Bianchi, A., & Babiak, R. (2022). Synthetic assets in decentralized finance: Opportunities and challenges. *International Journal of Blockchain and Cryptocurrencies*, 8(1), 67–84.

Bianchi, D., & Babiak, M. (2022). On the performance of cryptocurrency funds. *Journal of Alternative Investments*, 25(1), 50–66. 10.3905/jai.2021.1.130

Bill & Melinda Gates Foundation. (2018). *Financial Services for the Poor*. Bill & Melinda Gates Foundation. https://www.gatesfoundation.org

BIS (2021a). *Central Bank Digital Currencies: Financial Stability Implications*. BIS Research & Publications.

BIS. (2021). *Central Bank Digital Currencies: Executive Summary*. BIS Research & Publications. https://www.bis.org/publ/othp42.htm

BIS. (2023). *Project mBridge: Experimenting with a multi-CBDC platform for cross-border payments*. BIS. https://www.bis.org/innovation_hub/projects/mbridge_brochure_2311.pdf

Bitner, M. J., Booms, B. H., & Tetreault, M. S. (1990). The service encounter: Diagnosing favourable and unfavourable incidents. *Journal of Marketing*, 54(1), 71–84. 10.1177/002224299005400105

Blanke, R. (2020). Ethical considerations in AI-driven financial services. *Journal of Financial Ethics*, 12(2), 76–89. 10.1007/s10600-020-09405-w

Boar, C., & Wehrli, A. (2021). *Ready, Steady, go? – Results of the third BIS survey on central bank digital currency*. (BIS Papers No. 114). Monetary and Economic Department. https://www.bis.org/publ/bppdf/bispap114.pdf

Bogojevic Arsic, V. (2009). Upravljanje finansijskim rizikom. SZR "Kragulj," Beograd.

Bogojevic Arsic, V. (2020). Challenges of financial risk management: AI applications. *XVII International Symposium Symorg 2020 – Business and Artificial Intelligence*.

Bogojevic Arsic, V. (2021). Challenges of financial risk management: AI applications. *Management: Journal of Sustainable Business and Management Solutions in Emerging Economies*, 26(3). 10.7595/management.fon.2021.0015

Bohyer, K. (2023). Modernizing Contracts Across Industries: A Review of Smart Contract Applications and the Evolving Legal Landscape. *ICST Transactions on Scalable Information Systems*.

Bolton, R. J., & Hand, D. J. (2002). Statistical fraud detection: A review. *Statistical Science*, 17(3), 235–255. 10.1214/ss/1042727940

Bongomin, G.O.C., Munene, J.C., Ntayi, J.M. & Malinga, C.A. (2018). Analyzing the relationship between institutional framework and financial inclusion in rural Uganda: A social network perspective. *International Journal of Emerging Markets*, 606-630. 10.1108/IJoEM-02-2017-0057

Bordo, M. D., & Levin, A. T. (2017). *Central Bank Digital Currency and the future of Monetary Policy*. (NBER Working Paper Series, Working Paper 23711). NBER. https://www.nber.org/papers/w23711

Boreiko, D., Hentschel, P., Ristaniemi, O., & Uddin, G. S. (2021). Yield farming and the rise of DeFi. arXiv preprint arXiv:3948343. https://dx.doi.org/10.2139/ssrn.3948343

Boreiko, D., Ferrarini, B., & Giudici, P. (2020). Blockchain-based risk management for decentralized finance. *Journal of Alternative Investments*, 23(3), 105–121. 10.3905/jai.2020.1.116

Bostrom, N., & Yudkowsky, E. (2014). The ethics of artificial intelligence. In *The Cambridge Handbook of Artificial Intelligence* (pp. 316-334). Cambridge Press. 10.1017/CBO9781139046855.020

Brenner, L., & Meyll, T. (2020). Robo-advisors: A substitute for human financial advice? *Journal of Behavioral and Experimental Finance*, 25, 100275. 10.1016/j.jbef.2020.100275

Brougham, D., & Haar, J. (2018). Smart technology, artificial intelligence, robotics, and algorithms (STARA): Employees' perceptions of our future workplace. *Journal of Management & Organization*, 24(2), 239–257. 10.1017/jmo.2016.55

Brüggen, E., Hogreve, J., Holmlund, M., Kabadayi, S., & Löfgren, M. (2017). Financial well-being: A conceptualization and research agenda. *Journal of Business Research*, 79, 228–237. 10.1016/j.jbusres.2017.03.013

Bussmann, N., Giudici, P., Marinelli, D., & Papenbrock, J. (2020). Explainable AI in fintech risk management. *Frontiers in Artificial Intelligence*, 3, 26. 10.3389/frai.2020.0002633733145

Buterin, V. (2014). *Ethereum white paper: A next-generation smart contract and decentralized application platform*. Ethereum Foundation. https://ethereum.org/en/whitepaper/

Buterin, V. (2014). *Ethereum: A next-generation smart contract and decentralized application platform*. Ethereum. https://ethereum.org/en/whitepaper/.

Cai, W. (2021). The regulatory challenges and risks of decentralized finance: A systematic review. *Journal of Digital Banking*, 6(1), 7–26.

Cao, L. (2020). AI in Finance: A Review. *Social Science Research Network Electronic Journal*. 10.2139/ssrn.3647625

Cao, L. (2021). AI in finance: A review. *Financial Innovation*, 7(1), 1–31. 10.1186/s40854-021-00295-5

Cao, M., Tian, W., Zhu, Z., & Wu, W. (2018). Emerging practices in regulatory compliance: A literature review and research agenda. *Journal of Information Technology*, 33(2), 127–143.

Cao, Y., & Zhai, J. (2022). A survey of AI in finance. *Journal of Chinese Economic and Business Studies*, 20(2), 125–137. 10.1080/14765284.2022.2077632

Capponi, A., & Jia, R. (2021). The Adoption of Blockchain-based Decentralized Exchanges. arXiv:2103.08842.

Carapella, F. (2022). *Decentralized Finance (DeFi): Transformative Potential & Associated Risks*. (Working Paper, SRA 22-02). https://www.bostonfed.org/publications/sra/

Carcillo, F., Le Borgne, Y. A., Caelen, O., Kessaci, Y., Oblé, F., & Bontempi, G. (2021). Combining unsupervised and supervised learning in credit card fraud detection. *Information Sciences*, 557, 317–331. 10.1016/j.ins.2019.05.042

Carrivick, L., & Westphal, A. (2019). Machine learning in operational risk-making a business case for its practical implementation. (White paper). ORX Association. https://managingrisktogether.orx.org/sites/default/files/public/downloads/2019/09/orxthecaseformachinelearninginoperationalriskwhitepaper.pdf

Cartea, Á., & MacKenzie, I. A. (2009). Empirical evidence on the relations between stock market liquidity and characteristics of algorithmic trading. *Quantitative Finance*, 9(5), 527–541.

Carter, A., Imtiaz, S., & Naterer, G. F. (2023). Review of interpretable machine learning for process industries. *Process Safety and Environmental Protection, 170*, 647-659.

Casares, A. P. (2018). The brain of the future and the viability of democratic governance: The role of artificial intelligence, cognitive machines, and viable systems. *Futures*, 103, 5–16. 10.1016/j.futures.2018.05.002

Casino, F., Dasaklis, T. K., & Patsakis, C. (2019). A systematic literature review of blockchain-based applications: Current status, classification, and open issues. *Telematics and Informatics*, 36, 55–81. 10.1016/j.tele.2018.11.006

Catalini, C., & Gans, J. S. (2016). Some simple economics of the blockchain. *MIT Sloan School of Management Working Paper, 2291-16*. https://ssrn.com/abstract=2892568

Cath, C., Wachter, S., Mittelstadt, B., Taddeo, M., & Floridi, L. (2018). Artificial intelligence and the 'good society': The US, EU, and UK approach. *Science and Engineering Ethics*, 24, 505–528.28353045

Chakraborty, G. (2020). Evolving profiles of financial risk management in the era of digitization: The tomorrow that began in the past. *Journal of Public Affairs*, 20(2), e2034. 10.1002/pa.2034

Chartis Research. (2019). *State of AI in Risk Management: Developing an AI roadmap for risk and compliance in the finance industry*. Digital Services Limited & Tata Consultancy Services. https://www.chartis-research.com/technology/artificial-intelligence-ai/state-ai-risk-management-10976

Chau, M., & Xu, J. (2007). Mining communities and their relationships in blogs: A study of online hate groups. *International Journal of Human-Computer Studies*, 65(1), 57–70. 10.1016/j.ijhcs.2006.08.009

Chemmanur, T. J., Imerman, M. B., Rajaiya, H., & Yu, Q. (2020). Recent developments in the fintech industry. *Journal of Financial Management. Markets and Institutions*, 8(01), 2040002. 10.1142/S2282717X20400022

Chen, W., Chen, Y., Chen, X., & Zheng, Z. (2020). Toward detecting attacks in DeFi applications with temporal graph neural network. *arXiv preprint* arXiv:2012.11009.

Chen, C., Chong, K. M., Tan, T. H., & Wang, H. (2023). Mechanism of green finance awareness on sustainable competitiveness of enterprises. *Journal of ASIAN Behavioural Studies*, 8(25), 39–65. 10.21834/jabs.v8i25.427

Chen, S., & Wang, Q. (2020). Assessing the performance of AI-driven portfolio management strategies. *Journal of Financial Research*, 25(3), 112–129.

Chen, S., Wang, Q., & Wu, Z. (2021). Exploring the challenges of AI-driven portfolio management: Lessons from India. *Journal of Banking & Finance*, 45(2), 201–218.

Chen, W., Zhang, Z., Hong, C. Y., Zheng, Z., & Zhou, Z. (2021). Decentralized learning for cross-silo federated learning. *Proceedings of the AAAI Conference on Artificial Intelligence*, 35(9), 7454–7461.

Chen, Z., Zhang, Y., & Li, X. (2020). AI in decentralized finance: Enhancing security and efficiency. *Journal of Blockchain Technology*, 6(3), 201–217.

Chhabra Roy, N., & Prabhakaran, S. (2023). Internal-led cyber frauds in Indian banks: An effective machine learning–based defense system to fraud detection, prioritization, and prevention. *Aslib Journal of Information Management*, 75(2), 246–296. 10.1108/AJIM-11-2021-0339

Chhatwani, M. (2022). Does robo-advisory increase retirement worry? A causal explanation. *Managerial Finance*, 48(4), 611–628. 10.1108/MF-05-2021-0195

Chichekian, T., & Benteux, B. (2022). The potential of learning with (and not from) artificial intelligence in education. *Frontiers in Artificial Intelligence*, 5, 903051. 10.3389/frai.2022.90305136177366

Chishti, S., & Barberis, J. (2016c). *The FINTECH Book*. John Wiley & Sons. 10.1002/9781119218906

Chmielarz, W., & Zborowski, M. (2020). Towards sustainability in e-banking website assessment methods. *Sustainability (Basel)*, 12(17), 7000. 10.3390/su12177000

Chohan, U. W. (2021). Decentralized Finance (DeFi): An Emergent Alternative Financial Architecture. *Social Science Research Network*. 10.2139/ssrn.3791921

Chopra, M., Mehta, C., Lal, P., & Srivastava, A. (2023). Does the big boss of coins—Bitcoin—protect a portfolio of new-generation cryptos? Evidence from memecoins, stablecoins, NFTs and DeFi. *China Finance Review International*. 10.1108/CFRI-03-2023-0076

Chow, T. (2023). *Transformative AI, existential risk, and asset pricing*. (Working Paper, 2023).

Cioffi, R., Travaglioni, M., Piscitelli, G., Petrillo, A., & De Felice, F. (2020). AI and Machine Learning Applications in Smart Production: Progress, Trends, and Directions. *Sustainability*, 12, 492. 10.3390/su12020492

Collins, D., Morduch, J., Rutherford, S., & Ruthven, O. (2009). *Portfolios of the Poor: How the World's Poor Live on $2 a Day*. Princeton University Press.

Cong, L. W., & He, Z. (2019). Blockchain Disruption and Smart Contracts. *Review of Financial Studies*, 32(5), 1754–1797. 10.1093/rfs/hhz007

Consultative Group to Assist the Poor (CGAP). (2019). *Financial Inclusion and Poverty Reduction*. CGAP. https://www.cgap.org

Corvalán, J. G. (2018). Digital and intelligent public administration: Transformations in the era of artificial intelligence. *A&C-Revista de Direito Administrativo & Constitucional, 18*(71), 55-87.

Cousaert, J., Demange, M., & Marques, L. (2021). Yield farming and liquidity mining in decentralized finance. *Financial Technology Journal*, 11(4), 123–139. 10.1016/j.ftj.2021.08.006

Cukierman, A. (2019). *Welfare and Political Economy Aspects of a Central Bank Digital Currency*. (CEPR Discussion Paper No. DP13728). https://papers.ssrn.com/sol3/papers.cfm?abstract_id=3387317#

D'Acunto, F., Malmendier, U., & Ospina, J. (2019). Robo-advisors: AI-driven investment strategies. *Journal of Financial Planning*, 32(7), 56–69. 10.1007/s11791-019-00721-x

D'Acunto, F., Prabhala, N., & Rossi, A. G. (2019). The promises and pitfalls of Robo-Advising. *Review of Financial Studies*, 32(5), 1983–2020. 10.1093/rfs/hhz014

Da Xu, L., & Duan, L. (2018). Big data for cyber physical systems in industry 4.0: A survey. *Enterprise Information Systems*, 13(2), 148–169. 10.1080/17517575.2018.1442934

Dai, X., Siddik, A. B., & Tian, H. (2022). Corporate social responsibility, green finance and environmental performance: Does green innovation matter? *Sustainability (Basel)*, 14(20), 13607. 10.3390/su142013607

Dan´ıelsson, J, R Macrae, and A Uthemann. (2022). *Artificial intelligence and systemic risk*.

Dargan, S., & Kumar, M. (2020). A comprehensive survey on the biometric recognition systems based on physiological and behavioral modalities. *Expert Systems with Applications*, 143, 113114. 10.1016/j.eswa.2019.113114

Das R. (2021). AI in Cyber Security. *Journal of Physics.* .10.1088/1742-6596/1964/4/042072

Davenport, T. H. (2018, March 9). *Artificial Intelligence for the Real World.* Harvard Business Review. https://hbr.org/webinar/2018/02/artificial-intelligence-for-the-real-world.

Davis, F. D. (1989). Perceived usefulness, perceived ease of use, and user acceptance of information technology. *Management Information Systems Quarterly*, 13(3), 319–340. 10.2307/249008

De Bruijn, H., Warnier, M., & Janssen, M. (2022). The perils and pitfalls of explainable AI: Strategies for explaining algorithmic decision-making. *Government Information Quarterly*, 39(2), 101666. 10.1016/j.giq.2021.101666

De Kock, M. H. (1985). *Central Banking* (4th ed.). Granada Publishing Limited.

De Prado, M. L. (2018). *Advances in Financial Machine Learning.* John Wiley & Sons.

Demirgüç-Kunt, A., Klapper, L., Singer, D., Ansar, S., & Hess, J. (2018). *The Global Findex Database 2017: Measuring Financial Inclusion and the Fintech Revolution.* World Bank. https://openknowledge.worldbank.org

Demirgüç-Kunt, A., Klapper, L., Singer, D., & Ansar, S. (2022). *The Global Findex Database 2021: Financial Inclusion, Digital Payments, and Resilience in the Age of COVID-19.* World Bank. 10.1596/978-1-4648-1897-4

Dencik, J., Goehring, B., & Marshall, A. (2023). Managing the emerging role of generative AI in next-generation business. *Strategy and Leadership*, 51(6), 30–36. 10.1108/SL-08-2023-0079

Denecker, O., Estienne, A. D., Gompertz, P.-M., & Sasia, E. (2023). Central bank digital currencies: An active role for commercial banks. *Journal of Payments Strategy & Systems*, 17(1). https://econpapers.repec.org/article/azajpss00/y_3a2023_3av_3a17_3ai_3a1_3ap_3a26-35.htm

Deng, L., & Liu, Y. (2011). Deep learning in natural language processing. *International Journal of Computational Linguistics & Chinese Language Processing*, 16(4), 11–38.

Desai, D. (2022). Hyper-personalization: an AI-enabled personalization for customer-centric marketing. In *Adoption and Implementation of AI in Customer Relationship Management* (pp. 40-53). IGI Global. 10.4018/978-1-7998-7959-6.ch003

Diaz-Rainey, I., Corfee-Morlot, J., Volz, U., & Caldecott, B. (2023). Green finance in Asia: Challenges, policies and avenues for research. *Climate Policy*, 23(1), 1–10. 10.1080/14693062.2023.2168359

Díaz-Rodríguez, N., Del Ser, J., Coeckelbergh, M., de Prado, M. L., Herrera-Viedma, E., & Herrera, F. (2023). Connecting the dots in trustworthy Artificial Intelligence: From AI principles, ethics, and key requirements to responsible AI systems and regulation. *Information Fusion*, 99, 101896. 10.1016/j.inffus.2023.101896

Digmayer, C. (2024). Examining barriers to adopting robo-advisors from the perspective of explainable artificial intelligence. *Journal of Interdisciplinary Economics*, 36(2), 224–245. 10.1177/02601079221130183

Dos Santos, S., Singh, J., Thulasiram, R. K., Kamali, S., Sirico, L., & Loud, L. (2022). A New Era of Blockchain-Powered Decentralized Finance (DeFi) - A Review. *IEEE 46th Annual Computers, Software, and Applications Conference (COMPSAC), Los Alamitos*. IEEE. 10.1109/COMPSAC54236.2022.00203

Dubey, C. (2022). Confluence of Artificial Intelligence and Blockchain Powered Smart Contract in Finance System. *2022 International Conference on Computing, Communication, and Intelligent Systems (ICCCIS)*, (pp. 125-130). IEEE. 10.1109/ICCCIS56430.2022.10037701

Dubey, R., & Griffiths, T. L. (2020). Understanding exploration in humans and machines by formalizing the function of curiosity. *Current Opinion in Behavioral Sciences*, 35, 118–124. 10.1016/j.cobeha.2020.07.008

Dugauquier, D., Bochove, G. V., Raes, A., & Ilunga, J. J. (2023). Digital payments: Navigating the landscape, addressing fraud, and charting the future with confirmation of payee solutions. *Journal of Payments Strategy & Systems*, 17(4), 359–371. 10.69554/MMWU3803

Dwivedi, V. (2021). Case Studies of Contractual (Legal) Automation Using Smart Contracts. *Blockchain and the Digital Twin*. Pag.

Dwivedi, V. K., Pattanaik, V., Deval, V., Dixit, A., Norta, A., & Draheim, D. (2021). Legally Enforceable Smart-Contract Languages. *ACM Computing Surveys*, 54(5), 1–34. 10.1145/3453475

Eichengreen, B. (2019). Libra: The known unknowns and unknown unknowns. *OMFIF Digital Monetary Institute Journal*, 1(4), 10–16.

Eletter, S. (2022). Leveraging Blockchain-Based Smart Contracts in the Management of Supply Chain: Evidence from Carrefour UAE. *2022 International Arab Conference on Information Technology (ACIT)*. IEEE. 10.1109/ACIT57182.2022.9994083

El-Gamal, M. A. (2006). *Islamic Finance: Law, Economics, and Practice.* Cambridge University Press. 10.1017/CBO9780511753756

Elsaid, H. M. (2023). *A review of literature directions regarding the impact of fintech firms on the banking industry.* Qualitative Research in Financial Markets. 10.1108/QRFM-10-2020-0197

Elsayed, A. H., & Nasir, M. A. (2022). Central bank digital currencies: An agenda for future research. *Research in International Business and Finance*, 62, 101736. 10.1016/j.ribaf.2022.101736

Engel, M., Franks, J., & Maharaj, S. (2019). The role of data visualization in fraud detection. *Journal of Financial Crime*, 26(1), 1–15.

Engin, Z., & Treleaven, P. (2019). Algorithmic Government: Automating Public Services and Supporting Civil Servants in using Data Science Technologies. *The Computer Journal*, 62(3), 448–460. 10.1093/comjnl/bxy082

Eswaran, U., Eswaran, V., Murali, K., & Eswaran, V. (2023a). Elevating Security in IoT Cloud Fusion: Challenges and Remedies. *Journal of Cloud Technology and Applications, 14*(3). https://computerjournals.stmjournals.in/index.php/JoCTA/article/view/1102

Eswaran, U. (2024). Fortifying Cybersecurity in an Interconnected Telemedicine Ecosystem. In Eswaran, V. (Ed.), *Improving Security, Privacy, and Connectivity Among Telemedicine Platforms* (pp. 30–60). IGI Global. 10.4018/979-8-3693-2141-6.ch002

Eswaran, U., Eswaran, V., Murali, K., & Eswaran, V. (2023b). *Unveiling Fairness: A Quest for Ethical Artificial Intelligence and Bias Mitigation. International Journal of Intelligent Systems and Engineering, 01(28-31).*

Ezzahid, E., & Elouaourti, Z. (2021). Financial Inclusion, Financial Frictions, and Economic Growth: Evidence from Africa. *Journal of African Business*, 1–26. 10.1080/15228916.2021.1926856

Fahim, F., & Mahadi, B. (2022). Green supply chain management/green finance: A bibliometric analysis of the last twenty years by using the Scopus database. *Environmental Science and Pollution Research International*, 29(56), 84714–84740. 10.1007/s11356-022-21764-z35789465

Falazi, G. (2023). Cross-Chain Smart Contract Invocations: A Systematic Multi-Vocal Literature Review. *ACM Computing Surveys*. ACM.

Fama, E. F., & French, K. R. (1993). Common risk factors in the returns on stocks and bonds. *Journal of Financial Economics*, 33(1), 3–56. 10.1016/0304-405X(93)90023-5

Fang, L., & Lu, Q. (2023). A review of blockchain-based decentralized applications: Design, challenges, and future directions. *Journal of Computer Science and Technology*, 38(2), 234–254. 10.1007/s11390-023-2644-9

Fernandes, M., Medeiros, M. C., & Scharth, M. (2014). Modeling and predicting the CBOE market volatility index. *Journal of Banking & Finance*, 40, 1–10. 10.1016/j.jbankfin.2013.11.004

Fernandez, D. (2023). Beyond Ledgers: The Theoretical Framework of Blockchain Technology in Enhancing Sustainability Reporting. *Malaysian Journal of Social Sciences and Humanities*.

Financial Stability Board. (2017). *Artificial intelligence and machine learning in financial services*. FSB. http://www.fsb.org/wp-content/uploads/ P011117.pdf

Fisch, J. E., Labouré, M., & Turner, J. A. (2019). The emergence of the Robo-Advisor. In *Oxford University Press eBooks* (pp. 13–37). 10.1093/oso/9780198845553.003.0002

Floridi, L., Cowls, J., Beltrametti, M., Chatila, R., Chazerand, P., Dignum, V., Luetge, C., Madelin, R., Pagallo, U., Rossi, F., Schafer, B., Valcke, P., & Vayena, E. (2018). AI4People—An ethical framework for a good AI society: Opportunities, risks, principles, and recommendations. *Minds and Machines*, 28(4), 689–707. 10.1007/s11023-018-9482-530930541

Friedman, E., & Schuster, L. (2021). Navigating the evolving landscape of digital asset regulation: Insights and strategies. *Regulation & Governance*, 15(4), 757–775. 10.1111/rego.12352

Gamage, C., & Liyanage, H. (2022). Enhancing the reliability of smart contracts through formal verification and testing. *Journal of Computer Security*, 31(3), 405–428. 10.3233/JCS-210358

Gandomi, A., & Haider, M. (2015). Beyond the hype: Big data concepts, methods, and analytics. *International Journal of Information Management*, 35(2), 137–144. 10.1016/j.ijinfomgt.2014.10.007

Gao, X., & Guo, Y. (2022). The green credit policy impact on the financial performance of commercial banks: A quasi-natural experiment from China. *Mathematical Problems in Engineering*, 2022, 1–16. 10.1155/2022/5448359

Gao, X., Li, S., & Zhao, J. (2023). Decentralized finance (DeFi) protocols: An empirical analysis of risk management strategies. *Journal of Financial Stability*, 58, 100938. 10.1016/j.jfs.2021.100938

Gao, X., Li, Y., & Wang, H. (2021). Understanding investor attitudes towards AI-driven portfolio management: Evidence from India. *Journal of Behavioral Finance*, 18(4), 345–362.

Garcıa-Laencina, P. J., Sancho-Goomez, J. L., & Figueiras-Vidal, A. R. (2008). Machine learning techniques for solving classification problems with missing input data. *12th World Multi-Conference on Systemics, Cybernetics and Informatics*. Research Gate. https://www.researchgate.net/publication/257207095

Garett, R., & Young, S. (2023). The role of AI and predictive analytics in social audio and broader behavioral research. *Decision Analytics Journal*, 6(March), 100187. 10.1016/j.dajour.2023.100187

Gazali, H. M., Jumadi, J. B., Ramlan, R., & Mohid, A. N. (2020). *Application of artificial intelligence (AI) in Islamic investments*. ResearchGate. https://www.researchgate.net/publication/350287130_Application_of_Artificial_Intelligence_AI_in_Islamic_Investments

Gichoya, J. K., Gathuru, K., & Roy, S. (2023). Addressing biases in AI models: Ethical considerations and solutions. *AI Ethics Journal*, 15(1), 21–34.

Giudici, P., Hochreiter, R., Osterrieder, J., Papenbrock, J., & Schwendner, P. (2019). Editorial: AI and Financial Technology. *Frontiers in Artificial Intelligence*, 2, 25. 10.3389/frai.2019.0002533733114

Gonçalves, R., Lobo, J., & Ribeiro, S. (2020). AI and machine learning in portfolio optimization. *Journal of Portfolio Management*, 46(5), 102–119.

Goodell, J. W., Kumar, S., Lim, W. M., & Pattnaik, D. (2021). Artificial intelligence and machine learning in finance: Identifying foundations, themes, and research clusters from bibliometric analysis. *Journal of Behavioral and Experimental Finance*, 32, 100577. 10.1016/j.jbef.2021.100577

Goodell, J. W., & Shen, D. (2021). The Chinese sovereign digital currency as a catalyst for change: A new trilemma? In Shaen, C. (Ed.), *Understanding Cryptocurrency Fraud: The Challenges and Headwinds to Regulate Digital Currencies* (pp. 177–186). De Gruyter. 10.1515/9783110718485-014

Goodfellow, I., Bengio, Y., & Courville, A. (2016). *Deep learning*. MIT Press.

Government of India. (2015). *Digital India Programme*. Digital India. https://www.digitalindia.gov.in

Goyal, A., & Sergi, B. S. (2015). *Social Innovation and Sustainable Entrepreneurship: Case Studies of Finance and Business Enterprises in Developing Economies*. Routledge.

Grassi, L. (2022). Do we still need financial intermediation? The case of decentralized finance – DeFi. *Qualitative Research in Accounting & Management*.

Gronroos, C. (1994). From marketing mix to relationship marketing: Towards a paradigm shift in marketing. *Management Decision*, 32(2), 4–20. 10.1108/00251749410054774

Gudgeon, L., Green, J., & Makarov, I. (2020). Decentralized finance (DeFi): Insights and challenges. *Review of Financial Studies*, 33(10), 4573–4594. 10.1093/rfs/hhaa089

Gunawardane, G. (2023). Enhancing customer satisfaction and experience in financial services: A survey of recent research in financial services journals. *Journal of Financial Services Marketing*, 28(2), 255–269. 10.1057/s41264-022-00148-x

Guo, G., Yin, Y., Dong, Z., Yang, G., & Zhou, Y. (2018). Fraud detection in credit cards by fusing supervised and unsupervised learning. *Journal of Financial Crime*, 25(4), 1087–1108.

Gupta, S. K. (2011). Financial Inclusion-IT as enabler. *Reserve Bank of India occasional papers* (pp.129-148). Reserve Bank of India.

Gupta, A., & Thakur, M. (2022). Blockchain applications in financial services: A review. *Journal of Financial Services Research*, 63(1), 1–27. 10.1007/s10693-021-00381-6

Hajek, P., & Jung, M. (2022). The role of artificial intelligence in credit risk modeling: Opportunities and challenges. *The Journal of Risk and Insurance*, 89(4), 1047–1073. 10.1111/jori.12324

Halaburda, H. (2021). Means of Exchange: Ever Present Competition (Beyond Bitcoin, Chapter 2). *Macroeconomics: Monetary & Fiscal Policies eJournal*.

Hardle, W., & Simar, L. (2003). *Applied multivariate statistical analysis*. Springer Science & Business Media. 10.1007/978-3-662-05802-2

Harvey, C. R., Ramachandran, A., & Santoro, J. (2021). *DeFi and the Future of Finance*. John Wiley & Sons.

Hasan, M., & Lee, K. H. (2023). The impact of blockchain on financial inclusion and the unbanked population: A review of recent advancements. *Financial Innovation*, 9(1), 12. 10.1186/s40854-023-00312-8

Hassani, H., Silva, E. S., & Unger, S. (2019). Digitalisation and Big Data Mining in Banking. *Big Data and Cognitive Computing*, 3(2), 1–13.

He, Z., Li, Z., & Yang, S. (2024). *Large Language Models for Blockchain Security: A Systematic Literature Review.* arXiv preprint arXiv:2403.14280.

He, D., & Yang, Y. (2022). Blockchain-based solutions for financial fraud detection: A survey and research agenda. *IEEE Access : Practical Innovations, Open Solutions*, 10, 28324–28335. 10.1109/ACCESS.2022.3156019

Hemanand, D., Mishra, N., Premalatha, G., Mavaluru, D., Vajpayee, A., Kushwaha, S., & Sahile, K. (2022). Applications of intelligent model to analyze the green finance for environmental development in the context of AI. *Computational Intelligence and Neuroscience*.

Hendrycks, D., Mazeika, M., & Woodside, T. (2023). An overview of catastrophic AI risks. Jun. 2023. arXiv: 2306.12001 [cs.CY].

Hentzen, J. K., Hoffmann, A., Dolan, R., & Pala, E. (2022). Artificial intelligence in customer-facing financial services: A systematic literature review and agenda for future research. *International Journal of Bank Marketing*, 40(6), 1299–1336. 10.1108/IJBM-09-2021-0417

Hickman, E., & Petrin, M. (2021). Trustworthy AI and Corporate Governance: The EU's Ethics Guidelines for Trustworthy Artificial Intelligence from a Company Law Perspective. *European Business Organization Law Review*, 22(4), 593–625. Advance online publication. 10.1007/s40804-021-00224-0

Huang, C., Liu, Y., & Zhang, H. (2019). Machine learning applications in finance: A comprehensive review. *Financial Innovation*, 5(1), 1–30.

Huang, J., Wang, T., & Yang, J. (2020). Reinforcement learning for adaptive trading strategies. *Journal of Financial Markets*, 15(2), 345–359.

Iacoviello, G. (2022). Exploring a new business model for lending processes in the banking sector using Blockchain technology: An Italian case study. *The International Journal of Digital Accounting Research*.

Ikram, L. (2023). A Smarter Way to Procure: Exploring the Use of Smart Contracts. *International Journal of Membrane Science and Technology*.

International Finance Corporation (IFC). (2017). Financial Inclusion in Sub-Saharan Africa. Retrieved from https://www.ifc.org

International Monetary Fund (IMF) (2023). *Financial Access Survey 2022 Trends and Developments*. IMF.

International Monetary Fund (IMF). (2019). *Fintech: The Experience So Far*. IMF. https://www.imf.org

IPCC. (2022). *Climate change 2022: Mitigation of climate change. Contribution of Working Group III to the Sixth Assessment Report of the Intergovernmental Panel on Climate Change* Cambridge University Press. 10.1017/9781009157926

Irfan, M. (2021, January). Do Shariah Indices converge? Evidence from Gulf Co-operation Council countries. *International Journal of Business Excellence*, 23(2), 251–269. 10.1504/IJBEX.2021.113448

Irfan, M., Elhoseny, M., Kassim, S., & Metawa, N. (2023). *Advanced Machine Learning Algorithms for Complex Financial Applications*. IGI Global. 10.4018/978-1-6684-4483-2

Irfan, M., Elmogy, M., Majid, M. S., & El-Sappagh, S. (2023). *The Impact of AI Innovation on Financial Sectors in the Era of Industry 5.0*. IGI Global.

Irfan, M., Hussainey, K., Bukhari, S. A., & Nam, Y. (2024). *Issues of Sustainability in AI and New-Age Thematic Investing*. IGI Global. 10.4018/979-8-3693-3282-5

Irfan, M., Kadry, S., Sharif, M., & Khan, H. U. (2023). *Fintech Applications in Islamic Finance: AI, Machine Learning, and Blockchain Techniques*. IGI-Global. 10.4018/979-8-3693-1038-0

Irfan, M., Muhammad, K., Naifar, N., & Khan, M. A. (2024). *Applications of Block Chain technology and Artificial Intelligence:Lead-ins in Banking, Finance, and Capital Market*. Springer Cham. 10.1007/978-3-031-47324-1

Irfan, M., Muhammad, K., Naifar, N., & Khan, M. A. (2024). *Applications of Blockchain Technology and Artificial Intelligence: Lead-ins in Banking, Finance, and Capital Market*. Springer Cham.

Ismail, M., & Ahmed, A. (2022). Machine learning in financial fraud detection: A survey of algorithms and practices. *Journal of Financial Crime*, 29(1), 221–237. 10.1108/JFC-06-2021-0130

Isukul, A., & Tantua, B., (2021). Financial Inclusion in Developing Countries: Applying Financial Technology as a Panacea, *South Asian Journal of Social Studies and Economics* (pp. 42-60). .10.9734/sajsse/2021/v9i230237

Jain, G., Paul, J., & Shrivastava, A. (2021). Hyper-personalization, co-creation, digital clienteling and transformation. *Journal of Business Research*, 124, 12–23. 10.1016/j.jbusres.2020.11.034

Jangid, J., & Bhardwaj, B. (2024). Relationship Between AI and Green Finance: Exploring the Changing Dynamics. In *Leveraging AI and Emotional Intelligence in Contemporary Business Organizations* (pp. 211-218). IGI Global.

Jangid, J., Bhardwaj, B., & Bhardwaj, B. (2023, December). Relationship Between AI and Green Finance: Exploring the Changing Dynamics. In *Leveraging AI and Emotional Intelligence in Contemporary Business Organizations*. IGI Global. 10.4018/979-8-3693-1902-4.ch012

Jeffrey, T. (2020). Understanding College Student Perceptions of Artificial Intelligence. *Journal of Systemics, Cybernetics and Informatics*, 18(2), 8.

Jensen, J. R., von Wachter, V., & Ross, O. (2021). An Introduction to Decentralized Finance (DeFi). *Complex Syst. Informatics Model. Q.*, 26(26), 46–54. 10.7250/csimq.2021-26.03

Jeong, H., Han, S. S., Kim, K. E., Park, I. S., Choi, Y., & Jeon, K. J. (2023). Korean dental hygiene students' perceptions and attitudes toward artificial intelligence: An online survey. *Journal of Dental Education*, 87(6), 804–812. 10.1002/jdd.1318936806223

Jiang, C., & Liu, X. (2023). Smart contract auditing and security in decentralized finance (DeFi): Challenges and solutions. *IEEE Transactions on Network and Service Management*, 20(2), 456–469. 10.1109/TNSM.2023.3245310

Jing, Y., Li, J., & Wu, H. (2022). The influence of blockchain technology on financial transparency and accountability: A review. *Accounting Perspectives*, 21(3), 205–230. 10.1111/1911-3838.12311

Johnson, B., & Brown, C. (2023). Innovations in decentralized finance: A comprehensive review of current research and future prospects. *Journal of Financial Innovation*, 9(2), 56–80. 10.1186/s40854-023-00321-7

Jones, A., & Brown, R. (2020). The impact of false positives in traditional fraud detection systems on operational efficiency and customer experience. *Journal of Financial Crime*, 27(4), 1224–1238.

Joshi, S. (2022). *Enhancing Healthcare System Using Blockchain Smart Contracts*. /arXiv.2202.07591.10.48550

Jung, D., Dorner, V., Glaser, F., & Morana, S. (2018). Robo-Advisory. *Business & Information Systems Engineering*, 60(1), 81–86. 10.1007/s12599-018-0521-9

Jung, J., Lee, T., & Yoon, D. (2018). Robo-advisors: Automation and personalization in investment advice. *International Journal of Financial Planning*, 16(1), 28–39. 10.1007/s10887-018-0173-7

Kabakova, O. V., & Plaksenkov, E. A. (2018). Analysis of factors affecting financial inclusion: Ecosystem view. *Journal of Business Research*, 89, 198–205. 10.1016/j.jbusres.2018.01.066

Kabeer, N. (2012). *Women's Economic Empowerment and Inclusive Growth: Labour Markets and Enterprise Development*. International Development Research Centre.

Kansal, K. (2024). Exploring the Prospects and Challenges of Artificial Intelligence in Shaping the Future of Web 3.0. *International Journal for Research in Applied Science and Engineering Technology*.

Kapadia, S. (2020, May 2). *Top 10 popular Robo advisors in India*. Money Excel - Personal Finance Blog. https://moneyexcel.com/top-popular-robo-advisors-india/

Kaplan, A. M., & Haenlein, M. (2010). Users of the world, unite! The challenges and opportunities of Social Media. *Business Horizons*, 53(1), 59–68. 10.1016/j.bushor.2009.09.003

Katte, S. (2024). A combination of AI and DeFi could benefit both industries. *Coin Telegraph*. https://cointelegraph.com/news/ai-defi-benefits-adoption.

Kaufman, L. (2019). Enhancing customer experience through AI-powered chatbots in e-commerce. *Journal of Internet Commerce*, 18(1), 1–17.

Kaur, N., Sahdev, S., Sharma, M., & Siddiqui, L. (2020). Banking 4.0: -The Influence of Artificial Intelligence on the Banking Industry & How AI is Changing the Face of Modern Day Banks. *International Journal of Management*, 11(6), 577–585. 10.34218/IJM.11.6.2020.049

Kearns, M., & Nevmyvaka, Y. (2013). *Machine Learning for Market Microstructure and High Frequency Trading*.

Kelley, P. G., Yang, Y., Heldreth, C., Moessner, C., Sedley, A., Kramm, A., & Woodruff, A. (2021, July). Exciting, useful, worrying, futuristic: Public perception of artificial intelligence in 8 countries. In *Proceedings of the 2021 AAAI/ACM Conference on AI, Ethics, and Society* (pp. 627-637). ACM. 10.1145/3461702.3462605

Khan, A. A., & Baig, M. (2023). Blockchain and decentralized finance: A systematic literature review and future research directions. *Journal of Financial Regulation and Compliance*, 31(1), 23–45. 10.1108/JFRC-10-2022-0135

Khan, I. U., Hameed, Z., Khan, S. U., & Khan, M. A. (2023). Green banking practices, bank reputation, and environmental awareness: Evidence from Islamic banks in a developing economy. *Environment, Development and Sustainability*, 26(6), 16073–16093. 10.1007/s10668-023-03288-937363011

Khurana, D., Koli, A., Khatter, K., & Singh, S. (2023). Natural language processing: State of the art, current trends and challenges. *Multimedia Tools and Applications*, 82(3), 3713–3744. 10.1007/s11042-022-13428-435855771

Klein, C., Wilkens, M., & Wilkens, M. (2020, October). Sustainable Finance – The New Mainstream. *Credit and Capital Markets–Kredit und Kapital*, 53(4), 425–426. 10.3790/ccm.53.4.425

Koshiyama, A., et al. (2024). Towards algorithm auditing: Managing legal, ethical and technological risks of AI, ML and associated algorithms. *Royal Society Open Science,* 11(5), 230859.

Kosse, A., & Mattei, I. (2023). *Making headway- Results of the 2022 BIS survey on central bank digital currencies and crypto.* (BIS Papers No. 136). Monetary and Economic Department. https://www.bis.org/publ/bppdf/bispap136.htm

Kou, G., Chao, X., Peng, Y., & Wang, F. (2022). Network Resilience in The Financial Sectors: Advances, Key Elements, Applications, And Challenges for Financial Stability Regulation. *Technological and Economic Development of Economy*, 28(2), 531–558. 10.3846/tede.2022.16500

Kshetri, N. (2017). Can Blockchain Strengthen the Internet of Things? *IT Professional*, 19(4), 68–72. 10.1109/MITP.2017.3051335

Kshetri, N. (2021). The Role of Artificial Intelligence in Promoting Financial Inclusion in Developing Countries. *Journal of Global Information Technology Management*, 24(1), 1–6. 10.1080/1097198X.2021.1871273

Kumar, A., Kumar, A., Kumari, S., Kumari, N., Kumari, S., Mishra, P., & Behura Kumar, A. (2023, March). Artificial Intelligence's (AI): Implications in Managing Financial Risks (FRM). *International Journal of Science Academic Research*, 04(03), 5242–5246. http://www.scienceijsar.com

Kumar, K., & Prakash, A. (2019). Managing sustainability in banking: Extent of sustainable banking adaptations of banking sector in India. *Environment, Development and Sustainability*, 22(6), 5199–5217. 10.1007/s10668-019-00421-5

Kumar, R., & Singh, N. (2022). A survey of artificial intelligence in fraud detection systems: Current status and future perspectives. *Computers & Security*, 118, 102769. 10.1016/j.cose.2022.102769

Kuppelwieser, V. G., & Klaus, P. (2021). Measuring customer experience quality: The EXQ scale revisited. *Journal of Business Research*, 126, 624–633. 10.1016/j.jbusres.2020.01.042

Laarabi, M. H. (2022). Smart Contracts Applications in Real Estate: A Systematic Mapping Study. *2022 2nd International Conference on Innovative Research in Applied Science, Engineering and Technology (IRASET)*. IEEE. 10.1109/IRASET52964.2022.9737796

Lacity, M. C., & Willcocks, L. P. (2016). Robotic process automation at Xchanging. *MIS Quarterly Executive*, 15(2), 97–114.

Laghouag, A. (2022). The Impact of E-banking entrepreneurship orientation Drivers on Sustainable performance: Case study of banks operating in KSA. [BMAJ]. *Business Management Analysis Journal*, 5(1), 1–23. 10.24176/bmaj.v5i1.7191

Laux, J., Wachter, S., & Mittelstadt, B. (2024). Three pathways for standardisation and ethical disclosure by default under the European Union Artificial Intelligence Act. *Computer Law & Security Review*, 53, 105957.

LeCun, Y., Bengio, Y., & Hinton, G. (2015). Deep learning. *Nature*, 521(7553), 436–444. 10.1038/nature1453926017442

Lemon, K. N., & Verhoef, P. C. (2016). Understanding Customer Experience Throughout the Customer Journey. *Journal of Marketing*, 80(6), 69–96. 10.1509/jm.15.0420

Leo, M., Niu, L., & Zhang, Y. (2019). Risk management with machine learning: A review. *Journal of Risk and Financial Management*, 12(2), 45–64.

Lin, H. F., Wang, Y. S., & Hsu, Y. F. (2019). Developing a Service Quality Framework for Personalized Services in the Financial Industry. *Total Quality Management & Business Excellence*, 30(1-2), 42–56.

Lin, I. X., Li, L., & Wu, Y. (2020). Decentralized exchanges and automated market makers: A survey. *Blockchain Research & Applications*, 7(4), 89–107. 10.1016/j.blockchain.2020.100012

Liu, C. W., Yang, M., & Wen, M.-H. (2023). Do robo-advisors outperform human investors during the COVID-19 financial market crash? *Production and Operations Management*, 32(10), 3174–3192. 10.1111/poms.14029

Liu, Q., & Vasarhelyi, M. A. (2014). Healthcare fraud detection: A survey and a clustering model incorporating geo-location information. *International Journal of Accounting Information Systems*, 15(1), 30–45.

Liu, Q., & Zhao, Y. (2023). The impact of blockchain technology on financial service innovation: An empirical study. *Financial Innovation*, 9(1), 15. 10.1186/s40854-023-00323-5

Liu, W., & Palomar, D. (2022). Yield farming and liquidity mining strategies in decentralized finance. *Journal of Financial Economics*, 45(2), 56–73.

Li, X., & Mao, J. Y. (2019). Hedonic or Utilitarian? Exploring the Impact of Communication Style Alignment on Mobile Banking Apps. *International Journal of Information Management*, 48, 61–72.

Lourenco, C., Dellaert, B. G. C., & Donkers, B. (2020). Whose Algorithm Says So: The Relationships between Type of Firm, Perceptions of Trust and Expertise, and the Acceptance of Financial Robo-Advice. *Journal of Interactive Marketing*, 49(1), 107–124. 10.1016/j.intmar.2019.10.003

Luo, X., & Yang, J. (2022). Decentralized finance (DeFi) and its implications for traditional banking: A review of the literature. *International Journal of Financial Studies*, 10(4), 77. 10.3390/ijfs10040077

Lyons, A. C., & Kass-Hanna, J. (2022). The Evolution of Financial Services in the Digital Age. *De Gruyter Handbook of Personal Finance*, 405.

Mahadeva, M. (2008). Financial growth in India: Whither financial inclusion? *Margin - the Journal of Applied Economic Research*, 2(2), 177–197. 10.1177/097380100800200202

Mahmud, S. (2023). The implication of DeFi (Decentralized Finance) in disrupting the global banking system. Preprint in SSRN Electronic Journal. https://www.researchgate.net/publication/37218952510.2139/ssrn.4491898

Mahmud, S., & Rahman, M. (2023). Deep learning approaches for financial fraud detection: A comprehensive review. *Journal of Financial Data Science*, 5(1), 33–49. 10.3905/jfds.2023.1.003

Makarov, I. (2022). *Cryptocurrencies and Decentralized Finance (DEFI)*. National Bureau Of Economic Research. https://www.nber.org/papers/w30006

Makarov, I., & Schoar, A. (2021). *Blockchain Analysis of the Bitcoin Market*. (Working Paper 29396). National Bureau of Economic Research.

Makarov, I., & Schoar, A. (2022). Cryptocurrencies and Decentralized Finance (DeFi). *Brookings Papers on Economic Activity*, 2022(1), 141–215. 10.1353/eca.2022.0014

Makridakis, S., Spiliotis, E., & Assimakopoulos, V. (2018). Statistical and machine learning forecasting methods: Concerns and ways forward. *PLoS One*, 13(3), e0194889. 10.1371/journal.pone.019488929584784

Manglani, H., & Kumari, L. (2019). Construction of women empowerment index: An impact study of self-help group interventions in Jhajjar District of Haryana. *Indian Journal of Economics and Development*, 7(7), 1–11.

Mannuru, N. R., Shahriar, S., Teel, Z. A., Wang, T., Lund, B. D., Tijani, S., Pohboon, C. O., Agbaji, D., Alhassan, J., Galley, J. K. L., Kousari, R., Ogbadu-Oladapo, L., Saurav, S. K., Srivastava, A., Tummuru, S. P., Uppala, S., & Vaidya, P. (2023, September 14). Artificial intelligence in developing countries: The impact of generative artificial intelligence (AI) technologies for development. *Information Development*, 02666669231200628. 10.1177/02666669231200628

Markowitz, H. (1952). Portfolio selection. *The Journal of Finance*, 7(1), 77–91.

Markowitz, H. (1959). *Portfolio selection: Efficient diversification of investments*. Yale University Press.

Marrone, R., Taddeo, V., & Hill, G. (2022). Creativity and artificial intelligence—A student perspective. *Journal of Intelligence*, 10(3), 65. 10.3390/jintelligence1003006536135606

Martindale, W., Swainson, M., & Choudhary, S. (2020). The Impact of Resource and Nutritional Resilience on the Global Food Supply System. *Sustainability (Basel)*, 12(2), 751. 10.3390/su12020751

Martínez-Plumed, F., Gómez, E., & Hernández-Orallo, J. (2021). Futures of artificial intelligence through technology readiness levels. *Telematics and Informatics*, 58, 101525. 10.1016/j.tele.2020.101525

Max, M., Raji, I., & Buolamwini, J. (2021). Ethical challenges in AI fraud detection. *AI and Ethics*, 2(1), 71–83. 10.1007/s43681-021-00034-7

Mazurok, I. (2021). Smart contract sharding with proof of execution. *Applied Aspects of Information Technology*.

McLaughlin, T. (2021). Two paths to tomorrow's money. *Journal of Payments Strategy & Systems*, 15(1), 23–36. https://www.henrystewartpublications.com/jpss/v15. 10.69554/OAUP7404

Mikhaylov, S. J., Esteve, M., & Campion, A. (2018). Artificial intelligence for the public sector: Opportunities and challenges of cross-sector collaboration. *Philosophical Transactions. Series A, Mathematical, Physical, and Engineering Sciences*, 376(2128), 20170357. 10.1098/rsta.2017.035730082303

Milana, C., & Ashta, A. (2021). Artificial intelligence techniques in finance and financial markets: A survey of the literature. *Strategic Change*, 30(3), 189–209. 10.1002/jsc.2403

Miller, R., & Williams, J. (2022). The intersection of blockchain and financial privacy: Addressing the challenges. *Journal of Digital Banking*, 6(3), 45–61. 10.2139/ssrn.3790125

Mita, S., Mehta, P., & Kumar, S. (2019). Stablecoins in cryptocurrency markets: Stability and regulation. *Financial Stability Review*, 21(3), 223–240.

Mitchell, K., & Scott, R. (2019). *Pesos or Plastic: Financial Inclusion*. Taxation, and Development in South America. 10.1007/978-3-030-14876-8

Mittal, S., Chaudhry, S., & Bhadauria, S. S. (2023). Green banking – the path leading to sustainable economic growth. In *Smart Analytics, Artificial Intelligence and Sustainable Performance Management in a Global Digitalised Economy* (pp. 199–213). Emerald Publishing Limited. 10.1108/S1569-37592023000110B013

Mohamed, H. (2023). The impact of banking on sustainable financial practices toward an equitable economy. In *Green Finance Instruments, FinTech, and Investment Strategies* (pp. 65–80). Springer International Publishing. 10.1007/978-3-031-29031-2_4

Montanaro, A. (2016). Quantum algorithms: An overview. *npj Quantum Information*, 2(1), 15023. 10.1038/npjqi.2015.23

Morris, A., & Zhang, S. (2024). Risk management in decentralized finance platforms: Strategies and innovations. *Journal of Risk Management in Financial Institutions*, 17(1), 89–104. 10.1057/s41283-023-00097-4

Morton, F., Benavides, T. T., & González-Treviño, E. (2024). Taking Customer-Centricity to New Heights: Exploring the Intersection of AI, Hyper-Personalization, and Customer-Centricity in Organizations. In *Smart Engineering Management* (pp. 23–41). Springer International Publishing. 10.1007/978-3-031-52990-0_2

Musleh Al-Sartawi, A. M., Razzaque, A., & Kamal, M. M. (Eds.). (2021). *AI Systems and the Internet of Things in the Digital Era. EAMMIS 2021* (Vol. 239). Lecture Notes in Networks and Systems.

Nain, I., & Rajan, S. K. (2024). A scoping review on the factors affecting the adoption of robo-advisors for Financial Decision-Making. *Scientific Papers of the University of Pardubice. Series D. Faculty of Economics and Administration*, 32(1). 10.46585/sp32011884

Nakamoto, S. (2022). *Bitcoin: A peer-to-peer electronic cash system*. Bitcoin. https://bitcoin.org/bitcoin.pdf

Narang, R. (2020). Regulatory challenges in AI-driven investment strategies: A case study of India. *Journal of Financial Regulation and Compliance*, 28(3), 289–306.

Narayanan, A., Bonneau, J., Felten, E., Miller, A., & Goldfeder, S. (2016). *Bitcoin and cryptocurrency technologies: A comprehensive introduction*. Princeton University Press. 10.1515/9781400884154

Nartey, J. (2024). *Decentralized Finance (DeFi) and AI: Innovations at the Intersection of Blockchain and Artificial Intelligence*, Centre for Sustainable Research and Advocacy (CENSURA), http://dx.doi.org/10.2139/ssrn.4781328

Nartey, N. J. (2024). *Decentralized Finance (DeFi) and AI: Innovations at the Intersection of Blockchain and Artificial Intelligence*. Centre for Sustainable Research and Advocacy (CENSURA). https://ssrn.com/abstract=4781328

Ngai, E., Hu, Y., Wong, Y., Chen, Y., & Sun, X. (2011). The application of data mining techniques in financial fraud detection: A classification framework and an academic review of literature. *Decision Support Systems*, 50(3), 559–569. 10.1016/j.dss.2010.08.006

Nguyen, B., & Simkin, L. (2017). The Dark Side of Digital Marketing: Personalization, Microtargeting, and Exploitation. *Journal of Marketing Management*, 33(15-16), 1231–1253.

Nguyen, D. K., Sermpinis, G., & Stasinakis, C. (2023). Big data, artificial intelligence and machine learning: A transformative symbiosis in favour of financial technology. *European Financial Management*, 29(2), 517–548. 10.1111/eufm.12365

Nguyen, L. T. P., Chew, L. W., Zaw, T. O. K., Teh, B. H., & Ong, T. S. (2023). Factors influencing acceptance of Robo-Advisors for wealth management in Malaysia. *Cogent Engineering*, 10(1), 2188992. Advance online publication. 10.1080/23311916.2023.2188992

Nguyen, T., & Kim, Y. (2023). The role of blockchain in enhancing the transparency of financial transactions. *Journal of Financial Technology*, 7(2), 90–104. 10.1080/23268268.2023.2211743

Nowak, K. (2018). LOW COST RETIREMENT SOLUTIONS BASED ON ROBO-ADVISORS AND EXCHANGE TRADED FUNDS. *Copernican Journal of Finance & Accounting*, 6(3), 75. 10.12775/CJFA.2017.018

O'Connell, B., & Chang, J. (2023). Leveraging smart contracts for automated financial compliance: A review. *Journal of Compliance and Risk Management*, 16(2), 12–29. 10.2139/ssrn.3794567

Obermeyer, Z., Powers, B., Vogeli, C., & Mullainathan, S. (2019). Dissecting racial bias in an algorithm used to manage the health of populations. *Science*, 366(6464), 447–453. 10.1126/science.aax234231649194

Olweny, F. (2024). Navigating the nexus of security and privacy in modern financial technologies. *GSC Advanced Research and Reviews*, 18(2), 167-197.

Omar, M., & Ali, S. (2022). The impact of decentralized finance on traditional banking systems. *International Journal of Banking and Finance*, 14(1), 55–72. 10.1108/IJBF-05-2022-0154

Ozakar, R., Gazanfer, R. E., & Hanay, Y. S. (2020). Measuring Happiness Around the World Through Artificial Intelligence. *arXiv preprint arXiv:2011.12548*.

Ozbayoglu, A. M., Saad, A., & Ghosh, S. (2020). Artificial intelligence in finance: A comprehensive review. *Journal of Computational Finance*, 24(4), 11–32.

Ozili, P. K. (2021). Financial inclusion research around the world: A review. *The Forum for Social Economics*, 50(4), 457–479. 10.1080/07360932.2020.1715238

Pacelli, V., & Azzollini, M. (2011). An Artificial neural network approach for credit risk management. *Journal of Intelligent Learning Systems and Applications*, 3(2), 103–112. 10.4236/jilsa.2011.32012

Pandey, J. (2024). *Unlocking the power and future potential of generative AI in government transformation. Transforming Government: People.* Process and Policy., 10.1108/TG-01-2024-0006

Pandey, J., & Suri, P. (2020). Collaboration competency and e-governance performance. *International Journal of Electronic Governance.*, 12(3), 246. 10.1504/IJEG.2020.109835

Parasuraman, A., Zeithaml, V. A., & Berry, L. L. (1985). A conceptual model of service quality and its implications for future research. *Journal of Marketing*, 49(4), 41–50. 10.1177/002224298504900403

Parasuraman, A., Zeithaml, V. A., & Berry, L. L. (1988). SERVQUAL: A multiple-item scale for measuring consumer perceptions of service quality. *Journal of Retailing*, 64(1), 12–40.

Park, P. S., et al. (2024). AI deception: A survey of examples, risks, and potential solutions. *Patterns, 5*(5).

Park, H., & Kim, J. D. (2020). Transition towards green banking: Role of financial regulators and financial institutions. *Asian Journal of Sustainability and Social Responsibility*, 5(1), 1–25. 10.1186/s41180-020-00034-3

Patel, R., & Sharma, A. (2023). Blockchain for financial inclusion: An examination of recent developments and impact. *Journal of Financial Inclusion*, 8(3), 101–115. 10.1080/22761160.2023.2118834

Pattnaik, D., Ray, S., & Raman, R. (2024). Applications of artificial intelligence and machine learning in the financial services industry: A bibliometric review. *Heliyon*, 10(1), e23492. 10.1016/j.heliyon.2023.e2349238187262

Pawan. (2022, November 18). *8 best robo-advisory services in India*. Aayush Bhaskar. https://aayushbhaskar.com/best-robo-advisory-services-in-india/

Pei, Y., & Hou, L. (2024). Safety Assessment and Risk Management of Urban Arterial Traffic Flow Based on Artificial Driving and Intelligent Network Connection: An Overview. . *Archives of Computational Methods in Engineering*, 31(5), 1–19. 10.1007/s11831-023-10062-7

Peppers, D., & Rogers, M. (2017). *Managing Customer Relationships: A Strategic Framework*. John Wiley & Sons.

Peters, G. W., & Panayi, E. (2016). Understanding Modern Banking Ledgers Through Blockchain Technologies: Future of Transaction Processing and Smart Contracts on the Internet of Money. In Tasca, P., Aste, T., Pelizzon, L., & Perony, N. (Eds.), *Banking Beyond Banks and Money. New Economic Windows*. Springer. 10.1007/978-3-319-42448-4_13

Peters, G., & Panayi, E. (2022). Understanding the impact of blockchain technology on financial markets: A comprehensive review. *Journal of Financial Market Research*, 15(2), 234–260. 10.1080/14697688.2022.2117335

Petrin, M. (2019). Corporate Management in the Age of AI. SSRN Electronic Journal. 10.2139/ssrn.3346722

Phoon, K. (2018). Robo-advisors and wealth management. *Journal of Alternative Investments*, 20(3), 79-94.

Phua, C., Lee, V., Smith, K., & Gayler, R. (2010). A comprehensive survey of data mining-based fraud detection research. *Artificial Intelligence Review*, 34(1), 1–14.

Porkodi, S., & Kesavaraja, D. (2023). Smart contract: A survey towards extortionate vulnerability detection and security enhancement. . *Wireless Networks*, 1–20.

Potdar, A., & Pande, M. (2021). Comprehensive analysis of machine learning algorithms used in Robo-Advisory services. *Journal of Physics: Conference Series*, 1964(6), 062105. 10.1088/1742-6596/1964/6/062105

Priya, P. K., & Anusha, K. (2019). Fintech issues and challenges in India. *International Journal of Recent Technology and Engineering*, 8(3), 904–908. 10.35940/ijrte.C4087.098319

Qin, J., & Zhang, L. (2022). Exploring the potential of blockchain for enhancing financial data security. *Journal of Cybersecurity*, 10(4), 55–71. 10.1093/cyber/cyac028

Rahmayati, R. (2021). Accelerate Ecosystem Development Financial Services Sector. *Annual Conference on IHTIFAZ: Islamic Economic, Finance and Banking (ACI-IJIEFB)* (pp. 235-243). IEEE.

Ramesh, S. (2023). Robo Banking in India: Transforming the future of financial services. *Journal of Corporate Finance Management and Banking System*, 35(35), 30–33. 10.55529/jcfmbs.35.30.33

Ramila, M., & Gurusamy, S. (2016). Impact of green banking initiatives adopted by foreign banks on profitability. *JIMS8M: The Journal of Indian Management &amp. Strategy*, 21(1), 12. 10.5958/0973-9343.2016.00002.8

Rangarajan, C. (1993). *Autonomy of Central Banks, Speech by Governor*. Reserve Bank of India.

Rashid, M. M. (2022). A Blockchain-Based approach in Healthcare Supply Chain using Smart Contracts and Decentralized Storage Systems. *Proceedings of the 2022 ACM Conference on Information Technology for Social Good*. ACM. 10.1145/3524458.3547251

Rathore, S., & Lee, H. (2019). Cultural influences on investment decisions in India. *International Journal of Finance*, 12(4), 289–305.

Rats, O., & Alfimova, A. (2023). Green bonds as a perspective financial instrument for bank investment in Ukraine. *Development Management*, 21(1). 10.57111/devt/1.2023.08

Ravichandran, S., & Roy, M. (2022). Green finance: A key to fight with climate change. *Indian Journal of Economics and Finance*, 2(2), 34–38. 10.54105/ijef.B2526.112222

Ray, P. P. (2023). Benchmarking, ethical alignment, and evaluation framework for conversational AI: Advancing responsible development of chatgpt. *BenchCouncil Transactions on Benchmarks, Standards and Evaluations, 3*(3), 100136.

Reed, J., & Khatri, K. (2023). The evolving role of artificial intelligence in financial risk assessment. *AI in Finance Journal*, 6(1), 78–91. 10.2139/ssrn.3777210

Rekha, K., & Deepthi, Mrs. (2020). A Study On Portfolio Management. *Jetir, 7*(8), JETIRED06039.

Reserve Bank of India (RBI). (2020). *Financial Inclusion in India: Moving Beyond Jan-Dhan Yojana*. RBI. https://www.rbi.org.in

Risselada, H., Hillebrand, B., & Galenkamp, H. (2018). Data-driven customer experience in retail banking. *Journal of Financial Services Marketing*, 23(1), 17–28.

Robin Hui Huang, C. C. (2022). The development and regulation of robo-advisors in Hong Kong: Empirical and comparative. *Journal of Corporate Law Studies*, 22(1), 229–263. 10.1080/14735970.2021.2012884

Robo Advisors Essay - For reference - Robo-Advisors: A Portfolio Management Perspective Jonathan. (n.d.). Studocu. https://www.studocu.com/hk/document/hku-school-of-professional-and-continuing-education/introduction-of-accounting/robo-advisors-essay-for-reference/76929460

Robo advisory for investments in India. (2016, November 4). Groww. https://groww.in/blog/robo-advisory-india

Rogers, C., & Smith, T. (2022). Blockchain-based solutions for financial privacy: A critical analysis. *Journal of Digital Privacy*, 12(2), 100–115. 10.1016/j.jdp.2022.100022

Romanova, Anna. (2023). Development of Autonomous Artificial Intelligence Systems for Corporate Management. *Artificial societies, 18*. .10.18254/S207751800024942-5

Roncalli, T. (2020). AI and the future of portfolio management. *Journal of Portfolio Management*, 46(2), 78–92.

Rosenbaum, M. S., Ramirez, G. C., Campbell, J., & Klaus, P. (2021). The product is me: Hyper-personalized consumer goods as unconventional luxury. *Journal of Business Research*, 129, 446–454. 10.1016/j.jbusres.2019.05.017

Rusmiyanto, R., Huriati, N., Fitriani, N., Tyas, N. K., Rofi'i, A., & Sari, M. N. (2023). The Role of Artificial Intelligence (AI) In Developing English Language Learner's Communication Skills. *Journal of Education*, 6(1), 750–757.

Rutherford, S. (2000). *The Poor and Their Money*. Oxford University Press.

Sabharwal, C. L., & Anjum, B. (2018). *Robo-Revolution in the Financial Sector*. IEEE. *https://ieeexplore.ieee.org/xpl/conhome/8859311/proceeding*. 10.1109/CSCI46756.2018.00249

Sachs, J. D., Woo, W. T., Yoshino, N., & Taghizadeh-Hesary, F. (2019). *Why Is Green Finance Important? ADBI Working Paper 917*. Asian Development Bank Institute. https://www.adb.org/publications/why-green-finance-importa

Salami, A. (2021). The democratization of financial services through DeFi. *Journal of Financial Inclusion*, 3(2), 67–84.

Sánchez, F., Lara-Rubio, J., Verdu, A., & Meseguer, V. (2021). Research Advances on Financial Inclusion: A Bibliometric Analysis. *Sustainability (Basel)*, 13(6), 3156. 10.3390/su13063156

Sandner, P., Gans, J. S., & Kahlenborn, T. (2020). Blockchain technology and the tokenization of assets. *Review of Blockchain Studies*, 8(1), 33–48. 10.1016/j.rbst.2020.04.005

Sarvghad, S. S. (2018). Big Data and Predictive Analytics in Fraud Detection: A Case Study. *Journal of International Technology and Information Management*, 27(2), 45–57.

Satyanarayanan, M. (2017). The emergence of edge computing. *Computer*, 50(1), 30–39. 10.1109/MC.2017.9

Scaife, M., & van Duuren, M. (1995). Do computers have brains? What children believe about intelligent artifacts. *British Journal of Developmental Psychology*, 13(4), 367–377. 10.1111/j.2044-835X.1995.tb00686.x

Schär, F. (2021). Decentralized Finance: On Blockchain- and Smart Contract-Based Financial Markets. *RE:view*, 103(2). 10.20955/r.103.153-74

Schär, F. (2021). Decentralized finance: On blockchain and smart contract-based financial markets. *Review - Federal Reserve Bank of St. Louis*, 103(2), 145–159. 10.20955/r.103.145-159

Schwinn, R., & Teo, E. G. S. (2018). *Inclusion or exclusion? Trends in robo-advisory for financial investment services* (pp. 481–492). Elsevier eBooks. 10.1016/B978-0-12-812282-2.00021-8

Selbst, A. D., Boyd, D., Friedler, S. A., Venkatasubramanian, S., & Vertesi, J. (2019). Fairness and abstraction in sociotechnical systems. In *Proceedings of the Conference on Fairness, Accountability, and Transparency* (pp. 59-68). ACM. 10.1145/3287560.3287598

Shaikh, Z. H. (2024). *The Effect of Strategic Partnership on Innovation and Business: Performance of the Fintech Industry in Bahrain.* IGI Global. 10.4018/979-8-3693-1038-0.ch016

Shaikh, Z. H., Sarea, A., & Irfan, M. (2022). *Islamic Banking Strategies in the World of Fintech: Success Story of Bahrain* (Vol. 423). Springer., 10.1007/978-3-030-93464-4_10

Shaikh, Z., Irfan, M., Sarea, A., & Panigrahi, R. R. (2024). *The Emergence of Islamic Fintech and Bahrain: Prospect for Global Financial Sectors* (Vol. 503). Springer. 10.1007/978-3-031-43490-7_52

Sharma, M., & Choubey, A. (2022). Green banking initiatives: A qualitative study on Indian banking sector. *Environment, Development and Sustainability*, 24(1), 293–319. 10.1007/s10668-021-01426-933967597

Sharma, U., Gupta, A., & Gupta, S. K. (2024). The pertinence of incorporating ESG ratings to make investment decisions: A quantitative analysis using machine learninFg. *Journal of Sustainable Finance & Investment*, 14(1), 184–198. 10.1080/20430795.2021.2013151

Sharpe, W. F. (1964). Capital asset prices: A theory of market equilibrium under conditions of risk. *The Journal of Finance*, 19(3), 425–442.

Shen, A., Tong, R., & Deng, Y. (2018). Application of classification models on credit card fraud detection. *Procedia Computer Science*, 147, 343–348.

Shibly, M., Alawamleh, H. A., Nawaiseh, K. A., Ali, B. J., Almasri, A., & Alshibly, E. (2021). The relationship between administrative empowerment and continuous improvement: An empirical study. *Revista Geintec-Gestao Inovacao E Tecnologias*, 11(2), 1681-1699.

Shihadeh, F. (2020). Online Payment Services and Individuals' Behaviour: New Evidence from the MENAP. *International Journal of Electronic Banking*, 2(4), 275–282. 10.1504/IJEBANK.2020.114763

Shirole, A. (2023). Blockchain Technology and AI-A Review. *Recent Trends in Artificial Intelligence & it's Applications.*

Sicari, S., Rizzardi, A., Grieco, L. A., & Coen-Porisini, A. (2015). Security, privacy and trust in Internet of Things: The road ahead. *Computer Networks*, 76, 146–164. 10.1016/j.comnet.2014.11.008

Singh, I., & Kaur, N. (2017). Wealth Management Through Robo Advisory. *International Journal of Research - Granthaalayah*, 5(6), 33–43. 10.29121/granthaalayah.v5.i6.2017.1991

Singh, B., & Kaunert, C. (2024). Future of Digital Marketing: Hyper-Personalized Customer Dynamic Experience with AI-Based Predictive Models. In *Revolutionizing the AI-Digital Landscape* (pp. 189–203). Productivity Press. 10.4324/9781032688305-14

Singh, R., & Patel, M. (2022). The impact of decentralized finance on traditional financial institutions. *International Journal of Financial Services*, 19(2), 200–223. 10.1108/IJFS-04-2022-0054

Sissoko, C. (2021). The Nature of Money in a Convertible Currency World. *Review of Economic Analysis*, 13(1), 1–43. 10.15353/rea.v13i1.1771

Smith, J. K., & Johnson, L. M. (2018). AI-driven portfolio optimization: A comparative analysis. *Financial Engineering Journal*, 10(2), 45–62.

Smith, J., & Gupta, A. (2021). Challenges in rule-based fraud detection systems: Adapting to evolving fraud techniques. *Journal of Business Ethics*, 163(3), 543–558.

Smith, J., Patel, R., & Chen, Y. (2020). Assessing the performance of AI-driven portfolio management: A case study of Indian investors. *Journal of Financial Economics*, 28(4), 543–560.

Soderberg, G., Bechara, M., Bossu, W., Che, N., Kiff, J., Lukonga, I., Mancini-Griffoli, T., Sun, T., Yoshinaga, A. (2022). Behind the scenes of central bank digital currency: Emerging treFnds, insights, and policy lessons. *International Monetary Fund, Fintech Note*.

Solove, D. J. (2006). A Taxonomy of Privacy. *University of Pennsylvania Law Review*, 154(3), 477–564. 10.2307/40041279

Soltani, M., Braeken, A., Vandamme, J., & De Cock, M. (2018). A review on the state-of-the-art privacy-preserving approaches in e-commerce. *International Journal of Information Management*, 43, 193–207.

Soni, V., & kumar, D. (2019). (pp. 1–7). Role Of Artificial Intelligence in Combating Cyber Threats in Banking.

State Bank of India (SBI). (2020). *Financial Inclusion Initiatives*. SBI. https://www.sbi.co.in

Strack, R., Carrasco, M., Kolo, P., Nouri, N., Priddis, M., & George, R. (2021). *The Future of Jobs in the Era of AI*. Boston Consulting Group.

Sullivan, R., & Turner, L. (2023). Innovations in smart contract technology for financial applications. *Journal of Financial Engineering*, 11(3), 123–139. 10.1080/09720529.2023.2178564

Sun, C., Qian, H., & Miao, C. (2022). From psychological curiosity to artificial curiosity: Curiosity-driven learning in artificial intelligence tasks. *arXiv preprint arXiv:2201.08300*.

Suri, T., & Jack, W. (2016). The Long-Run Poverty and Gender Impacts of Mobile Money. *Science*, 354(6317), 1288–1292. 10.1126/science.aah530927940873

Sutton, R. S., & Barto, A. G. (2018). *Reinforcement learning: An introduction*. MIT Press.

Swan, M. (2015). *Blockchain: Blueprint for a new economy*. O'Reilly Media.

Tanwar, S., Bhatia, Q., Patel, P., Kumari, A., Singh, P. K., & Hong, W. C. (2020). Machine Learning Adoption in Blockchain-Based Smart Applications: The Challenges, and a Way Forward. *IEEE Access : Practical Innovations, Open Solutions*, 8, 474–488. 10.1109/ACCESS.2019.2961372

Tan, Y., & Yang, L. (2023). Blockchain technology and its applications in financial services: A review and future prospects. *Journal of Financial Technology and Innovation*, 9(2), 89–105. 10.2139/ssrn.3772123

Tapscott, D., & Tapscott, A. (2016). *Blockchain Revolution: How the Technology Behind Bitcoin Is Changing Money, Business, and the World*. Penguin.

Tapwal, R. (2022). CartelChain: A Secure Communication Mechanism for Heterogeneous Blockchains. *ICC 2022 - IEEE International Conference on Communications*. IEEE. 10.1109/ICC45855.2022.9838600

Terzi, S. (2019). Transforming the supply-chain management and industry logistics with blockchain smart contracts. *Proceedings of the 23rd Pan-Hellenic Conference on Informatics*. ACM. 10.1145/3368640.3368655

Thatikonda, R., Ponnala, J., Yendluri, D. K., Kempanna, M., Tatikonda, R., & Bhuvanesh, A. (2023). The Impact of Blockchain and AI in the Finance Industry. In *2023 International Conference on Computational Intelligence, Networks and Security (ICCINS)* (pp. 1-6). IEEE. 10.1109/ICCINS58907.2023.10450000

Thompson, A., & Jones, R. (2022). The intersection of AI and blockchain in financial services: Opportunities and challenges. *Artificial Intelligence in Finance*, 8(1), 47–63. 10.1016/j.aif.2022.100121

Timucin, T. (2023). The evolution of smart contract platforms: A look at current trends and future directions. *Mugla Journal of Science and Technology*.

Todd, T. M., & Seay, M. C. (2020). Financial attributes, financial behaviors, financial-advisor-use beliefs, and investing characteristics associated with having used a robo-advisor. *Financial Planning Review*, 3(3), e1104. Advance online publication. 10.1002/cfp2.1104

Tokmakov, M. (2021). *Artificial Intelligence in Corporate Governance.* .10.1007/978-3-030-60926-9_83

Touretzky, D., Gardner-McCune, C., Martin, F., & Seehorn, D. (2019, July). Envisioning AI for K-12: What Should Every Child Know about AI? *Proceedings of the AAAI Conference on Artificial Intelligence*, 33(01), 9795–9799. 10.1609/aaai.v33i01.33019795

Treleaven, P., Brown, S., & Yang, D. (2013). Algorithmic trading and artificial intelligence. *Financial Markets and Portfolio Management*, 27(2), 121–143.

Troisi. (2022). Blockchain-based Food Supply Chains: the role of Smart Contracts. *European Journal of Privacy Law & Technologies*.

Tsaih, R. (2018). Neural networks in finance: A review and evaluation of models. *Financial Innovation*, 4(2), 1–22.

Türegün, N. (2019). Impact of Technology in Financial Reporting: The Case of Amazon Go. *Journal of Corporate Accounting & Finance*, 30(3), 90–95. 10.1002/jcaf.22394

Tyson, L. D., & Zysman, J. (2022). Automation, AI & work. *Daedalus*, 151(2), 256–271. 10.1162/daed_a_01914

Ullah, F., & Al-turjman, F. M. (2021). A conceptual framework for blockchain smart contract adoption to manage real estate deals in smart cities. *Neural Computing & Applications*, 35(7), 5033–5054. 10.1007/s00521-021-05800-6

Ullah, N., & Khan, M. (2023). Blockchain for financial fraud prevention: Current trends and future directions. *Journal of Financial Crime*, 30(1), 55–73. 10.1108/JFC-01-2023-0005

UNEP. (2021). Renewables 2021 global status report. In *UNEP - UN Environment Programme*. UNEP. https://www.unep.org/resources/report/renewables-2021-global-status-report

Uzougbo, N. N. S., Ikegwu, N. C. G., & Adewusi, N. O. (2024). Regulatory Frameworks for Decentralized Finance (DeFi): Challenges and opportunities. *GSC Advanced Research and Reviews*, 19(2), 116–129. 10.30574/gscarr.2024.19.2.0170

Valdez Mendia, J. M., & Flores-Cuautle, J. D. J. A. (2022). Toward customer hyper-personalization experience—A data-driven approach. *Cogent Business & Management*, 9(1), 2041384. 10.1080/23311975.2022.2041384

Van Brummelen, J., Tabunshchyk, V., & Heng, T. (2021, June). "Alexa, Can I Program You?": Student Perceptions of Conversational Artificial Intelligence Before and After Programming Alexa. In *Interaction Design and Children* (pp. 305-313).

Van Vliet, B. (2018). *High-Frequency Trading: A Practical Guide to Algorithmic Strategies and Trading Systems*. Wiley.

Vargo, S. L., & Lusch, R. F. (2004). Evolving to a new dominant logic for marketing. *Journal of Marketing*, 68(1), 1–17. 10.1509/jmkg.68.1.1.24036

Vasquez, M., & Huang, Y. (2022). The potential of blockchain to disrupt financial trading systems: A review. *Journal of Financial Markets*, 13(4), 301–316. 10.2139/ssrn.3688520

Venkatesan, R., & Kumar, V. (2004). A Customer Lifetime Value Framework for Customer Selection and Resource Allocation Strategy. *Journal of Marketing*, 68(4), 106–125. 10.1509/jmkg.68.4.106.42728

Vijai, C. (2019). *The Blockchain Technology and Modern Ledgers Through Blockchain Accounting*. Technology.

Voigt, P., & Von dem Bussche, A. (2017). *The EU General Data Protection Regulation (GDPR): A Practical Guide*. Springer International Publishing. 10.1007/978-3-319-57959-7

Volz, U. (2021). Governing sustainable finance. *Asia Bond Monitor*. https://asianbondsonline.adb.org/documents/abm/abm_jun_2021_governing_sustainable_finance.pdf

Volz, U., Beirne, J., Ambrosio Preudhomme, N., Fenton, A., Mazzacurati, E., Renzhi, N., & Stampe, J. (2020). Climate change and sovereign risk. SOAS University of London, Asian Development Bank Institute. 10.25501/SOAS.00033524

W, S. & Jayakumar, D. S. (2022, June 1). *Portfolio Management, Classical and Robust Statistics. A literature Review*. ResearchGate. https://www.researchgate.net/publication/362902068_Portfolio_Management_Classical_and_Robust_Statistics_A_literature_Review

Wang, L. (2023). Memory-augmented appearance-motion network for video anomaly detection. *Pattern Recognition, 138*, 109335.

Wang, Y., Lucey, B.M., Vigne, S.A., & Yarovaya, L. (2022). The Effects of Central Bank Digital Currencies News on Financial Markets. *Technological Forecasting & Social Change, 180*, 1-39. 10.1016/j.techfore.2022.121715

Wang, J., & Li, H. (2023). A review of blockchain-based solutions for financial data integrity and security. *International Journal of Financial Engineering*, 10(2), 120–136. 10.1142/S2345678923500152

Wang, S., Li, B., Yang, M., & Yan, Z. (2019). Missing Data Imputation for Machine Learning. In Li, B., Yang, M., Yuan, H., & Yan, Z. (Eds.), *IoT as a Service*. Springer. 10.1007/978-3-030-14657-3_7

Wang, T., Lund, B. D., Marengo, A., Pagano, A., Mannuru, N. R., Teel, Z. A., & Pange, J. (2023). Exploring the Potential Impact of Artificial Intelligence (AI) on Higher Education. *Generative AI*, 13(11), 6716. 10.3390/app13116716

Watanabe, H., Ichihara, K., & Aita, T. (2024). *VELLET: Verifiable Embedded Wallet for Securing Authenticity and Integrity*. arXiv preprint arXiv:2404.03874.

Werbach, K. (2018). *The Blockchain and the New Architecture of Trust*. MIT Press. 10.7551/mitpress/11449.001.0001

Werner, S., Krämer, J., & Müller, S. (2021). Challenges and opportunities of decentralized finance. *Journal of Financial Technology*, 12(3), 215–232. 10.1016/j.ftj.2021.05.004

West, J., & Bhattacharya, M. (2016). Intelligent financial fraud detection: A comprehensive review. *Computers & Security*, 57, 47–66. 10.1016/j.cose.2015.09.005

Whitrow, C., Hand, D. J., Juszczak, P., Weston, D., & Adams, N. M. (2009). Transaction aggregation as a strategy for credit card fraud detection. *Data Mining and Knowledge Discovery*, 18(1), 30–55. 10.1007/s10618-008-0116-z

Wilkens, S. (2019). Machine Learning in Risk Measurement: Gaussian Process Regression for Value-at-Risk and Expected Shortfall. *Journal of Risk Management in Financial Institutions, 12*, 374-383. 10.2139/ssrn.3246131

Wöhrer, M., & Zdun, U. (2018). Blockchain-based smart contracts: Security and compliance. *Computer Science Review*, 30, 123–142. 10.1016/j.cosrev.2018.07.002

World Bank. (2018). *Financial Inclusion*. World Bank. https://www.worldbank.org

Wright, A., & Buterin, V. (2022). Ethereum: A blockchain platform for decentralized applications. *Journal of Blockchain Research*, 5(1), 101–118. 10.2139/ssrn.3715023

Wu, G., Wang, H. P., Lai, X., Wang, M., He, D., & Chan, S. (2024). A comprehensive survey of smart contract security: State of the art and research directions. . *Journal of Network and Computer Applications*, 226, 103882. 10.1016/j.jnca.2024.103882

Xiao, R., & Chen, L. (2023). Blockchain-based financial innovations: A review of recent advances. *Journal of Financial Innovations*, 7(2), 65–82. 10.1080/22761160.2023.2118325

Yahya, A. A., & Zargar, P. (2023). Achieving corporate sustainability through green human resource management: The role of CSR in the banking industry of a developing country. *Sustainability (Basel)*, 15(14), 10834. 10.3390/su151410834

Yang, C., & Masron, T. A. (2022). Impact of digital finance on energy efficiency in the context of green sustainable development. *Sustainability (Basel)*, 14(18), 11250. 10.3390/su141811250

Yang, W., & Wu, J. (2023). Machine learning and blockchain technology in financial fraud detection: A survey. *Journal of Financial Data Analysis*, 6(1), 21–38. 10.2139/ssrn.3772121

Yao, F., Qin, Z., & Wang, X. (2023). The influence of bank governance structure on green credit. *PLoS One*, 18(3), e0281115. 10.1371/journal.pone.028111536913350

Yap, S., Lee, H. S., & Liew, P. X. (2023). The role of financial inclusion in achieving finance-related sustainable development goals (SDGs): A cross-country analysis. *Ekonomska Istrazivanja*, 36(3), 2212028. 10.1080/1331677X.2023.2212028

Yin, G., Li, W., & Wang, J. (2019). The impact of DeFi on traditional financial systems: Opportunities and risks. *Journal of Financial Stability*, 39(4), 85–100.

Yoshino, N., Taghizadeh-Hesary, F., & Nakahigashi, M. (2018). Modelling the social funding and spill-over tax for Addressing the green energy financing gap. *Economic Modelling*. 10.1016/j.econmod.2018.11.018

Yuan, L., & Zeng, S. (2023). An empirical study on the impact of green credit on financial performance of china's listed banks. *Advances in Management and Applied Economics*, 89–110. 10.47260/amae/1325

Yunus, M. (2007). *Banker to the Poor: Micro-Lending and the Battle Against World Poverty*. PublicAffairs.

Zarsky, T. Z. (2016). Incompatible: The GDPR in the Age of Big Data. *Seton Hall Law Review*, 47, 995.

Zetzsche, D. A., Arner, D. W., & Buckley, R. P. (2020). Decentralized Finance (DeFi). *Journal of Financial Regulation*, 2020(6), 172–203. 10.1093/jfr/fjaa010

Zetzsche, D. A., Buckley, R. P., & Arner, D. W. (2020). The future of financial regulation: The role of DeFi and AI. *Journal of Financial Regulation*, 15(1), 65–84. 10.1093/jfr/fwaa011

Zhang, H., Su, H., Wu, X., & Yang, Y. (2024). Cross-Chain Interoperability and Collaboration for Keyword-Based Embedded Smart Contracts in Internet of Things. *IEEE Internet of Things Journal*, 11(6), 10791–10807. 10.1109/JIOT.2023.3328190

Zhang, Q., Li, H., & Wang, X. (2020). Fraud detection using machine learning: Techniques and applications. *International Journal of Data Science and Analytics*, 9(1), 45–63.

Zhang, X., & Zhou, T. (2022). The impact of decentralized finance on the future of global financial markets. *Journal of Financial Stability*, 59, 100943. 10.1016/j.jfs.2022.100943

Zhang, Z., & Ding, Y. (2023). The impact of green financial development on stock price crash risk from the perspective of information asymmetry in Chinese listed companies. *Environmental Science and Pollution Research International*, 30(37), 87199–87214. 10.1007/s11356-023-27771-y37418190

Zhang, Z., Liu, Y., Han, Z., & Liao, X. (2022). Green finance and carbon emission reduction: A bibliometric analysis and systematic review. *Frontiers in Environmental Science*, 10, 929250. 10.3389/fenvs.2022.929250

Zhou, Q., & Wu, J. (2023). Smart contracts in blockchain-based financial systems: A comprehensive review. *IEEE Transactions on Emerging Topics in Computing*, 11(1), 234–249. 10.1109/TETC.2023.3167461

Zhou, Z.-H. (2012). *Ensemble methods: Foundations and algorithms*. Chapman and Hall/CRC. 10.1201/b12207

Zuboff, S. (2015). Big other: Surveillance capitalism and the prospects of an information civilization. *Journal of Information Technology*, 30(1), 75–89. 10.1057/jit.2015.5

About the Contributors

Mohammad Irfan is presently working as an Associate Professor at School of Business and Management, Christ University, Bengaluru, India. Dr. Irfan has done his Ph.D. from the Central University of Haryana. He is MBA (Finance), M.Com (Account and Law), and MA (Economics). He has qualified UGC-JRF/SRF/NET in Management and Commerce. Dr. Irfan certified NSEs (NCFM) and BSEs certification. He has experience of more than sixteen years in the area of SAPM, Artificial Intelligence, Machine Learning, Blockchain, Cryptocurrency, Financial Engineering, Fintech, Green Finance, and Alternative Finance. He has to his credit more than 40+ Scopus Indexed articles, includes The Journal of Economic Cooperation and Development (Q2), International Journal of Business Excellence (IJBEX), International Journal of Economics and Management (IJEM), Montenegrin Journal of Economics (Q2), Cogent Business & Management (Taylor & Francis) (Q2), Indian Journal of Finance (IJF) and Journal of Islamic Monetary Economics and Finance (JIMF). His citations reached 301+ along with 12 H-index. Dr. Irfan has published 7 books in Springer, IGI Global Publication (Scopus indexed).

Mohammed Elmogy is a professor and head of the Information Technology Dept., Faculty of Computers and Information, Mansoura University, Egypt. He received his B.Sc. and M.Sc. from the Faculty of Engineering, Mansoura University, Mansoura, Egypt. He received his Ph.D. from Informatics Department, MIN Faculty, Hamburg University, Hamburg, Germany, in 2010. He worked as a visiting researcher from July 2016 to August 2019 at the Bioengineering Department, University of Louisville, Louisville, USA. He has authored/co-authored over 250 research publications in peer-reviewed reputed journals, book chapters, and conference proceedings. Most of his publications are in artificial intelligence, machine learning, computer vision, medical data analysis, and their applications. He has served as a reviewer for various prestigious international journals, such as Artificial Intelligence in Medicine, Computers in Biology and Medicine, Information Sciences, IEEE Journal of Biomedical and Health Informatics, and IEEE Access. He served as a technical program committee member in many workshops and conferences. He served as a member of the editorial board of many journals, such as Computers in Biology and Medicine, Journal of Software Engineering & Intelligent Systems, and International Journal of Advanced Computer Research. He is a senior member of the IEEE society, membership since 2008. He has been a professional member of the ACM society since 2011. He advised and co-advised more than 40 master's and doctoral graduates. His current research interests are artificial intelligence, computer vision, medical image analysis, machine learning, pattern recognition, and biomedical engineering.

Swati Gupta brings a wealth of experience, accumulating two decades of expertise in both the academic and corporate realms. Currently serving as an Associate Professor at Universal AI University, she has dedicated a significant portion of her career to shaping minds in the academic arena, specializing in finance and accounting. With a profound understanding of the subject matter, Dr. Gupta has been instrumental in delivering comprehensive education, offering courses such as Fintech, Rural Finance, Valuation, Merger & Acquisition, and Financial Modeling. Her pedagogical approach is enriched by practical insights gained through her extensive corporate experience. In the corporate sector, Dr. Gupta's acumen has been honed through active engagement with esteemed organizations. This dual perspective, blending academic rigor with real-world application, has not only defined her teaching philosophy but has also contributed to her success as a mentor for change. Beyond the classroom, Dr. Swati Gupta's influence extends to the international stage, marked by her presentations at numerous conferences and a prolific record of publications and book chapters in Scopus-indexed journals. Her journey over two decades reflects a seamless integration of academic excellence and corporate wisdom, making her a distinguished figure in both spheres.

Fahmi Khalifa, Ph.D., is an Assistant Professor of ECE, Morgan State University (MSU), Maryland USA, received. Dr. Khalifa received his BS and MS degrees in Electrical Engineering from Mansoura University, Egypt in 2003 and 2007, respectively, and his PhD degree in 2014 from ECE Department, University of Louisville (UofL), USA. He has more than 15 years of hands-on experience in the fields of artificial intelligence, image/signal processing, machine learning, biomedical data analysis, and computer-aided diagnosis with more than 190 publications appearing in prestigious journals and top-rank international conferences in addition to and five US patents. Dr. Khalifa is an associate editor for IEEE Access, IEEE JBHI, and Frontiers in Neuroscience; guest edited multiple special issues; and served a reviewer for 60+ journals and conferences. Dr. Khalifa's honors and awards include Mansoura University scholarship for distinctive undergraduate students for four consecutive years (1999–2002), Theobald Scholarship Award (ECE, UofL,2013), the ECE Outstanding Student award for two times (ECE, UofL, 2012 and 2014), the John M. Houchens award for the outstanding dissertation (UofL, 2014), the second-place Post-Doctoral Fellow award in Research! Louisville (UofL, 2014), PowerLIVE Award for Faculty commitment to students and their academic success (MSU, 2023), and Final list for the "Instructional Innovator of the Year" (MSU, 2023).

Rui Manuel Teixeira Santos Dias has a Postdoctoral degree in Finance at the State University of Feira de Santana (BR), Department of Exact Sciences. Doctor of Finance at the University of Évora—Institute of Research and Advanced Training (PT). Diploma of Advanced Studies in Doctoral Studies (DEA), at the University of Extremadura (ES), in the scientific area of Financial Economics.

***

Fatima Muhammad Abdulkarim obtained her bachelor degree in Business Administration (E-Commerce) from Infrastructure University of Malaysia and graduated with first class honors in 2011. She immediately joined National University of Malaysia (UKM) in the same year where she studied Masters in Business Administration majoring in Islamic finance. In 2013, she joined International Centre for knowledge in Islamic Finance (INCEIF) and studied PhD in Islamic Finance and graduated in 2016. Dr. Fatima then secured a job with Federal University Dutse in 2018 in the Department of Banking and Finance. In the same year, she was appointed to head Actuarial Science Department for two years in which her tenure expired in 2020. She has published numerous papers in high impact journals.

Jahanvi Bansal is currently working as Assistant Professor, School of Management Studies & Liberal Arts, GSFC University, Vadodara, Gujarat (India). Her research papers have been published in reputed national and international journals. She was honored with 'Emerald Literati Award- Highly Commendable Paper 2020' by Emerald Publishing House, United Kingdom. Her research interests include workforce diversity, business ethics, corporate social responsibility, and SDGs.

Ahu Coşkun was born in Istanbul in 1981. She graduated from Istanbul University, Department of Economics, the Ph.D.program in 2012 and she has been working as a faculty member at Marmara University since 2014. Dr.Coşkun Özer has publications on international trade and international political economy. Dr. Coşkun Özer edited 3 international scientific books for IGI Global Publishing. Dr.Coşkun Özer has written and published many research papers in the national & international Journal and Conferences. Dr.Coşkun Özer teaches courses on Introduction to Economics, Business Management, Entrepreneurship, Professional English.

Suchi Dubey currently works at the School of Business, Manipal Academy of Higher Education, Dubai. She is an experienced Associate Professor with a demonstrated history of working in the education management industry. She completed her Doctor of Philosophy (Ph.D.) focused in Finance from the University of Allahabad, India.

Vishal Eswaran is an accomplished Senior Big Data Engineer with an impressive career spanning over 6 years. His fervor for constructing robust data pipelines, unearthing insights from intricate datasets, identifying trends, and predicting future trajectories has fueled his journey. Throughout his tenure, Vishal has lent his expertise to empower numerous prominent US healthcare clients, including CVS Health, Aetna, and Blue Cross and Blue Shield of North Carolina, with informed business decisions drawn from expansive datasets. Vishal's ability to distill intricate data into comprehensive documents and reports stands as a testament to his proficiency in managing multifaceted internal and external data analysis responsibilities. His aptitude for synthesizing complex information ensures that insights are both accessible and impactful for strategic decision-making. Moreover, Vishal's distinction extends to his role as a co-author of the book "Internet of Things - Future Connected Devices." This book not only underscores his prowess in the field but also showcases his visionary leadership in the realm of Internet of Things (IoT). His insights resonate with a forward-looking perspective, emphasizing the convergence of technology and human life. As the author of "Secure Connections: Safeguarding the Internet of Things (IoT) with Cybersecurity," Vishal Eswaran's reputation as a thought leader is further solidified. His work is a manifestation of his commitment to ensuring the security of interconnected devices within the IoT landscape, a vital consideration in our digitally driven world. Vishal's dedication to enhancing the safety and integrity of IoT ecosystems shines through in his work.

Vivek Eswaran has 8 years of experience as a Senior Software Engineer specializing in front-end development, and brings a vital perspective to securing the Internet of Things (IoT). At Medallia, Vivek played an instrumental role in crafting engaging user interfaces and optimized digital experiences. This profound expertise in front-end engineering equips them to illuminate the crucial synergy between usability and cybersecurity as IoT adoption accelerates. In the new book "Secure Connections: Safeguarding the Internet of Things with Cybersecurity," Vivek combines their real-world experiences building intuitive and secure software systems with cutting-edge insights into strengthening IoT ecosystems. Drawing parallels between front-end best practices and security imperatives, they offer readers an invaluable guide for fortifying IoT without compromising usability. As businesses and consumers continue rapidly connecting people, processes, and devices, Vivek's contribution provides timely insights. Blending user empathy with security proficiency, Vivek empowers audiences to realize the potential of IoT through resilient and human-centered systems designed for safety without friction

Ushaa Eswaran is an esteemed author, distinguished researcher, and seasoned educator with a remarkable journey spanning over 34 years, dedicated to advancing academia and nurturing the potential of young minds. Currently serving as a Principal and Professor in Andhra Pradesh, India, her vision extends beyond imparting cutting-edge technical expertise to encompass the nurturing of universal human values. With a foundation in Electronics Engineering, Dr. Eswaran delved into the realm of biosensors, carving a pioneering path in nanosensor models, a remarkable achievement that earned her a well-deserved Doctorate. Her insights have been encapsulated in her acclaimed book, "Internet of Things: Future Connected Devices," offering profound insights into the evolving IoT landscape. Her expertise also finds its place in upcoming publications centered around computer vision and IoT technologies. Dr. Eswaran's commitment to literature is rooted in her unwavering passion to equip the younger generation with the latest knowledge fortified by ethical principles. Her book stands as a beacon of practical wisdom, providing a roadmap through the intricate IoT terrain while shedding light on its future societal impacts. Her forthcoming contributions unveil her interdisciplinary perspective, seamlessly integrating electronics, nanotechnology, and computing. Bolstering her scholarly contributions is her ORCID identifier, 0000-0002-5116-3403, a testament to her prolific research journey that encompasses over a hundred published papers. Dr. Eswaran thrives in merging her profound academic insights with her dedication to nurturing holistic student growth. Her tireless exploration of the dynamic interface between technology and human values continues to shape her works. As the author of "Secure Connections: Safeguarding the Internet of Things (IoT) with Cybersecurity," Dr. Ushaa Eswaran's voice emerges as a beacon of wisdom in the realm of IoT. Her work encapsulates her dedication to enhancing the interconnected world while ensuring its resilience against cyber threats.

Parul Garg is an accomplished educator and researcher, currently serving as an Assistant Professor at the Amity Global Business School, Noida. With a background in MBA from UPTU, M.A. in Economics, she brings a wealth of knowledge and experience to her role. She is also UGC NET qualified in Labour Laws and holds a Ph.D from Jiwaji University (NAAC Accredited A++ Grade State University), Gwalior, adding to her expertise in the field. With 11+ years of rich experience in teaching and research, she has established herself as a leading in the areas of Economics and Human Resource Management. In addition to her academic pursuits, Dr. Garg is dedicated to helping students succeed and reach their full potential. She has also published many research papers in National and International Journals of repute.

Ankit Goel is currently serving as Associate Professor at Maharaja Agrasen Institute of Management Studies, affiliated to Guru Gobind Singh Indraprastha University, New Delhi. With a PGDM (MBA) from Apeejay Institute and M.Com., Dr. Goel has a wealth of knowledge in the field of Commerce and Management. He has also qualified for UGC NET JRF in Commerce and UGC NET in Management. Dr. Goel's passion for finance led him to complete his Ph.D. in Finance from JIWAJI University (NAAC Accredited A++ Grade State University), Gwalior. He has published many research papers in National and International Journals of repute. Along with 12+ years of rich experience in teaching Accounts, Finance, Taxation, Economics, Share Market, he has also conducted numerous national workshops on TALLY Prime, MS Excel, Filing Income Tax Return and Investment decisions.

Mahadi Hasan serves as an Associate Professor and Head of the Department of Business Studies at the University of Information Technology and Sciences (UITS). He has been engaged in academia since 2010.

Vartika Jaiswal holds a Master's degree from Christ University, Bangalore India. Her interest lies in security analysis and evaluation.

Jugal Kishor is an Assistant Professor at the Central University of Rajasthan, Ajmer, India. He teaches postgraduate/undergraduate students in business administration. His research interest includes entrepreneurship and integrated marketing communication.

Early Ridho Kismawadi, Dr. S.E.I, MA, is a lecturer at the Department of Islamic Banking, Faculty of Islamic Economics and Business IAIN Langsa, Aceh, Indonesia, he has been a lecturer since 2013, he has completed a doctoral program in 2018 majoring in Sharia economics at the State Islamic University of North Sumatra. He was appointed head of the Islamic economics Law study program (2023) Islamic banking study program (2020) and Islamic financial management study program (2019) at Langsa State Islamic Institute (IAIN Langsa), Aceh, Indonesia. His research interests include financial economics, applied econometrics, Islamic economics, banking, and finance. He has published articles in national and international journals. In addition, he is also a reviewer of several reputable international journals such as Finance Research Letters, Financial Innovation, Cogent Business &; Management, Journal of Islamic Accounting and Business Research. He has also presented his papers at various local and international seminars.

Reenu Kumari is Assistant Professor in the Department of Management, KIET group of Institutions, ghaziabad Uttar Pradesh, (India). She has received Ph.D from Indian Institute of Technology, Roorkee in 2017. She has qualified UGC NET (JRF) in 2011. She has thirteen year experience in teaching as well as research also. Her area of specialization is Finance & Accounting. Her are of interest FDI, Education, Economic Growth, Digitalization and Trade Openness. She has written and published many research papers in the national; international Journal and Conferences. She has reviewer in various journals including Sage, Emerald, Inderscience, and Elsevier. International Journal of Emerging Markets (IJoEM), Management Research Review (MRR), International Journal of Comparative Management (IJoCM), the Third PAN-IIM World Management Conference, Human Development and Capabilities (JoHDC), the social science Journal (SSJ), Transnational Corporations Review (TCR), South Asian Journal of business studies. She has taken various guest lecturers on research methodology in repute institutions.

Mohammed Majeed is a Senior Lecturer at Tamale Technical University in Ghana. He is the Head of the Department for Marketing and his research interests include branding, hospitality and tourism, and social media in service organizations.

Naji Mansour Nomran, PhD, is currently Assistant Professor in Finance & Accounting Department, College of Business Administration, Kingdom University, Kingdom of Bahrain. His research interests include Islamic banking and finance, corporate governance, risk management, financial performance, and financial markets. His attention has recently shifted to a variety of topics, including the role that green finance plays in combating climate change and promoting sustainable development, examining issues related to cryptocurrencies, blockchain technology in finance, besides issues related to artificial intelligence and FinTech in finance. He has published several publications in international peer-reviewed journals as well as edited books.

Keerthana Murali has over 5 years of experience as a Site Reliability Engineer at Dell. Keerthna Murali has honed an intricate expertise in maintaining and optimizing robust digital infrastructures. On the frontlines of ensuring seamless online experiences, Keerthna specialized in troubleshooting complex issues and proactively enhancing system performance and availability. These capabilities uniquely position them to tackle the critical challenge of security for rapidly emerging IoT ecosystems. In their new book "Secure Connections," Keerthna channels their real-world experiences maintaining enterprise-scale platforms into a compelling vision for building security into the foundation of IoT systems. Blending software engineering best practices with cybersecurity insights, they offer a prescient guide for developers, IT leaders, and security experts seeking to realize IoT's potential while mitigating its risks.

Madhusudan Narayan is an accomplished researcher and educator with a background in marketing. Holding a Ph.D. and MBA in Marketing, along with a PGD in International Business, Dr. Narayan's expertise encompasses various facets of marketing, including Digital Marketing, Rural Marketing, and Entrepreneurship. With over several years of teaching experience, Dr. Narayan has made significant contributions to academia through his research endeavors. He has published extensively in prestigious journals indexed in Scopus, Web of Science, and UGC-Care lists, demonstrating his commitment to scholarly excellence. Furthermore, Dr. Narayan's influence extends beyond his research publications. He actively serves as a member of several Editorial Boards and as a reviewer for esteemed national and international journals, contributing to the dissemination of knowledge and the advancement of the academic community. Dr. Narayan brings a wealth of academic and professional experience to his research pursuits. His dedication to exploring diverse areas within Marketing and Entrepreneurship, along with his contributions to teaching and research, underscores his commitment to academic excellence and innovation

S. Padma is PhD in Management She has 22 years of experience in molding management graduates post graduate students and guiding PhD scholars. She has 31 publications in various UGC/Scopus/ABDC/ other peer reviewed journals. She presented papers in various national and international conferences. She is a reviewer for many international journals. She is a resource person for data analytics using excel, and other research topics like 'how to prepare synopses, and 'Data analysis using SPSS'. She has three books to her credit, co-author for Organizational Behaviour and Managerial Economics.

Yanamandra Ramakrishna has an impressive career spanning three decades in teaching, research, and consultancy, specializing in Operations, Project Management, Logistics, and Supply Chain Management. He earned his PhD in Supply Chain Management from Jawaharlal Nehru Technological University (JNTUH), Hyderabad, India. Currently, he serves as the Program Chair and Associate Professor at the School of Business, Skyline University College, Sharjah, UAE. He has published numerous research articles in reputed indexed journals and has presented many research papers at international conferences, focusing on circular, responsible, and sustainable supply chain and operations management. He has conducted extensive training and consultancy programs for both faculty and industry professionals in Supply Chain Management across India, the UK, and the UAE. His edited books published through IGI Global have all been indexed in Scopus.

Satya Pavan Kumar Ratnakaram is an accomplished academician currently employed as an Assistant Professor in the Faculty of Business and Logistics, Bahrain Polytechnic since September 2022. Prior to this, he has worked as a Program Manager and IQA member in the Commercial Studies Division, Bahrain Training Institute, Kingdom of Bahrain for more than 16 years. With over two decades of teaching/training/industry experience across three countries, published more than 15 articles in national and international journals in the field of banking, insurance, accounting, and CSR.

Dhana S is a vibrant, enthusiastic professional with nearly 13 years of Academic, Research and Industry experience in various institution approved by AICTE/UGC. Ample experience in academic, research, also curriculum design in Management, Tourism and Travel Management courses. Author for book "Multirater Feedback for Succession Planning: A Study on Banking Sector". Contribute regularly in articles for Journals. Proven researcher on various aspects of Management especially Human Resource, Marketing, Tourism and Hospitality Journals. She has published many articles in international and national journals few of the articles in UGC Care List, WOS, Scopus and reputed Journals. She is serving as Editorial Member and Reviewer for Elsevier and Reputed Journals.

Jyoti Sah An M Com, M Phil passed out from Department of Commerce, Dibrugarh University in the year 2012, and in the year 2021, she has been awarded with Ph.D. degree from the same university. She has presented papers in 9 national seminars and 4 publications in various research journals of repute so far to her credit. Apart from the above she has been working as Assistant Professor on part time basis in the Department of Commerce and CME (BBA) of Tinsukia College Assam since 2015. She has joined as full time in Faculty of Commerce & Business Studies, Motherhood University, Roorkee, Dehradun Road Vill- Karoundi, Post-Bhagwanpur, Dist- Haridwar, Uttarakhand since 21st July, 2022 to 10th October 2023. Currently working as Assistant Professor-III, in Amity Business School, Amity University Maharashtra, Mumbai - Pune Expressway Bhatan, Somathne, Panvel, Mumbai, Maharashtra 410206 since 19th October 2023.

Ankit Saxena is currently working as associate professor at Institute of Business Management, GLA University, Mathura. He is a Director Medalist from Dayalbagh Educational Institute, Agra. He qualified NET-JRF (UGC). He has excellent academic background and a rich experience of 17 years in research and academics. He has published number of research papers and contemporary business case studies. His area of interest comprises Strategic Financial Management and behavior of market participants.

Zakir Shaikh is an Assistant Professor, Department of Accounting and Finance, School of Business Administration, Kingdom University, Bahrain. Prior to this, he worked more than 28 years in commercial and academic industry. He has published numerous articles in referred journals and presented many papers in various conferences, both local and abroad in the different area of Accounting, management and Islamic Banking and Finance. He has also participated in a variety of seminars, forums, workshops and international conferences. He obtained his Ph.D. (Islamic Banking and Finance) from India in 2018. His doctoral thesis explored the entrepreneurial phenomenon from an Islamic perspective and argued for profit and loss sharing (PLS) contracts as viable alternatives to conventional interest-based financing instruments. He holds Master degree in Commerce, Business Administration & Finance and Control. He is a member of AAA, Chartered Institute of Islamic Finance Professionals (CIIF), Malaysia; Indian Accounting Association; Orissa Commerce Association, India and associated with Accounting & Auditing Organization for Islamic Financial Institution (AAOIFI), Bahrain

Sofia Devi Shamurailatpam has a Ph.D. in Economics with specialization in the area of Banking and Financial Economics. Currently she is serving as an Assistant Professor in the Department of Banking and Insurance, Faculty of Commerce, The Maharaja Sayajirao University of Baroda. She has published several research papers in her credit and authored a book entitled "Banking Reforms in India: Consolidation, Restructuring and Performance, published by Palgrave Macmillan, UK (2017). Her major research area of interests includes Economics of Banking, Financial Economics, Agricultural Economics and Development Economics particularly Contemporary issues on Sustainability.

Komal Sharma is Assistant Professor in the Department of Management, Ghaziabad She has received Ph.D from CCS university, Meerut. She has thirteen year experience in teaching as well as research also. Her area of specialization is Finance & Accounting.

Swati Sharma is an Assistant Professor at the School of Business and Commerce, Manipal University Jaipur, Rajasthan, India. She teaches to undergraduate and postgraduate management students. Her research interest includes SMEs, e-banking and financial inclusion.

Parag Shukla is an Assistant Professor in Commerce at Maharaja Sayajirao University of Baroda, India, specializing in Marketing Management. He earned his bachelor's and master's degrees from the same university, focusing on Marketing Management. Dr. Shukla's research centers on Retailing, and he has a background in content analysis within the television and media research industry. He teaches management courses at various levels and has published extensively in national and international journals and conferences. His current research project titled "An Empirical Investigation of Experiential Value vis-a-vis Usage Attitude of Selected Mobile Shoppers in Gujarat." Dr. Shukla is notable for receiving the Silver Medal at the 68th International All India Commerce Conference for his research, earning the Best Business Academic of the Year Award, a significant recognition in Indian Education and Retail Industry.

Tapsi Srivastava, is an accomplished academic professional specializing in finance. NISM V-A Certified, she is pursuing a Ph.D. in Finance at the University of Lucknow and has cleared the NTA NET in Commerce with high percentiles. With 4.5 years of teaching experience she began her career at Sherwood College of Professional Management, where she served as Class Coordinator and directed the Student Cultural Team. She then joined IILM Academy of Higher Learning, where she chaired the Finance Area, collaborated with the Placement Team, and coordinated the Mentoring Coordination Team. Currently, she is an Assistant Professor at Amity Global Business School, Amity University, Noida. Her research focuses on Wealth-tech, Fintech, and Banking, with notable publications including "Unravelling the Metaverse: A Bibliometric Review" and "Evolution Acceptance and Adaptation of Fintech: A Road Map towards Sustainable Development" published in databases like EBSCO, PRO-QUEST, Google Scholar and J-Gate. She has presented papers at various international and national conferences, earning recognition for her contributions. Tapsi has received accolades such as the Best Paper Award at the International Conference on Integrating AI Spirituality Healthcare and Management for Sustainable Well Being organized by Amity University in 2023 and first prizes in multiple debate competitions. Fluent in English and Hindi, she is committed to continuous learning and fostering financial knowledge and inclusion.

Pankaj Kumar Tripathi is working as an Assistant Professor in the Department of Accounting and Financial Management, Faculty of Commerce, The Maharaja Sayajirao University of Baroda, Vadodara. He has vast experience in academics, worked in different states of India adding varied multicultural experience to his career. He holds PhD in Finance and Accounting. His areas of expertise include financial accounting, financial economics, business economics and business administration. He has various papers in National and international journals.

Deepika Upadhyay is currently working as an Associate Professor in the Department of Commerce at Christ University, Bangalore. Her research interest lies in behavioural finance, studies on the stock market, capital structure, sustainability, entrepreneurship etc. Dr Upadhyay holds a Doctoral degree in Commerce from the Faculty of Commerce, Banaras Hindu University and has published papers in journals of repute. In addition to this, she is passionate about teaching and guiding students, mentoring, and community outreach.

Index

A

Adoption of Ai 62, 64, 80, 89, 95, 113, 152, 203, 267, 268, 318, 320, 321
AI-driven solutions 55, 102, 206
ANOVA 289, 293, 299
artificial intelligence 1, 2, 3, 5, 7, 9, 10, 11, 13, 15, 16, 17, 19, 20, 21, 22, 23, 24, 26, 27, 28, 29, 30, 31, 35, 38, 40, 41, 42, 44, 45, 46, 48, 49, 68, 87, 88, 89, 91, 92, 93, 95, 103, 104, 105, 106, 107, 108, 109, 110, 112, 113, 114, 115, 116, 117, 118, 119, 121, 127, 129, 130, 132, 133, 134, 135, 136, 137, 138, 139, 143, 144, 145, 150, 151, 152, 154, 158, 159, 162, 163, 164, 166, 168, 169, 176, 178, 179, 199, 202, 206, 207, 208, 222, 223, 225, 228, 233, 235, 245, 246, 247, 248, 250, 252, 253, 254, 256, 257, 259, 260, 261, 263, 264, 265, 269, 270, 271, 289, 290, 291, 292, 293, 294, 296, 297, 299, 300, 301, 302, 318, 319, 320, 334
Artificial Intelligence (AI) 206
Asia 183, 198, 200, 303, 309
awareness index 289, 293, 294, 298, 299

B

Bahrain 112, 113, 114, 115, 116, 118, 119, 121, 125, 127, 129, 130, 132, 133, 134, 135, 136, 137, 138
Banks 3, 7, 12, 14, 15, 22, 25, 26, 29, 30, 33, 35, 39, 42, 90, 94, 105, 119, 146, 151, 162, 165, 169, 175, 181, 182, 183, 184, 185, 186, 187, 188, 189, 190, 191, 192, 193, 194, 195, 196, 197, 198, 199, 200, 203, 204, 205, 206, 207, 215, 216, 222, 232, 233, 250, 255, 259, 263, 273, 274, 275, 276, 277, 278, 279, 281, 283, 284, 285, 286, 288

Behavioral Aspects 318
Blockchain 3, 4, 5, 6, 8, 9, 10, 11, 12, 16, 17, 18, 22, 23, 24, 27, 41, 45, 47, 49, 50, 53, 57, 69, 77, 87, 88, 90, 92, 94, 103, 104, 105, 106, 107, 108, 109, 110, 111, 119, 137, 138, 142, 146, 153, 156, 158, 165, 204, 222, 226, 227, 228, 229, 230, 231, 232, 233, 234, 235, 236, 237, 238, 239, 240, 241, 242, 243, 244, 245, 246, 247, 248, 249, 250, 251, 254, 255, 258, 259, 260, 261, 268, 269, 270, 271, 272, 311, 316
Blockchain Technology 3, 4, 5, 6, 8, 9, 10, 11, 12, 22, 24, 41, 49, 50, 53, 77, 90, 92, 94, 105, 108, 109, 110, 111, 119, 137, 153, 204, 226, 227, 228, 229, 231, 232, 233, 234, 235, 236, 239, 240, 241, 248, 249, 250, 251, 254, 255, 259, 260, 261

C

cryptocurrency 6, 11, 17, 95, 104, 109, 230, 288
Customer Experience 19, 21, 22, 23, 24, 25, 28, 32, 34, 35, 36, 37, 41, 42, 45, 47, 159, 204, 207

D

Data Analytics 19, 20, 21, 23, 24, 26, 27, 33, 35, 39, 40, 41, 42, 43, 103, 146, 147, 204, 207, 302, 308
Decentralized Autonomous Organizations 52, 80, 226, 228, 239, 240, 246, 247, 248
Decentralized finance 5, 7, 15, 16, 17, 18, 41, 48, 49, 64, 76, 81, 86, 87, 89, 90, 91, 92, 93, 94, 95, 96, 100, 101, 102, 103, 104, 105, 106, 107, 108, 109, 110, 111, 225, 226, 227, 228, 229, 230, 231, 233, 236, 238, 245, 246, 247, 248, 249, 250, 254, 255, 257, 258, 259, 260, 261, 262, 265, 268, 269, 270, 271, 272
Decentralized Finance (DeFi) 5

DeFi 1, 2, 3, 4, 5, 6, 7, 8, 9, 10, 11, 12, 13, 14, 15, 16, 17, 18, 41, 48, 49, 50, 51, 52, 53, 54, 55, 56, 57, 58, 59, 61, 62, 63, 64, 65, 66, 67, 68, 69, 70, 71, 72, 73, 74, 75, 76, 77, 78, 79, 80, 81, 82, 83, 84, 85, 86, 87, 89, 90, 91, 92, 93, 94, 95, 96, 97, 98, 99, 100, 101, 102, 103, 104, 105, 106, 107, 108, 110, 111, 225, 226, 227, 228, 229, 230, 231, 232, 236, 238, 245, 246, 247, 248, 249, 250, 252, 253, 254, 255, 256, 257, 258, 259, 260, 261, 262, 263, 265, 266, 267, 268, 269, 270, 271, 315

DeFi Applications 5, 6, 10, 50, 53, 94, 105, 230, 259, 261

Digital Currency 6, 11, 273, 274, 275, 278, 279, 281, 283, 287, 288

Digital economy 116, 117, 139, 140, 141, 142, 143, 144, 145, 146, 147, 155, 156, 157, 225, 234, 235, 240, 246

Digital Financial Technology 201, 202, 208, 218, 219

E

Efficient Governance 112, 113, 132

environmental 12, 68, 87, 181, 182, 183, 184, 185, 186, 187, 188, 189, 190, 191, 192, 193, 194, 195, 196, 198, 199, 200, 276, 302, 303, 304, 308, 309, 310, 311, 312, 313, 314, 315

Ethical AI 48, 51, 63, 67, 68, 70, 74, 75, 80, 85, 154, 234, 313

F

Financial Inclusion 7, 11, 12, 13, 32, 92, 107, 109, 110, 163, 165, 176, 177, 189, 201, 202, 203, 204, 205, 206, 207, 208, 209, 210, 211, 212, 213, 214, 215, 216, 217, 218, 219, 220, 221, 222, 223, 224, 230, 232, 269, 273, 274, 275, 279, 281, 283, 284, 285, 288

Financial Markets 13, 14, 18, 26, 107, 109, 110, 111, 161, 166, 170, 178, 221, 256, 259, 260, 271, 272, 288, 308, 309, 319, 320, 334

Financial Services 2, 3, 5, 7, 8, 9, 10, 11, 12, 13, 14, 19, 20, 21, 22, 23, 24, 25, 26, 27, 30, 31, 32, 33, 34, 35, 36, 37, 38, 39, 40, 41, 42, 43, 44, 45, 46, 47, 64, 70, 71, 79, 86, 90, 92, 94, 104, 107, 110, 114, 118, 119, 164, 165, 168, 169, 174, 176, 177, 178, 180, 189, 202, 203, 204, 205, 206, 207, 209, 210, 211, 212, 213, 214, 215, 216, 217, 218, 219, 221, 223, 229, 230, 231, 232, 233, 234, 254, 255, 256, 258, 259, 260, 261, 267, 270, 274, 320

Financial Stability 17, 106, 109, 111, 183, 185, 188, 211, 219, 230, 264, 270, 274, 275, 278, 279, 281, 284, 287

financial system 2, 3, 4, 12, 13, 14, 90, 92, 198, 201, 202, 205, 206, 209, 217, 218, 255, 256, 257, 259, 260, 262, 269, 274, 275, 276, 279, 280, 283, 284, 285, 309

Fraud Detection 4, 8, 10, 15, 18, 26, 30, 31, 51, 55, 56, 85, 89, 90, 91, 92, 93, 94, 95, 96, 97, 98, 99, 100, 101, 102, 103, 105, 107, 108, 111, 132, 133, 139, 140, 141, 142, 143, 144, 145, 146, 147, 148, 149, 150, 151, 152, 153, 154, 155, 156, 157, 158, 159, 160, 207, 228, 235, 236, 246, 253, 265, 266, 267

Fraud Prevention 35, 91, 96, 97, 99, 100, 110, 140, 145, 146, 151, 152, 219, 308

G

Green banking 181, 182, 183, 184, 185, 186, 187, 188, 189, 190, 191, 192, 193, 194, 195, 196, 197, 199, 315

Green Finance 181, 183, 184, 185, 186, 187, 188, 189, 198, 199, 200, 302, 303, 304, 305, 309, 310, 311, 312, 313, 314, 315, 316

H

Hyper-personalization 19, 20, 21, 22, 23, 24, 27, 28, 29, 30, 31, 32, 33, 34, 35,

36, 37, 38, 39, 40, 41, 42, 44, 45, 46, 47

I

Indian investors 318, 321, 322, 332, 333, 334
Innovative approach 115, 254
Interoperability 11, 146, 216, 227, 228, 233, 236, 237, 238, 245, 246, 247, 251, 276, 281, 282
Investment Landscape 170, 318, 319, 332
Investments 27, 104, 161, 166, 170, 179, 180, 182, 183, 185, 186, 188, 191, 193, 194, 195, 203, 211, 215, 218, 262, 270, 304, 309, 310, 313, 325, 334

M

Machine Learning 4, 5, 7, 8, 10, 15, 16, 17, 18, 19, 21, 22, 23, 26, 30, 31, 32, 34, 41, 43, 45, 46, 52, 55, 57, 58, 62, 77, 79, 80, 81, 82, 87, 88, 89, 91, 93, 94, 95, 97, 98, 99, 100, 101, 102, 105, 106, 107, 108, 111, 114, 115, 119, 136, 137, 138, 139, 143, 144, 145, 146, 147, 149, 150, 151, 152, 153, 154, 155, 156, 167, 176, 179, 204, 207, 222, 226, 228, 233, 245, 246, 247, 249, 252, 264, 265, 270, 271, 272, 292, 302, 305, 306, 307, 313, 315, 316, 319, 334
Machine Learning Algorithms 4, 8, 10, 16, 19, 26, 30, 31, 34, 41, 45, 58, 87, 91, 95, 99, 107, 136, 143, 147, 150, 151, 152, 167, 179, 222, 249, 264, 271, 302, 313, 315
Multi-Chain Smart Contracts 226, 228, 236, 238, 246, 247

N

Natural Language Processing 4, 7, 31, 34, 43, 89, 91, 93, 94, 97, 100, 101, 102, 148, 153, 158, 305, 306, 312, 316

P

perception index 289, 294, 296, 297, 299
Perception of AI 290
Portfolio management 5, 14, 32, 106, 110, 162, 163, 164, 167, 168, 169, 172, 176, 180, 207, 318, 319, 320, 321, 322, 323, 324, 325, 328, 329, 330, 331, 332, 333, 334
Power of AI 49, 86, 267
Predictive Analytics 7, 8, 10, 19, 20, 27, 30, 32, 33, 34, 35, 43, 49, 50, 51, 53, 56, 58, 59, 85, 132, 144, 146, 147, 148, 151, 155, 156, 159, 207, 307, 315
principle component analysis 289

R

Regulatory Compliance 4, 9, 26, 40, 43, 44, 53, 65, 71, 74, 80, 81, 84, 87, 95, 98, 101, 102, 148, 151, 154, 207, 215, 233, 234
Risk Management 4, 10, 12, 13, 14, 15, 20, 26, 27, 30, 32, 33, 41, 48, 49, 51, 52, 53, 54, 57, 58, 59, 62, 63, 75, 78, 79, 82, 83, 85, 86, 88, 90, 92, 95, 104, 105, 106, 108, 109, 142, 162, 183, 221, 230, 235, 252, 256, 257, 258, 260, 261, 262, 263, 264, 265, 266, 267, 268, 269, 270, 272, 293, 319
Robo-advisors 5, 22, 104, 105, 108, 161, 162, 163, 164, 165, 166, 167, 168, 169, 170, 171, 172, 173, 174, 175, 176, 177, 178, 179, 180, 204, 206

S

SDGs 181, 182, 184, 194, 196, 197, 214, 224, 303, 304, 310
Security 4, 5, 8, 9, 10, 12, 14, 22, 23, 24, 26, 27, 35, 37, 38, 39, 41, 42, 48, 49, 50, 51, 52, 53, 54, 55, 57, 58, 61, 65, 66, 69, 70, 74, 77, 78, 79, 81, 82, 84, 85, 86, 87, 88, 89, 90, 91, 94, 95, 98, 99, 100, 101, 102, 103, 104, 105, 106, 107, 108, 109, 110, 111, 113, 114, 115, 121, 133, 142, 146, 147, 149,

151, 152, 153, 155, 156, 160, 163, 169, 170, 176, 191, 205, 207, 210, 211, 216, 227, 228, 232, 234, 235, 236, 238, 241, 242, 245, 254, 255, 257, 259, 262, 263, 266, 267, 268, 272, 273, 274, 276, 282, 283, 285, 307, 308, 315, 325

Smart Contracts 2, 3, 5, 6, 8, 10, 11, 12, 13, 16, 22, 49, 50, 52, 53, 54, 55, 57, 58, 81, 94, 95, 97, 99, 106, 109, 111, 225, 226, 227, 228, 229, 230, 231, 232, 233, 234, 235, 236, 237, 238, 239, 240, 241, 242, 243, 244, 245, 246, 247, 248, 249, 250, 251, 254, 255, 259, 267, 268

social 13, 14, 15, 16, 19, 20, 28, 29, 31, 32, 33, 34, 35, 44, 97, 100, 112, 113, 115, 118, 142, 143, 159, 163, 166, 167, 168, 169, 178, 182, 183, 185, 188, 189, 190, 193, 194, 196, 198, 199, 200, 204, 207, 208, 221, 222, 223, 249, 250, 257, 260, 261, 288, 292, 302, 303, 304, 309, 310, 311, 312, 315, 332

Sustainability 1, 4, 6, 17, 45, 69, 88, 104, 107, 121, 137, 164, 181, 184, 185, 186, 187, 189, 190, 191, 192, 193, 194, 195, 196, 197, 198, 199, 200, 222, 223, 249, 254, 259, 260, 262, 263, 266, 271, 303, 304, 305, 308, 309, 310, 311, 312, 313, 314, 315, 316

Sustainable Finance 183, 188, 198, 200, 273, 274, 285, 309, 310, 313, 316

T

Traditional Portfolio Management 318, 319, 320, 321, 322, 323, 324, 328, 329, 330, 331, 332, 333

Publishing Tomorrow's Research Today

Uncover Current Insights and Future Trends in
Business & Management
with IGI Global's Cutting-Edge Recommended Books

Print Only, E-Book Only, or Print + E-Book.
Order direct through IGI Global's Online Bookstore at **www.igi-global.com** or through your preferred provider.

Developmental Language Disorders in Childhood and Adolescence
ISBN: 9798369306444
© 2023; 436 pp.
List Price: US$ 230

The Sustainable Fintech Revolution: Building a Greener Future for Finance
ISBN: 9798369300084
© 2023; 358 pp.
List Price: US$ 250

Cases on Enhancing Business Sustainability Through Knowledge Management Systems
ISBN: 9781668458594
© 2023; 366 pp.
List Price: US$ 240

5G, Artificial Intelligence, and Next Generation Internet of Things: Digital Innovation For Green and Sustainable Economies
ISBN: 9781668486344
© 2023; 256 pp.
List Price: US$ 280

The Use of Artificial Intelligence in Digital Marketing
ISBN: 9781668493243
© 2024; 318 pp.
List Price: US$ 250

AI and Emotional Intelligence for Modern Business Management: Bridging the Gap and Nurturing Success
ISBN: 9798369304181
© 2023; 415 pp.
List Price: US$ 250

Do you want to stay current on the latest research trends, product announcements, news, and special offers?
Join IGI Global's mailing list to receive customized recommendations, exclusive discounts, and more.
Sign up at: www.igi-global.com/newsletters.

Scan the QR Code here to view more related titles in Business & Management.

www.igi-global.com | Sign up at www.igi-global.com/newsletters | facebook.com/igiglobal | twitter.com/igiglobal | linkedin.com/igiglobal

Ensure Quality Research is Introduced to the Academic Community

Become a Reviewer for IGI Global Authored Book Projects

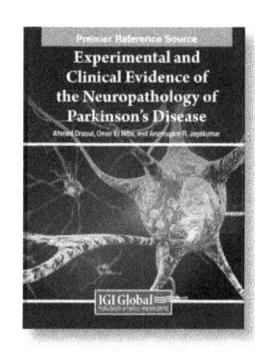

The overall success of an authored book project is dependent on quality and timely manuscript evaluations.

Applications and Inquiries may be sent to:
development@igi-global.com

Applicants must have a doctorate (or equivalent degree) as well as publishing, research, and reviewing experience. Authored Book Evaluators are appointed for one-year terms and are expected to complete at least three evaluations per term. Upon successful completion of this term, evaluators can be considered for an additional term.

If you have a colleague that may be interested in this opportunity, we encourage you to share this information with them.

IGI Global
Publishing Tomorrow's Research Today
www.igi-global.com

IGI Global
Open Access
Journal Program

Publishing Tomorrow's Research Today

IGI Global's Open Access Journal Program

Including Nearly 200 Peer-Reviewed, Gold (Full) Open Access Journals across IGI Global's Three Academic Subject Areas: Business & Management; Scientific, Technical, and Medical (STM); and Education

Consider Submitting Your Manuscript to One of These Nearly 200 Open Access Journals for to Increase Their Discoverability & Citation Impact

Web of Science Impact Factor 6.5
Journal of Organizational and End User Computing

Web of Science Impact Factor 4.7
Journal of Global Information Management

Web of Science Impact Factor 3.2
International Journal on Semantic Web and Information Systems

Web of Science Impact Factor 2.6
Journal of Database Management

Choosing IGI Global's Open Access Journal Program Can Greatly Increase the Reach of Your Research

Higher Usage
Open access papers are 2-3 times more likely to be read than non-open access papers.

Higher Download Rates
Open access papers benefit from 89% higher download rates than non-open access papers.

Higher Citation Rates
Open access papers are 47% more likely to be cited than non-open access papers.

Submitting an article to a journal offers an invaluable opportunity for you to share your work with the broader academic community, fostering knowledge dissemination and constructive feedback.

Submit an Article and Browse the IGI Global Call for Papers Pages

We can work with you to find the journal most well-suited for your next research manuscript.
For open access publishing support, contact: journaleditor@igi-global.com

Publishing Tomorrow's Research Today
IGI Global
e-Book Collection

Including Essential Reference Books Within Three Fundamental Academic Areas

Business & Management
Scientific, Technical, & Medical (STM)
Education

- Acquisition options include Perpetual, Subscription, and Read & Publish
- No Additional Charge for Multi-User Licensing
- No Maintenance, Hosting, or Archiving Fees
- Continually Enhanced Accessibility Compliance Features (WCAG)

| Over **150,000+** Chapters | Contributions From **200,000+** Scholars Worldwide | More Than **1,000,000+** Citations | Majority of e-Books Indexed in Web of Science & Scopus | Consists of Tomorrow's Research Available Today! |

Recommended Titles from our e-Book Collection

Innovation Capabilities and Entrepreneurial Opportunities of Smart Working
ISBN: 9781799887973

Advanced Applications of Generative AI and Natural Language Processing Models
ISBN: 9798369305027

Using Influencer Marketing as a Digital Business Strategy
ISBN: 9798369305515

Human-Centered Approaches in Industry 5.0
ISBN: 9798369326473

Modeling and Monitoring Extreme Hydrometeorological Events
ISBN: 9781668487716

Data-Driven Intelligent Business Sustainability
ISBN: 9798369300497

Information Logistics for Organizational Empowerment and Effective Supply Chain Management
ISBN: 9798369301593

Data Envelopment Analysis (DEA) Methods for Maximizing Efficiency
ISBN: 9798369302552

Request More Information, or Recommend the IGI Global e-Book Collection to Your Institution's Librarian

For More Information or to Request a Free Trial, Contact IGI Global's e-Collections Team: eresources@igi-global.com | 1-866-342-6657 ext. 100 | 717-533-8845 ext. 100